Understanding youth:

perspectives, identities and practices

Youth: perspectives and practice

This book forms part of an innovative series of structured teaching texts from The Open University, aiming to improve readers' understanding of young people's lives at a time of rapid social change, and to encourage critical and reflective practice in work with young people. The series consists of two books, *Understanding Youth: Perspectives, Identities and Practices*, edited by Mary Jane Kehily, and *Youth in Context: Frameworks, Settings and Encounters*, edited by Martin Robb. The two books form the core texts for The Open University's third-level undergraduate course KE308 *Youth: Perspectives and Practice*.

The two books share a number of key features:

- a biographical and holistic emphasis on young people's lives and lived experience, with extensive use of young people's voices and perspectives

- a dynamic focus on change in young people's lives, including the changing experience of youth, changes in ways of working with young people, and young people as agents of change

- an emphasis on diversity and inequalities in young people's experience, for example on the basis of class, gender, ethnicity and disability.

Understanding youth:
perspectives, identities and practices

Edited by Mary Jane Kehily

The Open University

⑤SAGE Publications
London • Thousand Oaks • New Delhi

Published by

Sage Publications
1 Oliver's Yard
55 City Road
London EC1Y 1SP

in association with

The Open University
Walton Hall
Milton Keynes MK7 6AA

Edited and designed by The Open University.

Typeset by S&P Enterprises (rfod) Limited, Lydbrook, Glos.

Printed and bound in the United Kingdom by The Alden Group, Oxford.

This book forms part of an Open University course KE308 *Youth: Perspectives and Practice*. Details of this and other Open University courses can be obtained from the Student Registration and Enquiry Service, The Open University, PO Box 197, Milton Keynes MK7 6BJ, United Kingdom: tel. +44 (0)870 333 4340, email general-enquiries@open.ac.uk

A catalogue record for this book is available from the British Library.

Library of Congress Control Number: 2006924444.

ISBN 978-1-4129-3064-2 (hardback)

ISBN 978-1-4129-3065-9 (paperback)

1.1

Contents

About the authors

Mary Jane Kehily is Senior Lecturer in Childhood and Youth Studies at The Open University. She has a background in cultural studies and education and has research interests in gender and sexuality, narrative and identity, and popular culture. She has published widely on these themes. Recent publications include *Sexuality, Gender and Schooling: Shifting Agendas in Social Learning* (Routledge, 2002); (edited with Joan Swann) *Children's Cultural Worlds* (Wiley/The Open University, 2003); and *An Introduction to Childhood Studies* (McGraw-Hill/Open University Press, 2004).

Heather Montgomery is Lecturer in Childhood Studies at The Open University. She is a social anthropologist who has worked in Thailand and is the author of *Modern Babylon? Prostituting Children in Thailand* (Berghahn, 2001).

Martin Robb is Lecturer in the Faculty of Health and Social Care at The Open University. He is co-editor of *Relating Experience: Stories from Health and Social Care* (Routledge, 2005), *Communication, Relationships and Care* (Routledge, 2004) and *Understanding Health and Social Care* (Sage, 1998), and has published articles and book chapters on a wide range of topics, with a recent focus on issues of fatherhood, masculinity and childcare. Before joining The Open University he worked in informal and community education projects with adults and young people.

Rachel Thomson is Professor of Social Research in the Faculty of Health and Social Care at The Open University. She has 15 years' experience of researching young people's lives including major studies of heterosexuality, values, consumption and the formation of adult identities. She has published widely in these areas and in the fields of qualitative methodology and theories of gender identity. She also has experience of policy and practice development in the field of youth, having worked for the National Children's Bureau between 1990 and 1999 and maintaining an involvement in the development of personal, social and health education, sex education and sexual health strategies. Her published work includes five books, two edited collections, two special issues of international journals, 26 chapters in books and 26 refereed journal articles. Recent publications include: (2004) '"An adult thing"? Young people's perspectives on the heterosexual age of consent', *Sexualities*, vol. 7, no. 2; (2004) 'Inventing adulthoods: a biographical approach to understanding youth citizenship', *Sociological Review*, vol. 52, no. 2; (2005) *All You Need is Love? Sexual Morality Through the Eyes of Young People*, National Children's Bureau.

Other contributors

This book has grown out of debates and discussions in the KE308 course team at The Open University. Besides the named authors, other team members who have contributed to the development of the book include Linda Camborne-Paynter, Jo Dawson, Helen Evans, Andy Rixon and Danielle Turney. The Open University course team would like to thank critical readers and developmental testers for their valuable comments on earlier draft chapters, and especially Robert MacDonald who, in his capacity as external assessor, provided insightful and timely comments at every turn.

Introduction

Mary Jane Kehily

Definitions of 'youth' in Western societies usually refer to the life stage between childhood and adulthood, the transitional period between being dependent and becoming independent. As Simon Frith (2005) points out, youth is a sociological category rather than a biological one. As such it is a more flexible concept than 'adolescent' or 'teenager'. Frith suggests that at the end of the twentieth century the notion of youth could describe a young person, an attitude and an established social institution. In contemporary times the transition from childhood to adulthood is increasingly protracted, commonly lasting much longer than adolescence or the 'growing up' years. This book attempts to understand and explore the changes and points of continuity that characterise contemporary youth. Central to our developing understanding is the need to place young people within their everyday social context as peers, family members and active participants in local and global cultures. Our approach emphasises connectedness, relationships and modes of belonging.

The lives of young people in the UK, as elsewhere in the world, have changed in dramatic ways in recent years. There is evidence that transitions from youth to adulthood are now substantially different from those experienced by previous generations, and also that they are increasingly unequal. Recent years have seen important changes in the social structures and processes shaping young people's lives, including changes in schooling and in higher education, the loss of the traditional youth labour market, and shifts in the nature of family and intimate relationships. Research has kept pace with these changes, developing new ways of theorising young people's lives, including placing greater emphasis on biographical approaches and on representing the voices and perspectives of young people themselves. The same period has seen a major focus on young people in social policy, with important initiatives in the fields of health, education and youth justice. There has been a parallel shift of emphasis in work with young people, with a greater emphasis on inter-agency collaboration, a drive towards professionalisation and the emergence of new hybrid professionals and new professional frameworks. For the first time the UK has what can be described as a coherent youth policy. There is a need for educational resources that reflect these social, policy and practice changes to support the development of critical thinking and reflective practice in work with young people.

This volume focuses on ways of understanding the changing experiences of young people in the contemporary period. The approach is holistic and interdisciplinary, drawing extensively on empirical research that showcases biographical case studies of young people in order to make sense of the ways in which social change, personal experience and agency may be negotiated and configured in young people's lives. The book provides a clear and comprehensive overview of youth in late modernity across ten chapters. Collectively, the chapters contribute to an understanding of changing conceptualisations of youth, issues of identity and key social practices that give shape to young people's lives. In order to develop insights into the concept of youth and the varied experiences of young people, the book is divided into three sections: perspectives, identities and practices.

The first part of the book, 'Perspectives', presents three different ways in which youth can be conceptualised and understood: cultural, comparative and biographical. Taking the three chapters together, the approaches outlined in each can be seen as different lenses for viewing young people in society. Each perspective offers a way of looking that generates particular insights and understandings. Underpinning Part 1 is the intention that these three approaches can be productively applied to the study of youth in different contexts. Each chapter profiles a different way of understanding young people's lives. The approaches are not in competition with each other as definitive and exclusive 'scoops' on the story of youth. Rather, they can be seen as complementary, offering rich and diverse ways of understanding youth as well as discussing the significant features of social change that have shaped young people's lives in the late modern period.

Chapter 1, 'A cultural perspective', highlights social constructionist and cultural approaches to youth informed by the interdisciplinary field of cultural studies. Defining culture as 'everyday social practice', a cultural perspective suggests that young people make sense of the world and take their place in it through participation and engagement with the routine social practices of everyday life. The chapter examines some of the differences between the concepts of adolescence and youth. Looking at young people culturally positions them as active meaning-makers in their own lives. Through negotiations with the social world and the exercise of agency, young people can be seen to develop their own cultures. The concept of youth culture and subculture is defined and explored throughout the chapter, drawing on several illustrative examples of subcultures in action.

A comparative perspective to youth is developed and explored in Chapter 2. The chapter takes an anthropological approach to understanding young people, demonstrating that Western categories cannot be regarded as biological or universal. Drawing on cross-cultural examples of young people in non-Western societies such as West Africa and Samoa, the chapter illustrates the limits of Western perspectives as culturally specific knowledges that do not readily apply outside their culture of origin. Social anthropology relies on ethnographic research methods, requiring researchers to spend a long time observing and participating in the culture they are studying. The chapter discusses the many ways in which an ethnographic approach can help us to understand young people's lives by offering us a unique insight into the social world of respondents themselves. Social anthropological approaches to youth suggest that this transitional period in the life course carries different meanings in different cultures. The idea of 'rites of passage' is discussed in the chapter as a way of marking and giving meaning to the social process of becoming an adult.

The final chapter of Part 1 develops a biographical perspective on young people's lives. Drawing on late modern social theory, Chapter 3 explores the significance of the biographical in developing an awareness of young people's lives. A biographical approach to young people can help us to develop a holistic account of individuals: who they are, what they think and feel. However, biographical approaches move beyond a focus on the self to enable us to place individuals in a societal context. Understanding a life intergenerationally and cross-generationally forms a productive part of biographical perspectives. The chapter outlines and discusses a number of key theoretical concepts important for understanding youth in contemporary times such as the reflexive project of self, individualisation, and 'normal' and 'choice' biographies. Collectively, these terms point to the ways in which the notion of a biographical self has become a key feature of the modern world, recognised across a range of sites including social policy and practice. Finally, the chapter considers how a biographical approach can be usefully applied to aspects of policy and practice when working with young people. Crucially, biographical perspectives encourage us to acknowledge the importance of timing and 'critical moments' in young people's lives that may suggest appropriate forms of intervention and support.

Part 2 of the book, 'Identities', considers issues of self and identity and the complex and shifting patterns of identification in young people's lives. Chapter 4 deals specifically with matters of gender as an aspect of identity that is central to young people's developing sense of self. Taking young men and the notion of masculinity as a main focus, the chapter examines the ways in which young people develop a sense of gender identity. It considers the relationships between youth, gender and identity at a time of rapidly changing ideas and expectations. At a time when young men are getting a bad press as emotionally inarticulate underachievers, prone to thuggery and suicide, the chapter asks, in what ways are young masculinities changing? What models of masculinity are available to young men in the UK today and how are they embodied? The chapter discusses key features of contemporary young masculinity, including young men's experiences of emotions, relationships and physicality/embodied experience. A fascinating feature of the chapter is the sustained discussion of forms of embodiment. How young men live in their bodies and think about themselves as embodied beings provides a revealing and generative insight into the complexities of developing an identity as young and masculine.

Chapter 5 considers a further aspect of identity, belonging. This chapter explores what belonging means to young people. The many different dimensions of belonging discussed include: group membership; regional, national and ethnic affiliations; forms of recognition and identification; forms of dis-identification and exclusion. The chapter begins with an extended discussion of a controversial and much publicised event: the banning of the headscarf in French schools. This event is drawn on in order to illustrate and explore the contradictory ways in which belonging may be interpreted. The chapter also considers further examples of belonging in discussions of nationhood and national belonging and what it means to belong to a sexual community. The idea of belonging can be viewed as an active force in young people's lives, generating powerful feelings while engaging them in forms of identity work and moments of dis-identification. The chapter concludes by discussing how a sense of belonging can be fostered in work with young people.

The final chapter of Part 2 focuses on issues of wellbeing. Chapter 6 examines current debates about young people's wellbeing, including concerns about obesity and eating disorders, mental health and emotional health. Young people's wellbeing has been the subject of much media interest and policy making in recent years. The general picture is a gloom-ridden one of young people increasingly prone to eating disorders and mental health problems. The chapter considers the ways in which media discourse and public policy have constructed young people's health, and the implications of these constructions for young people and those who work with them. Using a range of theoretical frameworks, the chapter analyses the notion of wellbeing for young people and explores the influence of factors such as class, gender and ethnicity on physical and mental health. The chapter explores the contours of what an alternative, holistic, critical framework for understanding young people's wellbeing might look like and considers the implications of such an approach. Finally, the chapter discusses the measures being taken to promote young people's health and critically examines the concept of 'resilience'.

Part 3 of the book explores young people's everyday 'practices', by which we mean the day-to-day activities that give shape to their lives. Chapter 7, 'Working', explores the practice of work in young people's transitions to adulthood. The chapter begins with a discussion of what work may mean to young people in the UK and elsewhere, before critically engaging with arguments concerning the changing nature of the youth labour market.

Biographical examples of young people balancing work and education are documented and serve to provide a valuable first-hand account of young people's experience of work and how it fits with the rest of their lives and their aspirations for the future. Their involvement in paid and unpaid work may reflect inequalities between young people and, indeed, may have the effect of compounding existing inequalities. The chapter considers the significance of local economies for young people in transition and the ways in which remaining local and maintaining local connections may shape the choices available to them. For some young people the boundaries between work and leisure become blurred by their pursuit of a 'pleasure that pays' lifestyle. Most young people, however, struggle to combine earning enough money with their other interests and aspirations. The chapter concludes with a discussion of how youth policy and practice seek to engage with young people's working lives.

As a companion chapter to 'Working', Chapter 8 focuses on the role of playing and leisure in young people's lives. The chapter introduces the notion of play as a social practice that young people engage in. It looks at issues of leisure, pleasure, sport and consumption as key practices that constitute play for young people. Most studies of children and young people use the term play to refer to children's activities, while young people are viewed as engaging in leisure activities rather than play. Children's play is commonly viewed as benign: imaginative, exploratory and a 'safe' way of dealing with difficult emotions. By contrast, young people's play/leisure is frequently cast as potentially threatening and disturbing. The chapter explores the practice of play and leisure in young people's lives by suggesting that youth at play can be seen as an imaginative expression of late childhood and early adulthood that has many points of continuity with children's play.

Chapter 9 is concerned with the practice of moving and the significance it may have for young people. It deals with the importance of travel, mobility and movement in young people's lives. Moving through physical space, relocating or spending time abroad may represent a significant event for young people, sometimes acting as a powerful catalyst for change and social development. The chapter discusses three case studies of young people on the move: refugees and asylum seekers travelling involuntarily to the UK; young people leaving care; and gap year students. Through these three very different accounts of how young people move and why, it is possible to glean insights into the practice of moving as a potentially enhancing or troubling experience. For some young people local and national boundaries appear fluid and can be crossed with ease, while for others moving may be disruptive, traumatic and potentially damaging.

The final chapter of the book focuses on the practice of relating. Chapter 10 explores the key relationships in young people's lives and the ways in which these are changing. The chapter discusses the meanings that personal relationships have for different groups of young people and the ways in which relationships may be differentiated on the basis of gender, ethnicity and other social factors. Young people's experience of relationships within families forms a significant part of the discussion, with an exploration of the impact of extended dependency on relationships with parents, and a discussion of the experience of young parents. The second part of the chapter looks at the differing role of friendships and the peer group in the lives of young men and women. This discussion also considers the changing nature of the meaning of intimate and sexual relationships for young people.

Although this book has been written for Open University students, it will be of interest to a much wider audience concerned to understand youth in changing times. Uniquely combining sociological approaches with biographical detail and matters of practice, the book provides a valuable resource for those studying or working with young people. As a teaching text, each chapter of the book includes a range of activities. These commonly call on readers to reflect on personal experience or test out ideas in relation to their own experience. Activities act as interactive learning tools that aim to consolidate the main teaching points for the chapter. They are, of course, optional for general readers. Finally, in order to help *all* readers and to make the text as accessible as possible, key terms are emboldened and explained at the point when they are first discussed.

Reference

Frith, S. (2005) 'Youth' in Bennett, T., Grossberg, L. and Morris, M. (eds) *New Keywords: A Revised Vocabulary of Culture and Society*, Oxford, Blackwell.

Part 1
Perspectives

Chapter 1

A cultural perspective

Mary Jane Kehily

Introduction

The three chapters in this first part of the book aim to introduce you to three different perspectives for studying youth and understanding young people. The three perspectives are:

- the cultural
- the comparative
- the biographical.

These perspectives aim to provide you with conceptual tools for studying youth and understanding young people's lives. They are intended to be complementary, each offering fresh insights and new ways of looking at young people in the past and the present. When looking at particular case studies of young people you may find that the perspectives collide or overlap in interesting ways.

In this chapter the focus is the *cultural* perspective on youth. The chapter will take a cultural approach to youth as a concept and will point to ways in which this perspective can provide useful tools for understanding young people's lives in the past and the present.

The chapter poses the following core questions:

- How does the concept of youth help us to make sense of the life stage from late childhood to young adulthood?
- How has the study of young people changed over time?
- How has the concept of youth subcultures brought young people into focus?
- What are some of the strengths and limitations of viewing young people from a cultural perspective?

While not intending to present a history of youth, the chapter takes a historical approach that is informed by the interdisciplinary field of cultural studies.

But first a word about culture; the term culture has a wide range of meanings in both academic and everyday discourse. It can refer to the traditions of a particular society or community, but it can also be used more narrowly to refer to artistic forms and practices, in the sense of 'high culture'. From a cultural studies perspective, culture can be defined as *everyday social practice*. The idea of culture is extended to include the commonplace routines and practices that characterise and bind together a particular group or community. No distinction is made between 'high' and 'low' culture and their associated practices. Culture, in this sense, can be observed and studied in day-to-day engagements with the social world. This way of conceptualising culture draws on the work of literary and cultural critic Raymond Williams (1961, 1989), who insisted that *culture is ordinary*. Williams referred to the 'everydayness' of culture as a *way of life* that makes sense to individuals involved in a particular community. This perspective also sees culture as a form of action: it is not just something that people *have*, it is also what people *do*. The anthropologist Brian Street (1993) argued that 'culture is a verb', indicating that it can be seen as a dynamic process rather than a fixed entity. Culture is something that people actively produce in their day-to-day activities. Applying these ideas to young people has important consequences for understanding youth. A cultural perspective suggests that young people make sense of the world and take their place within it through participation and engagement with everyday social practices. Viewing young people culturally also positions them as active meaning-makers in their own lives. Through negotiations with the social world and the exercise of agency, young people give shape to their lives and actively ascribe meanings to events. In this way young people can be seen to develop their own cultures. Indeed, the term 'youth culture' is commonly used as shorthand to describe these processes.

1 Young people in time and place

Youth as a life phase in Western cultures is commonly seen as socially significant and psychologically complex. But how did it become so? Large scale socio-economic changes in Europe and North America such as industrialisation, mass education and legislation regulating child labour created the conditions for children and young people to be separated, to some extent, from the adult world. Schooling, for example, organises children and young people into age-based cohorts, subjects them to similar experiences and, of course, delays the onset of economic activity. Within the changing social context of the late nineteenth century, in which the young spent less time with adults and more time with each other, the emergent discipline of psychology played a part in constructing the concept of 'adolescence' rather than youth. American psychologist G. Stanley Hall was influential in charting adolescence as a stage of development within the life course (Hall, 1904).

Hall described adolescence as a transitional period in the journey from childhood to adulthood. He drew on the notion of *recapitulation* – the idea that individual development mirrors the development of humankind throughout history – from primitive being to civilised adult. Hall is best known for his characterisation of adolescence as a period of storm and stress:

> It is the age of natural inebriation without the need of intoxicants, which made Plato define youth as spiritual drunkenness. It is a natural impulse to experience hot and perfervid psychic states, and it is characterised by emotionalism. We see here the instability and fluctuations now so characteristic.
>
> (Hall, 1904, vol. 2, pp. 74–5)

For Hall, adolescence was marked by physiological change and bodily development that conjures up an image of the stereotypical teenager, subject to 'raging hormones', mood swings and an inability to communicate with adults. Hall's account of adolescence and the contemporary image of the teenager in popular culture imply that young people are at the mercy of biological change that they are not entirely in control of. The biological basis of adolescence inherent in Hall's account powerfully suggests that young people are in the grip of hormonal and psychological changes that produce an erratic range of feelings and behaviour.

Approaches associated with understanding youth from a cultural perspective have been critical of research traditions associated with adolescence. The two contrasting terms *adolescence* and *youth* signal some of the differences between the perspectives. Although both terms refer to young people in the same age range (roughly from 13 to the early twenties), the term adolescence is usually used by researchers, like Hall, in the fields of biology, psychology and human development. From this perspective adolescence is viewed as a developmental stage. This idea will be discussed in more detail in the next section of the chapter. The term youth, on the other hand, suggests a more social orientation, a concern with young people as a socially constituted group and an interest in the ways in which young people are positioned and defined within society. This approach is commonly associated with **social constructionism**, a set of ideas and theories that explore the ways in which concepts are made and shaped by society. A social constructionist approach to youth examines beliefs, ideas and images of young people, including those generated by scientific and biological approaches. Social constructionists suggest that what can be known about young people is the product of cultural knowledge that changes over time and place. This idea is discussed further in Chapter 2 where you will be introduced to comparative perspectives that illustrate the diverse ways in which young people are positioned in society and understood.

1.1 Adolescence as a stage of development

The idea of adolescence as a stage of development has been influential in shaping many psychological and psychotherapeutic studies of young people. D.W. Winnicott (1896–1971) for example, drawing on his experience as a psychotherapist in the UK, placed emphasis upon adolescence as a period of psychological growth. Winnicott's ideas are premised on a dynamic notion of individual growth that occurs within what he termed a 'facilitating environment'. Central to the idea of a facilitating environment is a theory of childcare subscribed to by Winnicott and others that emphasises the need for continuity of care in the early years in order to give children and young people a sense of continuity in their own lives. A particular concern of Winnicott's was unconscious motivation. He cited the children's game 'I'm the king of the castle' to illustrate what he meant by this. The game is accompanied by the rhyme: 'I'm the king of the castle, And you're the dirty rascal'. During the course of the game the 'king' kills all rivals and establishes dominance, only to be deposed by the 'dirty rascal'. Winnicott suggested that we need to translate this game into the language of the unconscious motivation of adolescence and society. In psychological terms, becoming an adult is achieved 'over the dead body of an adult' (Winnicott, 1989 [1968], p. 141). The material that underlies the play can be seen as unconscious fantasy, informing and giving shape to family relations and the game itself:

> If, in the fantasy of early growth, there is contained *death*, then at adolescence there is contained *murder*. Even when growth at the period of puberty goes ahead without major crises, one may need to deal with acute problems of management because growing up means taking the parent's place. *It really does*. In the unconscious fantasy, growing up is inherently an aggressive act ... there is to be found death and personal triumph as something inherent in the process of maturation and in the acquisition of adult status.
>
> (Winnicott, 1989 [1968], pp. 144–5)

Seen from this perspective, adolescence involves the individual in the psychological drama of killing parents in order to emerge as an independent adult. Winnicott was keen to point out that being rebellious, immature and irresponsible are normal and healthy features of adolescence that will pass over time. Winnicott's advice to adults was to remain responsible and in control; like the king of the castle, to remain dominant for as long as possible until deposed and above all not to abdicate as they are about to be killed. Winnicott argued that abdicating responsibility will give adolescents a sense of 'false maturity' that strips them of their greatest asset – the freedom to have ideas and act on impulse.

A contrasting perspective on psychological development during adolescence can be found in the work of Erik Erikson (1902–94). Erikson focused on the concept of identity as it emerged and changed in developmental stages across the life course. He used the term 'identity confusion' to describe the conflict of adolescence in which young people appear to be at war with themselves and the society they live in. Erikson's account of the development of identity begins in infancy when the child incorporates adult images that arise in the trustful parent–child relationship. Later childhood is marked by 'identification': the incorporation of roles and values of others who are most admired. Adolescence places emphasis on identity formation in which the individual retains some earlier childhood identifications and rejects others in accordance with their developing interests and values. Erikson's account of adolescent development is distinctive in that he considers young people within the context of their society, paying attention to work, prevailing ideologies and cultural milieu:

> As technological advances put more and more time between early school life and the young person's final access to specialized work, the stage of adolescing becomes an even more marked and conscious period and, as it has always been in some cultures in some periods, almost a way of life between childhood and adulthood. Thus in the later school years young people, beset with the physiological revolution of their genital maturation and the uncertainty of adult roles ahead, seem much concerned with faddish attempts at establishing an adolescent subculture with what looks like a final rather than a transitory or, in fact, initial identity formation. They are sometimes morbidly, often curiously, preoccupied with what they appear to be in the eyes of others as compared with what they feel they are, and with the question of how to connect the roles and skills cultivated earlier with the ideal prototypes of the day. In their search for a new sense of continuity and sameness, which must now include sexual maturity, some adolescents have to come to grips again with crises of earlier years before they can install lasting idols and ideal guardians of final identity ...

> In any given period in history, then, that part of youth will have the most affirmatively exciting time of it which finds itself in the wave of a technological, economic or ideological trend seemingly promising all that youthful vitality could ask for ... In general it is the inability to settle on an occupational identity which most disturbs young people. To keep themselves together they temporarily overidentify with the heroes of cliques and crowds to the point of an apparently complete loss of individuality.
>
> (Erikson, 1968, pp. 128–32)

Erikson notes the significance of the broader context in which young people experience their teenage years and comments on some of the interrelationships to be found. A striking feature of Erikson's account is the way in which he views youth subcultures as 'faddish' and disruptive cliques that young people may be in danger of over-identifying with. The accounts of adolescent development presented by Winnicott and Erikson treat young people as an important category that requires attention. In their analyses adolescence is seen as a life phase that is both socially significant and psychologically complex. A shared feature of both accounts is a concern with young people as individuals. Understanding young people and taking them seriously is regarded as important for parents, other adults and society as a whole. Winnicott and Erikson both place emphasis on psychological development in adolescence; for Winnicott this is couched broadly in terms of psychiatric health, while Erikson focuses on matters of identity formation. In the next section of the chapter you will be asked to consider some of the differences between psychological and cultural approaches to young people. This will involve completing an activity on the terms adolescence and youth.

Key points

*   In Western cultures youth is regarded as socially significant and psychologically complex.

*   The terms adolescence and youth emerge from different research traditions that have focused on young people between the ages of 13 and 25.

*   Understanding young people and taking them seriously is regarded as important for parents, other adults and society as a whole.

2   Adolescence or youth? Two sides of the same research subject

In the previous section we discussed adolescence as a time of growth and development and considered some of the themes in research literature in this field. We pointed out that cultural approaches to young people tend to use the term youth rather than adolescence. In this section the aim is to explore further the difference between adolescence and youth, this time focusing more on the cultural perspective.

Activity 1	Young people in focus

Allow 30 minutes   The following extracts take a historical approach to describe some of the ways in which young people in the West have been represented in research literature and in everyday discourse. Read the extracts and make a note of the main points in each passage, then try to identify some of the differences between seeing young people as either 'youth' or 'adolescents'.

From 1880 to 1980: the story continues

Since the 1880s, dominant ideologies about 'youth' and 'adolescence' have been characterized by a series of tensions and realignments between biological determinism and social constructionism, with the storm-and-stress model providing a recurrent element in psychological and sociological texts ...

Few contemporary historians of youth dwell on the 1940s, yet the foundations of the 1960s counter-culture were emerging in African-American urban life. The 'Harlem Renaissance' saw the emergence of the many African-American cultural forms from which the youth groups of the 1950s and 1960s drew so much of their inspiration (Tyler, 1989). In addition moral panics over Frank Sinatra's young female fans meant that 'Sinatrauma' predated 'Beatlemania' by some twenty years (Shaw, 1968, Griffin, 1987) ...

Adolescence has been defined via an uneasy mixture of the biological and the social, with biology positioned as the major determining element, and puberty onset defined as the starting point of adolescence. The biological dimension generally refers to the development of 'normal' genital (hetero)sexuality,

reproductive capacity (especially for young women) and/or more generalized hormonal surges. In practice, the identification of puberty onset is notoriously difficult to define, especially in young men (Muuss, 1968). The age of menarche is usually taken as the agreed criterion for young women, but there is not necessarily a neat transition into (or out of) menstruation (Ussher, 1989). The latter is not a solely physiological process of course, since physical maturation and menarche are closely associated with nutrition levels (Laslett, 1971). The social dimension of youth/adolescence often appears at its end-point, referring to economic transition points such as entry to the job market and/or marriage and independence from the family of origin (Springhall, 1986) ...

We can still see this uneasy combination of the biological and the social in contemporary psychological and sociological texts on adolescence and youth (e.g. Marsland, 1986). Contemporary crises over 'youth' are frequently attributed in the mainstream literature to a mismatch between the biological and social boundaries of this age stage.

(Griffin, 1993, pp. 18–20)

The penny theatre

One of the first English middle-class 'cycles of outrage' at nineteenth-century forms of popular entertainment intended primarily for the youth market was directed against the penny theatre – a rehearsal for similar and more recent campaigns. Journalist James Grant was convinced in 1838 that 'a very large majority of those who afterwards find their way to the bar of the Old Bailey, may trace the commencement of their career in crime to their attendance in Penny Theatres' ...

The penny theatre or 'gaff' (any form of amusement was liable to be called the 'gaff' in Cockney or coster

slang) was hence generally found in previously vacant premises such as a shop or a warehouse taken over for cheap, staged entertainment intended primarily for wage-earning children and adolescents of both sexes aged from about eight to twenty...

Police harassment of penny gaffs provided a rehearsal for subsequent campaigns against presumed cultural incitements to criminality, convenient scapegoats to account for the errand boy who robbed his employer or the scullery maid who turned to prostitution.

(Springhall, 1998, pp. 9–13)

Comment

Christine Griffin posits the idea that young people have been seen either in biological terms or in terms of social constructionism and that a tension exists between these two approaches. The biological perspective generally views young people as 'adolescents' undergoing an intensive period of physical growth and hormonal change that marks the transition from childhood to adulthood. Social constructionist perspectives on young people are more likely to use the term 'youth' rather than 'adolescence' and regard the teenage years as shaped culturally by the society in which young people live. The storm and stress model referred to by Griffin draws on Hall's approach to biology, discussed earlier, which suggests that young people may have difficulty adjusting to rapid biological changes and the social demands of developing an identity as a young adult. Griffin makes the point that young people are always seen in relation to their society. In fact, concerns expressed about young people at any given time can be understood as a comment on broader social changes affecting the population as a whole. Researchers who have studied youth cultures often refer to key moments of cultural activity that help to define young people as a distinct cultural group. The hippy movement associated with 1960s counter-culture and the phenomenon of Beatlemania are frequently referred to as powerful influences that young people embraced and through which they defined themselves. Subsequent youth cultures such as punk and rave can be seen as a response to these earlier forms of youth culture. Griffin points out that Beatlemania and the 1960s counter-culture have historical precedents in the USA and should not be regarded as the first youthful expressions of a postwar generation of young people with money to spend and time to protest. Furthermore, Griffin suggests that young people in the West do not exist in isolation from other societies but actually draw inspiration from events and movements in other countries. Finally, Griffin suggests that defining adolescence in terms of a combination of the biological and the social produces a tense and less than comfortable alliance that usually prioritises the biological as fundamental to young people's development and the social as something to aspire to: adult status as defined by sexual and economic norms.

The extract by John Springhall introduces further themes that are significant to a cultural approach. Cultural perspectives take an interest in young people as a social group, what they do and how this is viewed by others in society. Springhall points out that the activities of young people as a social group have a patterned history; they have been regarded as a source of concern by adults and continue to be seen in this way. Frequently, expressed concerns have moral overtones. A rich source of anxiety relates to young people's engagement with popular culture and adult fears of corruption and criminality. Springhall points out that young people's enjoyment of popular culture is often seen as causal: the root of contamination that inevitably leads to deviance and destruction. Finally, Springhall alludes to police harassment as a societal response to adult fears and anxieties – a response that provides explanations by creating scapegoats. Police intervention, as in the case of the penny theatres can, with hindsight, be seen as a recurrent feature – the regulation of youth cultures by the state.

The following subsection takes up many of the themes introduced by Springhall in a discussion of youth and 'moral panics'.

2.1 Youth and 'moral panics'

As the extracts from Griffin and Springhall suggest, the activities of young people have long been a cause for concern among adults. There are many ways in which youth and the activities of young people have been cast as 'deviant' in the postwar period. Young people's reluctance to conform to societal norms has routinely been seen as a form of deviance incorporating moments of rebellion and/or criminality. The notion of 'moral panics' can be seen as a counter interpretation, an attempt to understand the activities of young people in ways that do not pathologise them. As Springhall (1998) points out, the term 'moral panic' describes the disjuncture between reactions to social or cultural phenomena that appear out of proportion to the actual threat posed. The term is drawn from the research of Stanley Cohen. Taking a sociological approach, Cohen (1972) focused on the emergence of two UK based youth subcultures with contrasting modes of dress and lifestyle.

Cohen's study of mods and rockers in south east England illustrates the ways in which media coverage of their activities turned young people into

Mods and rockers in the UK in the 1960s

'folk devils' and thus generated widespread 'moral panic' about their behaviour:

> A crucial dimension for understanding the reaction to deviance both by the public as a whole and by agents of social control, is the nature of the information that is received about the behaviour in question. Each society possesses a set of ideas about what causes deviation – is it due, say, to sickness or to wilful perversity? – and a set of images of who constitutes the deviant – is he an innocent lad being led astray, or is he a psychopathic thug? – and these conceptions shape what is done about his behaviour. In industrial societies, the body of information from which such ideas are built, is invariably received at second hand. That is, it arrives already processed in the mass media and this means the information has been subject to alternative definitions of what constitutes 'news' and how it should be gathered and presented. The information is further structured by the various commercial and political constraints in which newspapers, radio and television operate.
>
> (Cohen, 1972, p. 16)

Cohen turns his attention to the now infamous encounters between mods and rockers at south coast holiday resorts on Bank Holiday weekends in the mid-1960s. He documents the journalistic styles of exaggeration, melodrama and distortion that 'enter into the consciousness and shape societal reaction at later stages' (Cohen, S., 1972, p. 33). In a detailed analysis of the events and media coverage of them, Cohen powerfully suggests that the activities of young people do not exist as reportable stories of youthful rivalry: 'The mods and rockers didn't become news because they were new; they were presented as new to justify their creation as news' (Cohen, S., 1972, p. 46). Through the act of reporting, mods and rockers acquire ideological meaning as symptomatic of imminent social breakdown. In a further study elaborating on Cohen's thesis, Geoffrey Pearson (1983) presents a carefully worked history of moral panics from the mid-1880s to the 1980s. His argument, based on textual analysis of historical documents and contemporary representations, suggests that every 20 years or so there is a moral panic about youth. Pearson indicates that a new moral panic commonly repeats the themes of previous moral panics. Just when the panic is fading from popular memory, it re-emerges in a similar form to be visited upon the next generation of young people. Both studies point to the ways in which young people are positioned in society and offer explanations based on adult concerns and anxieties.

2.2   Youth and subcultures

The publication of Cohen's *Folk Devils and Moral Panics* marked the emergence of a new and highly influential approach to youth: the subcultural. The concept of 'subculture' is important in understanding the social lives of young people. In simple terms a subculture can be seen as a group within a group. The social group frequently referred to as 'youth' has thrown up many subgroups over the years which come to be regarded as subcultures. Over time these subcultures acquire names and identities such as teddy boys, skinheads, punks and goths. There is a rich vein of research that uses the concept of subculture to illustrate the many ways in which young people can be observed and studied. It is through the concept of subculture that the activities of many young people have become visible.

The following activity is intended to help you identify some features of a subculture and the role it may play in young people's lives.

Activity 2   The case of Wanda

Allow 25 minutes

Read the following extract written in 1932 which describes a social practice comparable to table dancing or lap dancing. Make a note of the main points in the passage and try to identify why the world of the taxi-dance hall may be regarded as a subculture: a group within a group.

The life-cycle of a taxi-dancer

Taxi-dance halls are relatively unknown to the general public. Yet for thousands of men throughout the United States who frequent them they are familiar establishments. Located inconspicuously in buildings near business centers of many cities, these taxi-dance halls are readily accessible ...

The girl employed in these halls is expected to dance with any man who may choose her and to remain with him on the dance floor for as long a time as he is willing to pay the charges. Hence the significance of the apt name 'taxi-dancer' ... Like the taxi-driver with his cab, she is for public hire and is paid in proportion to the time spent and the services rendered ...

[the] case of Wanda ... reveals the way in which the girl's scheme of life may be completely altered through the brief sojourn in the world of the taxi-dance hall.

Wanda, American-born but of Polish parents, at fifteen ... secured work in a cigar factory, telling her employer that she was eighteen. Shortly after, she left home and no trace of her was found until four months later, when she was found married to a young Filipino. He said his wife told him that she was nineteen and that he had no reason to doubt her. Wanda met him in the taxi-dance hall in which she had been employed. They had known each other only a month before their marriage.

According to Wanda's story, she left the cigar factory because the work was monotonous. All day long she wrapped cigars until after a month she could endure it no longer. Through a friend in the factory she secured employment in the dance hall, dignified by the name of a 'dancing school for men' ... Wanda was rather embarrassed at first at the prospect of dancing with so many strange men, but before the end of the first evening she found herself thoroughly enjoying it and turned in more tickets than any other girl on the floor. She began to look forward to the evenings in the dance hall; she 'got a thrill' from meeting so many new people ...

But her clientèle began to fall off. She learned that several of the other girls, jealous of her success, were circulating tales that she was a 'bad sport' and a prude. To rectify this Wanda resorted to the wiles of the other girls; she rouged heavily, darkened her eyes, and shortened her skirts. Again she achieved popularity, also the other girls grew more tolerant of her.

One evening she danced with Louis, a Filipino. His peculiar accent intrigued her, and she accepted an invitation to supper. Their friendship grew. He told her of his childhood in his native islands, and she confided her growing dislike of the dance hall. They agreed that they would like to 'settle down', and so one evening Wanda 'resigned' and they drove to Indiana and were married.

(A Chicago social worker quoted by Cressey, 1932, in Gelder and Thornton, 1997, pp. 28–32)

Comment

The first point you may have noticed is the presence and location of the taxi-dance hall itself. Although centrally placed in the business district of most American cities, the taxi-dance hall was relatively unknown to the general public. In other words the world of the taxi-dance hall can be seen as a subculture within the larger culture of business and commerce that flourished in the everyday life of the city. This may lead us to consider the 'sub' status of subcultures, a prefix that usually means below or underneath. Researchers who have studied subcultures suggest that subcultural groups often have a subordinate relationship to the broader culture, that in some ways they can be seen as underground or subterranean. The subculture, therefore, exists within the wider culture but occupies a neglected or marginal status.

The practice of taxi-dancing also has borderline status as a form of employment for young women and as a business enterprise more generally. Like massage parlours and escort agencies, taxi-dancing challenges the conventions of the wider society and exists in the blurred boundaries between personal services and the illicit world of prostitution. In the context of 1930s Chicago, the norms and values associated with sexual relationships privilege the idea of romantic love as a basis for all forms of intimacy. Romantic love is an ideal that is assumed to be outside the realm of the economy and free from monetary transactions. This makes taxi-dancing a seemingly out of the ordinary practice, transgressing the norms and values operating in the rest of society.

Wanda's behaviour can be viewed as transgressive in many other ways: she leaves a dull but respectable job to dance for men in exchange for money; she leaves her family; and finally she marries a man from another culture whom she has known for only a month. These factors, reported as they are by a social worker, can be cited from a social care perspective as evidence that Wanda has 'gone off the rails' or at least strayed a little from the path deemed acceptable for working class young women.

Participants in subcultures often see themselves, and are seen by others, as different or oppositional in some way. Youth subcultures frequently seek to define themselves as against the culture that exists around them and particularly against the values they associate with the parental home. It could be argued that there is a tendency in traditional studies of subcultures to emphasise the unconventional, deviant and nonconformist aspects of subcultural groups. However, within the context of nonconformity, participation in subcultures also demands a considerable amount of conformity. You may have noticed that Wanda found herself under pressure from the other taxi-dancers to fit in, to behave and dress like the other girls. In this case fitting in involved bodily adornment: wearing short skirts and the heavy use of eye make-up and rouge. Subcultural groups are commonly marked by their distinctive appearance, a particular style, mode of dress and adornment that make the participants look different, sometimes even spectacular and shocking. In the context of subcultural groups style takes on a particular meaning as 'the means by which cultural identity and social location are negotiated and expressed' (O'Sullivan *et al.*, 1994, p. 305).

It is also interesting to note the emotions and the experience of being a member of a subculture. In the passage Wanda's feelings are discussed initially in terms of embarrassment; she is reported to have felt self conscious at the thought of dancing with so many strange men. However, during the course of her first evening the embarrassment gives way to enjoyment. This is followed by feelings of anticipation and excitement, getting a thrill out of dancing, being popular and earning money. Being a member of a subculture, then, is not about being a victim. Although Wanda can be seen as a victim of her circumstances in many ways, she also exercises choice and experiences pleasure. Individuals involved in subcultural activity often speak of the highs and lows of life as part of a subculture; the mundane inertia of 'doing nothing' contrasted with moments of risk and excitement when something happens (Corrigan, 1979). Taxi-dancing offers Wanda some, albeit temporary, feelings of enjoyment and self worth. Through taxi-dancing she finds an escape from the monotonous routine of factory work and access to an independent income. For working class young women like Wanda, being a taxi-dancer is both a struggle for survival and a search for pleasure.

Key points

- A subculture may be seen as a group within a group that traditionally has occupied an underground or marginal status in society.

- Subcultures may challenge the conventions of the wider society and may be regarded as transgressive or oppositional.

- Members of a subculture do not regard themselves as victims.

- Subcultural activities and practices may engage with mainstream culture and in some cases may blur the boundaries between the two.

3 Defining subcultures

The example of Wanda provides a way of understanding subcultures as a group within a group. Participants in a subculture usually have things in common with one another that serve to distinguish them from other social groups. This section considers further what makes a subculture by drawing on the accounts of researchers working in this field. This is followed by a closer look at the notion of 'youth subcultures'. Milton M. Gordon, an American sociologist writing in 1947, proposed that the concept of subculture refers to:

> a subdivision of a national culture, composed of a combination of factorable social situations such as class status, ethnic background, regional, rural or urban residence, and religious affiliation, but *forming in their combination a functioning unity which has an integrated impact on the participating individual.*
>
> (Gordon, 1947, in Gelder and Thornton, 1997, p. 41)

Gordon's definition suggests that a subculture can be identified as a set of cultural patterns of behaviour carried by a segment of the population in any one country. This early definition allowed sociologists and cultural anthropologists to look at aspects of diversity within Western societies, particularly in the USA. Albert K. Cohen (1955) further explored the concept of subculture and the ways it can aid understanding of the social world. He suggested that subcultures can help us to understand and explain *what people do*. In Cohen's analysis subcultures arise when people with similar problems get together to look for solutions. Through interaction with one another, Cohen argues, members of a subculture come to share a similar outlook on life and evolve collective solutions to the problems they experience. This process, however, often creates a distance between the subculture and the dominant culture. Indeed, achieving status within a subculture may entail a loss of status in the wider culture. Classic studies of subcultures from the 1950s elaborated on Cohen's analysis by seeking to explain the contrast between the dominant values of society and the values of marginal groups such as ethnic minority communities as in William Whyte's study (1943) *Street Corner Society: The Social Structure of an Italian Slum* and Jock Young's later study (1971) *The Drugtakers: The Social Meaning of Drug Use*. Both illustrate that subcultures may be connected to a sense of place or location, in Whyte's case the youth of Boston's North End, as well as to particular activities and practices like drug use or taxi-dancing.

O'Sullivan *et al.* (1994) offer the following contemporary definition of subculture:

> As the prefix implies, *sub*cultures are significant and distinctive negotiations located within wider cultures ... The term and its supporting theory have developed almost exclusively in the study and explanation of youth ...
>
> The concept hinges on several important assumptions. First, that Western societies are characterized principally by their division into social **classes**, based on inequalities of **power** and wealth, and their consequent relations of dominance and subordination. Second, that these unequal and conflicting divisions and relations are realized and articulated in the form of class **cultures**, themselves sets of complex cultural responses to particular social class positions. Third, within these class cultures ... youth negotiate and advance 'their own' distinctive and especially symbolic *subcultural* responses to the problems posed not only by age or generational status, subordination and control, but also by class position and inequality, particularly as they are experienced and combined in the spheres of education, work and leisure ... Within this framework, subcultural analysis has generated and continues to propose an important way of deconstructing and understanding the appearance, behaviour and significance of differing youth groups in the postwar UK.
>
> (O'Sullivan *et al.*, 1994, pp. 307–8)

This definition makes it clear that the subcultures exist in relationship to the society from which they emerge and that their existence may provide an insight into the experiences of young people, especially in the areas of education, work and leisure. A final point of definition we suggest is that many contemporary subcultures are involved in the act of self definition: groups of young people may collectively develop ways of differentiating themselves from others and, in the process of doing so, constitute and define themselves as a subcultural group.

3.1 The cultural studies approach to youth subcultures

The cultural studies approach to youth subcultures is largely associated with the Centre for Contemporary Cultural Studies (CCCS) based at the University of Birmingham, UK from 1964 until 2002. CCCS researchers focused on subcultural formations among young people in 1970s and 1980s Britain.

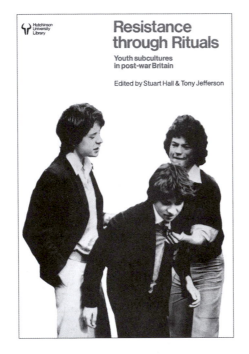

In an influential collection of studies, the CCCS researchers explore youth subcultures as expressive forms of resistance that make connections between everyday experience, social class, culture and the wider society (Hall and Jefferson, 1976). Engaging in subcultural activity involves young people in acts of 'articulation', the bringing together of different elements in particular contexts, in ways that make sense to the individuals concerned. Hall and Jefferson suggest that working class youth subcultures involve young people in a 'double articulation', first with their parents' culture and second with the broader culture of postwar social change. In Chapter 3 we take up the theme of intergenerational change and the ways in which young people shape their biographies in relation to their peers and their parents. To view youth subcultures as adolescent rebellion is to underestimate the extent to which young people seek to address and comment on generational change and social structures. From a cultural studies perspective, youth subcultures are purposeful interventions, imbued with meaning. An example of this is the skinhead subculture, discussed below as a case study.

More recent postmodernist approaches to youth culture have critiqued earlier definitions and challenged the concept of subculture itself. We're all mainstream now, the argument goes; the increased commodification and commercialisation of all areas of social life close down the possibility of subcultural space for young people. Besides, the notion of a 'dominant culture' is also changing and fragmenting, creating multiple cultures rather than the mainstream and the subcultural. Steve Redhead's (1997) study asserts that subcultures have been replaced by 'clubcultures'. Redhead's analysis signals the impact of **globalisation** on youth culture. Globalisation is a feature of contemporary life marked by the flow of multinational corporations, Western capitalism and Western culture across the globe. Redhead defines clubcultures as global and fluid youth formations that are based on the media and the niche marketing of dance music as a youth-culture-for-all. He refers to clubbing as 'hedonism in hard times' (1997, p. 4) suggesting that it is both an escape from and a riposte to political realities, including forms of police regulation. There are parallels here with Springhall's description of the regulation of penny theatres in the nineteenth century. Sarah Thornton (1995) provides a complementary approach to Redhead's in her study of club cultures. Thornton suggests that through engagement with different styles of dance music, young people define themselves in relation to their peers. Drawing on the work of Bourdieu (1984), Thornton develops the idea of 'subcultural capital' to analyse the forms of taste and distinction that characterise the club scene. Further studies have critiqued the concept of subculture and tried to find other terms to express young people's activity, relationship to culture and self expression. Contenders for the new, reconfigured subcultural crown include 'scenes' 'tribes' and 'neo tribes'. 'Scenes' is a term used widely in studies of popular music to explore musical collectivities. 'Tribes' and 'neo tribes' draw on the work of Maffesoli (1995) to describe loose groups of young people whose stylised tastes and lifestyles come together during moments of shared interest (see Bennett 1999, 2000, Blackman, 2005 and Hesmondhalgh, 2005 for a further discussion of these terms). Recent studies of youth formations indicate that definitions of subculture cannot be fixed in terms of earlier studies or socio-cultural moments. Like other sociological concepts, they are subject to change and redefinition.

We now look at the development of a subcultural group, skinheads, and consider some of the ways in which subcultures change and develop over time.

Skinheads: a case study

Skinhead style emerged in 1960s Britain at a time of social and economic change. Phil Cohen's (1972) study of subcultures in the East End of London describes the breakdown of traditional working class communities as old, run-down and cramped terraces were demolished and replaced by new housing developments. Long established communities were uprooted, dispersed and finally rehoused in new environments which, although brighter and more hygienic, were often considered to be unfriendly and even alien. Workplaces and traditional forms of employment were also disrupted during this period and many young men had no choice but to find work outside the area. The disruption of family life, kinship patterns and working relations has been well documented. In this literature the focus on the East End prior to redevelopment often conjures up an imaginary past, the 'classic white slum' as Hebdige (1987) describes it. At the same time the structure of British society was undergoing change due to the impact of postwar immigration from former colonies in the Asian subcontinent and the Caribbean. Changes in social relations were also taking shape that can be understood in terms of the emergence of a new sexual agenda. Questions were being asked about the position of women in society and their rights in relation to men. Such questions inevitably challenged the dominance of the white heterosexual male. Within this context the skinhead appeared to represent the concerns of the present couched in the myth of the past. Cohen describes the skinhead style of dress as 'a kind of caricature of the model worker' (Cohen, P., 1972), ready for manual work but actually spending leisure time.

Skinhead style

The following activity based on an extract by John Clarke explores some of these themes.

Activity 3   Skinheads

Allow 20 minutes   Read the following extract and make notes on the reasons the author gives for the emergence of the subculture and on the defining features of the subculture, for example how the participants look, behave and feel.

Skinheads and the magical recovery of community

Our basic thesis about the skinheads centres around the notion of community. We would argue that the skinhead style represents an attempt to re-create through the 'mob' the traditional working class community, as a substitution for the *real* decline of the latter. The underlying social dynamic for the style, in this light, is the relative worsening of the situation of the working class, through the second half of the sixties, and especially the more rapidly worsening situation of the lower working class (and of the young within that) ...

But the skinheads felt oppressed by more than just the obvious authority structure; they resented those who tried to get on and 'give themselves false airs', people from within the neighbourhood who had pretensions to social superiority; they resented the 'people on our backs' ...

However, the skinhead style does not revive the community in a real sense; the postwar decline of the bases of that community had removed it as a real source of solidarity; the skinheads had to use an *image* of what that community was as the basis of their style. They were the 'dispossessed inheritors'; they received a tradition which had been deprived of its real social bases. The themes and imagery still persisted, but the reality was in a state of decline and disappearance. We would suggest that this dislocated relation to the traditional community accounts for the exaggerated and intensified form which the values and concerns of that community received in the form of the skinhead style ...

Finally, we would like to exemplify this relation between the skinheads and the image of the community through some of the central elements of the skinhead style. One of the most crucial aspects is the emphasis on territorial connections for the skinheads – the 'Mobs' were organised on a territorial basis, identifying themselves with and through a particular locality (e.g. the 'Smethwick Mob', etc.). This involved the Mobs in the demarcation and defence of their particular 'patch', marking boundaries with painted slogans ('Quinton Mob rules here', etc.), and maintaining those boundaries against infractions by other groups ...

We may see these three interrelated elements of territoriality, collective solidarity and 'masculinity' as being the way in which the skinheads attempted to recreate the inherited imagery of the community in a period in which the experiences of increasing oppression demanded forms of mutual organisation and defence. And we might finally see the intensive violence connected with the style as evidence of the 'recreation of the community' being indeed a 'magical' or 'imaginary' one, in that it was created without the material and organisational basis of that community and consequently was less subject to the informal mechanisms of social control characteristic of such communities. In the skinhead style we can see both the elements of continuity (in terms of the style's content), and discontinuity (in terms of its form), between parent culture and youth subculture.

(Clarke, 1976, in Hall and Jefferson, 1976, pp. 99–102)

Comment

John Clarke suggests that skinhead subcultures emerged as a response to the decline of traditional working class communities in the UK in the postwar period. For Clarke, skinhead groups defining themselves as 'mobs' represent an attempt not just to mourn the loss of working class community but actually to recreate it. The term 'mob' and its associations with revolutionary zeal and criminal activity captures a sense of proletariat energy and protest that is forceful and purposeful. Skinheads had things to be angry about and this anger provided them with a collective cause or solidarity. Elsewhere in the text Clarke documents the many ways in which the skinheads feel oppressed by the environment they find themselves in and the people around them: the police and the legal system; schools and youth clubs; social workers and middle class 'do-gooders'; the aspiring working class; hippies; ethnic minority groups and gays. Such a wide ranging list is indicative of the extent of their anger and suggests that skinheads as a group feel alienated and besieged. They have a sense of belonging to a community that is, from their perspective, fragmenting and in decline. Their sense of marginalisation leads to feelings of frustration and aggression. The skinheads' concern over territory, the marking and regulation of their neighbourhood by their presence and their graffiti, also points to a constant need to defend what is theirs – to say this part of the city, estate or street is our space, *we rule here*. This assertion of authority in certain localities also brings into sharp focus the skinheads' feelings of dispossession and dislocation at a more general level which could be interpreted as: *we rule here cos we don't rule anywhere else*.

Do skinheads hate everything and everybody, or is there anything they enjoy? Elsewhere in his account Clarke suggests that the skinheads enjoy the rituals of football and fighting. Within these spheres of activity they can display a style of masculine prowess premised upon being physically tough and being together. Clarke describes the skinheads' uncompromising stance in the face of violence and the highly prized feelings of group loyalty which make it important to support each other when 'trouble' erupts. 'Paki-bashing' and 'queer bashing' provide an arena for the values of the skinhead group to be displayed and consolidated. Clarke suggests that these practices can be understood as defensive reactions to the breakdown of cultural homogeneity and traditional forms of masculinity. Ethnic minority groups and gays become scapegoats for the skinheads' sense of loss and feelings of powerlessness in the face of social change.

3.2 Changing skinhead style

Contemporary research on skinhead youth indicates that skinhead style can be appropriated and interpreted in different ways. In the context of 1980s Britain, anti-racist activists sought to challenge and invert the stereotypical image of the skinhead by appropriating the skinhead 'look'.

A notable rebranding of the skinhead image can be found in the band The Redskins. As members of the Socialist Workers Party and the Anti Nazi League, the band took up the skinhead look to promote anti-racism through grassroots political activism and popular social movements such as Rock Against Racism. Rock Against Racism was spearheaded by rock bands through gigs, rallies and mass demonstrations, and achieved success and widespread support as an energetic campaign to promote racial equality and celebrate diversity.

A further reworking of the skinhead look can be seen in Murray Healy's (1996) study of working class gay men in Europe and the USA. Healy documents the ways in which his respondents adopted the signature skinhead haircut and mode of dress to assert their working class homosexual masculinity. The gay skinheads in Healy's study were keen to demonstrate that being gay did not necessarily involve a compromise with white class-coded masculinity and its associations with strength and resilience. The gay skinheads sought to distance themselves from middle class homosexuals who frequently adopted an effeminate 'camp' style, the embodiment of the stereotypical limp-wristed 'queen'. The gay skinheads, however, unlike their predecessors in Clarke's study, did not espouse racist views and were not associated with racial violence. Anoop Nayak's (1999) study of skinheads in the Kempton Dene area of Birmingham, UK points to other ways of understanding skinhead style. Nayak suggests that although ethnicity remains a much studied aspect of black minority groups, little is known about the ethnicity of white youth and the way in which racism may feature in their lives. In the light of this omission, his study aims to explore the process whereby explicitly racist young men evoke whiteness within their suburban neighbourhoods in relation to their two obsessions: being authentic and being British.

Skinhead movements – dance of the paleface

The nostalgic portrayals of white working-class men are voiced in bodily descriptions of them as 'the backbone of the nation', 'the salt of the earth', 'the heart of the country', etc. Such earthy corporeal metaphors not only articulate notions of class and gender, but are premised on static notions of a rooted white community. Rather than seeing whiteness as the unchanging, anatomical identity fetishised here, I want to suggest that white masculinities are given the appearance of substance in *embodied* action and synchronised routines ...

[...]

In Kempton Dene, the haircut became the main signifier of difference between skinheads and other youth groups ...

Paradoxically, the fashion of the skinheads from 'the Dene' re-worked black cultural style, though they were a far cry from the 'braces-'n'-bovver-boots' appearance of previous periods. The interviewees frequently wore loose checked shirts, training shoes, baggy jeans and hooded anoraks; familiar accessories found in the wardrobes of many African/Caribbean males in Birmingham. The monocultural whiteness the young men chose to celebrate, disguised the hybrid exchanges that had occurred in their appropriation of dissonant styles. Consequently, the 'skins' were engaged in a 'post-imperial mode of mimicry' (Mercer, 1994, p. 123), adopting elements of black cultural style and synthesising this into a white working-class repertoire of style. Where former skinhead cultures looked to reggae, bluebeat and ska for inspiration, the young men in this study looked to the equally contradictory black influence of 'rave', ragga and hip-hop. The alteration in styles of dress and music by contemporary skinheads in outer-city Birmingham is possible, as these are 'plastic' forms not directly produced by the subculture but selected and invested with subcultural value (Cohen, P., 1972, p. 23). Thus hardcore 'rave' music could be appropriated as a white working-class youth culture, while its black cultural roots were overlooked. This suggests that skinhead style has developed, while continuing to be in 'dialogue' *with* and *against* black culture.

Skinhead style as a manifestation of white pride is, at once, structured in contradiction. Hebdige (1987) metaphorically notes how skinheads bleached the black roots embedded in their stylistic identities. The haircuts of the Kempton Dene males ranged from 'no. 1' (the severest grade on an electric shaver), through to 'crew cuts' and 'flat tops'. These cuts drew upon the black soulboy look of the mid-1960s, so as a motif of white authenticity remain highly suspect (Mercer, 1994). Effectively, the genuine 'trademark' that the Kempton 'skins' hope to achieve only produces a synthetic whiteness, as the style was fabricated through black/white interaction. Rather, the skinhead style remains, to all purposes, an inverted parody of blackness, what Kobena Mercer (1994, p. 123) has compared to 'a photographic negative'. Here, the shadowy image of a black 'Other' is the film through which whiteness is constituted. In other words, essentialising blackness to trace and locate an authentic white being, only produces another ephemeral imitation, a copy of a copy. It seems that behind the dazzling dance of the paleface may lurk the smudged shadow outline of black history.

(Nayak, 1999, pp. 76–84)

Nayak's study is an illustration of the ways in which subcultures develop and change. The skinheads of Kempton Dene shared features in common with skinheads of earlier periods but there were also significant differences. Nayak points to the variations in haircut, clothes and musical influences to indicate the diversity and fluidity within the subculture. Furthermore, Nayak makes visible an account of white ethnicity that has not been central to earlier studies. Seeing skinheads through the lens of white ethnicity highlights the many points of engagement between black and white cultures and reveals the contradictions inherent in skinhead identity.

Key points

- Subcultures exist in relationship to the societies in which they take shape.
- Subcultures may be a response to changing social and economic relations.
- Subcultural activity may be understood as an attempt to resolve some of the contradictions faced by young people in particular social and economic circumstances.
- Members of a subculture may celebrate certain aspects of their lives and identities such as ethnicity and class consciousness.
- Subcultures change and develop over time.

4   What about girls?

Looking at subcultural groups such as skinheads provides us with striking accounts of the differences between the subculture and the dominant culture as well as giving a glimpse into the lifestyle and outlook of young people who participate in subcultures. You may have noticed that the subcultures we have looked at so far have been populated mainly by young men. Cressey's work on the taxi-dance hall is an exception to this and is, in itself, an unusual study for the period. Women working in the field of youth challenged the masculine bias that was assumed in many studies of youth subcultures and asked the question, what about girls and subcultures? Joyce Canaan (1991), in an influential critique 'Is "doing nothing" just boys' play?', asked whether girls have a presence in youth subcultures and, if so, why they are absent from so many contemporary accounts. The following extract considers the status of girls in relation to youth subcultures and provides a valuable insight into young people's cultural worlds from a gendered perspective.

Activity 4   Girls, girls, girls

Allow 25 minutes   What are the main points in the following passage? Make notes on how a focus on gender changes the contours of youth subcultures and on what we learn about young people and gender relations during this period.

Girls and subcultures

Though girls participated in the general rise in the disposable income available to youth in the 1950s, girls' wages were not as high as those of boys. Patterns of spending were also structured in a different direction. Girls' magazines emphasised a particularly feminine mode of consumption and the working class girl, though actively participating in the world of work, remained more focused on home and marriage than her male counterpart. Teddy-boy culture was an escape from the claustrophobia of the family, into the street and the 'caff'. While many girls might adopt an appropriate way of dressing, complementary to the teds, they would be much less likely to spend the same amount of time on the streets. Girls had to be careful not to 'get into trouble' and excessive loitering on street corners might be taken as a sexual invitation to the boys. The double standard was probably more rigidly maintained in the 1950s than any other time since then. The difficulty in obtaining effective contraception, the few opportunities to spend unsupervised time with members of the opposite sex and the financial dependency of the working class woman on her husband, meant that a good reputation mattered above anything else. As countless novels of the moment record, neighbourhoods flourished on rumours and gossip and girls who spent too much time on the street were thought to be promiscuous.

At the same time the expanding leisure industries were directing their attention to *both* boys and girls. Girls were as much the subject of attention as their male peers when it came to pin-up pictures, records and magazines. Girls used these items and activities in a different context from those in which boys used them. Cosmetics were of course worn outside the home, at work and on the street, as well as in the dance-hall. But the rituals of trying on clothes, and experimenting with hair styles and make-up were home-based activities. It might be suggested that girls' culture of the time operated within the vicinity of the home, or the friend's home. There was room for a great deal of the new teenage consumer culture within the confines of the girls' bedrooms. Teenage girls did participate in the new public sphere accorded by the growth of the leisure industries, but they could also consume at home, upstairs in their bedrooms.

(Based on McRobbie and Garber, 1975)

Comment

Angela McRobbie and Jenny Garber draw attention to the ways in which girls have been overlooked or misrepresented in studies of youth subculture. They argue that gender, like social class, is a structural inequality that materially affects the life chances and experiences of individuals. It is from this perspective that they discuss the role of girls in youth subcultural settings. A starting point for McRobbie and Garber is the social space that girls occupy in society generally. They speculate that the absence of girls in subcultures may be because girls are more centrally involved in the 'private' domestic sphere of home and family life than the public world of the street where most subcultural activities seem to occur. Looking at girls in subcultures, therefore, shifts the focus from oppositional forms to a consideration of modes of conformity. There are dangers for girls in hanging around on the streets. Beyond the obvious danger of physical assault, girls' presence on the street could be associated with sexual promiscuity and carry the ensuing risk of a damaged reputation. McRobbie and Garber discuss the significance of mass culture to the lives of young people and particularly the ways in which boys and girls were targeted by companies as potential buyers of their products. For girls, new patterns of teenage consumption engaged them in more home based activities: experimenting with changes of clothes, hairstyles and make-up, often in the confined space of the bedroom.

McRobbie and Garber go on to profile and discuss three images of girls as participants in subcultures: the motorbike girl, the mod girl and the hippy girl. These three images illustrate the range of ways in which girls may have had a presence in subcultures and the overwhelming tendency to associate girls with issues of sexuality. In fact, young women are frequently defined in terms of their sexuality; their physical attractiveness, sexual availability and reproductive capacities become tropes for the general appraisal of girls as individuals and as a social group. The authors conclude that it is important to look at the ways in which young women interact among themselves to form distinctive cultures of their own. Engagements with teenage magazines and participation in 'teenybopper' culture are some of the ways in which young women create and structure their own cultural worlds.

But what about girls in the present period? How has the experience of being a girl changed since the 1970s when McRobbie and Garber were writing? Contemporary research on girlhood indicates that there are different ways of being a girl and that femininity is no longer so rigidly defined. In fact, it may be helpful to suggest that there are now *femininities*: multiple ways of living and identifying as female. Sinikka Aapola, Marnina Gonick and Anita Harris (2005) suggest that the lives and experiences of young women in the contemporary period can be understood in relation to two competing **discourses**: 'girl power' and 'reviving Ophelia'. Discourse describes a way of looking at the world, combining an expression of knowledge and power. The girl power discourse has gained currency in popular culture through girl bands and girl power attitude. Girl power suggests to young women that they can get what they want and do what they want. In this respect the girl power discourse exists as a seemingly new version of femininity that can be seen as an assertive and individualised expression of power. Drawing on a best-selling book of the same name (Pipher, 1994), the reviving Ophelia discourse articulates a set of moral and social concerns in relation to young women such as loss of sense of self, pregnancy and sexually transmitted disease, drug taking, involvement in crime and other forms of crisis. Within the context of these competing discourses, Aapola *et al.* suggest that young women are active in shaping their own identities in new and interesting subcultural spaces. The authors argue that the internet has become an important site for girls to express themselves as individuals and, through dialogue with other girls, develop a collective identity and attitude.

Illustration from a girlzine publication

Since electronic communication allows for the reformulation of various sorts of cultural activity, it becomes clear that subcultures do not necessarily need to be face-to-face or local. The proliferation of electronic magazines, written by and for girls, points to a level of energy and agency that is active in redefining feminine identities and provides a commentary on contemporary girlhood. Significantly, the activities that Aapola *et al.* document play an important part in reshaping and redefining subcultures and subcultural space.

'Girl power' and 'Riot Grrrls'

The origin of the term [girl power] is usually traced back to the early 1990s, in the US to a loosely formed movement of young, mainly white and middle class women ... who called themselves 'Riot Grrrls'. With their roots in punk rock music and their motto 'Grrrls need guitars', the riot grrrls reclaimed the word girl, using it strategically to distance themselves from the adult patriarchal worlds of status, hierarchies and standards (Hesford, 1999, p. 45). Its usage also marks a celebration of both the fierce and aggressive potential of girls (the 'grrr' stood for growling) as well as reconstitution of girl culture as a positive force embracing self-expression through fashion, attitude and a Do It Yourself (DIY) approach to cultural production ...

Many grrrls used their bodies to convey this ironic melding of style with political expression by, for example the juxtaposition of gendered signs (for example '1950s dresses with combat boots, shaved hair with lipstick, studded belts with platform heels' (Klein, 1997, p. 222)) and through writing politically loaded words such as 'rape', 'shame' and 'slut' on their arms and stomachs (Japenga, 1995, p. 30 as in Jacques, 2001, p. 49). By most accounts the movement was a response to the sexism, elitism and violence of local masculinist punk scenes where girls were considered less than full members ...

In addition to regular face to face meetings, gigs, workshops and conventions, the Riot Grrrls network through zines, which are self written and designed photocopied publications they hand out and mail to other girls. The writings take up a full range of themes and styles: angry, supportive, advice-giving, on issues like relationships, harassment, mental, physical and verbal abuse, and rape ... Zines are often attempts to forge new communities beyond their locales. The capacity to build a global grrrl movement through these media is critical to many zine creators.

Girls are also turning to cyberspace and the creation of e-zines as a alternative site for self-expression. In comparison to print zines, online zines have the advantage of limited production and distribution expense after the initial investment of a computer ...

(Aapola *et al*., 2005, pp. 20–2)

McRobbie (1994) has attempted to trace some of these changes in her later work. She suggests that a new social order is emerging and that the dramatic changes in contemporary youth cultures may be responses to such change. Key changes at a societal level cited by McRobbie include de-industrialisation, class de-alignment, gender relations, changing patterns of work and leisure and the reality of HIV/AIDS. By detailing some of the activities involved in being part of a subculture, McRobbie suggests that the distinction between mainstream society and the separate sphere of the subculture is not so easy to maintain. In the following activity you are asked to consider the impact of social change on youth subcultures and to reflect on the changing status of subcultures themselves.

Activity 5   Key changes in youth subcultures

Allow 30 minutes   What are the key changes in youth culture identified by McRobbie in the following extract? Do you think that youth subcultures now constitute part of mainstream society? Suggest reasons for your answer.

Girls, cultural production and youth culture

Let us start by saying that there have been some key changes in youth culture in the last decade. In fact things were never the same after punk. The turning point it marked meant that youth subcultures, whatever guise they had taken, could no longer be seen as occupying only a 'folk devil' position in society. There were too many of them, and they were increasingly able to counter whatever charges were made against them by the mass media since they had at their disposal – partly as a result of the availability of cheaper technology – the means to defend themselves and to discuss the issue with a wider audience than themselves ...

... magazines produced by fans, music produced by DJs, the clothes bought, sold and worn by subcultural 'stylists', do more than just publicize the subculture. They also provide the opportunity for learning and sharing skills, for practising them, for making small amounts of money; more importantly, they provide pathways for future 'life-skills' in the form of work or self-employment. To ignore the intense activity of cultural production as well as its strongly aesthetic dimension (in graphics, fashion design, retail and music production) is to miss a key part of subcultural life – the creation of a whole way of life, an alternative to higher education (though often a 'foundation' for art school), a job creation scheme for the culture industries. The point is that far from being merely the commercial, low ebb of the subculture, as far removed from resistance as it is possible to imagine, these activities can be seen as central to it. They are also expressions of change and social transformation. ... involvement can be an empowering experience, particularly for young people with no access to the skills and qualifications acquired as a matter of course by those other young people destined for university and for the professions. Subcultures are often ways of creating job opportunities as more traditional careers disappear. In this undocumented, unrecorded and largely 'hidden economy' sector, subcultures stand at one end of the culture industry spectrum and the glamorous world of the star system and the entertainment business at the other.

(McRobbie, 1994, pp. 159–62)

Comment

McRobbie cites punk as a turning point for youth subcultural forms. There were lots of inversions embedded within punk. Fans formed bands, created their own record labels, produced magazines for other fans and collectively engaged in a range of practices that broke down some of the boundaries between mainstream culture and commercial practices and the subculture. Emerging in the late 1970s, during a period of high unemployment in the UK, punks refused to be marginalised. McRobbie suggests that punk attitude and activity changed youth subcultures. Participants began to engage in mainstream practices such as making, buying and selling, and then imported these practices into the subculture. Such activities provided young people with skills to use in the mainstream while also offering alternatives to the mainstream. McRobbie concludes that the 'hidden economy' of subcultural life becomes an active and life-enhancing feature of mainstream cultural production.

Key points

- Early studies of subcultures focused more on the participation of young men than young women.

- Girls have traditionally been associated with the domestic sphere of the home rather than public spaces such as the street and the city centre.

- The subcultural activities of girls can be seen in terms of conformity to, and rejection of, the gender roles available to them.

- The internet has redefined subcultures in ways that have been productive for girls and young women.

- Through subcultural activity girls may provide a social commentary on girlhood, gender relations and feminine identities.

Conclusion

In this final part of the chapter you will consider ways of evaluating the concept of youth culture. The chapter concludes by considering how the concept of subculture may shape our understanding of youth as a social group.

Activity 6	Evaluating subcultures

Allow 25 minutes

Divide a piece of paper into two columns. Drawing on the material in this chapter, in one column jot down what you consider to be some of the strengths of seeing young people as participants within distinct subcultural groups. In the other column suggest some of the limitations of this approach. Do any key themes or points emerge?

Comment

You may have identified the following strengths of the youth subcultures approach:

1 Youth subcultures make young people visible and provide an insight into their position in society and their perspectives.

2 Ethnographic accounts such as Nayak (1999) give voice to youth and offer ways of making sense of their experiences.

3   Many accounts of subcultural forms acknowledge the importance of the cultural perspective and offer ways of reading cultural artefacts.

Did you note any of these limitations of the youth subcultures approach?

1   Youth subcultures are not necessarily full time: they overlap with other spheres of young people's lives such as family, work and college.

2   There is a tendency to focus on the deviant and the spectacular; this overlooks groups of young people who 'conform' or who do not stand out.

3   Young people's activity tends to be interpreted as a form of protest or resistance rather than as a form of self expression such as play or leisure.

Sarah Thornton (1997) points out that in the process of portraying social groups, researchers inevitably construct them and bring them into being. This process of construction through observation and analysis could apply to all the youth cultures studied in this chapter. Subcultures such as the skinheads, rastas and punks are given shape and substance not least because they are labelled, objectified and analysed through the media and the research process. What can we say about youth from the cultural perspective? Andy Bennett (1999) has pointed out that participants in subcultures tend to be defined by their subcultural identity rather than by other identities that may shape their lives such as being a member of a family, having a relationship or being a student. Christine Griffin points to other implications when she suggests that, in Western societies, the category 'youth' is 'treated as a key indicator of the state of the nation itself' (Griffin, 1993, p. 9). The values, behaviour and attitudes of young people can be read as a comment on society at present and can also be seen to hold the key to the nation's future. Viewed in these terms, youth as a social category represents something bigger than the young people themselves.

References

Aapola, S., Gonick, M. and Harris, A. (2005) *Young Femininity: Girlhood, Power and Social Change*, Basingstoke, Palgrave.

Bennett, A. (1999) 'Subcultures or neo-tribes? Rethinking the relationship between youth, style and musical taste', *Sociology*, vol. 33, no. 3, pp. 599–617.

Bennett, A. (2000) *Cultures of Popular Music*, Maidenhead, Open University Press/ McGraw-Hill.

Blackman, S. (2005) 'Youth subcultural theory: a critical engagement with the concept, its origins and politics, from the Chicago School to postmodernism', *Journal of Youth Studies*, vol. 8, no. 1, pp. 1–20.

Bourdieu, P. (1984) *Distinction: A Social Critique of the Judgement of Taste*, London, Routledge and Kegan Paul.

Canaan, J. (1991) 'Is "doing nothing" just boys' play? Integrating feminist and cultural studies perspectives on working-class masculinities' in Franklin, S., Lury, C. and Stacey, J. (eds) *Off-Centre: Feminism and Cultural Studies*, London, Routledge.

Clarke, J. (1976) 'The skinheads and the magical recovery of community' in Hall, S. and Jefferson, T. (eds) *Resistance through Rituals: Youth Subcultures in Postwar Britain*, London, Hutchinson.

Cohen, A.K. (1955) *Delinquent Boys: The Culture of the Gang*, New York, The Free Press.

Cohen, P. (1972) 'Subcultural conflict and working class community', *Working Papers in Cultural Studies 2*, University of Birmingham, Centre for Contemporary Cultural Studies.

Cohen, S. (1972) *Folk Devils and Moral Panics*, London, Paladin.

Corrigan, P. (1979) *Schooling the Smash Street Kids*, London, Macmillan.

Cressey, G. (1932) *The Taxi-Dance Hall*, New York, Greenwood Press.

Erikson, E. (1968) *Identity, Youth and Crisis*, New York, Norton & Co.

Gelder, K. and Thornton, S. (1997) *The Subcultures Reader*, London, Routledge.

Gordon, M. (1947) 'The concept of the subculture and its application', *Social Forces*, October.

Griffin, C. (1987) 'Broken transitions: schooling to the scrap heap' in Allatt, P., Keil, T., Bryman, A. and Bytheway, B. (eds) *Women and the Life-Cycle: Transitions and Turning Points*, London, Macmillan.

Griffin, C. (1993) *Representations of Youth*, Cambridge, Polity Press.

Hall, G.S. (1904) *Adolescence: Its Psychology, and its Relations to Physiology, Anthropology, Sociology, Sex, Crime, Religion and Education* (2 vols), New York, Appleton.

Hall, S. and Jefferson, T. (eds) (1976) *Resistance through Rituals: Youth Subcultures in Postwar Britain*, London, Hutchinson.

Healy, M. (1996) *Gay Skins: Class, Masculinity and Queer Appropriation*, London, Cassell.

Hebdige, D. (1987) *Subculture: The Meaning of Style*, London, Methuen.

Hesford, W. (1999) *Framing Identities: Autobiography and the Policies of Pedagogy*, Minneapolis, University of Minnesota Press.

Hesmondhalgh, D. (2005) 'Subcultures, scenes or tribes? None of the above', *Journal of Youth Studies*, vol. 8, no. 1, pp. 21–40.

Jacques, A. (2001) 'You can run but you can't hide: the incorporation of riot grrrl into mainstream culture', *Canadian Women's Studies*, 20/21.

Japenga, A. (1995) 'Punk girls groups are putting the self back into self-esteem', *New York Times*, 15 November, p. 30.

Klein, M. (1997) 'Duality and redefinition: young feminism and the alternative music community' in Heywood, L. and Drake, J. (eds) *Third Wave Agenda: Being Feminist, Doing Feminism*, Minneapolis, University of Minnesota Press.

Laslett, P. (1971) 'Age of menarche in Europe since the eighteenth century', *Journal of Interdisciplinary History*, vol. 2, no. 2, pp. 221–36.

Maffesoli, M. (1995) *The Time of the Tribes: The Decline of Individualism in Mass Society*, London, Sage.

Marsland, D. (1986) *The Theory of Youth in Sociology and in Practice*, paper presented at British Sociological Association annual conference, Loughborough University.

McRobbie, A. (1994) *Postmodernism and Popular Culture*, London, Routledge.

McRobbie, A. and Garber, J. (1975) 'Girls and subcultures' in Hall, S. and Jefferson, T. (eds) (1976) *Resistance through Rituals: Youth Subcultures in Postwar Britain*, London, Hutchinson.

Mercer, K. (1994) *Welcome to the Jungle: New Positions in Black Cultural Studies*, London, Routledge.

Muuss, R.E. (1968) *Theories of Adolescence* (2nd edn), New York, Random House.

Nayak, A. (1999) 'Pale warriors: skinhead culture and the embodiment of white masculinities' in Brah, A., Hickman, M. and Mac an Ghaill, M. (eds) *Thinking Identities: Ethnicity, Racism and Culture*, Basingstoke, Macmillan.

O'Sullivan, T., Hartley, J., Saunders, D., Montgomery, M. and Fiske, J. (1994) *Key Concepts in Communications and Cultural Studies*, London, Routledge.

Pearson, G. (1983) *Hooligan: A History of Respectable Fears*, Basingstoke, Macmillan.

Pipher, M. (1994) *Reviving Ophelia: Saving the Selves of Adolescent Girls*, New York, Riverhead Books.

Redhead, S. (1997) *Subcultures to Clubcultures*, Oxford, Blackwell.

Shaw, A. (1968) *Sinatra: A Biography*, New York, W.H. Allen.

Springhall, J. (1986) *Coming of Age: Adolescence in Britain, 1860–1960*, Dublin, Gill and Macmillan.

Springhall, J. (1998) *Youth, Popular Culture and Moral Panics: Penny Gaffs to Gangsta Rap, 1830–1996*, Basingstoke, Macmillan.

Street, B. (1993) 'Culture is a verb: anthropological aspects of language and cultural process' in Graddol, D., Thompson. L. and Bryam, M. (eds) *Language and Culture: British Studies in Applied Linguistics 7,* Clevedon, Multicultural Matters.

Thornton, S. (1995) *Club Culture*, Cambridge, Polity Press.

Thornton, S. (1997) 'Introduction to Subcultures' in Gelder, K. and Thornton, S. (eds) *The Subcultures Reader*, London, Routledge.

Tyler, B.M. (1989) 'Black jive and white repression' *Journal of Ethnic Studies*, vol. 16, no. 4, pp.1–66.

Ussher, J. (1989) *The Psychology of the Female Body*, London, Routledge.

Whyte, W.F. (1943) *Street Corner Society: The Social Structure of an Italian Slum*, Chicago, University of Chicago Press.

Williams, R. (1961) *The Long Revolution*, London and New York, Columbia University Press.

Williams, R. (1989) *Resources of Hope: Culture, Democracy, Socialism*, London, Verso.

Winnicott, D.W. (1989 [1968]) 'Contemporary concepts of adolescent development and their implications for higher education' in *Playing and Reality*, New York, Routledge.

Young, J. (1971) *The Drugtakers: The Social Meaning of Drug Use*, London, Paladin.

Chapter 2

A comparative perspective

Heather Montgomery

Introduction

This chapter takes a different approach to studying youth – a comparative one – which will examine anthropological understandings of young people. Through the use of example, it will show that young people's lives vary widely throughout the world and that categories that are often taken for granted in Western terms are not universal or biologically based, but are embedded in culture and mean very different things in different contexts. In this chapter cross-cultural contexts will generally mean non-Western or traditional societies. There are problems with these labels, as will be explained further on, but some of the examples chosen will be from highly unfamiliar societies and groups of people living very different lives. This is not to set up non-Western cultures as interesting exotica but to show, by the use of stark contrasts, that certain categories, such as youth, are not based on scientific fact, on chronological age or universal life stages, but are categories created and given meaning by society, and that we cannot understand them unless we acknowledge, and are aware of, the social and cultural context in which they are formed.

The chapter will address the following core questions:

- How does an ethnographic approach to research help us to understand young people's lives?
- Why are youth and adolescence not the same thing?
- Why is youth seen as a time of storm and stress?
- What are rites of passage and why are they important?

The chapter will start by discussing social anthropology and how it can inform studies of young people. It will briefly discuss a couple of examples of anthropological accounts of young people's lives in traditional societies. There will then be an extended discussion about rites of passage and whether or not such a concept is meaningful in discussing contemporary young people's lives. The chapter will also pose the question as to whether young people are a problem for society or whether it is social attitudes towards young people that cause the difficulties.

Activity 1   What defines youth?

Allow 20 minutes   Write a brief description of how you define youth. What are the most salient features, in your mind, of young people's lives, and do you assign any particular attributes to young people?

Comment

This might seem at first a rather simplistic exercise, but it is important to recognise that 'youth' is a loaded term and carries with it many connotations and assumptions. It is also worth pointing out that if you asked a friend or relative to do the same, they might come up with very different definitions or features. If your friend or relative had a different cultural heritage from your own, you might find that they used very different criteria from yours, emphasising, for example, the importance of a social or religious ritual such as a bar mitzvah as the dividing point between childhood and youth.

Nevertheless, I asked four white, middle class female friends in their mid-thirties this question and found that certain key features were mentioned.

- Youth was tied to chronological age: everyone stated quite confidently that it began at 13. There was less uniformity about when it ended, with some saying 18 – the legal age of adulthood – while others thought that 19 or 20 was more realistic.

- Youth was also seen as having some connection to puberty, and also to sexuality. Adolescents were different from children because their bodies were changing but they lacked the social maturity to handle these changes.

- Youth was linked to social and political change in that young people were allowed greater freedoms, both personal (there was less restriction on where they travelled and at what times) and political: they were allowed some civil or social freedoms such as the ability to open bank accounts, take on part time jobs and so on.

Having come up with these statements, we all found the attributes of youth more difficult. I was surprised at how negative our associations were. We came up with words and phrases like 'sulky', 'spotty', 'petulant', 'full of raging hormones', 'obsessed with sex', 'grunting', 'whinging' and 'irresponsible'. We found it much harder to come up with positive views of young people, and even when we did and thought of their political engagement, their concern with equality, these were mentioned with a knowing smile at their naivety.

Maybe you were not as harsh as my friends and I were, but, nevertheless, it emphasises that young people are often seen as a problem, as unsettling, as troublemakers or nuisances that have to 'grow up'.

As discussed in the previous chapter, the term adolescence has a strong biological and chronological basis and it is interesting that most people define adolescence as being bounded by chronological age and biological maturity. However, it should be stressed that while biological explanations and definitions of adolescence are some of the most powerful, they are not always adequate, especially when we look at young people's lives in a cross-cultural perspective. The association between adolescence and biological change is very strong and adolescence is often seen as having a biological basis in that it usually coincides with puberty and with clearly observable physical changes in both boys and girls, such as the onset of menstruation, the growth of body hair, the breaking of a boy's voice. Yet it is important not to overstate the role of biology in these processes, and dismiss the very complex transitions and changes in young people's lives as being down to 'biology' or 'hormones'. It is the social significance and understanding of these changes that is crucial to comprehend as it is this that gives them meaning. Perhaps the most useful way of looking at young people from an anthropological perspective is to emphasise that youth is a period of transition – the in-between or liminal phase between childhood and adulthood – which like many transitional phases is understood as a time of stress, disruption and social change. As Tom Hall has argued:

> The enduring power of the young to disconcert owes something to the ambiguity of youth as an intermediary and transitional phase. Young people are betwixt and between. No longer children and not yet adults, they do not quite fit or fully belong; and this makes youth a rolling moment of social tension and unease. But no one stays forever young. Young people grow older; they leave their youth and younger days behind them and move to maturity, majority and social integration. That is what is supposed to happen, at least; but this move does not always come easy.
>
> (Hall, 2003, p. 117)

1 What is social anthropology?

Social anthropology is a relatively new academic discipline. It was not until the late Victorian period that anthropology was formally recognised by universities and integrated into the social sciences. At its heart is an interest in the traditional, non-industrial, tribal societies outside Europe and the different beliefs and world views held by the members of these societies. Put very simply, social anthropology is the study of human beings: their behaviour, their beliefs, their family lives, the social and political organisation of their communities and their relationships with each other. That definition, however, could apply to other subjects as well, from the study of English literature to developmental psychology. What differentiates anthropology from these other disciplines is its study of people's cultural lives, acknowledging and celebrating the diversity of different peoples throughout the world, and recognising that, while we share some biological similarities, these have little meaning outside our cultural beliefs and understandings of the world.

The other differentiating feature of anthropology, which will be discussed shortly, is the importance of fieldwork. Doing Activity 1 in other parts of the world would result in some very different answers. While everyone might acknowledge that young people go through certain changes at puberty, what these changes mean, how society should deal with them and what impact they have on the individual would be understood very differently according to the different beliefs held in a society about the nature of humanity, the role of young people and the competencies and attributes that might be expected from a person at any given stage in the lifecycle. It is these understandings and world views that are of particular interest to anthropologists; as a discipline anthropology does not seek out right or wrong answers to questions such as what is a child, a young person or an adult. Rather anthropologists attempt to understand what the members of a community think about particular issues, regardless of their own views.

Malinowski with the Trobriand islanders

1.1 The role and importance of fieldwork

In its earliest days, anthropology was concerned with comparisons between the 'primitive' and the 'civilised'. Social anthropologists were reliant on the reports of travellers, missionaries and colonial administrators, which they read at second hand and then used to make assumptions about the nature of societies they had never visited. Such methods were quickly discredited, however, and anthropologists began to rely on first-hand evidence, going themselves to distant countries, spending time with informants and using this as their primary source of data. Social anthropologists realised that the best way to understand the patterns of life in other societies was to spend time in them, that the best informants about a particular way of life were those who lived it, and that an anthropologist should, as far as possible, produce an account written from the inside rather than the outside: an **ethnography**. Such ideas were set down most explicitly by pioneers such as Bronislaw Malinowski, who promoted the use of fieldwork and a method known as 'participant observation'. In 1922 he published his book *Argonauts of the Western Pacific*, a study of people who lived in the Trobriand islands of Papua New Guinea. He lived with these people for four years, learned their language, participated in their social, economic and religious life and aimed to view their society as an insider.

The key method used by anthropologists is still based on Malinowski's insistence on fieldwork and participant observation. It remains as central to the discipline today as it was in the early years of the twentieth century when Malinowski first conducted fieldwork. Roger Keesing describes fieldwork and ethnography as follows:

> For most anthropologists, the immediate problems of understanding and the sources of data come from what has come to be known as fieldwork: intimate participation in a community and observation of modes of behavior and the organization of social life. The process of recording and interpreting another people's way of life is called *ethnography* ...

> Most essentially, [fieldwork] entails a deep immersion into the life of a people. Instead of studying large samples of people, the anthropologist enters as fully as possible into the everyday life of a community, neighborhood, or group. These people become a microcosm of the whole. One learns their language and tries to learn their mode of life. One learns by participant observation, by living as well as viewing the new patterns of life.

(Keesing, 1981, pp. 5–6)

Despite the practical and theoretical problems with participant observation, few anthropologists can get a postgraduate qualification in the discipline without doing ethnographic fieldwork. It is a central feature of the discipline, and central to many anthropologists' identity. It is important to understand therefore that what anthropologists mean by ethnographic research differs substantially from what other disciplines mean. Ethnography is sometimes used by other disciplines as a shorthand for qualitative research in general, so that, for example, if a researcher goes into a classroom and talks to young people once a week for a few weeks, they may claim this as ethnographic research – a term a social anthropologist would totally reject. Nevertheless, ethnography is no longer the preserve of anthropologists, and some sociologists, cultural studies and educationalists are now increasingly using anthropological methods of participant observation and fieldwork in their ethnographies. Ethnography to an anthropologist implies the following:

- immersion into a culture

- living, as far as possible, alongside the members of a culture or community with which the researcher is working

- learning the language and working within that language

- long term participation (researchers used to spend between four and five years in the field, but now the time is much shorter).

Activity 2	Anthropology at home

Allow 30 minutes   In the past anthropologists have focused exclusively on non-Western cultures, particularly former British colonies. Since the 1960s, however, they have begun to return 'home', arguing that the same understandings of social life and social processes that they brought to the study of non-Western peoples could be usefully applied to more complex, industrial societies (Jackson, 1987).

One recent ethnography based on fieldwork conducted 'at home' has been Tom Hall's study of youth homelessness in the UK. He lived and worked in a hostel for young homeless people (the Lime Street hostel) in a town in the UK, called by its pseudonym Southerton. Hall adopted the classic anthropological technique of participant observation. Below is an account of his methods, the problems he found, and the ways he gradually built up relationships of trust and mutual reliance with his informants.

As you read this though, make notes of the various methods Hall used. To what extent is he participating in these young people's lives and to what extent observing them? Why do you think using a tape recorder was problematic? What do you find distinctive about Hall's approach? What are its benefits? Take care to read the footnotes as well as they contain important data on his fieldwork methods.

In the field

What does an ethnographer, a participant observer, do all day? Those engaged in ethnographic research can employ a number of strategies and techniques; for my part I was neither innovative nor exhaustive in my approach. I determined, simply enough, to spend as much time as I could in the company of, and in conversation with, those young people I first met at the Lime Street hostel, keeping a daily written record of things said and done. On arrival in Southerton I rented a small bedsit room five minutes' walk from Lime Street and spent the best part of most days and every evening visiting the hostel. Over time, I was introduced to a wider ambit of young people, and my itinerary expanded to include the high street and shopping centre, the Department of Social Security (DSS) office and the bedsits of those who have moved on from the hostel. Eventually my own room became a venue for residents and ex-residents alike, some of whom even stayed there overnight when they had nowhere else to go.

I had no carefully worked out itinerary for the weeks and months as they passed. My movements on any given day were, by and large, determined by those I happened to be with or bump into. I was probably more sociable than most, trying to make and maintain a wide circle of contacts, and keep in touch with as many of those passing through the hostel as I could[1]. But even so, my daily round – calling in on friends, meeting up at the hostel, hanging out in the town centre – was little different from that of the majority of those I was spending time with. Letting the hours unfold in this way, rather than attempting to direct the action or prompt events, made for a fair amount of dull repetition. I passed a good part of each day doing very little – talking about nothing much in cramped bedsit rooms, standing on Lime Street watching passers-by, fidgeting on the fixed seats in the DSS; and although this was often time spent in good company it could be desperately tedious all the same. At other times things got much more exciting and stressful for all concerned, with events racing ahead of my ability to keep track and the young people's ability to cope. My first and lasting impression of those who passed through the

Lime Street hostel during the year I spent in Southerton was one of restlessness and inertia combined; time spent with them could be unpredictable and eventful and yet it was somehow always the same[2]...

In the first few months of fieldwork I made use of a tape recorder, sometimes arranging to sit down with individuals and conduct 'unstructured interviews'. Conducting interviews gave me something to do whilst I worked on developing the relationships that I hoped to build my fieldwork around; it also made a certain sort of sense to the residents at the hostel, who were beginning to wonder what I was doing just hanging around all day. But, encouraging as it was to transcribe the tapes and see the sheets of 'data' produced, I was never all that happy with these interviews and eventually stopped doing them altogether. I did not seem to be able to find questions that asked what it was that I really wanted to know; and the answers I got did not always 'ring true'. I was not the only one to feel that these interviews were a little deliberate and forced sometimes.

Richie: Ask Susan to come in, and interview her without her knowing about the tape. And then say to her 'I've taped you and if you want me to I'll wipe it.' It's better that way, innit, cos they react like normal.

Craig: And then pass the tape to me so I can put it on the stereo out loud and really embarrass her.

Richie [to Susan who has just walked in the room]: He wants to ask you a couple of questions. We've asked each other a couple of questions – about the hostel, about money and that, and, like, where you're going to live after, and jobs and that.

Susan [sarcastic]: Oh, really.

Richie [trying to keep a straight face]: We are, that's what we're doing. Cos he's doing a project thing, or something. Don't look at me like that, I'm being serious.

I also tried to use the tape-recorder in a less formal way, toting it around with me and recording casual discussion of the sort I was constantly involved in. Here again, I felt that conversations conducted with the tape recorder on tended to be a little stilted (only subtly so sometimes, but perhaps the more misleadingly for that) or at any rate different from those that I had when the machine was not there to speak into. It may be that I should have set aside my misgivings and persevered ... But, as it was, I pretty much stopped using my tape-recorder after the first few months of fieldwork, and was glad to do so ...

Rather than transcripts of recorded conversations, it was fieldnotes that comprised the bulk of the data I took away with me from Southerton, and I have relied on these as my primary source in writing this book. Fieldnotes are hard work. I spent several hours of almost every day in Southerton writing in my notebooks, anxious to get everything down but sometimes fed up with the time it took to do so. I seldom took detailed notes in company, because it proved impractical to do so. I couldn't keep up with events and conversations if I was simultaneously recording these with paper and pen; and even if this had been possible I would have felt uncomfortable doing so, for the same reasons I was uncomfortable

carrying the tape recorder around. But I did keep a small notebook with me at all times in which I made (surreptitiously) scribbled notes and jottings whenever the opportunity presented itself. These served as a valuable *aide-mémoire* when, last thing at night or first thing in the morning, I sat down in my room to write.

[1] In all, over the course of a year spent in Southerton I got to know just over a hundred young people, almost all of whom had at some time stayed at the hostel on Lime Street. Some, I knew only briefly; others I saw regularly, almost daily, and grew close to.

[2] On a more trivial level, another lasting impression I have of fieldwork is of music and cigarette smoke. Each day, it seems to me now, was played out to a soundtrack of chart music, rave or reggae – ticking and fizzing from personal stereos or played loud on brand new hi-fi obtained from the mail order catalogue, with little thought as to how to meet the repayments. Cigarettes were also ubiquitous, an essential accompaniment to any activity: something to burn up time with when sitting alone, or to share with others when you could afford a whole pack; something to 'scrounge' off others when you were broke; something to calm you down after an argument; an accessory on the street, to be held in a certain way and then placed casually in the corner of your mouth or wedged behind your ear, unlit, for later on.

(Hall, 2003, pp. 9–12)

Comment

This passage has been quoted at length because it provides an honest and reflexive account of some of the difficulties associated with the fieldwork process. Hall describes very well the tensions between being part of the young people's lives he is studying (a participant) but also an observer, having to take notes, write things down and attempt to discern significance in sometimes random patterns of social life. Much fieldwork is indeed rather boring, not much happens, and yet the anthropologist has to be there, recording everything, hoping that eventually it will make sense and can be seen in terms of larger cultural patterns. To try to force events, or to direct the action, distorts this process and this is why Hall found using a tape-recorder problematic. Many people become self-conscious when they feel they are being recorded and cannot act 'naturally'. Although Hall is aware that his very presence sometimes makes people act unnaturally, ideally the long term nature of fieldwork means that anthropologists can form relationships with their informants, and while acknowledging the complexities of people's lives and characters, can gain a more rounded picture of people's lives, looking at what they do, as well as what they say.

The reciprocity between anthropologist and informant is also crucial to the process. Because Hall let the young people stay with him, because he shared and cadged cigarettes, the distance between researcher and researched was diminished. As the rest of the book goes on to detail, Hall obviously had very good relationships with the young people he worked with. There is little sense of him studying them, but a fine description of the relationships between the young people, in which he is central. The benefits of this type of ethnography therefore are the limiting of distance between the 'expert' and the subject, the trust that is built up and the ethical foundations of such research, which enable those who are its subjects to influence the agenda.

The other issue which is implicit in this passage is the dissolution of the boundaries between the professional ethnographer and the informant. While in many cases this is a strength, it is also a challenge to many people who work with young people as it goes against many ideas of professional distance. The ethnographer has a very different relationship to young people than many other professionals; he is taking part in their lives, drinking and smoking with them, and on occasions endorsing harmful behaviour in order to be accepted by them. An ethnographer makes no attempt to change young people's lives and thus this way of working with young people is often radically different to other ways of becoming involved in young people's lives.

1.2 Youth as a social construction

Having looked at the methods used by anthropologists, this chapter will now turn to some of the perspectives that anthropologists in the past have brought to the study of young people. Some of this ethnography is out of date and the societies it describes have changed beyond all recognition, yet the fundamental point remains that terms such as youth must be understood as the products of culture, and must be seen as cultural constructions. To illustrate this, we can compare different conceptions of the lifecycle and the different words used to describe the various stages. There is an activity on this shortly, but to give an idea of the complexity of views about this, consider the case of the age sets among Kiswahili-speaking communities in Tanzania. The stages in the lifecycle are complex, but each one is recognised as a distinct phase of life, and a person is referred to by different terms depending on their stage in the lifecycle.

Birth to between 3 and 6 months	Very young child, baby, literally in the early stage of growth
7 months to 2 years	Suckling child
3–6 years	Small child
7–9 years (girls)	Child
7–14 years (boys)	Child
10–12 years (girls)	Pre-pubertal girl
13–15 years	Pubertal girl/boy
16–24 years	Youth – post puberty (boys and girls)
25–35 years	Whole/mature person
36–50 years	Mature person
51–65 years	Old
More than 65 years	Very old

(Source: based on Ahmed *et al.*, 1999, p. 103)

Looking at this chart, it is obvious that there are several stages that might be covered by the English word 'youth', yet Kiswahili speakers specify further. They also make important distinctions between boys and girls so that a boy remains a child until 13, while a girl ends her childhood at around nine.

Activity 3   Cultural constructions of youth and the lifecycle

Allow 20 minutes

How do you see the lifecycle in modern Britain? How many phases would you divide it into? What names would you give to these stages?

Read through the following table, which sets out the different categories used to describe young people among the Sereer of West Africa. What do you notice about these descriptions compared with your own categorisations? How is each of these stages defined by the Sereer?

Comment

It is difficult to write down all the stages in the lifecycle in contemporary Britain. Some phrases are embedded in everyday use – baby, toddler, young person – but terms change and other terms, often based on advertising or marketing demographics, come into use and then fade away again. Tweenies (or pre teenagers) are now a recognised category, and

Boys				
Name of stage	SISSIM	GAYNAK	PES	WAYABAN E
	Young of the tribe	Shepherds	Young people	Youth and adults
Age	8 to 11 years	12 to 18 years	19 to 26 years	27 to 35 years
Socialisation activities	Education about what not to do	Preparation for circumcision	Circumcision, initiation	Marriage

Girls			
Name of stage	FU NDOG WE	NOG WE	MUXOLARE
	Young girls	Adolescents	Adults
Age	7 to 10 years	11 to 18 years	19 to 26 years
Socialisation activities	Education through numerous prohibitions	Tattooing	Marriage, initiation

(Source: Gravrand, 1983, quoted in Ennew *et al.*, 1996, p. 88)

advertisers and manufacturers are continually chasing the 'middle youth' market: people in their thirties and forties who think of themselves as young people but have the spending capacity that young people themselves rarely have. What is clear though is that the lifecycle can be divided in a number of ways: by age, by consumption habits or by self definition. Stages in the lifecycle and progression from one stage to another are not clear-cut or unambiguous.

Among the Sereer there seems more certainty. There is nothing particularly remarkable about the Sereer, and this example has been chosen because it emphasises so well the point that many of the societies traditionally studied by anthropologists have very different concepts of the stages of the lifecycle. Here, the lifecycle is seen in terms of social roles and social competencies. Progression through the lifecycle depends on being competent in the role assigned to you at a particular age. A boy, for instance, is not referred to as a shepherd because of reaching a particular age, but because he successfully fulfils his socially assigned role.

It is also relevant that unlike the gender neutral terms 'young people' or 'child', such a blurring of categories is simply not possible among the Sereer. To represent the different stages of life requires two entirely separate grids for boys and girls. Except for the very earliest years, girls and boys are socialised to be radically different, and conceptually they have entirely different lives as young people.

In a sense they grow up in different worlds, so we cannot properly speak of conceptualisations of youth but of expectations of gender related competence at various ages. The expectations of boys and girls entail differential ages for entry into adult maturity, which is closely tied to reproductive maturity. Thus, for example, where women and children are largely economically dependent on men, a girl's passage to womanhood may take place far earlier, at a chronological age fairly close to the average age of puberty for her social group. Boys, on the other hand, may have to wait far beyond physical maturity to become recognised as men who can build their own house and support their own wife and children.

Key points

- This section has introduced basic premises behind the discipline of social anthropology. It has focused on the method of participant observation in which the outsider tries to understand the culture from the inside. It has also introduced the concept of ethnography – the way of describing a culture from within.

- It has shown that ideas about youth are socially and culturally constructed. Different cultures have very different understandings of the concept of youth and what behaviours can be expected of young people.

2 Youth as a time of storm and stress?

To look at some of the classic examples of young people in anthropology we have to contextualise these in the cultural settings of the people under discussion while also acknowledging that anthropologists are seeing these people through a particular lens. As discussed in the previous chapter, it was G. Stanley Hall who, in 1904, first labelled adolescence as a distinct social phase of life characterised by 'storm and stress', when children turn away from their families and towards their peer groups, when they begin to experiment with sex, gain some financial independence and start the transition from childhood to adulthood. This idea was highly influential but contested by several anthropologists, who rejected the idea that adolescence was a recognisable, biological stage characterised by storm and stress, both for the individual and for society.

One of the founders of American anthropology, Franz Boas, suggested to his student Margaret Mead that she challenge this view of universal social and biological development and, on his instigation, she travelled to

Street fight

Western Samoa to work among young people there, looking at the ways in which adolescence was understood and managed in a society radically different to contemporary North American society. In the early 1920s she conducted fieldwork among the young women in Samoa, with the explicit aim of refuting the idea that the effects of puberty were necessarily a source of stress and tension and that they could be managed very differently. Most importantly, she rejected the idea that problems in adolescence were the result of changes within individuals brought on by the biological changes which occurred during puberty and instead argued that any problems that young people had during this period were the result of sexual repression in society and of society's handling of young people. Her findings showed that the stresses of adolescent life for American teenagers focused in part on the denial and disapproval surrounding adolescent sexuality, pressures that were unknown in Samoan society. She also claimed that American adolescents were bombarded with choices and options which made their lives more difficult as they had to decide what they wanted from life. In contrast, young people in Samoa had very limited choices which revolved around staying in their villages with their families, marrying and having children in due course and remaining within their communities until they died.

Sexuality was not a source of stress for teenagers because there was no limit on premarital sex and no sexual repression. According to Mead, the girls whose lives she studied had several lovers, beginning just after puberty. Usually a girl's lover would be a boy some years older than herself or a much older man, and before her marriage she would expect to have many lovers or casual sexual partners. Sexuality was identified as a source of pleasure rather than tension as it was in the USA, and without a battle to control sexuality, many of the problems that she identified among American teenagers were completely absent in Samoa. She wrote:

> Adolescence represented no period of crisis or stress, but was instead an orderly developing of a set of slowly maturing interests and activities. The girls' minds were perplexed by no conflicts, troubled by no philosophical queries, beset by no remote ambitions. To live as a girl with as many lovers as long as possible and then to marry in one's own village, near one's own relatives, and to have many children, these were uniform and satisfying ambitions.
>
> (Mead, 1972 [1928], p. 129)

Mead's work has been much debated since and some scholars feel that by going to Samoa with such an explicit agenda, she interpreted all she saw in the light of her hypothesis that sexuality, and sexual repression, were at the heart of adolescent conflict in the USA. In doing so, she overlooked many of the sources of tension within the community. Nevertheless, Mead's work makes the important point that the 'problems' of youth are not necessarily the problems of individuals or families but may be the problems of a society putting unnecessary pressures and stresses on young people; society rather than teenagers may well be the problem.

It is also undoubtedly true that sexuality among adolescents is perceived very differently cross-culturally and there is much evidence that it need not necessarily be seen as a problem for young people or have implications for wider society. Although Mead may have been wrong in some of her specific claims about Samoa, there are many communities in the world where premarital sex among adolescents is understood as a normal and healthy part of their development. The issues surrounding teenagers and young people as they grow up cannot be divorced from their cultural context and, once again, it is important to emphasise that while physical changes are occurring around puberty, it is the ways in which these changes are managed and understood by society that gives them meaning. Puberty for young women is a much more obvious set of processes than it is for boys. It is possible to point to first menstruation as marking the onset of puberty (although girls' bodies will have changed before that) and many societies mark the menarche with rituals designed to show the girl that she is now an adult woman and ready to take on the burdens of maturity, be they marriage, childbearing or other signs of social adulthood.

Even in societies that see menstruation as dangerous or polluting, although first menstruation is not necessarily celebrated, it is marked with rituals and girls are made aware of a very significant change in status between their previous lives and their new roles. In the UK, however, few would argue that first menstruation signalled an entry into adulthood and there are no rituals or ceremonies associated with it. Among girls themselves, however, first menstruation may exist as a common talking point and marker of status within the peer group (Kehily *et al.*, 2002). Other researchers who have looked at girls' responses to their first menstruation, such as Shirley Prendergast, have noted the lack of celebration, finding that girls are much more likely to talk in terms of embarrassment or hassle (Prendergast, 1989). Menstruation is generally seen as a problem of individual management rather than a matter of social concern.

Activity 4	Storm and stress in contemporary society

Allow 45 minutes

You should now read another long description of anthropological fieldwork. Like Hall's work quoted earlier, this description by anthropologist Philippe Bourgois takes place in a community plagued by social problems and poverty. He based his study around the crack houses of East Harlem (New York) and the ways in which young people were inculcated into the world of drugs and crimes, whether they wanted to be or not. As well as providing a similar description of the challenges and opportunities of fieldwork among such marginal people, this passage also shows how easy it is for young people to lose the sympathy usually accorded to children in poverty.

As you read through this passage, make notes on the assumptions made about these young people, both by the anthropologist and the wider society. Why do you think these young people are seen as a problem rather than as young people with problems? To what extent do you think that, in this situation, adolescence is a time of storm and stress?

Families and children in pain in a US inner city

When the shrieks of crying children rose through the heating pipes in my tenement in East Harlem, New York, I fretted: Was I ethnocentrically misreading the expressively aggressive child-rearing practices of my second- generation Puerto Rican immigrant neighbors? Or was I failing to be a decent human being by not running downstairs to intervene? For almost four years, I lived with my family opposite an immense conglomeration of high-rise housing projects in a crumbling apartment with inadequate heat, inconsistently running water, and abundant vermin. At first I thought I was going to study the underground economy through the life stories of some two dozen or so Puerto Rican drug dealers who all worked for Ray, the owner of a discount franchise of crack houses that operated on and around my block. Soon, however, I found myself spending much of my time documenting the gendered violence and social suffering of the family lives of these crack sellers. I could not avoid becoming deeply immersed in their family lives, because family life is what is most important, painful and rewarding to them. It is a crucial, intimate arena for struggling for self-respect, love, meaning and personal power. It is also the institution most polemically heralded by pundits, politicians, academics, and clergy as being in crisis. Almost every day, the children, lovers, newborns, and even the aunts, uncles, and grandfathers of the crack dealers came by the crack houses where we spent most of our time ...

On a personal level, the most stressful dimension of living in El Barrio's street scene was witnessing the destruction of the children of my friends and neighbors. I watched dozens of little girls and boys fall apart as they passed from childhood to adolescence. Under my eye, energetic, bright-eyed children were ground up by the dozens into what the United States calls its 'underclass'. Within five short years, my little neighbor Gigi metamorphosed from an outgoing, cute, eager-to-please eight-year-old, who gave me a construction-paper Valentine's card every year, into a homeless, pregnant, crack-using thirteen-year-old 'teenager'. Meanwhile, her older brother, Hector, was transformed from a shy, giggling, undersized twelve-year-old into a juvenile inmate, guilty of 'assault with a dangerous weapon' ...

I began organizing biweekly trips for local street kids to cross New York's invisible apartheid barriers to visit museums, the FAO Schwartz toy store, and the Trump Tower. They loved the Andy Warhol exhibit at the Museum of Modern Art, and Angel even assured me that the Frick Museum collection of Dutch Masters was 'not boring at all'.

The full force of the racial and class boundaries confining the children of El Barrio became glaringly clear on these outings. In the museums, for example, we were usually flanked by guards with hissing walkie-talkies. Often I was eyed quizzically as a suspected pedophile parading my prey. Angel was particularly upset at the Joan Miro exhibit at the Guggenheim when he asked one of the guards – who was himself Puerto Rican – why he was being followed so closely and was told 'to make sure you don't lift your leg'.

On our way home from the Miro exhibit, I brought Angel and his friends to my mother's apartment in the Upper East Side's silk-stocking district, located less than twenty blocks from our tenements. I was sobered by Angel's simple but naive wish: 'I'm planning on

moving my mother into a building like this when I grow up, too. I wish my mom lived here'. I engaged him in a discussion of the inadequacies of the education system. I asked, 'What's the matter? You got mean teachers?' Angel focused on the destructive behavior of the victims themselves: 'No, it's the kids I'm afraid of. They be mugging people in the hallways'.

Later that evening, Angel complained to me that his mother's boyfriend had broken open his piggy bank and taken the twenty dollars' worth of tips he had saved from working as a delivery boy at the supermarket on our block. He blamed his mother for having provoked her boyfriend into beating her and robbing the apartment when she invited another man to visit her in her bedroom: 'I keep telling my mother to only have one boyfriend at a time, but she won't listen to me.' In these expressions of vulnerability, I recognized the brutal dynamic whereby tender victims internalize the social structures that dominate them. This was forcefully portrayed in the hauntingly sad and violent pictures that the children drew when I provided them with paper and crayons on the car hoods in front of my tenement after dark.

As my youthful friends grew older, Ray's franchise of crack houses gradually merged as central institutions in their lives. They were socialized into the 'normalcy' of drug dealing. In El Barrio, the crack house is virtually the only adolescent space that is heated in the winter and air-conditioned in the summer. There are simply no other healthy social scenes to frequent if one has limited resources and wants to be where the action is. Many – if not most – East Harlem apartments are overcrowded, plagued with vermin, poorly heated in the winter and stiflingly hot in the summer. The street or the crack house, consequently, offers a more comfortable alternative living room. Junior, the son of Candy, one of only two women dealers in Ray's network[1], was the first boy I watched graduate into crack-dealer status. When I first asked him at the age of thirteen what he wanted to be when he grew up he dreamed of being a 'cop'. He also wanted, however, to have 'cars, girls, and gold chains – but no drugs; a big roll [of money] and rings on all my fingers'. A year later, Junior had become a bona fide drugs courier without realizing it. He thought of the job simply as 'running errands'. Junior was more than eager to be helpful, and Primo, the manager of the crack house next to my tenement, would send him to pick up ten dollar packets of powder cocaine from around the corner or to fetch cans of beer from the bodega two doors down. Junior was not using drugs; he was merely behaving like any eager teenager flattered by the possibility of hanging out with the grown ups. Before his sixteenth birthday, Junior began filling in for Caesar, Primo's lookout, when Caesar's crack binges kept him from coming to work on time. Soon Ray promoted Junior to working at another one of his crack houses as a permanent lookout on weekends. He was replacing his Uncle Luis (a compadre of Ray), who had just been fired. Luis's crack use had rendered him an unacceptably erratic employee. Although Junior had dropped out of school by this time and already had a juvenile record for hot-wiring a car, he was a strict teetotaler and an obedient worker. He was only available to run errands and work lookout at night, however, because Candy often made him baby-sit his little sister during the day while she looked for work or visited friends.

When I tried to make Junior realize that he was being sucked into a life of drug dealing, the conversation merely degenerated into a display of how crack house logic maintains its hegemony in the daily lives even of those children who want to be good.

Philippe: So, Junior, if you don't want to be a drug dealer, what are you doing working here for Primo tonight?

Junior: Nah, I'm only lookin' out. I ain't touching no product. My mom knows about it; she said it was OK. Besides, I know drugs is wack. They just put you in hospital.

Philippe [smiling at Primo]: Junior, what's gonna happen to you? Are you just gonna turn into another scum-of-the-earth drug dealer like Primo? [In a serious tone] And keep on selling drugs and get yourself arrested?

Junior: No, not no more, 'cause if I get busted again, I get in a lot of trouble.

Primo [interrupting]: No, not the first time, Junior.

Junior: But I could get sent to a home, 'cause of that shit with the car.

Primo [condescendingly]: If you get busted selling drugs now, you'll be all right. It's the second time that you'll get fucked. [Turning to me reassuringly] He'll have someone lookin' out for him; someone who will send him bail – [giggling] most likely.

[1] The only other woman dealer, Jaycee, was a sister-out-of-law to Ray via a woman Ray had separated from. Jaycee spent much of her time working at the crack house knitting a shawl for her newborn baby girl. She quit after a year when she had saved enough money for the first and last month's rent on a subsidized apartment.

(Bourgois, 1998, pp. 331–9)

Comment

It is interesting to note that Bourgois refers to these young people as children. Generally, to talk of young people as children is to place them conceptually in a cherished category to which certain well-defined expectations and entitlements apply, whereas to position young people beyond childhood, but short of adulthood, is to assign them to a more ambiguous phase. Thus, while the guards at the museum see these young people as a problem (and in even more pejorative terms than that), the anthropologist claims they retain certain childhood privileges which should enable us to see them with more sympathy.

Clearly, these young people are living in a state of storm and stress but it is harder to know if this is because of their adolescence or because of the circumstances they find themselves forced into. The crack house is the only available comfortable space for them to hang out in. It provides both an enjoyable physical experience and also a social one, with opportunities for growing up, being seen as 'hard' and of obtaining the markers of respect: 'cars, girls, and gold chains'. It makes more sense to argue here that it is not that adolescence is a time of storm and stress (despite the horrendous toll that it seems to take on these young people), but that social forces conspire to push these young people on to a certain path, which it is then very hard for them to get off. Young people are often associated with criminality, and in this context the fact that they are poor and Puerto Rican makes others (even other Puerto Ricans) regard them as criminals, even when they have done nothing wrong. Yet as Bourgois shows so clearly, these are young people actually trying to make the best of their world; even when sucked into the drug culture, they attempt not to let it overwhelm them. Being young is not the problem in their life; rather it is poverty, discrimination, racism and a lack of any other available or worthwhile choices for them. There is undoubtedly storm and stress in their lives, but they do not necessarily generate it.

Key points

- The idea that youth is necessarily a time of storm and stress is based on Western understandings, and is not universally applicable.

- Social problems may cause the storm and stress of youth, rather than vice versa.

3 Rites of passage

One of the most lasting contributions that anthropologists have made to the study of youth is in popularising the concept of rites of passage, and for many years this was how anthropologists most often studied young people. One of the earliest and most influential social anthropologists was Arnold Van Gennep, who first coined the term. He claimed that all social and individual life could be understood as the process of crossing a series of ritual thresholds. In his words, 'Life itself means to separate and to be reunited, to change form and condition, to die and to be reborn. It is to act and to cease, to wait and rest, and then to begin again, but in a different way' (Van Gennep, 1960, p. 189). What he meant by this was that people continually changed states throughout their lives; they moved from one role to another and this transition was marked by a series of rituals of separation and reincorporation into the social body. The transition from one stage of life to another was marked symbolically and publicly, and these transitions, he argued, often occurred at times of crisis in people's lives, such as birth, puberty, marriage, childbirth and death, and while these rites of passage may differ between cultures, or be celebrated at different phases, they were features of all cultures. He argued that all true rites of passage occurred in three stages, and had three separate components:

1   separating from the familiar and leaving it behind
2   a liminal stage, meaning an in-between stage, during the transition from the old state to the new one
3   return and reintegration into the original social structure.

For Van Gennep, rites of passage were similar in structure and function wherever they occurred in the world, and always concerned similar elements. They occurred at transitional points in life, and people undergoing rites of passage were entering exclusive groups so that after this ritual they attained a higher social status. Although rites of passage occur at various times in people's lives, some of the best documented have occurred around adolescence and these will be discussed before looking at how rites of passage still occur at transitional points in young people's lives.

Activity 5   Nelson Mandela's initiation

Allow 20 minutes

Nelson Mandela in Xhosa dress

In many traditional societies rites of passage are clearly marked and observed, and there are very set practices that young people have to go through in order to attain adulthood.

Young people have a clear sense of purpose about their teenage years and look forward to rites of passage that will transform them from children to adults. One of the most famous accounts we have of a rite of passage is that written by Nelson Mandela in his book *Long Walk to Freedom* in which he describes his initiation into Xhosa manhood (Mandela is a member of one of South Africa's largest tribal groups, Xhosa, and an *ingcibi* is a man who traditionally ritually circumcises the young men). Read through the account and identify the three elements that constitute a rite of passage according to Van Gennep. In what ways do you think these tests and trials might have a positive effect on young people?

Becoming a man

When I was sixteen, the regent decided that it was time that I became a man. In Xhosa tradition, this is achieved through one means only: circumcision. In my tradition, an uncircumcised male cannot be heir to his father's wealth, cannot marry or officiate in tribal rituals. An uncircumcised Xhosa man is a contradiction in terms, for he is not considered a man at all, but a boy. For the Xhosa people, circumcision represents the formal incorporation of males into society. It is not just a surgical procedure, but a lengthy and elaborate ritual in preparation for manhood. As a Xhosa, I count my years as a man from the date of my circumcision ...

Early in the new year, we journeyed to two grass huts in a secluded valley on the banks of the Mbashe River, known as Tyhalarha, the traditional place of circumcision for Thembu kings. The huts were seclusion lodges, where we were to live isolated from society. It was a sacred time; I felt happy and fulfilled taking part in my people's customs and ready to make the transition from boyhood to manhood ...

At dawn, when the stars were still in the sky, we began our preparations. We were escorted to the river to bathe in its cold waters, a ritual that signified our purification before the ceremony. The ceremony was at midday, and we were commanded to stand in a row in a clearing some distance from the river where a crowd of parents and relatives, including the regent, as well as a handful of chiefs and counsellors, had gathered. We were clad only in our blankets and as the ceremony began, with drums pounding, we were ordered to sit on a blanket on the ground with our legs spread out in front of us. I was tense and anxious, uncertain of how I would react when the critical moment came. Flinching or crying out was a sign of weakness and stigmatized one's manhood. I was determined not to disgrace myself, the group or my guardian. Circumcision is a trial of bravery and

stoicism, no anaesthetic is used; a man must suffer in silence ...

Suddenly I heard the first boy cry out '*Ndiyindoda*!' ('I am a man!'), which we had been trained to say at the moment of circumcision. Seconds later, I heard Justice's strangled voice pronounce the same phrase. There were now two boys before the *ingcibi* reached me, and my mind must have gone blank because, before I knew it, the old man was kneeling in front of me. I looked directly into his eyes. He was pale, and though the day was cold, his face was shining with perspiration. His hands moved so fast they seemed to be controlled by an otherworldly force. Without a word, he took my foreskin, pulled it forward, and then, in a single motion, brought down his *assegai*. I felt as if fire was shooting through my veins; the pain was so intense that I buried my chin in my chest. Many seconds seemed to pass before I remembered the cry, and then I recovered and called out, '*Ndiyindoda*!'

I looked down and saw a perfect cut, clean and round like a ring. But I felt ashamed because the other boys seemed much stronger and firmer than I had been; they had called out more promptly than I had. I was distressed that I had been disabled, however briefly, by the pain, and I did my best to hide my agony. A boy may cry; a man conceals his pain.

I had now taken the essential step in the life of every Xhosa man. Now I might marry, set up my own home and plough my own field. I could now be admitted to the councils of the community; my words would be taken seriously. At the ceremony, I was given my circumcision name, Dalibhunga, meaning 'Founder of the Bungha', the traditional ruling body of the Transkei. To Xhosa traditionalists, this name is more acceptable than either of my two previous given names, Rolihlahla or Nelson, and I was proud to hear my new name pronounced: Dalibhunga.

(Mandela, 1994, pp. 24–6)

Comment

Mandela's description of his circumcision clearly shows the three stages of a rite of passage as characterised by Van Gennep. The first stage – the leaving behind of the familiar – occurs when Mandela and his friends of a similar age leave their families and live in the bush for several months. There is both a physical and conceptual separation of the young men from the rest of the community. Second, there is a period of living away from the community – a liminal time – when the young men live together in isolation from others in their community and when they are expected to perform certain feats of bravery to show that they are ready for the trials of manhood. They are then ritually circumcised by a traditional circumciser – an *ingcibi* – and expected to show no pain or fear at this, and are deeply disgraced if they do. Once this has been done and they have become men, they can return home to their villages as adults, are acknowledged by everyone as such and are allowed to take on adult duties such as marriage. This is the final stage: reintegration. The following year a new cohort of young men will go through the same process and in this way society reproduces itself.

Many societies have such ceremonies for both boys and girls in which their transition from one stage of life to another is publicly acknowledged and celebrated. Some of these may sound harsh and problematic to Western audiences and often do seem to involve pain and challenges. Yet they are very necessary both to the social organisation of the society and to the individuals. It is very rare for young people to refuse to go through initiation because, as Mandela says, it is impossible to be an adult without undergoing them. Rites of passage, even when they involve pain, can therefore be seen as a positive force for good, they can give young people a sense of purpose and achievement when they have completed them, and they can also have a levelling effect. If every person in a community has to undergo these rites, regardless of status, wealth or privilege, then there is greater social equality. As Mandela describes, all his cohort were men, and equals. Celebrating the attainment of adulthood in this way also means that young people do not have to spend many years 'in between', not quite children and not yet adults. There is a fixed end point to their childhood and these rituals enable them to prove themselves as adults definitively and then take up the responsibilities and privileges of adulthood.

It is not known how common these forms of initiation still are today. In South Africa young Xhosa men are still circumcised and still spend time away from their families in the bush, but these rituals take less time, it is illegal to perform them before a boy's 18th birthday and they are usually now held in the school holidays, by *ingcibi* who are expected to have basic hygiene and basic medical knowledge as well as religious or ritual qualifications. Such examples are useful, however, in that they clearly show the importance of Van Gennep's basic structure in understanding rites of passage. Anthropologists today still use this formula in analysing rites of passage and in helping them to understand the ways in which children make the transition to adolescence and young people to adulthood.

3.1 Rites of passage in contemporary society

Using the example of Nelson Mandela, it is easy to see Van Gennep's tripartite structure in action. It is much harder to see such patterns in the contemporary UK. It could be claimed that certain points of transition, such as an 18th birthday, passing the driving test, the loss of virginity, coming out as gay, religious conversions or getting a first job, are rites of passage, but they are not marked by public social rituals. Indeed, many of the major stages and transitions in young people's lives are constrained by adult-controlled, external forces, particularly those of bureaucracy. The move from childhood to adulthood is marked by the growing accumulation of legal rights so that a young person can consent to sex at 16, learn to drive at 17, attain full voting rights at 18 and stand as an MP at 21. Conversely, young people also acquire more legal responsibilities as they get older. Under the age of ten, a young person cannot be prosecuted for a crime in England and Wales. Once they have reached this age, they are deemed responsible for their actions and are regarded as knowing the difference between right and wrong, and are expected (with certain safeguards in place) to stand trial for any wrongdoing. None of these stages is marked by any recognisable rite of passage, and such bureaucratic boundaries become relevant only when young people fall foul of them. They are arbitrary markers set on general assumptions about the average ten-year-old or 16-year-old. No one is suggesting that a young person of 16¾ is necessarily any less able to learn to drive than a person of 17 and a day, only that the markers of adulthood and legal responsibility in the UK are largely bureaucratic ones. They might have enormous impact on young people's lives but they are essentially a bureaucratic convenience. Unlike the rite of passage undergone by a Xhosa boy such as Nelson Mandela, bureaucratic rights are accrued accumulatively and passively because of a young person's age. There is no challenge to them, no sense of achievement at the end of them, and even when childhood ends legally at the age of 18, there is limited social or individual recognition that a young person is now an adult, with adult responsibilities. They may lose some of the legal privileges accorded to children but there is little positive celebration at this point, no sense, as in Mandela's autobiography, that a boy has become a man and can take his place among adults.

Even more blurred are the social and economic transitions that occur as children grow into adults, and which in a capitalist society are some of the cornerstones of independence and adulthood. Although children are now targeted as consumers, this lies not in their purchasing power, but in their 'pester power': encouraging their parents to buy products for them that they have seen advertised. Young people, on the other hand, are making their own choices and enacting them, and their economic power is an important force in the economy. Whether they are starting to earn their own money (and in the UK children are legally allowed to do light work such as paper rounds from the age of 13), or are given an allowance by their parents, the youth market is a huge one. Even so, few young people are economically independent. Pocket money, whether earned through work or an allowance, is not expected to contribute to family income or be enough to live on independently. Similarly, student grants or loans, extra money to stay on in post-GCSE[1] education and other government policies are not designed to make young people economically independent and they rest on the assumption that the vast majority of young people have the resources of their parents to call on until well into their twenties. It is also notable in this respect that there is a different minimum wage for under and over 18-year-olds, and employers are allowed to discriminate on age grounds and pay under 18s less, even for the same job. The assumption is always that the proper place for under 18s is in education, supported by their parents, and that any money they earn is 'extra' money which can be used for luxuries but is not intended to live on.

It is in the economic sphere therefore that young people find it hardest to 'grow up'. Paul Willis once argued that 'the wage packet is the provider of freedom and independence' (Willis, 1977, p. 150), but this is no longer true now, and even when young people make the transition from being educated to working, they are now likely to find that a pay packet does not give them the independence and adulthood they had hoped. There is an emphasis in the UK, unlike in many other European societies, that young people should leave home and be financially independent at the first opportunity. This means that young people are encouraged to live on their own and, coupled with another British obsession, to buy a place of their own to live in as soon as possible. Since the majority of people in Europe rent their homes and less stress is placed on living independently, some of these pressures are avoided and there are very different demographics, so that, for example, 25 per cent of Italian men over 30 still live with their parents, a situation that would seem very strange in the UK. Adulthood in the UK is closely tied to ideas about financial independence, owning a home and holding down a job. The reality is that this is impossible for

---

[1] General Certificate of Secondary Education, the qualifications that mark the end of compulsory education in the UK.

many young people and getting harder. As house prices increase, the average first time buyer is well over 30, will probably have to be helped financially by parents and may have lived at home for many years after the age of 18. Increasingly, early entrance into adulthood is a preserve of the better-off and those without money are marginalised. It has also meant that on some levels the definition of the term youth is broadening; young people are expected to remain financially dependent on their parents until a much later age.

Activity 6	Creating rites of passage

Allow 20 minutes   Given the often negative view of young people, there are some small-scale attempts to introduce more positive and celebratory rites of passage into the lives of modern young people. Read through the account below and analyse your own response to this. Would you have liked a similar rite of passage as a young person? Do you think that such rituals would be helpful to young people, both in themselves and in order to promote a better understanding of them in society generally?

Boom boxes and ribbons

How one enterprising group of women invented a new ritual for teenage girls.

Anyone who's ever tried to put a ritual together for a teenager knows that many just aren't interested: the idea of being the center of a rite of passage is right up there with chaperoned dates. But I live in cohousing – an intentional community that a group of us built and live in together, in Amherst, Massachusetts. Of the 84 people, there are 31 kids under the age of 15, and the adults wanted a ritual to bring the teenagers into our circle. Having lived in the community since I was 19 (I'm now 24), I've often felt I span the gap between teenagers and adults. So I knew how important it was to invite the older kids into the 'adult' side of community living (meetings, work teams, and support councils), as well as to recognize their maturity.

We decided the women would come up with a ritual to welcome the girls that were ready to become part of a community of women. The challenge was to create something that would please adults and teens alike.

When I first heard the idea, I cringed; I remembered being 13, when the last thing I wanted to do was spend time with adults. I assumed that most of the girls would feel the same way. But almost immediately, I realized how wonderful it was that we could support them through what I remembered as the trials of adolescence. We just needed to get them to participate.

Our first step was to ask the three girls who had come of age (13 or older and menstruating) what they wanted. Their response: no talk of periods and go light on the spirituality. Nor did they want the spotlight directly on them. Mark the passage, not the girl, allow them to bring a boom box, and they would – reluctantly – join us.

On a Saturday afternoon, close to 25 of us met the girls and their mothers for a silent walk to a nearby meadow. Each girl held one end of a ribbon while her mother held the other. With the mother/daughter pairs walking far behind us, the other adults arrived at the meadow, stopped, and formed a circle. We began calling to the pairs, inviting them to run into our circle. The girls, being younger, ran much faster than their mothers, ripping the ribbons from their mothers' hands. In their palms and hearts, the three women felt the bittersweet break of their exclusive bonds. The girls rushed in – smiled, hugged, joined our circle. Their mothers held each other, happy to have a community to receive their daughters.

We spent the night around a campfire sharing food, stories, and wisdom and listening to groups like the Back Street Boys and Barenaked Ladies. Each girl was given a handmade book, filled with poetry, stories, and thoughts on being a woman, each page created by a different woman. The ritual seemed to work. Even though they didn't really want to talk about it (they were still teenagers, after all), one girl later said, 'It was nice to be able to talk to people other than my parents.' But we all got something: I had felt isolated for so long, not knowing my place in either age group; now the distance between the generations seems shorter. I agree with the mother who said, 'We intended to give a gift to our young women and found ourselves receiving one. It increased our caring and connection to each other.' And perhaps best of all, two of the three girls are already planning next year's ritual.

(Reid, 1999)

Comment

Your initial reaction to this may have been as unenthusiastic as that of some of the teenagers. Certainly, I would have utterly hated the idea of skipping with a ribbon with my mother at 13! I find it hard to read this account without a slight cringe at the combination of new-age earnestness, lack of authenticity, and sentimentality. Even so, the idea behind it – to celebrate the transitions in young people's lives as positive events – is a good one and gets away from the idea that adolescence is necessarily a time of stress, of difficulty, and that young people are a problem for society and being a teenager is problematic for the young people themselves. Whether or not created rites of passage are the way to change perceptions of young people is highly debatable, but the fact remains that there are very few celebratory rituals for today's young people.

The following chapter will examine critical moments in young people's lives and the ways in which young people make sense of them through a biographical perspective. What is noticeable, however, is the lack of contemporary rites of passages in their lives. Although they identify some of the critical moments, such as passing a driving test, gaining GCSEs or losing their virginity, as important moments in their own personal biographies that often had far-reaching consequences, there is an obvious lack of public recognition of these changes. Changes are individualised and to be made sense of by the young person themselves, and they receive little support from society.

Key points

- The classic anthropological descriptions of rites of passage involve separation, a liminal stage and then reintegration. In traditional societies these stages help give a structure to young people's lives and mark a clear boundary between childhood and adulthood.

- The West has few rites of passage for young people to go through, and few ways of positively celebrating different stages of the lifecycle.

Conclusion

Social anthropology offers another way of looking at young people's lives. Its emphasis on methods, particularly ethnography and participant observation, means that taking an ethnographic approach can illustrate and illuminate young people's lives in a way that questionnaires or interviews, for example, cannot hope to do. The two major pieces of ethnographic work discussed in this chapter show the benefits of such an approach and stand out as major contributions to the study of young people in the UK and elsewhere. This is not to claim that anthropology has always got young people right or that other disciplines cannot make an equally valid contribution to the study of young people. Rather it is to emphasise that anthropological methods remain one of the best ways of getting information about the daily lives of young people. Ethnography allows a comparative perspective which challenges any notions that adolescence is a universal stage predicated on biological changes, and stresses the point that adolescence must be seen as a cultural construction. Bringing in a cross-cultural perspective can show that adolescence is a problem not only for young people themselves but for society in general, and it can be seen as a problem that society has created. Margaret Mead has been criticised, but she did at least acknowledge that adolescence was what social, cultural and economic forces dictated it should be – an insight that is as relevant now as it was 80 years ago.

References

Ahmed, S., Bwana, J., Guga, E., Kitunga, D., Mgulambwa, A., Mtambalike, P., Mtunguja, L., Mwandayi, E., with Sumra, S. and Ennew, J. (1999) *Children in Need of Special Protection Measures: A Tanzanian Study*, Dar es Salaam, Tanzania, UNICEF.

Bourgois, P. (1998) 'Families and children in pain in the US inner city' in Scheper-Hughes, N. and Sargent, C. (eds) *Small Wars: The Cultural Politics of Childhood*, Berkeley and Los Angeles, University of California Press.

Ennew, J., Gopal, K., Heeran, J. and Montgomery, H. (1996) *Children and Prostitution: How Can We Measure and Monitor the Commercial Sexual Exploitation of Children?*, background papers and annotated bibliography for the World Congress on the Commercial Sexual Exploitation of Children, Oslo, Childwatch International.

Gravrand, H. (1983 *La civilisation Sereer: Cosaan (les Origines)*, Dakar, Les Nouvelles Editions Africaines.

Hall, T. (2003) *Better Times Than This: Youth Homelessness in Britain*, London, Pluto Press.

Jackson, A. (ed.) (1987) *Anthropology at Home*, London, Tavistock.

Keesing, R. (1981) *Cultural Anthropology*, New York, Holt, Rinehart and Winston.

Kehily, M.J., Mac an Ghaill, M., Epstein, D. and Redman, P. (2002) 'Private girls and public worlds: producing femininities in the primary school', *Discourse: Studies in the Cultural Politics of Education*, vol. 23, no. 2, pp. 167–77.

Malinowski, B. (1922) *Argonauts of the Western Pacific*, London, Routledge.

Mandela, N. (1994) *Long Walk to Freedom*, London, Little, Brown.

Mead, M. (1972 [1928]) *Coming of Age in Samoa*, London, Penguin.

Prendergast, S. (1989) 'Girls' experience of menstruation in school' in Holly, L. (ed.) *Girls and Sexuality, Teaching and Learning*, Milton Keynes, Open University Press.

Reid, S. (1999) 'Boom boxes and ribbons: how one enterprising group of women invented a new ritual for teenage girls', *Ms Magazine*, October, www.beliefnet.com/story/1/story_194_1.html

Van Gennep, A. (1960) *The Rites of Passage*, Chicago, Chicago University Press.

Willis, P. (1977) *Learning to Labour: How Working Class Kids Get Working Class Jobs*, London, Saxon House.

Chapter 3

A biographical perspective

Rachel Thomson

Introduction

In the previous chapters we have explored the distinction between historical constructions of 'adolescence' and constructions of 'youth' that are more situated in place and time. In this chapter we will add another layer to this understanding by thinking of young people's transitions from childhood to adulthood in biographical terms. The chapter will help you understand how an approach centred on the individual can provide a holistic understanding of young people's lives that is historically and sociologically connected. So although this perspective enables us to listen to and think about how young people may feel and act, we are not simply trapped in a myriad of individual stories. We will explore how a biographical perspective can lead us to ask important questions about resources, about the operations of institutions and the role of professionals. The chapter will introduce some new and possibly unfamiliar ideas, and through activities and examples will help you apply these to your own life and the lives of young people.

The structure of this chapter is as follows: Section 1 will set the scene for the chapter, suggesting that contemporary Western cultures have undergone a 'biographical turn' (Chamberlayne et al., 2000) that has implications for popular culture, youth policy and practice. Section 2 will provide an introduction to late modern perspectives. In doing so, we will discuss a number of theoretical concepts including: the reflexive project of self; individualisation; 'normal' and 'choice' biography. Section 3 will explore shifts in biographies across generations, including intergenerational change and continuity. Section 4 will show what a biographical perspective might reveal. Drawing on my own research with young people I will introduce you to some components of a biographical approach including a focus on 'competence, recognition and investment' and a discussion of 'critical moments'. Throughout the chapter I will consider how this kind of perspective might contribute to a biographically informed practice.

The chapter will address the following core questions:

- How can late modern sociological theories help us to understand young people's lives?

- What is the shape of contemporary young people's biographies, and how may material inequalities be manifest in the form of their biographies?

- What are the changes and continuities of youth biographies over the course of several generations?

- How can a biographical perspective help us understand the ways in which young people think, feel and act?

1   The biographical turn

The simplest definition of biography is 'the history of the life of a person'. It is only in relatively recent times that the lives of ordinary individuals have been represented in this way, as traditionally biographies would only be written (or told) about the lives of people of great social and political importance and influence, such as monarchs, warriors and leaders. The democratisation of print and communications has been paralleled by a democratisation of the biographical form. Turn on the television, open a magazine, go into a bookshop or online and you are likely to find intimate accounts, or stories, about ordinary lives, both biographical (stories about other individuals' lives) and autobiographical (stories about the author).

It appears that popular culture is increasingly dominated by what has been described as 'mass produced confessional tales' in the form of reality television shows and 'the self on the shelf', that is, the self-help manual (Plummer, 2001, p. 97). But if we look more closely we find that the biographical form is more than a vehicle of self improvement and entertainment. Producing stories about who we are, where we come from and where we are going has become an unavoidable part of contemporary living. It has been argued that the autobiographical form is now *institutionalised* through practices such as the curriculum vitae, the job interview and the doctor's consultation (Silverman, 1993). UK sociologist Ken Plummer suggests that what he calls the 'autobiographical society' is double-edged: on the one hand it enables the expression of marginal voices, but on the other it leads to the commodification of the life story form where 'life stories become controllable, calculable, predictable, efficient' (Plummer, 2001, p. 98).

Governing of the self is the idea that, to be civilised, individuals must regulate and control their habits, passions, thoughts and actions. The role of biography in the governing of the self is explored by another UK sociologist, Nikolas Rose, who argues that this focus on the self is the result of the discursive dominance of what he terms 'psy' and therapeutic discourses (Rose, 1996, 1999). Following in the footsteps of French philosopher Michel Foucault, Rose has explored the growing influence

Your views & experiences on camera & online

VIDEOARCHIVE

Contributor:
Ben Borthwick

Ben Borthwick from Hull has become quite enamoured with the media. One of the highlights of working with BBCi Humber Video Diaries was a trip to the studios of the BBC's Newsround programme. Ben is now pursuing his media aims by taking up a course of media studies.

Ben Borthwick's diaries

Date	Title
01-12-04	Gifts
18-11-04	Games
02-11-04	College
01-09-04	GCSE
25-08-04	CV
18-08-04	Bowling
13-07-04	Party
29-06-04	Uncle Ben
22-06-04	Record
07-06-04	Revision
04-12-03	College decisions
01-09-03	Ben goes camping
13-08-03	School Trip to London
01-08-03	"BeautifHull"
01-07-03	Ben's personal view on asylum
24-07-03	Dave the Hamster
23-06-03	Holidays

Video diaries are one way in which people have been able to tell their own stories to a wider public

of ideas about the self derived from psychology and psychotherapy in a range of public institutions as well as in popular culture. For Rose, these ideas are associated with a 'normative individualism' in which the individual is responsible for regulating themselves. Where once power would be exercised directly by the state, be that through the operation of the medical, welfare or criminal justice systems, it is increasingly the job of the individual to regulate themselves – as a good student, worker, citizen, client. Can you think of examples of policies directed towards young people that encourage self government in this way? One example might be the proliferation of initiatives that seek to encourage young people to look after themselves and to stay healthy, and the gradual withdrawal of school based health services such as free school milk, health checks and so on. Another example might be the shift away from generic youth and community based programmes that seek to take young people off the streets towards a proposal for a Youth Opportunities 'smart card' that rewards socially desirable behaviour. Can you think of others?

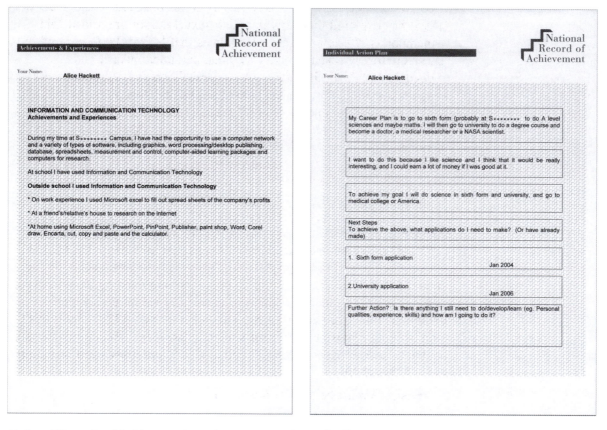

National Records of Achievement can be seen as a form of self governance

In recent years a 'biographical turn' has also taken place in social research, reflecting the process through which the examination of the self has become a key feature of the modern world and of social policy and practice (Chamberlayne *et al.*, 2000; Miller, 2000; Plummer, 2001; Roberts, 2001). The terms 'biographical methods' and 'life history research' encompass a wide range of approaches, defined most simply through a common starting point: the collection and analysis of biographical or autobiographical accounts. This includes a number of research traditions, often with distinct aims, fields and methods of enquiry. Common to all approaches is a methodological and theoretical tension between realist and constructionist positions – the tricky relationship between the life that is lived and the life that is told. Those who stand at the realist end of the continuum believe that it is possible to use biographical accounts to find out about what actually happens in the world – to document experience. Those who stand at the constructionist end of the continuum tend to question this belief, suggesting that the narratives that people generate may tell us most about what it is possible (in a particular time and place) to imagine and to speak about.

A controversial example of this relates to stories of sexual abuse. Plummer (1995) has explored the ways in which sexual stories are told within contemporary Western cultures. He argues that before the forging of 'survivor stories' sexual abuse was unnamed, unarticulated and undocumented. With the advent of women's liberation it became possible to speak out about abuse. The particular kinds of stories that were forged were associated with survivor identities, and together these shaped how individuals experienced abuse and recast the experience. A different kind of narrative may produce a different kind of 'experience'. This example alerts us to one of the most challenging aspects of a narrative or constructionist approach: that experience is always mediated. There is no such thing as a simple 'testimony'; rather, accounts are always shaped by narrative form, and the rules and context of the stories' telling. But this loss of simplicity that is associated with a narrative approach is countered by a gain in critical insight. By alerting us to the kinds of stories or narratives it is possible to tell, we also notice the kinds of stories or narratives that are *not* told. For example, if we are thinking about racism, rather than asking the question 'who is racist?', we might ask the questions: 'where are stories of explicit racism being told?'; 'why is this?'; 'who is/are the audience(s) for the stories?'; 'are there other stories that are unable to find expression?' As Plummer (1995) observes, for a new story to be successful:

- First, we must be able to *imagine* it.

- Second, we must be able to *articulate* it.

- To do this we need to be able to form *identities* that enable us to become storytellers.

- For a story to be told it must be heard, and the vital fourth criterion is the existence of communities of support who will form the *audience* for the story.

Plummer's argument should sensitise us to methods that are employed to elicit stories and produce biographical accounts. The production of survivor accounts of sexual abuse is closely related to the practices of consciousness raising associated with second wave feminism. Social research can also be understood as a method for the elicitation of stories, where the primary methodology is the semi-structured interview, that may be repeated over time in longitudinal studies. Visual methods such as video and photo diaries are increasingly being used in research with children and young people, resulting in a very different kind of biography and one that may or may not provide young people with more control over the final product. Whatever the methods employed to create auto/biographies in research or practice interventions, the medium itself has an impact on the kinds of stories and identities produced. Although those at the constructionist end of the continuum doubt researchers' ability to deduce experience directly from narratives, they do suggest that the stories that people tell in turn shape experience.

Over the course of this chapter and the rest of the book, repeated reference is made to the *Inventing Adulthoods* research project that I have been involved in with colleagues. It is a qualitative longitudinal study of young people's lives conducted over a ten-year period. The methods employed in the study include repeat individual interviews (up to five for each young person), focus groups, questionnaires and personal diaries (memory books). The study has been conducted in five contrasting localities of the UK including a Northern Irish city and, in England, an isolated rural location, an inner city locality, an affluent commuter belt locality, and a disadvantaged public housing estate. (For more information see Henderson *et al.*, 2007; London South Bank University, 2006.)

The biographical turn described above has made an impact on youth studies. This has been influenced by two drivers.

- On the one hand, researchers interested in the identities of particular groups of young people have looked towards the stories that they tell in order to understand who and what it is possible to be. For example, it may be very difficult for a young person to articulate an identity as sexually knowledgeable and competent in a culture where such stories are seen as evidence of immorality.

- On the other hand, mainstream sociologists have turned towards biography as a way of understanding wider processes of social change. Those researching youth have, in turn, drawn on these theories, concentrating on describing and categorising the kinds of biographies that young people have.

In the next section we will consider the second of these drivers, the ideas that are grouped together under the term 'late modern perspectives', and the impact that these ideas have had on those studying young people's lives.

2 Late modern perspectives

> Individualization ... means that each person's biography is removed from given determinations and placed in his or her hands, open and dependent on decisions. The proportion of life opportunities which are fundamentally closed to decision-making is decreasing and the proportion of the biography which is open and must be constructed personally is increasing. Individualization of life situations and processes thus means that biographies become *self-reflexive*; socially prescribed biography is transformed into biography that is self-produced and continues to be produced. Decisions on education, profession, job, place of residence, spouse, number of children and so forth, with all the secondary decisions implied, no longer can be, they must be made. Even where the word 'decisions' is too grandiose, because neither consciousness nor alternatives are present, the individual will have to 'pay for' the consequences of decisions not taken ...
>
> In the individualized society the individual must therefore learn, on pain of permanent disadvantage, to conceive of himself or herself as the center of action, as the planning office with respect to his/her own biography, abilities, orientations, relationships and so on.
>
> (Beck, 1992, p. 135)

Ulrich Beck is an influential German sociologist. His book *Risk Society*, published in 1992, suggests that we are living in a society where nothing can be taken for granted; we must make decisions about our future or face the consequences of failing to do so. The assumption underpinning the statement quoted above is that if we simply drift along in life we will fail to identify and realise opportunities and thus disadvantage ourselves and those who depend on us. It is a picture that emphasises uncertainty, competition and the threat of downward social mobility. But are things really getting more difficult? Are there really more pressures to make the right choices? Was it so different for earlier generations? In order to answer some of these questions we will take a journey which begins with theory and ends with young people's lives. We will work through the theory in a gradual way, attempting where possible to make sense of it in terms of real life examples. Concepts may not make complete sense at first sight, but by the end of the chapter you should have got a taste for ideas that will be returned to over the course of this book.

Sociologists such as Ulrich Beck, Zygmunt Bauman and Anthony Giddens argue that contemporary Western cultures have entered a period of **late modernity** in which the economic and social processes that brought about the industrial revolution (and what we understand as the modern liberal state) have continued to evolve to their logical conclusion. The post-industrial era is seen as being marked by risk, uncertainty and the breakdown of traditional values. It is argued that we now live in a globalised economic system in which the nation state is increasingly less important and a new relationship between the individual and the social is emerging. Each of the late modern theorists emphasises different aspects of this process of change. For example, Bauman paints a rather pessimistic picture of the ethical consequences of our transformation from citizens into consumers, pointing to the dangers of 'social deskilling', 'a neglect to learn the skills of discussing and negotiating the ways out of trouble with others' (Bauman and Tester, 2001, p. 114).

2.1 The reflexive project of self

Anthony Giddens is more optimistic than Bauman, focusing on the two ends of the process: exploring on the one hand the political consequences of globalisation (and his arguments for a 'third way' between left and right wing positions) and on the other how this affects the way in which individuals see themselves and others. As traditions fade, Giddens suggests that we are each responsible for our own **reflexive project of self**, a story of who we are and who we will be in the future. He describes it as 'the process whereby self identity is constituted by the reflexive ordering of self narratives' (1991, p. 244). Storytelling (to ourselves and others) is central to the construction of a reflexive project of self. As we rework existing narratives and forge new ones, we invent and reinvent who it is possible to be.

Contemporary culture increasingly demands an active building of self identity. Where in the past this may have been part of the life phase understood as adolescence, increasingly it is a demand also made of adults. In a flexible and uncertain employment market, those without secure resources are expected to engage in lifelong learning, reskilling and reinvention of self. Think of the curriculum vitae (Miller and Morgan, 1993) and the Record of Achievement that is linked to the UK National Curriculum (Cremin, 2005). The demand to create individualised personal development 'plans' is entwined with assessment tools through which professionals elicit what is deemed to be 'relevant' information. The demand to create or 'submit' to these kinds of self evaluations ranges from the voluntary (for example, the choice to develop a personal website), through the 'recommended advice' that we identify our personal 'learning style', to the compulsory demand for assessment and pathway planning among those moving through health and welfare systems. Each can be understood as technologies through which we explicitly make and revise our 'reflexive project of self', yet with varying degrees of formality or informality and personal control. The production of self identity is increasingly demanded by our participation in public institutions such as work, education and welfare, but we also work on self identity in private: in conversations with our parents, partners and friends, through reading self-help literature, magazines and horoscopes, which equip us with resources that are reworked in our conversations with our intimates. If we think back to the work of Plummer, discussed in the Introduction, we can also think of the reflexive project of self as resourced by narratives, culturally specific stories about the kind of person it is possible to be. In the following activity you will explore how useful the idea of the reflexive project of self might be for understanding young people's lives.

Activity 1	Ordering self narratives

Allow 20 minutes

In the *Inventing Adulthoods* study (Henderson *et al.*, 2007) the researchers asked young people regularly about change in their lives. The kinds of things that they reported as triggers to this kind of self-conscious change included bereavement, becoming a parent, starting full time work, losing their virginity, going to university. Two examples follow: first Sheila talks about the experience of becoming a mother and then Sam talks about how he is different when he is single and when he is in a relationship. As you read these extracts, make notes on how these young people's lives might be understood in terms of reflexive projects of self. In particular, see if you distinguish between 'old self narratives' and new ones that have been reworked from the old.

> Sheila: I've grown up a lot. I'm not the person I was last year, I'm just completely, I look at things a lot differently now, I was put through so much in pregnancy ... This time last year I just hadn't a care in the world, I was getting ready for my friend's 18th birthday, going out, going to work, having a really good social life, whereas this year, tied down, I have a full time responsibility of a baby to look after and I'm living in my own house, and in terms of adulthood I've grown up so much. I have a different perspective on things altogether and I realise that it's just not me any more. I'm a lot more adult than I was and I know that myself, you know, in the way I've handled certain situations – I would have handled them all differently a year ago. Even sitting down last week and talking out my problems with Jimmy. Last year I wouldn't have done that, I would have roared at him for not listening to what I was going to say and walked out and slammed the door. I know I've definitely grown up a lot. I know more about myself now than I did, if you know what I mean.

> Sam: But I realise that my personality changes when I'm in a relationship. As soon as I'm not, I'm very, very loud and very – I'm a party animal when I'm single. I'm out till five/six in the morning most nights and not up till three in the afternoon. As soon as I've got a boyfriend – I don't ever mean to – I just stop, it's just that my attention is completely focused on them, really. I dunno, I didn't

really think I would be like that. But hmm, but it's quite nice in a way, I like it. It means that every once in a while I get to calm down. I think deep down I really do enjoy settling down and mellowing out with someone. But I think that's why sometimes I fall so deeply, 'cos it's also the idea of having that stability. But then when I'm in there I want to go out and party all the time [laughs].

Comment

Although these examples are very different, they both show young people constructing a self identity, and in the process forging a set of narratives, or stories, about themselves. The shift in identity that motherhood has entailed for Sheila is dramatic, and she is in the process of reconstructing her project of self, bringing her narratives of the past in line with a new identity in which responsibility, self knowledge and maturity are emphasised. Sam is beginning to construct an identity as a gay man, experimenting with narratives about the kind of person he is, or could be. He juxtaposes an identity of calmness, focus and stability while in a relationship with an extrovert and chaotic identity while single. These identities are presented as ongoing options rather than in terms of a permanent transition from one to another. Both Sam's and Sheila's extracts need to be understood as accounts of the self, produced in the context of a research interview, rather than windows into the lives and identities of these two young people. Their stories of self change over time, and in the context of their telling. Yet, all is part of the process of self creation.

What do you think about this argument? Can you think of any examples from your own life that fit with Giddens's claims? Do you have a reflexive project of self? Have you had experiences in your life that changed you, that gave rise to new stories of self?

For Giddens and other late modern theorists, this kind of incessant work by the self on the self (what he calls 'reflexivity') is new. It is work that ultimately transforms interaction between parents and children, between lovers, between friends, and between teachers and pupils, as we slowly renegotiate the expectations and norms of tradition. In the past the authority of elders may have been accepted at face value (think of the account offered by Nelson Mandela in Chapter 2). Yet research with young people suggests that they value relationships with adults that are characterised by an 'ethic of reciprocity' in which authority is earned rather than simply asserted (Thomson and Holland, 2002). Reflexivity understood in this way encompasses an awareness of power, and of the self, and is increasingly recognised as a skill that is central to professional practice (Turney, 2007).

Many people have criticised Giddens's arguments for being simplistic, even wishful thinking. They cite continuing evidence of coercion and force within relationships, where people fail miserably to negotiate but rather impose their will on others. They also point to the important difference between 'feeling' that you are in control and the reality of self determination. Questions have also been raised as to whether Giddens's approach universalises what is in fact a very white, middle class and Western narrative style (Skeggs, 2002). The ability to 'story' the self may in fact be a form of privilege, and while some young people may not have the requisite resource to produce these kinds of accounts of the self, others may positively resist the demand on them to do so. So, even though the idea of a 'reflexive project of self' may be a useful way of thinking about how individuals plan their lives, it may be that the concept encourages us to overplay the agency of the individual and underplay the significance of other factors that affect their lives such as resources, inequalities, discrimination and oppression. Think again about your own reflexive project of self: can you see ways in which your identity (the stories you tell yourself and others about who you are) may protect you from facing how little power you may have to control your life? This is an important (if unsettling) insight and one that is crucial in developing a biographical perspective that has some psychological depth. The stories that we tell about ourselves cannot be simply taken at face value.

2.2 Individualisation

The argument presented by Beck (1992) avoids some of the pitfalls that beset Giddens's perspective. Beck argues that contemporary Western societies have been shaped by a process of **individualisation**. This term is not the same as 'individualism'; in creating a verb (individualise) from the noun (individualism), Beck is deliberately moving our attention away from a discussion of conduct and feelings centred on the self. Individualisation is used to denote a fundamental shift in the relationship between the individual and the society, underwritten by new economic and technological processes. Beck characterises individualisation through three aspects:

* disembedding (removal from tradition, local and familial ties and connections), which he calls the 'liberating dimension'

* loss of traditional security with respect to practical knowledge, religious faith and guiding norms, which he calls the 'disenchantment dimension'

* re-embedding, the creation of a new type of social commitment, which he calls the 'reintegration dimension'.

Individualistic values may dominate in an individualised society, and an individualised society may be one in which choices taken or not are highly consequential. But not everyone is in a position to be able to put their own choices into practice. Beck argues that the process of individualisation impacts both on the objective life situation and on subjective identities, but it does this in a range of ways.

For Beck, individualisation is a historical process, transforming among other things the relationship between generations. Let us think for a moment how we might use notions of 'disembedding', 'loss of security' and 're-embedding' to think about how understandings of and practices of youth and adulthood are changing.

	Youth	Adulthood
Disembedding	Young people may access what previously were considered 'adult' behaviours at younger ages (consumption, technological competence, sexual awareness)	Becoming an adult no longer means giving up youthful practices and identities such as 'play'
Loss of security	Anxiety caused by lack of clarity as to the boundaries between childhood and adulthood, expressed in terms of 'loss of innocence' as young people are drawn into the world of adult preoccupations and responsibilities	Old certainties of what adulthood means disappear. Economic independence, citizenship and moral autonomy no longer come as a 'package'. Extended dependency and resequencing of the key indicators of adult status make adulthood hard to achieve
Re-embedding	Young people seek those forms of 'competence' and 'recognition' that are available to them. Institutions such as schools, colleges, training programmes, welfare regimes have significant influence on the kinds of identities forged	New forms of adult identity begin to appear, reflecting the resources that particular groups and families have access to. New forms of inequality emerge. Emergence of a significant generation gap as parents have to rethink themselves as adults and their own expectations of the life course

Beck suggests that these three aspects (disembedding, loss of security and re-embedding) are associated with corresponding *dimensions*: the 'liberating' dimension, the 'disenchantment' dimension and the 'reintegration' dimension. So disembedding liberates us from tradition; the loss of security that this brings disenchants (or renders mundane and threatening) those practices it affects; as we create ways of acting (re-embedding) we experience new forms of integration and community.

Let us try now to apply this to a concrete area of young people's lives: communications and the use of mobile telephones.

Gains, losses and new
forms of community

Activity 2   Individualisation and the mobile phone

Allow 30 minutes   Try to fill in the following table, outlining the impact of the different
processes of individualisation in relation to mobile phones.

Process	Disembedding	Loss of security	Re-embedding
Dimension	Liberating	Disenchantment	Reintegration
Mobile phones			

Comment

The impact may be on young people, adults, or both. I thought that the
liberating dimension of the mobile phone for young people primarily
involved the ability to have communication that is private. The phone may
also enable more physical freedom, especially significant for girls, as
parents allow their children to be unsupervised as long as they are
contactable by phone. The disenchantment dimension can be sensed in
the series of moral panics surrounding mobile phones, from fears of cancer
to new forms of bullying. So, although something is being gained with the
advent of this personalised technology, there is also a sense of something
being lost. The reintegration dimension could be identified in the new social
practices that are growing up around mobile phones, for example forms of
parenting that assume the ability to contact children and new forms of
sociality in which young people are at the centre of individualised networks.

In the next subsection we will go on to use Beck's notion of individualisation as a way of understanding the emergence of new kinds of biography, and the tensions that may exist between biographies across generations.

2.3 Normal and choice biography

Beck has written about the impact of individualisation in terms of a shift from **'normal' biographies** to **'choice' biographies**. The term normal biography refers to a life pattern defined by convention and shared expectation. For those living a normal biography there are few questions about what to do next, or who to be. Rather, we do as is expected of us. In contrast, a choice biography refers to a life pattern in which much more appears to be within the orbit of individual determination. Things happen because we make them happen, and if we do not exert agency, they may not happen at all.

Changing gender identities and relationships are a key motif and mechanism of these wider transformations (as will be discussed in Chapter 4). Put simply, traditional normal biographies tend to be highly gender specific – with men and women, girls and boys having clearly defined roles and distinct if complementary destinies. Many of the anthropological examples explored in Chapter 2 can be seen to be underpinned by normal biographies. The choice biography has been characterised as non gender specific, that is, the kind of biography that could be pursued by a man or woman, girl or boy.

So, for example, in a UK context a traditional gender specific biography might be illustrated by a pattern where:

- after compulsory education both sexes enter work
- on marriage women leave work to dedicate themselves to full time parenthood and men become the breadwinners.

A non gender specific choice biography might be illustrated by a transition to adulthood with the following characteristics:

- dependence on parents is extended
- work and studying continue alongside each other through to the end of higher education
- the onset of sexual relationships does not result immediately in either marriage or parenthood, but rather 'settling down' is deferred to the distant future
- leaving home may be an incremental process involving several returns.

Where the normal biography is *linear* and takes place in clear stages, the choice biography is *synchronic* (all aspects of transition move alongside each other) and is *reversible* (a young person might leave home and then return, leave school and later return to education, move in with a partner and then move out again).

Much of the academic literature on normal and choice biography comes from northern Europe where, due to the existence of highly developed welfare states and strong economies, socio-economic differences are not extreme. For example, the Dutch sociologist Manuela Du Bois-Reymond (1998) uses ideas of individualisation, the reflexive project of self and 'partial life projects' to describe the kinds of transitions pursued by young people in the Netherlands. In these countries the non gender specific choice biography appears to be becoming dominant. However, in countries with greater social polarisation (such as the UK and the USA) or countries with different family and/or welfare structures (such as Spain and Portugal), the picture is quite different. So, for example, the choice biography may be characteristic of the transitions of middle class young people in the UK and the Republic of Ireland, but much less so of those from more socially disadvantaged backgrounds, or those who are first or second generation migrants or who have grown up in cultural or religious communities whose values are distinct from the popular culture. It is important to recognise that this does not mean that these young people are somehow 'stuck in the past' or dominated by tradition, but rather it may be that the underlying process of individualisation manifests itself in very different ways depending on context. Individuals, families and communities *react* to individualisation, particularly the loss of security that it entails. The new forms of social commitment that arise as re-embedding takes place may be diverse and characterised by new forms of inequality. Social class, ethnicity, locality and sexuality all make a difference to young people's expectations of the future. Whether they believe that they can 'have it all' or that they have to 'do it all' will depend on many factors, including the resources that they can draw on as well as the values of their families and communities.

Key points

- In this section we have considered the contribution of late modern theory, focusing on Anthony Giddens's notion of the reflexive project of self and Ulrich Beck's concept of individualisation.

- We have explored the processes that constitute individualisation – disembedding, loss of security and re-embedding – and have started thinking about how these ideas might be applied to understanding the changing relationship between young people and adults.

- We have distinguished between a normal biography and a choice biography, the former being linear and defined by tradition, the latter being synchronic, reversible and non gender specific.

3 Intergenerational change

Detraditionalisation?

Commentators have suggested that a division between normal and choice biographies characterises the relationship between generations in contemporary Western culture. In a recent study of parenting practices in families with teenagers, Gill Jones *et al.* (2005) argue that this generation are experiencing a very different kind of transition from that experienced by their parents. Where their parents' transition to adulthood had been abrupt, with most leaving home and marrying at the same time, the children's transitions are more extended and incremental. The researchers are interested in how parents adopt and adapt parenting styles in order to manage this incongruence between their own experience and that of their children. They observe that parents are moving away from the notion that a successful transition to adulthood is achieved by doing the 'right thing in the right order' (linear transition) towards the idea that what their children need is the 'right relationship'. The right relationship is defined in terms of the kind of social networks that it brings to the family, the extent to which it is an equitable relationship and, most significantly, whether the relationship fits with and supports their child's educational plans. Relationships that draw children away from educational achievement are looked at with suspicion by parents. From this research it sounds as if parents are getting to grips with the 'synchronic' and 'reversible' choice biography described above.

Activity 3   **Your own transition to adulthood**

Allow 30 minutes   Think about your own transition to adulthood and write a short account (no more than one side of A4 paper). Try to focus on issues of dependence/ independence and the ways in which your parents or carers responded to them.

Now read your account and try to answer the following questions:

• Is your experience best described by either the linear normal biography or the synchronic and reversible choice biography?

- Was there a generation gap of the type discussed above between you and your parents?

- How did they deal with it?

- What kind of parenting strategies did they employ?

- Was it hard for them?

- If you are a parent yourself, are you now struggling to bridge the experience of your transition to adulthood with that of your own children?

Comment

I did this exercise with a group of colleagues and we found a wide range of experiences. For some of us, there was a big generation gap and very little discussion about it. This is a kind of parenting characterised by silence and fear of disapproval. For others of us, the differences between our parents' teenage years and our own was very much a topic for discussion. Our parents positively welcomed many of the changes that had taken place and were open to talking and negotiating boundaries. This does not mean that things were always easy or that rebellion did not take place. Jones *et al.* (2005) observe that the individualised approach to relationships that characterises the choice biography can be hard work. Parenting in this context demands a great deal of communication between parents and their children. It is ironic that in a period when so much anxiety is expressed about the loss of moral certainty, the presence of choice brings with it increased levels of ethical labour. Some of us found that reflecting on our youth in this way could make us feel sad, realising how little choice we may have had in decisions and that our views were not taken into account. In practice, it may also be difficult to categorise our transitions as either linear or synchronic. As we will find later, it may be necessary to look across several generations in order to identify the kinds of changes suggested by late modern theories.

3.1 Thinking through continuity

The two main criticisms levelled against Beck's account of individualisation are that:

- it makes untenable generalisations

- it overemphasises change at the expense of continuity.

The charge of generalisation is one to which social theories are always vulnerable. To his credit, Beck does not argue that the process of individualisation creates uniformity; rather he is clear that this underlying social process translates into different biographies, depending on circumstance. In relatively homogenous societies such as Norway and the Netherlands, individualised biographies may be relatively easy to categorise. In more diverse cultures such as the UK and increasingly the Republic of Ireland, this is much less easy. So rather than thinking of choice biographies as following the same pattern, it may be better to think of them as *characterised* by processes of disembedding and loss of certainty. How particular communities and individuals then re-embed (create new identities, values and traditions) depends on their circumstances, resources and resourcefulness. From this perspective it may be possible to make sense of a young person becoming increasingly committed to a religion such as Christianity or Islam, not as an example of a normal biography, but as an example of a choice biography: making new forms of commitment in the face of loss of certainty and the need to actively construct a self identity.

It is less easy to defend Beck's work against the second criticism. In emphasising change, he fails to take into account the extent to which we are tied to the past, be that through institutionalised inequalities that are reproduced over time or through our emotional connections to the biographies of others, particularly our parents. In that sense Beck overplays the extent to which our biographies are separate and subject to our control. A valuable corrective to this has been provided by the Norwegian scholars Harriet Bjerrum Nielsen and Monica Rudberg, who develop a more psychologically nuanced understanding of individualisation, capturing the factors that may interact to constrain change (Bjerrum Nielsen and Rudberg, 1994). Drawing on an empirical study of three generations of women, they distinguish between:

- gender identity (a sense of the kind of woman they want to be)
- gender subjectivity (the kind of woman they are, laid down in childhood and unconsciously influenced by the subjectivity of their mother)
- the cultural and social possibilities offered by the society at any time.

They argue that at the point of adolescence there is always a lack of 'contemporaneity' or 'fit' between these three dimensions, which gives rise to unique **biographical problems**, that is, problems arising from the particular circumstances of an individual's life. The character of this lack of fit is different for different generations. For example, girls growing up in the 1960s and 1970s experienced contradictions between a modern gender identity (the kind of women they consciously wanted to be) and an 'old-fashioned gendered subjectivity (the notion that autonomy is gained through relationships with men)' (Bjerrum Nielsen and Rudberg, 1994, p. 109). For their mothers, who were girls in the 1940s and 1950s, the contradiction was between a modern gender identity and restricted cultural possibilities. For girls in the 1980s and 1990s the contradiction was between gender subjectivity and the wider cultural and social possibilities that still make it difficult for women to combine motherhood and career.

The intergenerational break or magical recovery

In the researchers' words, the modern girl may not 'acknowledge her sex as a limitation – she wants everything and believes she can do anything. But is that possible?' (Bjerrum Nielsen and Rudberg, 1994, p. 111).

Activity 4	Mapping a three-generational chain

Allow 1 hour

For this exercise you need to choose a three-generational chain of men or women: a daughter or son, a mother or father, and a grandmother or grandfather. They can come from your own family or from a family you know. It might even be a family you know from a book, radio or television programme.

Try to fill in the following table, describing;

- gender identity (the kind of man or woman they wanted to be)

- gender subjectivity (the kind of man or woman they are)

- the social and cultural possibilities of the time

- the main biographical problem that they faced.

Be warned, this is not a simple exercise and it may take many conversations to complete. But it is also possible to think your way through the activity. I have tried to complete a version myself to give you an idea. Now you have a try.

	Daughter	Mother	Grandmother
Gender identity	Career woman, free, individual	Earth mother: liberal parenting, companionate wife, 'bohemian'	Dutiful wife and competent mother, 'colonial'
Gender subjectivity	Good mother and good worker	Dutiful daughter and good mother	?
Possibilities	Educational opportunity taken, a partner prepared to take parenting responsibility	Lack of educational opportunity, reliance on breadwinner	Good education but no possibility of paid work. High level of biographical disruption due to war and migration
Biographical problem	Exhaustion, doing it all	Frustrated potential	Keeping her family together

	Daughter/son	Mother/father	Grandmother/grandfather
Gender identity			
Gender subjectivity			
Possibilities			
Biographical problem			

Comment

Did you find it difficult to fill in all of the categories the further you went back in time? Whether you were able to talk to the people involved will have made a big difference to how you experienced the activity. Inevitably, you will have had to draw on mediated accounts, whether this was by 'the media' or by what it was possible or appropriate to talk about with someone from an older generation. You may have been surprised by the connections that you made between the biographies of different generations, in terms of both the gaps and the continuities. Whether you chose a male or female chain is likely to have had an impact on this as the lives and expectations of women have transformed most dramatically in recent history. Within a single family siblings may have taken different routes (perhaps in part a response to each other). Thinking about the different circumstances and opportunities faced by each generation is likely to have been revealing for you. It may have involved you in conversations that you don't usually have.

When I did the exercise I realised how little I knew about my grandmother, who died when I was a young child. But what I did know about her made me realise that living through the war and living in several different countries meant that there were social and cultural possibilities open to her that were not open to my mother. It also made me realise that my mother probably invested more in parenting than my grandmother did, for whom being a dutiful wife and running a household were the priority. I also recognised the investment that my mother placed on being a good mum, and a very different kind of mum from her own. Yet she also felt frustrated by not having a 'career', even though she did work. All this has contributed to my own biographical problem of trying to 'do it all' and feeling exhausted by it.

My intergenerational chain reflects a very particular history: white, middle class and downwardly mobile. Your intergenerational chain will no doubt be very different, showing the importance of factors such as gender, social class (and mobility), ethnicity, nationality, migration, religion and so on when taking a biographical perspective. For example, the norm of combining motherhood and employment may be historically new for the middle classes but is an established tradition for working class and African-Caribbean families.

If we read across the table from left to right or right to left we can see how social change is mediated through families. Social and cultural possibilities can be seen as objective changes, yet whether we are able to engage with those opportunities at the level of biography is mediated both by our identities (who we want to be – something close to Giddens's reflexive project of self) and also by our subjectivity – our feelings and emotions, much of which will be unconscious.

Members of each generation have their own biographical problems, which are uniquely connected to their own family, yet which may also be generalised to their wider historical cohort (those born at the same time). For example, Bjerrum Nielsen and Rudberg (2000) have written about how the accounts of the three generations of women they interviewed differed in broad terms. The grandmothers by and large talked in highly pragmatic terms about their childhood. They did not question their parents' motives nor interpret why they acted as they did. Theirs were primarily descriptive accounts of 'doing', set in the Norwegian countryside. The accounts that their daughters produced of their adolescence were very different. As the first generation to make the journey to the city, to urban life, further education and work, they produced complicated accounts that were highly psychological. By and large they were critical of their mothers, wanting to be very different kinds of women, and their narratives suggested a highly reflexive mode of analysis and interpretation. Their daughters' accounts were strangely like those of the grandmothers, yet with an ironic twist. Like the grandmothers, the daughters were accepting of their own mothers and did not want to be different from them in any major way. This account draws our attention to the unevenness of historical change. In biographical terms there may be moments when continuity dominates and moments when change is felt more acutely. The moment of time captured by the mothers' adolescence was a time of rapid social and cultural change in Norway and this generation had to forge something anew, even if they did so from a set of familiar resources. This was the moment of second wave feminism and a rejection of the past. In both earlier and subsequent generations the picture is more one of continuity, connection and stability.

The complexity of the relationship between generations can also be expressed indirectly through youth cultural forms. In Chapter 1 ('A cultural perspective') you heard about John Clarke's idea of the 'magical recovery', which seeks to show how oppositional youth cultures attempt to resolve, albeit magically, some of the contradictions of their parents' generation. Phenomena such as the mods, punks, goths or skaters can be understood in terms of a conversation with the culture of the parents' generation, where issues are encountered indirectly. Because these contradictions are bound up with the lives of earlier generations, they are unlikely to be within the power of young people to resolve. What then is 'magical' about the recovery is that the contradictions are engaged with symbolically and that, as a result, some kind of movement (if not resolution) is achieved. In biographical terms this may translate into a form of biographical momentum, even though the underlying contradictions remain and are likely to resurface again in a different way at another point in time. It may be possible to understand social movements such as feminism in part as complex 'magical recovery' to the biographical problems posed by an earlier generation.

Activity 5   'Magical recoveries'

Allow 20 minutes   Look back now at your three-generational chain exercise. Can you think of any examples of individual or collective 'magical recoveries' through which one generation responded to a biographical problem encountered by the earlier generation?

Comment

As with all these biographical activities, thinking about intergenerational dynamics may well raise complicated emotional feelings. It may be that conflict becomes condensed in magical recoveries, which as a result may not seem or feel that 'magical'. In thinking of something as a magical recovery we also move away from the interpretation of those directly involved. As one reader who did this activity observed of her skinhead brother: 'Maybe he was trying to fulfil a need to be autonomous and different from our parents. Trying to recreate the traditional working class community through his "mob". I bet he would laugh if I suggested this is what he was trying to do!' In searching for magical recoveries we may also find intergenerational cultural motifs: practices that are returned to over generations and through which family narratives are reworked. Another reader talked about how 'golfing' operated as an intergenerational motif in their family. Her father grew up next to a golf club but was unable to enter it – a symbol of social exclusion for the family. His son ended up working with professional golfers and achieving some of the things his father had not been able to, as someone who lacked the necessary 'resources', material and otherwise. In another family dancing was a intergenerational motif, representing an area of autonomy for women. A great aunt had been a professional dancer. Her niece had wanted to be a dancer too, but her ambitions were thwarted by her father, who insisted that she went to work in an office. The only dancing she did was at parties, until she met her husband, who didn't dance. After that she danced in front of *Top of the Pops* with the kids. Her daughter became a passionate dancer in the era of discos and raves, dancing all night, on podiums, in fields, on rooftops. Dancing provided them all with a feeling of independence in ways that were culturally and historically specific.

Key points

- In this section we explored how the shift from 'normal' to 'choice' biographies could be understood in historical and intergenerational terms, with consequences for parents' attempts to understand and support their children.

- In seeking to understand change as mediated by families we distinguished between gender identity, subjectivity and the social and cultural possibilities of any one historical time.

- Lack of fit between these elements gives rise to biographical problems. Where such biographical problems are experienced collectively, they may give rise to 'magical recoveries' at a symbolic and cultural level.

In the next section we will look more closely at what a biographical approach may mean in practice and how it may be applied in policy and practice approaches to working with young people.

4 Applying a biographical approach

One of the impacts of individualisation, it is argued, is that we begin to see the world from the perspective of the individual rather than simply in terms of institutional systems and social structures. For social analysts (including policy makers and practitioners) this involves a significant shift towards understanding all fields of action, both public and private, as interrelated parts of an individual's biography. This does not mean that social structures, systems and institutions are no longer important; rather we have to be aware of new ways in which the individual and the social interact. The emergence of 'institutional biographical patterns' is another characteristic of the process of individualisation described by Beck. Paradoxically, as we all become increasingly 'free' from tradition, we also become increasingly dependent on and defined by institutional processes:

> The apparent outside of the institution becomes the inside of the individual biography ... The liberated individuals become dependent on the labour market and *because of that*, dependent on education, consumption, welfare state regulations and support, traffic planning, consumer supplies, and on possibilities and fashions in medical, psychological and pedagogical counselling and care ... Individualization becomes the *most advanced* form of societalization dependent on market, law, education and so on.
>
> (Beck, 1992, pp. 130–1)

Beck's argument here is that although we may feel more and more like individuals, and we may be making more and more choices, the process of individualisation leads to new and often closer forms of governance. One example of the way in which institutional processes become written into biographies can be seen in the field of education. As traditional formations of social class reconfigure, it is argued that educational success and educational decision making become the central focus of young people's biographies, and the axis of subsequent inequalities. In biographical terms we can see young people as falling into two camps:

- The non gender specific extended educational transition: associated with middle class culture, post-16 academic study, extended dependency and extended youth, university and professions.

- The more gender specific accelerated transition: associated with working class cultures, leaving school early, low paid work, unemployment, early parenthood and the search for traditional forms of adulthood. It is these kinds of transitions that are the focus of much government policy including concerns with keeping young people in some form of education or training, punishing 'antisocial behaviour' and discouraging welfare dependency.

This kind of understanding of youth transitions is influential within contemporary UK government policy. It is founded on a notion of discreet but interlocking 'careers': for example a school to work career, a leisure career, a family career, a housing career. These careers overlap and compete and fall into different kinds of patterns: for example the patterns of extended dependency and the accelerated transition outlined above. We can think of these as 'typologies' of biographical patterns with characteristic career components. Clearly, the development of these kinds of typologies is useful for policy and practice, enabling the focusing of resources on particular groups of young people. However, reliance on such typologies also has a downside, and it is important to understand their weaknesses. For example, such typologies can:

- be static (representing single moments in time)

- be fragmented (privileging certain strands of transition, for example education and work, and ignoring others, for example personal relationships and leisure)

- focus on the system/structure rather than the young person's account

- obscure understanding of how and why particular courses of action take place, and thus how issues of resources and timing are implicated.

Ideally, a biographical approach to youth transitions can be holistic and dynamic, working with the meanings that young people attribute to their own lives, and revealing of issues of timing and circumstance.

4.1 Competence, recognition and investment

In the *Inventing Adulthoods* study (Henderson *et al.*, 2007) the researchers explored youth transitions through the eyes of 100 young people over a ten-year period. From the perspective forged in this study we imagine young people's biographies as composed of a number of different and competing fields. The extent to which young people **invest** in a particular field – the personal and symbolic significance they attach to it – depends on the extent to which they experience themselves as **competent** and are recognised as such by others. Being competent here means possessing personal skills that give them access to resources and cultural capital. Investments in one field are likely to be associated with dis-investments in another; we only have so much energy, time and personal resources. So, for example, young people who do not experience themselves as competent at school are more likely to be attracted to forms of recognition available to them in work or in leisure. This is illustrated vividly by the case of Cheryl.

Cheryl: 'You can't have the best of both worlds'

At her first interview Cheryl was 16 years old, living at home with her parents and sister and studying for her GCSEs[1] at school ... At this point she looked to education as a source of personal development, expressing the hope that she would go on to take A levels[2] and possibly on to a nursing course. She expressed no ambitions to move beyond her neighbourhood. Much of her energy went into an eight month old relationship with her twenty-year old boyfriend, through whom she vicariously accessed some of the material culture of adult life – a car, money and a social life. She also had two part time jobs that together earned her £50 per week.

Cheryl's eighteen year old sister had recently had a baby, and this had provoked Cheryl to reflect on the kind of adulthood that she wanted for herself. She explained that she was in 'no hurry' to become an adult with all of the associated responsibilities and in particular wanted to delay motherhood. At this point she was enjoying a life without commitments, but with many of the 'trappings' of adulthood made accessible through her boyfriend ... Her investment in education was offset by feelings of maturity gained through her relationship and practices such as cooking her boyfriend dinner and saving for joint holidays.

By her second interview this balance had shifted substantially. Having passed five GCSEs Cheryl decided to continue in a newly formed school sixth form, pursuing an NVQ[3] course. She reported being very frustrated by the school's failure to recognise the greater maturity of the members of the sixth form. According to her the school treated them like children. At the same time her relationship with her boyfriend had become more domestic and 'adult-like'. As a couple they made regular visits to relatives and family, shared cosy nights in together where Cheryl would cook, and talked about getting engaged and buying a car. Her plans for her future had also shifted. In this interview she was more focused on a future as a housewife, staying at home looking after children while her husband worked outside the home.

With more demands at school Cheryl had given up her part time work and found it difficult being dependent on her parents, and being treated as a child at school. Whilst still committed to her educational training, she also talked about being tempted by the world of work and the financial and emotional independence that this seemed to offer. So although Cheryl was still attending school, the only arena of her life in which she experienced any adult-like competence, or was recognised as having any, was in her relationship with her boyfriend. [However, the relationship became increasingly domestic and Cheryl described her life as increasingly boring and routine.] ...

At her third interview we discovered a very different young woman for whom 'everything' had changed ... The pressures and frustrations that were evident in her second interview had come to a head. Cheryl had left the sixth form two months before completing her NVQ to take up a full time clerical job paying £140 per week. She explains that she 'just got claustrophobic, you know, with the school sort of treating us really like children' ...

She explained this decision in terms of frustrations at her lack of freedom and spending power in comparison to her friends. The school had proved to be very inflexible in response to her situation. A plea by the careers teacher for her to be allowed to complete the course in the evening was denied by the head teacher. 'And I told her [careers teacher] that I just wasn't happy and I wanted money and wanted to be able to enjoy myself, I didn't like having to still have to do things at night and all and my parents were still treating me like a child and all because I was still at school ... But he just said you can't have best of both worlds.'

[...]

The decision to move into employment can be understood as the catalyst for a whole series of changes. In the same week that Cheryl took up her job she also moved out of her parental home, renting a room in the house of another woman who was working. Soon after this her relationship with her boyfriend came to an end, partly as a result of Cheryl's frustration with his parents' refusal to treat their relationship as sufficiently adult ...

As a result Cheryl was no longer staying at home and living for the future, but going out, partying and living for the moment ... Work not only provided her with the material resources to become independent of her boyfriend and parents, but also with access to social and cultural networks that made different forms of adulthood available to her ... Significantly, in this interview Cheryl was again talking about university as a possible option for the future. She recognised that her recent choices may have made the route to university harder and longer, but for her the informal gains that she had made in this period were more significant than any that she would have made at school.

[1] General Certificate of Secondary Education, the qualifications that mark the end of compulsory education in the UK.

[2] Advanced Level qualification, the academic post-16 qualification that has traditionally been a prerequisite of university education in the UK.

[3] National Vocational Qualification.

(Thomson *et al.*, 2004, pp. 229–32)

Children or adults?

In many ways Cheryl's story is typical of many working class young people in the *Inventing Adulthoods* study for whom the educational pathway is seen as offering insufficient immediate rewards in contrast to the world of work and consumption that they see many of their peers enjoying. Parenthood can also provide an alternative site of competence in a way that is particularly resonant for young women. If Cheryl had become pregnant, she might have easily been drawn into a local form of adulthood defined through parental and domestic responsibility. From a biographical perspective it becomes possible to understand the competing pull and push factors that affect young people's choices. Central to their choices is the pursuit of a sense of competence: of being good at something and recognised by others as such. Cheryl gained a sense of competence both in her relationship and as a worker, yet at school she felt like a child. From this perspective it is not possible simply to fit Cheryl into either a normal or choice biography category. Rather we can see her as pursuing a 'reflexive project of self' with limited resources and a compelling need to achieve satisfaction and belonging in the process. Insights gained by following an individual over time, through the different twists and turns of their transitions, encourage a move away from notions of successful/ unsuccessful transitions towards asking questions about resources and timing.

4.2 Critical moments

Shifting to a biographical approach from a focus on transitions involves thinking in a different way.

*   First, it involves a recognition of subjective experience, what things 'feel like'.

*   Second, it involves looking at investments, what is it that young people value and put energy into.

*   Third, it involves an awareness of temporality, including 'critical moments' within a project of the self.

The choice to leave education for work was a highly consequential 'critical moment' in Cheryl's biography (Thomson *et al.*, 2002). It enabled her to evacuate both education and relationships as sites of investment, and to pursue a more individualised and less localised forms of recognition as a worker and independent consumer. Earlier in the chapter we also heard from Sheila, for whom having a baby was a 'critical moment' involving a reordering of her project of self. Critical moments understood in this way are defined by their role in providing biographical momentum and structure. They can be seen as an individualised version of the rites of passage discussed in Chapter 2 in that they provide structure to the transition between childhood and adulthood. Yet critical moments are not necessarily institutionalised at the level of the whole society, and they may be experienced in a very individual way.

Activity 6	Identifying critical moments
Allow 20 minutes	Think about your own transition to adulthood. Can you think of any critical moments that were highly consequential? Focus on one such moment.
	If things had happened differently, or you had made a different choice, would your life have turned out differently?
	Did the intervention of a parent, friend, neighbour or professional make a difference? Could it have?

To what extent was this a shared or collective experience, or something you experienced as an individual?

Comment

The concept of the critical moment may help you relate your own experience to the theoretical framework outlined in this chapter. It may also help you remember the kinds of feelings associated with your own youth, helping you to empathise with young people today. Doing this exercise may also help you grasp the powerful biographical 'logic' that lies behind people's experiences and decisions. As one student who did this exercise observed, 'I don't think any type of intervention would have made a difference to my becoming a parent at 18'.

In the *Inventing Adulthoods* study we asked young people to identify critical moments in their biographies. The following list outlines the kinds of things that young people came up with (Thomson *et al.*, 2002). The critical moments they identified reflected the localities in which they were growing up.

Family

Being kicked out of home; parents splitting up; disclosing abuse; father remarrying; falling out with step-parents; parental unemployment; disowned by mother; parents splitting; one parent leaving the home; parental repartnering; reconciliation with estranged parent.

Death and illness

Death of a parent; aunt committing suicide; loss of a baby; diagnosis of dyslexia; diagnosis of chronic illness; death of grandparents; depression; falling ill; births; death of friend; death of mother, father, friends, grandparents, niece, aunt; grandmother moving away; rejection by mother; diagnosis of rheumatoid arthritis; near-death experience.

Education

Sitting GCSE exams; choosing GCSEs; failing GCSE exams; dropping out of school/college; excluded from school; bullying at school; changing/leaving school; starting college; careers advice; conflict with teacher; staying on in education; being rejected by university of choice; going to university; returning to college and to school; poor GCSE results; good GCSEs; career choice; visiting a university; 'getting real' and downgrading ambitions; failing and succeeding in selection for pro football.

Rites of passage

Eighteenth birthday; passing driving test; 'coming out' and subsequent fallout re leaving home; religious conversion; doing a CV and resulting revaluation of self; getting a job; losing virginity; growing and reaching puberty.

Trouble

Getting caught taking drugs; getting arrested; getting pregnant; father going to jail; getting into drugs; reforming self; disclosure of sexual abuse; dangerous experiences – 'home alone' stories.

Leisure and consumption

Becoming involved in gay community; joining amateur dramatic society; starting to go to the pub; going clubbing; getting a mobile phone; getting a car; becoming a goth/skater; going travelling; passing driving test; piercings/tattoos; youth club closing.

Moving

Moving town; moving house; moving country; siblings leaving home; becoming mobile – passing driving test; going to university in England.

Relationships

New boyfriend; falling out with best friend; making new friends; being excluded from friendship group; changing friendship group; breaking up with girlfriend; girlfriend going to university; sexual experience; changing friendships via college; splitting up with boyfriend; steady girlfriend; losing virginity; 'learning how to handle lads'; pet dying; falling out with sister over a boy; developing sexual relationships; unrequited love; betrayal; becoming bisexual.

These are very different lists from those we might have obtained had we generated a list of issues that 'affect young people'. Here we can see those experiences and events that have biographical salience, both positive, negative and neutral. Some of these experiences are clearly within the remit of policy and practice interventions, for example getting arrested, getting pregnant, disclosing abuse, dropping out of school. Others (such as getting a mobile phone, falling out with a friend or experiencing the death of a grandparent) are unlikely to come to the attention of policy makers or practitioners. These are seen as a mundane and everyday part of growing up and being young.

Some of the critical moments reported by young people in the study were linked to institutional processes such as schooling. Others are more individual.

Activity 7   Mapping critical moments

Allow 15 minutes   It is also possible to distinguish those critical moments that are more or less within the control of an individual and those that are outside their control. Look again at the critical moments mentioned by the young people and identify which ones are likely to be associated with making choices and which are likely to be associated with factors beyond the control of the individual and with feelings of disempowerment.

Comment

This is an exercise designed to encourage thinking. There are no right or wrong answers. When analysing this list of critical moments the *Inventing Adulthoods* research team found that middle class, affluent young people were more likely to report critical moments associated with leisure and consumption, while young people from more disadvantaged backgrounds were more likely to report critical moments associated with death and illness, reflecting the realities of the environments in which they were growing up. Some of the critical moments in young people's biographies are the results of decisions taken by others (often parents). Yet young people may respond to similar events in very different ways. For example, for one young person the experience of bereavement may be the beginning of a downward spiral, for another who is well resourced, it may be equally painful, yet become an opportunity for reflection and growth. This also draws our attention to how and why certain events are perceived as critical for the individuals involved.

In another study of young people from a socially deprived neighbourhood Robert MacDonald, Jane Marsh and colleagues also identified critical moments in young people's accounts (MacDonald and Marsh, 2005; Webster *et al.*, 2004). These could be particular events that marked a shift in a young person's fortune or identity, often resulting in a reconstituting of their social networks. Ill health, parental separation and bereavement were found to be a relatively common experience among the young people studied, giving rise to significant if unpredictable outcomes. But although young people in the study tended to emphasise how much had changed in their lives (for example new relationships, changing leisure practices, shifts in drug and criminal activity), the dead-end socio-economic position of most of the young people in the study remained relatively consistent. As the authors observe, 'In this context getting a job that paid £4.50 an hour rather than £3.50 an hour was counted as a good outcome and potential jobs in call centres or as bus drivers were regarded as a step up' (Webster *et al.*, 2004, p. 410).

We can see from this example that although a biographical approach draws attention to young people's agency it should not, in the process, obscure the enduring importance of structural inequalities. A focus on critical moments implicit in a biographical approach encourages us to take issues of timing seriously as well as the way in which factors (many of them very ordinary) can combine or configure. It also demands that we look beyond recognised policy categories to find out what actually matters to young people themselves. If we ask and listen we may be surprised by what they say.

Key points

- A youth 'transitions' approach tends to focus on typologies (for example extended and accelerated transition) and policy related 'careers'. A biographical approach sees these elements as interrelated domains of an individual's life.

- Exploring the relationship between a sense of competence, recognition and investment can help us understand why young people may act as they do.

- A biographical perspective encourages us to focus on issues of timing, circumstance and subjective feelings, and we explore these through considering how 'critical moments' structure biographies and may provide opportunities for providing support.

- A biographical approach translates into youth policy and practice through an awareness of 'institutionally patterned biographies' and a commitment to joined up practice.

Conclusion

In this chapter we have outlined a biographical perspective on young people's lives. The approach that we have taken has as its starting point late modern theories of individualisation, which suggest a historical shift from normal to choice biographies. In the detraditionalised society the reflexive project of self is of increasing importance as disembedding and a resultant loss of security take their toll. In looking more closely at what a biographical perspective might reveal, we have explored the significance of a sense of competence and gaining recognition in determining the kind of investments young people make. In this respect questions of feelings and timing become crucial, with critical biographical moments operating as turning points in young people's lives.

In exploring the components of a biographical perspective we have cautioned against the tendency for such an approach to result in over-generalisation about societies, nations or historical periods. Ideally, a biographical approach is one that pays attention to detail, to context and to the changing shape of individuals' stories. Change is only one part of the story, and in outlining intergenerational processes and dynamics we hope to have drawn attention to the importance of continuity and our less conscious investments that mark the limits of choice.

References

Bauman, Z. and Tester, K. (2001) *Conversations with Zygmunt Bauman*, Cambridge, Polity Press.

Beck, U. (1992) *Risk Society: Towards a New Modernity*, London, Sage.

Bjerrum Nielsen, H. and Rudberg, M. (1994) *Psychological Gender and Modernity*, Oslo, Scandinavian University Press.

Bjerrum Nielsen, H. and Rudberg, M. (2000) 'Gender, love and education in three generations: the way out and up', *European Journal of Women's Studies*, vol. 7, no. 4, pp. 423–53.

Chamberlayne, P., Bornat, J. and Wengraf, T. (eds) (2000) *The Turn to Biographical Methods in Social Science: Comparative Issues and Examples*, London, Routledge.

Cremin, C. (2005) 'Profiling the personal: configuration of teenage biographies to employment norms', *Sociology*, vol. 39, no. 2, pp. 315–32.

Du Bois-Reymond, M. (1998) '"I don't want to commit myself yet": young people's life concepts', *Journal of Youth Studies*, vol. 1, no. 1, pp. 63–79.

Giddens, A. (1991) *Modernity and Self Identity: Self and Society in the Late Modern Age*, Cambridge, Polity Press.

Henderson, S., Holland, J., McGrellis, S., Sharpe, S. and Thomson, R. (2007) *Inventing Adulthoods: A Biographical Approach to Youth Transitions*, London, Sage (Set Book).

Jones, G., O'Sullivan, A. and Rouse, J. (2005) 'Young adults, partners and parents: individual agency and the problems of support', unpublished article.

London South Bank University (2006) *Inventing Adulthoods*, www.lsbu.ac.uk/inventingadulthoods [accessed 20/02/06].

MacDonald, R. and Marsh, J. (2005) *Disconnected Youth? Growing Up in Britain's Poor Neighbourhoods*, Basingstoke, Palgrave.

Miller, R. (2000) *Researching Life Stories and Family Histories*, London, Sage.

Miller, N. and Morgan, D. (1993) 'Called to account: the CV as an autobiographical practice', *Sociology*, vol. 27, no. 1, pp. 133–43.

Plummer, K. (1995) *Telling Sexual Stories: Power, Change and Social Worlds*, London, Routledge.

Plummer, K. (2001) *Documents of Life 2: An Invitation to a Critical Humanism*, London, Sage.

Roberts, B. (2001) *Biographical Research*, Buckingham, Open University Press.

Rose, N. (1996) 'Authority and the genealogy of subjectivity' in Heelas, P., Lash, S. and Morris, P. (eds) *Detraditionalization*, Oxford, Blackwell.

Rose, N. (1999) *Governing the Soul: The Shaping of the Private Self*, London, Free Association Books.

Silverman, D. (1993) *Interpreting Qualitative Data: Methods for Analysing Talk, Text and Interaction*, London, Sage.

Skeggs, B. (2002) 'Techniques for telling the reflexive self' in May, T. (ed.) *Qualitative Research in Action*, London, Sage.

Thomson, R., Bell, R., Holland, J., Henderson, S., McGrellis, S. and Sharpe, S. (2002) 'Critical moments: choice, chance and opportunity in young people's narratives of transitions, *Sociology*, vol. 36, no. 2, pp. 335–54.

Thomson, R. and Holland, J. (2002) 'Young people, social change and the negotiation of moral authority', *Children and Society*, vol. 16, no. 2, pp. 103–15.

Thomson, R., Holland, J., McGrellis, S., Bell, R., Henderson, S. and Sharpe, S. (2004) 'Inventing adulthoods: a biographical approach to understanding youth citizenship', *The Sociological Review*, vol. 52, no. 2, pp. 218–39.

Turney, D. (2007) 'Critical practice' in Robb, M. (ed.) *Youth in Context: Frameworks, Settings and Encounters*, London, Sage/The Open University (Course Book).

Webster, C., Simpson, D., MacDonald, R., Abbas, A., Cieslik, M., Shildrick, T. and Simpson, M. (2004) *Poor Transitions: Young Adults and Social Exclusion*, Bristol, Policy Press. Free pdf download available from Joseph Rowntree Foundation www.jrf.org.uk [accessed 20.02.06].

Part 2
Identities

Chapter 4

Gender

Martin Robb

Introduction

This part of the book is about young people's identities – the ways in which young people view themselves and make sense of their lives – and how those identities are negotiated against a background of social change. The first chapter in this part of the book focuses on an aspect of identity – gender – which is central to young people's developing sense of themselves. Transitions to adulthood are inescapably gendered: they are about becoming a man or a woman, rather than simply an adult. Another reason for beginning an exploration of young identities with gender is that it is an aspect of identity that has undergone dramatic changes in recent years. It also offers a lens through which to view some other key aspects of young people's identities, such as sexuality and attitudes to the body. Furthermore, although other important aspects of identity, such as ethnicity and class, are not the main focus of the chapter (they will be discussed more fully in Chapter 5, 'Belonging'), the approach taken in this chapter will be one that views gender identity as closely interwoven with other forms of social identity.

Within this general focus on young people and gender, the chapter has a more specific focus on young masculinities. Throughout the chapter there will be references to young women's experience and to the ways in which young masculinities and young femininities are worked out in relation to each other. However, there are good reasons for taking young men's experience as the main subject for a discussion of young gender identities. One reason is that, until recently, most work in this area has focused, understandably, on the experience of young women as the main 'victims' of the gendering of young people's lives. In this context the gendered identities of young men have remained largely invisible and have been seen as somehow 'natural'. As we shall see in later sections of this chapter, this situation has begun to change, with the appearance of a number of key research studies focusing on young masculinities, and the emergence of young men as an object of concern for policy.

This new policy focus, with its tendency to construct young men as a 'problem' on a number of fronts, offers a second reason for taking young masculinities as a focus of the chapter. There is a sense in recent policy and media debates that 'becoming a man' is now a less straightforward and more problematic experience than the transition to adult femininity, and certainly than it was for past generations of boys. Exploring the ways in which young masculinity is constructed in current public discourse, and then comparing these with the ways in which young men themselves negotiate their masculinity, can provide an insight into how gender identities are changing for both young men and young women.

Earlier chapters have described the ways in which young people in general have become a focus of wider public concerns, for example about crime and social order. Although young women's behaviour has certainly become an increasing subject of concern, young men remain the principal target of these problematising discourses. Here are two examples of recent media stories that have young men and young masculinity as their focus.

The lost boys: one in four lads say, 'we are just yobs'

A staggering one in four teenage lads admit to being 'serious or prolific' yobs, according to a terrifying Home Office report yesterday.

A shock crime survey revealed that 510,000 kids aged 14 to 17 across the country are lawless louts.

They have committed at least six crimes – including disorder, vandalism and shoplifting – in the last year. A hard core of teen crooks aged as young as 14 are behind burglary, robbery, joyriding, knife attacks and drug crime.

The teen crooks are fuelling a soaring violent-crime rate that has leapt by six per cent, the latest official survey reported. Ministers fear huge numbers of teenagers now have zero respect for law and order.

Last night, Home Secretary Charles Clarke confessed that the youth crime figures were 'appalling'.

The report means every secondary school classroom contains an average of four persistent tearaways – with many on the way to becoming career criminals.

[...]

Lout of order

[...]

Schoolboy Louis Bibby, aged just 12, gives law and order the finger as he is locked away for breaching the terms of an Asbo.

The tearaway from Leigh Park, Hants – who began offending when he was just eight – was sent to a detention centre for six months last year by a court.

(Hall, in *Daily Star*, 26 January 2005, pp. 8–9)

Young men 'failed over suicide'

No effective action is being taken to tackle the rising tide of male suicides, a report says.

The Men's Health Forum describes the loss of thousands of men's lives as 'tragic and needless' and calls for better targeting of action.

Glossy men's magazines have also been blamed for creating a false image of a male-dominated society that no longer exists, and which prevents young men from adapting to the modern world.

The report, published on Tuesday by the All Party Parliamentary Group on Mental Health, said the fact that men take more risks with their physical and mental health should be taken into account.

Three times as many young men as young women take their own lives – a total of 3,640 in 1996, up 2% on 1982. The number of women committing suicide fell by 41% during the same period.

(BBC News, 17 April 2000)

Activity 1   Stories about young men

Allow 30 minutes   Read these two media reports again. How do they represent young men? What similarities and differences do you notice in the ways young men are portrayed in the two reports? Make a note of your thoughts.

Comment

Both reports present young men as an urgent cause for concern. The first report suggests that a significant number of young men are 'yobs', involved in antisocial behaviour, whereas the second report purports to show that young men experience an enhanced risk of committing suicide. In the first report, there is a sense of moral panic about young men's impact on the wider society, while in the second there is a concern about the impact of contemporary society on young men. In other words, both reports represent young men as a 'problem'. However, whereas the first report presents young men as a problem to other people and society in general, the second suggests they may be a problem to themselves.

Young men have been portrayed as 'problems' by the media

Underlying both reports is a sense that being a young man in the UK today is somehow troubling, that there is something problematic about the state of young masculinity. These two media reports are not random or isolated examples. They have been chosen because they represent two common strands of recent public concern about young men and young masculinity. The reports present differing but complementary stories about young masculinity. They construct narratives which position young men in particular ways, both reflecting and reproducing powerful public discourses about the state of young masculinity.

These discourses are important for two reasons. First, they help to shape social attitudes towards young men, at an everyday level but also at an institutional level, influencing government policies and the practices of statutory agencies such as education and the justice system. So, indirectly, these discourses about young masculinity shape the experiences of young men themselves. Second, they have a more direct impact, providing frameworks within which young men themselves make sense of their own experience.

The narrative represented by the *Daily Star* story reflects the most common discourse about young masculinity currently in circulation, and its effect can be seen in a plethora of government initiatives in the field of youth justice, as well as more recent measures to deal with antisocial behaviour. The second story is typical of a number of recent narratives that portray young men as victims. They have been portrayed not only as being at greater risk of mental health problems, but also as more likely to be victims of violence. Another important example of the 'young men as victims' discourse has been what Victoria Foster *et al.* (2001) describe as the 'moral panic' about boys' supposed educational underachievement.

The current 'story' about young men, whether reflected in media discourse or embedded in policy statements, is made up of a number of contradictory strands. Are young men aggressors or victims, a threat to others or a problem to themselves? Is the 'problem' with young men, if it exists, the fault of something external to them, such as feminism or social change, or is there something intrinsically problematic about the nature of young masculinity itself? Do boys need to adapt and become more like girls, or do they need to recover a distinctive masculine identity, as argued by writers such as Robert Bly (1991) and Steve Biddulph (1997)?

Activity 2	Young men and media stories

Allow 2 hours   Over the next week or so, look out for media reports (in newspapers, magazines, on radio and TV) that feature young men. Observe closely how young men are represented in these stories. Are they presented as a problem to others or to themselves, or in some other way? Are there contradictions in the way young men are represented? What do the stories seem to be saying, either overtly or implicitly, about the current state of young masculinity?

Comment

Although it is not possible to anticipate what might be in the media stories that you select, I would guess that some of the themes discussed above will feature. However, it may be that new themes have emerged in the period since this chapter was written, perhaps displaying new ways of 'problematising' young men and young masculinity.

Having set out some of the changing and often contradictory ways in which young men are constructed in public discourse, the remainder of the chapter will explore how boys negotiate their gender identities in the context of these debates. Given the pervasive atmosphere of moral concern about young masculinity, what is it like to be young and male in the UK today? What is the relation between 'external' discourses and young men's own ways of making meaning out of their experience?

The chapter as a whole will attempt to address the following core questions:

- In what ways are young people's gender identities changing?
- What are some of the main features of contemporary young masculinities?
- How do young masculinities intersect with class, ethnic and sexual identities?
- How are young masculinities embodied?
- How does masculinity shape young men's emotional lives and personal relationships?
- What are the implications for supporting and working with young men and young women?

The first section of the chapter will set out a theoretical framework for thinking about young people's gender identities, and consider some of the ways in which those identities have changed in recent years. The remaining sections will draw on recent research work with young men to explore some key aspects of contemporary young masculinities, and the implications of these both for work with young men, and more broadly for policy and practice relating to young people and gender.

Key points

- Young people's lives are inescapably gendered and gender is a key, if changing aspect of young identities.
- Young men have become a focus of public debate and concern in recent years.
- Media and policy discourses tend to construct young masculinity as a 'problem', either for society or for young men themselves.

1 Ways of thinking about young gender identities

What kinds of theoretical frameworks can we use to understand young gender identities and young masculinities in particular? Part 1 of the book explored different ways of understanding and constructing youth. Despite their differences, the three chapters in Part 1 shared an explicit or implicit critique of the developmentalist theories of G. Stanley Hall (1904) and others. A developmentalist approach tends to see young people's gender identities as based on innate characteristics – as developing in a 'straight line', as it were, from biological sex – and as following patterns that are fairly universal. This **essentialist** approach to gender, which sees it as biologically or psychologically determined, working mainly 'from the inside out', is echoed in more recent accounts from neuroscience which argue that sexual differences are 'hardwired' into the brain (e.g. Baron-Cohen, 2003).

Social constructionist approaches pose a challenge to these accounts by viewing gender as something that is produced in diverse and dynamic social contexts. From this perspective ideas about what constitutes masculinity or femininity have changed over time and differ between societies, as well as between groups within a given society. A useful example is provided by men's involvement in the care of young children, which in twentieth-century Western societies was viewed as definitely unmasculine. However, in the pre-industrial West men were much more closely involved in childcare, as they are in many non-Western societies today. An example of this is provided by the writer Helena Norberg-Hodge from her experience of working with traditional communities in Ladakh in the Himalayas:

> Taking responsibility for other children as you yourself grow up must have a profound effect on your development. For boys in particular, it is important since it brings out their ability for caring and nurturing. In traditional Ladakh, masculine identity is not threatened by such qualities; on the contrary, it actually embraces them.
>
> (Norberg-Hodge, 2000, p. 66)

Central to this more social perspective on gender is the notion that gender identities are plural and diverse, and that they intersect with other social identities such as ethnicity and class. Young masculinities and femininities are shaped by the diverse and changing social contexts in which they are negotiated. The Australian sociologist Bob Connell (1995) has been influential in shifting attention away from the notion of masculinity as a singular, universal essence and towards the idea of *masculinities* as plural and socially situated. Thus it becomes possible to talk about black masculinities, or nineteenth-century masculinities, for example – or, for that matter, young masculinities. However, Connell also argues that in any given context certain versions of masculinity become dominant – or **hegemonic**. In the context of a secondary school, for instance, it is possible to identify a range of different ways of 'doing' masculinity, perhaps associated with different groups of boys. However, there will probably be one model that is more powerful than others, to which all boys need to aspire to achieve social acceptance. At the same time, hegemony is never achieved once and for all, and alternative versions of young masculinity may resist the dominant model and take part in a continuing struggle for social power.

In the Introduction we noted the importance of media and policy discourses in framing the ways in which young men and masculinity are seen in society. Social constructionist perspectives see gender identity as something that is achieved in and through language, drawing on culturally available discourses. **Discourse analysis** – investigating the ways in which meanings are made in language – has become an important field of enquiry in recent social research (Potter and Wetherell, 1987; Wetherell *et al.*, 2001). Margaret Wetherell and Nigel Edley carried out research into the ways in which young men construct their identities through talk, and Edley has argued that gender is something that is 'accomplished in the course of social interaction', while masculinity needs to be seen 'not as permanent or fixed, but as constantly remade on a moment-to-moment basis' (Edley, 2001, pp. 192–3). In other words, young men's gender identities are worked out in their interactions with others, rather than existing prior to those interactions.

However, this social constructionist emphasis on the external, social aspects of young gender identities needs to be complemented by an attention to the part played by internal, unconscious processes. Although some psychoanalytic writing has tended to reproduce a form of gender essentialism, the work of psychoanalytic feminists has attempted to describe the interplay of unconscious processes with changing social contexts. For example, Nancy Chodorow has argued that what appear to be 'specific personality characteristics in men' need to be seen as the product of the isolated nuclear family in contemporary capitalist society (Chodorow, 1978, p. 181), and Jessica Benjamin has suggested that changes in gender relations might lead to changes in the nature of masculinity and femininity: 'the changing social relations of gender have given us a glimpse of another world, of a space in which each sex can play the other and so accept difference by making it familiar' (Benjamin, 1998, p. 169).

1.1 Changing gender relations?

If young people's gender identities are produced in particular social contexts, in what ways have recent social changes impacted on young masculinities and young femininities? One of the most persistent recent 'stories' about young people and gender paints a picture of a feminised world in which girls' achievement is outstripping that of boys and in which young men are the victims of widespread social change. According to this narrative, changes in the economy have removed many of the jobs for which young men were traditionally prepared. At the same time, many new jobs in the information and service economies appear to demand more 'feminine' skills, and women seem to be making advances in the workplace to the detriment of men and of traditionally masculine skills and aptitudes. As a result, it is suggested that boys face a less certain future than their fathers and experience a crisis of expectation, in which they are unconvinced of the relevance of formal education, and in which traditional routes of socialisation into young manhood, such as apprenticeships, no longer exist (see Chapter 7, 'Working', for a more detailed discussion of young people's changing experience of work). In the school context, as we noted in the Introduction, there has been a 'moral panic' (Foster *et al.*, 2001) about boys' supposed underachievement relative to girls. However, some writers have challenged this dominant narrative of girls' success and boys' underachievement. According to Valerie Walkerdine *et al.* (2001) class is a decisive factor:

> Girls from professional families are doing very well at school and boys from families from lower occupational groups are doing badly. This is often presented as girls' good performance versus boys' poor performance, but this is far from the case. Boys from professional families, generally speaking are not allowed to fail ... while girls from lower-income families are not doing very well at all.
>
> (Walkerdine *et al.*, 2001, p. 16)

According to Sinikka Aapola *et al.* (2005) although girls appear to be the 'new success stories of contemporary times' and policy makers assume that recent social changes have been more advantageous to young women than to young men, this rosy picture needs to be complemented by other less optimistic stories:

> Whilst we hear about phenomenal schoolgirl success and the triumphs of girl power, we are also told of increasing incidents of girls' violence, self-esteem problems, and propensity for self-harm.
>
> (Aapola *et al.*, 2005, p. 9)

Aapola *et al.* state that the apparent feminisation of the workplace and the increasing preference of the new labour market for 'the expressive, well-groomed, mobile negotiator' (Aapola *et al.*, 2005, p. 62) are usually represented as problems for young men and as unproblematically advantageous for young women. However, they argue that the picture is more complex than this: for example, many of the new opportunities for young women in the new economy are poorly paid, casualised and short term.

Drawing on the work of Lisa Adkins, Walkerdine *et al.* suggest that women who enter male professional and business domains find it difficult

Girls' achievement in education is said to be outstripping that of boys

or impossible to take on the required 'masculine' traits, and it can be 'easier for men to inhabit feminine corporeality and performativity than it is for women to do the opposite' (Walkerdine *et al.*, 2001, pp. 55–6). Walkerdine *et al.* also point to the difficulties for young women in outpacing boys' achievement in the classroom, which may require girls to masquerade as 'one of the boys'. In their research they found that 'a pushy and argumentative girl was not understood in the same way as a pushy and argumentative boy'. Elsewhere they argue that 'the entry of middle class girls into masculine norms of rational academic excellence comes at a price. It is not achieved easily and indeed is produced out of the suppression of aspects of femininity and sexuality' (Walkerdine *et al.*, 2001, p. 178).

These challenges to popular discourses about boys' and girls' relative achievement suggest that recent social changes have affected young men and young women in complex ways. While changes in education and the labour market appear to have had a positive impact on many young women's lives, change has not affected all young women equally and both schools and the workplace remain deeply gendered environments. At the same time, despite the current problematising of boys, and the negative impact of labour market changes on particular groups such as working class and black young men (Archer, 2001), in many ways young masculinity remains privileged in current gender relations. As we shall see in the remaining sections of the chapter, gendered inequality continues to play an important part in the ways in which young men negotiate their masculine identities.

Key points

- Essentialist approaches see gender as biologically or psychologically determined, whereas social constructionist approaches view gender identities as plural, dynamic and produced in diverse social contexts.

- Psychoanalytic feminism has drawn attention to the ways in which unconscious processes interact with social context in the production of gender identities.

- Although it is widely assumed that recent social changes have benefited young women and worked to the disadvantage of young men, the situation is complex and gendered inequality persists.

2 Researching young masculinities

Research on young masculinities has become a growth area in recent years, with a number of important studies appearing in the UK, USA and Australia. Much of this research has taken place in schools and there has been a strong focus, to date, on the part played by peer groups, both within and outside schools, in the negotiation of young masculine identities. An early example of such research was Paul Willis's groundbreaking work (1977), and many of the findings of Willis's research with young, working class men have been echoed in more recent studies. By comparison, there has been little work to date on the family as a site for the reproduction of young masculinities, or for that matter on young men's personal relationships more generally, although research in this area is beginning to appear (see, for example, Peter Redman's work on young men and 'romance', which is discussed in more detail in Chapter 10).

Mairtin Mac an Ghaill's (1994) pioneering study explored the ways in which masculinities and sexualities were reproduced in a Midlands secondary school, focusing on the ways in which student and teacher cultures interacted to reproduce diverse but also hegemonic masculinities and sexualities. This was followed by the study carried out by Mike O'Donnell and Sue Sharpe (2000) which examined issues of masculinity, ethnicity and class in London comprehensive schools. A similar setting was the focus for important research carried out by Stephen Frosh, Ann Phoenix and Rob Pattman (Frosh et al., 2002), which explored a variety of issues with 11–14-year-old boys in a range of schools.

Some of the findings in these studies have found echoes in research by Wayne Martino and Maria Pallotta-Chiarolli (2003) with boys in Australian secondary schools.

What kind of picture do these studies present of the masculine identities available to young men today, and of the ways in which they negotiate them? Do they confirm a sense of dramatic change in young masculinities or reinforce traditional stereotypes? What is the relationship between boys' own understanding of themselves and the wider discourses and debates about the state of young masculinity that we have been exploring?

Below we discuss some of the key findings from these and other research studies. However, by way of introduction, it will be useful to draw out some of the general conclusions made by researchers into young masculinity. Frosh *et al.* found that the boys they interviewed had 'a sophisticated understanding of the current contradictions associated with the negotiation of masculine identities' (Frosh *et al.*, 2002, p. 10). They also reported that the young men they talked to were only too aware of the negative way in which boys and young men are represented in the mass media and elsewhere. To summarise their overall findings about the current state of young masculinity Frosh *et al.* list what they describe as a number of major **'canonical narratives'** (a term coined by Bruner, 1990, meaning stories about how lives may be lived in the culture) about masculinity current in London schools, as articulated by young men themselves:

1 Boys must maintain their differences from girls (and so avoid doing anything that is seen as the kind of thing girls do).

2 Popular masculinity involves 'hardness', sporting prowess, 'coolness', casual treatment of schoolwork and being adept at 'cussing'.

3 Some boys are 'more masculine' than others. This involves both racialised and class consciousness.

(Frosh *et al.*, 2002, p. 10)

In the sections that follow we will examine these key features of 'popular (young) masculinity' in more detail, drawing on evidence and examples from a range of research studies.

2.1 Hegemony and diversity in young masculine identities

Frosh *et al.* noted that young men themselves are aware of the ways in which factors of ethnicity and class intersect with masculine identities. From a social constructionist perspective, young masculinities need to be seen as located in diverse social contexts and as varying along lines of class and ethnicity. As Frosh *et al.* remark:

> One compelling finding ... is the impossibility of understanding masculinities in isolation from other constituting features of boys' lives. At least in our London sample, it is clear that masculinities are constructed out of a complex network of identity factors, including 'race', ethnicity, social class and sexuality.
>
> (Frosh *et al.*, 2002, p. 258)

This reinforces the point that contemporary young masculinity is not a singular entity, and that it cannot be understood in isolation from other aspects of young men's social identities. Another implication is that the models of masculinity which are influential for young men have powerful class and 'racialised' inflections. The most obvious example in the study by Frosh *et al.* was that African-Caribbean boys were routinely seen as more 'masculine' than boys from other ethnic groups, and as representing a model of masculinity that was desirable for other boys. Mary Jane Kehily's research into sexuality and gender in two Midlands secondary schools identified a similar interweaving of masculinities and ethnicities, with young Asian men feminised by comparison with young men from African-Caribbean backgrounds (Kehily, 2002, p. 158). Mac an Ghaill reports similar findings, at the same time pointing to the ways in which racialised young masculinities intersect with sexualities. Here is one boy from his study, Rajinder, talking:

> You see there's a lot of sexuality in there. The African Caribbeans are seen as better at football and that's really important in this school for making a reputation. And it's the same with dancing, again the black kids are seen as the best. And the white kids and the Asians are jealous because they think that the girls will really prefer the black kids. So, the 'race' thing gets all mixed up with other things that are important to young kids.
>
> (Mac an Ghaill, 1994, p. 86)

However, the relationship between masculinity and ethnicity is a complex one. In attempting to understand young black masculinity and its appeal for young white men, we need to remember the context of wider power relations. According to Claire Alexander, 'black masculinity is ... perhaps best understood as an articulated response to structural inequality, enacting and subverting dominant definitions of power and control, rather than substituting for them' (Alexander, 2002, p. 94).

Masculinity also carries strong class associations for young men. One of the 'canonical narratives' identified by Frosh *et al.* was that popular young masculinity involves physical 'hardness', sporting prowess, 'cussing' and hostility to schoolwork. These attributes have marked working class associations and can be seen as resistant to the predominantly middle class, academic culture of the secondary school. Unlike Frosh *et al.*, Mac an Ghaill (1994) does not identify a single, hegemonic masculinity, but rather describes a diversity of masculine cultures within a particular school. Nevertheless, it is clear from his research that one group of boys, the 'Macho Lads', with their declared devotion to the three 'F's – 'fighting, fucking and football' – had achieved a kind of hegemony in the school (Mac an Ghaill, 1994, p. 56). Diane Reay's case study of one boy, Shaun, caught between his mother's academic aspirations and his white, male, working class peer group, identifies a similar set of values among that peer group (Reay, 2002). In their analysis of the experience of 'Peter' in a boys' grammar school in the late 1970s and early 1980s, Redman and Mac an Ghaill (1997) also identify both a plurality of masculinities and at the same time the dominance of white working class masculinity:

> the predominantly white working-class/lower middle-class catchment area of the school meant that pupils' cultures tended to reproduce and validate masculinities that revolved around forms of white working-class male credibility: opposition to academic work and school authority, a taken-for-granted racism, football, 'the pub', girlfriends and, to a lesser extent (given the more academic orientation of the school), fighting.
>
> (Redman and Mac an Ghaill, 1997, p. 168)

Activity 3   Diverse gender identities

Allow 30 minutes   Think about your own experience of being at secondary school and try to identify the different ways of being a young man or a young woman that were available to you and your peers. What were the connections between these diverse gender identities and class, ethnicity or other factors? Which forms of masculinity or femininity were dominant among your peers and which were endorsed by the official culture of the school?

Comment

In doing this activity you may have identified both similarities to and differences from the findings of the research studies discussed above. Note that some of the studies were conducted some time ago – Mac an Ghaill's research, for example, was published in 1994. You may want to compare your own experience and the findings of these studies with the experience of any young people that you are in contact with now, whether professionally or as a parent, to see what has changed and what has remained the same.

Why is it that the cultures of groups that are subordinate in the wider society (such as working class and black young men) apparently provide such powerful models for all groups of young men? Tackling this question can perhaps help to throw light on the contexts in which young masculinities are produced.

Perhaps the first point to note is that these findings derive from studies among young male peer groups within schools. Remembering our earlier discussion of the contextual nature of gender identities, we might speculate that different models of young masculinity will be hegemonic in other contexts: at home, for example, or in local communities beyond the school. Within schools, too, it is important to remember that there are a range of locations where different kinds of masculinity might be possible. In the secondary school context that he studied, Mac an Ghaill identifies other young masculine cultures that were in contention with the Macho Lads – groups he identifies as the Academic Achievers, the New Enterprisers and the Real Englishmen (Mac an Ghaill, 1994). While boys in these groups acknowledged the power of the Macho Lads, and to some extent defined themselves in relation to them, they were also able to create spaces within which they could express different versions of young masculinity. Similarly, Redman and Mac an Ghaill describe how 'Peter' managed to carve out an alternative masculine identity, revolving around an interest in literature and ideas, through his identification with a particular history teacher (Redman and Mac an Ghaill, 1997, p. 168).

Once again, it is also important to remember the situated nature of these research studies, in secondary schools in specific geographical areas, with particular class and ethnic mixes of students. Research among boys in other geographical areas, with a different ethnic and class mix in the population, might well produce different identifications and affiliations.

Another way of understanding the hegemony of subordinated masculinities among boys is to refer back to our earlier discussion of young men's changing expectations. In a context where the value of school based education has been undermined by changes in the nature of work, it is possible to see the dominance of a 'macho' culture among young men as a culture of resistance, a generalising of the phenomenon first noticed by Willis in the 1970s (Willis, 1977). As will be noted later in the chapter, some commentators have argued that the unsettling of gender differences in recent years has produced a need for some men to assert the boundaries of masculinity more forcefully.

Finally, we suggested earlier in the chapter that gender identities are negotiated through speech (Edley, 2001), with talk a means of establishing masculine identity. It could be argued that the methodology of some research studies actually encourages the discursive reproduction of a certain kind of macho masculinity, especially where group interviews are the main method used, providing a stage on which more defensive versions of masculinity are performed for other members of the peer group. A psychodynamic analysis would go further, arguing that if a key feature of current constructions of young masculine identity is a disavowal of feelings that may be construed as 'feminine', then the discourse of young men in these research contexts will tend to rigorously exclude these aspects, even if they are privately important for the young men concerned. It is interesting that Frosh *et al.* suggest that the responses of the young men in their studies often differed markedly depending on whether they were taking part in individual or group interviews (Frosh *et al.*, 2002, p. 32).

If young masculinities are diverse in terms of class and ethnicity, they also intersect with diverse sexualities. As we have already seen, sexuality is closely interwoven with both ethnicity and class in the ways in which young men construe their own and each other's identities. As with class and ethnicity, an awareness of diversity needs to be complemented by a sense of the dominance of particular identities within young men's local cultures: in this case, the hegemony of heterosexual masculinity.

One of the difficulties of researching diverse sexual identities among young men is the apparent centrality of homophobia to many young male cultures – something that will be explored further in the next section. Another difficulty, which will also be discussed later, is the seeming reluctance of many young men to engage in discussion of intimate relationships. Certainly, open discussion of affection between young men appears to be 'off limits' within the context of the secondary school. Referring to one of the schools where he carried out his research, Mac an Ghaill notes:

> At Parnell School most of the young men appeared to find it difficult to talk about male affection in relation to sex. In interviews, they defensively could not or would not talk to me about how they might be linked.
>
> (Mac an Ghaill, 1994, p. 99)

However, Mac an Ghaill's study also includes interviews with young men who openly identified themselves as gay. Rajinder described how his sexuality was both made invisible and rejected by the school:

> At school there's no such thing as sexuality, so it seems. Then one day you come out and say you're gay and then you find out that it's the most important thing in the world. The teachers try everything to change you. 'It's a phase, you need psychiatric help, it's unnatural, it's against your religion, your parents won't accept you, your friends will reject you, you won't get a job.' I've heard it all. I think that teachers feel more threatened by gays than by any other group.
>
> (Mac an Ghaill, 1994, p. 153)

Janet Holland *et al.* (1998) have argued that achieving heterosexuality is central to the production of 'normal' masculinity. As Rajinder suggests, this process appears to include a routine defensiveness towards homosexuality – something that will be explored in Section 3.

Key points

- 'Hegemonic' young masculinity appears to involve physical 'hardness', sporting prowess and hostility to schoolwork.

- Young masculinities are diverse and are shaped by other aspects of young men's identities, such as class and ethnicity.

- The dominance of particular models of young masculinity needs to be seen as shaped by context and by wider social relations.

3 Policing the boundaries of young masculinity: young men and homophobia

One of the common findings of recent research studies has been the persistence of routine homophobia among young men. Frosh *et al.* report that homophobia was extremely pervasive among the 11–14-year-olds that they interviewed, and they describe boys as policing each other's masculine identities by positioning particular boys as 'transgressing gender boundaries, rendering them effeminate or gay' (Frosh *et al.*, 2002, p. 12). As we have already seen, one of the 'canonical narratives' identified by the same study was that 'Boys must maintain their differences from girls (and so avoid doing anything that is seen as the kind of thing girls do)' (p. 10). The authors claim that

> the construction of hegemonic masculinity as a contrast with a repudiated 'gay' identity is a major feature of young men's talk. Homophobia is one clear marker for much emergent masculinity in this age group, suggesting that the struggle to establish oneself as 'normatively heterosexual' is a very significant feature of identity formation for these boys.
>
> (Frosh *et al.*, 2002, p. 258)

This finding is echoed in other studies, which report that boys tend to construe non-masculine behaviour extremely broadly, to include being bad at games or showing too much interest in schoolwork. Writing about their own research into young men and homophobia, Anoop Nayak and Mary Jane Kehily quote one boy, Miles, talking about homosexuality:

> It's sort of a stigma, ain't it? A quiet person in a class would be called 'gay' or summat. I was for a time 'cos I was fairly quiet in the classroom and for a while everyone was calling me gay.
>
> (Nayak and Kehily, 1996, p. 214)

As the authors comment: 'Aspects of imagined gay behaviour are projected onto certain young men who are seen to deviate from the acceptable codes of masculine behaviour' (Nayak and Kehily, 1996, p. 214). Mac an Ghaill reports that: 'Alongside the heterosexual male students' practices of compulsory heterosexuality and misogyny, many of them displayed virulent public modes of homophobia' (Mac an Ghaill, 1994, p. 94). He quotes from an interview with one heterosexual boy:

Jim: I just hate 'bum boys'. When I think of them, it makes me want to puke. When I see two guys holding hands or pecking each other on the cheek, I have to turn away. I feel sick.

M.M: Have you ever seen any gays doing this?

Jim: No. But if I did I would. They must be looking at you, undressing you in their minds. They're just sick.

M.M: Why do you feel gays are so bad?

Jim: They just are. It's a strong feeling inside of me, inside any normal people.

(Mac an Ghaill, 1994, p. 95)

Some researchers emphasise the discursive nature of homophobia in defending against the appearance of femininity in talk within the young male peer group, while others draw attention to the ritualistic nature of young men's hostility. Nayak and Kehily describe the way that boys in their study made a crucifix sign with their fingers, as if warding off vampires, when the conversation turned to homosexuality (Nayak and Kehily, 1996, p. 217).

The impact of homophobia on the lives of young men and women who do not fit the norms of compulsory heterosexuality should not be underestimated. According to Sue Sharpe, gay and lesbian young people 'have to try and fit themselves into these powerful discourses with which they are so at odds, such as the perceptions about homosexuality involving predatory behaviour, or being something contagious' (Sharpe, 2002, p. 272). Like 'Devon' in the following quotation, they may even internalise aspects of the surrounding homophobic culture and so struggle to view their emergent sexuality in a positive light:

> I know I was homophobic when I was 14 ... I was thinking that no, it's completely unnatural. I really did think I was the only person in

the world who had that problem, because I'd heard about someone being gay, but I never actually thought there were people out there, who were like that. So I thought that gay was just an expression. I didn't think they existed at that age and I was just like, NO! NO WAY! NO WAY! I thought it was like a disease you – not a disease, but like a – a thing that you shouldn't be thinking. A thing that should be got rid of.

(Quoted in Sharpe, 2002, p. 273)

How can we account for the routine expression of homophobia among young men, and its place in the maintenance of young masculine identities? Nayak and Kehily draw on Judith Butler's (1990) notion of gender as performance to argue that young men's homophobia is a ritualised display that uses the 'othering' of women and gays to defend against a sense of emptiness at the core of masculinity:

> For many of the young men who engage in these oppressive actions, heterosexual masculinities are consolidated through display. The performance provides a fantasy of masculinity which can only be sustained through repetition, yet always resonates the echo of uncertainty.

(Nayak and Kehily, 1996, p. 227)

The authors explicitly link homophobia with misogyny, arguing that it is a 'means of consolidating sexuality and gender through the traducing of femininity, and its association with homosexuality', and they suggest that 'Young men may worry about being gay, and being called gay, in part due to the intense hostility expressed towards women and femininity' (Nayak and Kehily, 1996, p. 213).

From this perspective 'normal' young masculinity and heterosexuality are inseparable. Holland *et al.* argue that there is a link between normative, heterosexual masculinity and misogyny: 'being a "normal" man implies the exercise of power over women, whether or not this is recognised, acknowledged or desired by an individual man' (Holland *et al.*, 1998, p. 10). Psychoanalytic feminists such as Chodorow have argued that masculine development in contemporary society has taken the path of repressing what is perceived to be feminine:

> For children of both genders, mothers represent regression and lack of autonomy. A boy associates these issues with his gender identification as well. Dependence on his mother, attachment to her, and identification with her represent that which is not masculine; a boy must reject dependence and deny attachment and identification. Masculine gender role training becomes much more rigid than feminine. A boy represses those qualities he

takes to be feminine inside himself, and rejects and devalues women and whatever he considers to be feminine in the social world.

(Chodorow, 1978, p. 181)

Similarly, **queer theory** – a body of theory that suggests that gender and sexual identity are socially constructed – has argued that heterosexuality, while assumed to be 'natural', is something that needs to be achieved and sustained, particularly for men (Simpson, 1994). This involves the systematic and repeated repudiation of any suspicion of sexual attraction between men (Sedgwick, 1985).

However, in understanding homophobia as an unconscious defence 'built into' young masculine identity, it is important not to overlook the social context of young men's practices. Redman argues that the notion of homophobia 'tends to imply that boys' anti-lesbian and gay talk and practice can be explained solely in terms of the unconscious processes of individuals'. Instead he advocates seeing 'psychic and the social dynamics as mutually constitutive', which would involve 'thinking through the ways in which individual biography, unconscious dynamics and social relations interact to locate boys in differing positions in relation to the repertoire of masculinities available in the "little cultural worlds" of the school' (Redman, 2000, p. 496).

This attention to the contextual nature of young men's homophobia also needs to take account of wider changes in gender relations. For example, Anthony Giddens argues that gender divisions no longer have the authority that they did in the past and that traditional gender roles now 'demand discursive justification' (Giddens, 1994, p. 105). Commenting on this, Rachel Thomson has suggested that gender identities are more brittle than they once were and require more work to sustain them (Thomson, 2004).

If 'compulsory heterosexuality' shapes young men's gender identities, it is also important for young women. According to Aapola *et al.*:

Discourses of compulsory heterosexuality are part of a network of power relations governing women's lives, and they have traditionally been crucial for girls and young women in positioning themselves as properly 'female' and mature.

(Aapola *et al.*, 2005, p. 147)

While not minimising the persistence of homophobia among some groups of young women, the same authors suggest that the greater acceptance of physical intimacy in girls' friendships 'may sometimes lead to more consciously sexual contacts between young women'. They add: 'It may also be easier for girls to hide their erotic relationships with other girls, as sleep-overs and physical closeness are traditionally regarded as part of girls' culture' (Aapola *et al.*, 2005, p. 155). Sue Sharpe's research into young people's perceptions of homosexuality found that girls 'took a much more liberal stance' than boys, although attitudes among both girls and boys were also influenced by other factors such as class, religion and locality (Sharpe, 2002, pp. 264–5).

As we have already noted, young men's gender and sexual identities intersect with class identities in complex ways. David Buckingham and Sara Bragg's (2004) research on young people's attitudes to the representation of sex in the media concluded that class was an important factor in responses to diverse sexualities. They found support for gay rights among older and more middle class teenagers, who were often critical of the lack of gay representation in the media. The authors argue that this evidence of liberal tolerance among some young people may be part of investing in a 'metropolitan' identity which construes prejudice as undesirable and 'lower class'. Among working class young men they found less tolerance and suggest, interestingly:

> Perhaps 'homosexual awareness' became elided with other agents of professional control and expertise, imposed against their culture and values, and homophobia became a channel for resentment and a sense of class injuries ... Their homophobia may thus express a grasp of – and a misdirected anger about – the fact that, despite an apparent extension of social tolerance, there had been no real shift in power relations in their own life experience.
>
> (Buckingham and Bragg, 2004, p. 90)

Thus young men's homophobia needs to be understood in the context of wider and changing gender and social relations. It is important to explore why some young men, in particular contexts, feel such an urgent need to defend against what is perceived to be 'feminine'. This question will be pursued further in Section 4, which explores the part played by emotions and personal relationships in the production of young masculinities.

Key points

- Homophobia appears to be a routine feature of contemporary young men's performance of masculinity.

- Young men's homophobia can be seen as a response to the unsettling of traditional gender roles and a need to reinforce the boundaries of young masculinity.

- Some theorists argue that masculine identity is a defensive structure founded on hostility to anything perceived as feminine.

4 'Why doesn't he say that he loves me?' Young men, emotions and relationships

Some writers have suggested that the corollary of young men's denial of 'feminine' qualities in themselves is an emotional emptiness in boys' lives and relationships. Frosh *et al.* report that 'despite bravado and claims to the contrary on the part of boys themselves, they very frequently communicate a lack at the centre of their masculine identities' (Frosh *et al.*, 2002, pp. 259–60). Men and boys are often characterised as emotionally inexpressive, and this is sometimes linked to the 'victim' discourse mentioned in the Introduction, with an inability to express feelings seen as having negative consequences for mental health and for boys' educational achievement. According to Australian researcher Julie McLeod:

> The growth of the men's movement and the question of 'What about the boys?' have ... focused attention on emotions and gender difference. One of the qualities boys appear to lack and men want to reclaim is the experience of being in touch with their feelings, of being expressive and able to forge close bonds with one another ... In other words, the desire now is for men and boys to be able to conduct their personal and social relations with the kind of emotional openness said to characterise women's personal and social interactions. Educational programmes designed to assist boys often target the development of their social, emotional and communication skills.
>
> (McLeod, 2002, p. 213)

Whatever the reality behind the stereotype of boys as emotionally inexpressive, researchers on young masculinity certainly report a lack of emotional openness in the groups they encountered. Mac an Ghaill refers to the 'fragility' of young heterosexual masculinities and the 'bleaker' side of experience in young male peer groups (Mac an Ghaill, 1994, pp. 96–7). Holland *et al.* describe the 'unsupportive' nature of talk in boys' peer groups, with their 'collective pressure to express and define themselves in a particular way in order to prove their manhood' (Holland *et al.*, 1998, pp. 12–13).

The young men in Mac an Ghaill's study described the loneliness and confusion that they experienced with their male friends:

> During the research they reflected on their difficulty in expressing personal feelings with each other, resulting from their learning to hide from others and themselves what they felt ... One of the main themes that emerged out of the heterosexual male students' accounts was their emotional illiteracy. In personal interviews, they frequently returned to two connected issues: first, that there was no

safe space within which they could talk about how they felt; second, that the absence of an emotional language greatly influenced the development of their sexual identities.

(Mac an Ghaill, 1994, p. 97)

He quotes from two of the young men whom he interviewed:

Daniel: We've never really talked to each other about anything, you know anything important. Like when Patrick's father died, none of us could really talk to him. I had one talk when he was really sad but we never talked again. You see if you were really open, you just couldn't trust another bloke that the next day that he wouldn't tell everyone and then that would be the end of you.

Tony: You can't talk to men intelligently, only to women. You are talking to men seriously for a while, then they see a girl and say to each other, I'd give her eight out of ten.

(Mac an Ghaill, 1994, p. 98)

However, Frosh *et al.* found the boys they interviewed only too willing to talk about personal issues when given the opportunity: 'The image of the angrily grunting and inarticulate teenager is not one which stands up to scrutiny when one looks at what can happen when boys are given the opportunity to reflect on their experiences and are encouraged to talk' (Frosh *et al.*, 2002, p. 256). The authors conclude that 'when faced with an

Young men's family relationships remain largely unexplored by researchers

adult who did work hard in order to listen to them, they showed great life and fun, and considerable emotional as well as intellectual intelligence' (p. 257).

How can we reconcile these apparently contradictory findings? The implication of the quotation from Frosh *et al.* is that there is nothing innate or inevitable about young men's emotional inexpressiveness: it is largely a matter of context and opportunity. Mac an Ghaill's examples confirm this, suggesting that there is something in the defensive and performative nature of masculinity in the young male peer group that militates against emotional openness.

Jessica Benjamin explains young men's emotional inexpressiveness in terms of their early development in the context of gendered family relations. She describes boys as losing a sense of a 'vital source of goodness inside' when they separate from their mothers:

> The boy who has lost access to inner space becomes enthralled with conquering outer space.
>
> [...]
>
> The denial of identification with the mother ... tends to cut the boy off from the intersubjective communication that was part of the primary bond between mother and infant. Emotional attunement, sharing states of mind, empathically assuming the other's position, and imaginatively perceiving the other's needs and feelings – these are now associated with cast-off femininity. Emotional attunement is now experienced as dangerously close to losing oneself in the other; affective imitation is now used negatively to tease and provoke. Thus the intersubjective dimension is increasingly reduced, and the need for mutual recognition must be satisfied with mere identification of likeness ... The devaluation of the need for the other becomes a touchstone of adult masculinity.
>
> (Benjamin, 1998, pp. 163, 170–1)

However, other feminist writers have cautioned against pursuing this line of argument too vigorously. Lynne Segal, for example, questions why it is that men, who are still the more powerful gender, should be seen as 'vulnerable', and speculates that men might fear femininity not because of early experience of the engulfing mother, but 'because they rightly perceive the association between femininity and powerlessness' in current gender relations (Segal, reported in Edley and Wetherell, 1995, pp. 67–8). Segal's critique reminds us of the importance of seeing masculinities as constructed in the context of continuing inequalities between men and women.

As we noted earlier, some writers have argued that young men's homophobia is a symptom of a deeper devaluing of women and the feminine. Frosh *et al.* argue that this misogyny is also present, in an inverted form, in the way in which many boys idealise girls and their emotional expressiveness:

> A number of boys seemed to project on to girls a capacity for closeness and sympathy which they denied in boys. We also found that the construction of heterosexual desire seemed to involve a positive affirmation of these gendered oppositions; that is, gender difference was eroticised.
>
> (Frosh *et al.*, 2002, p. 12)

Drawing on his research into notions of love and romance among sixth-form boys, Redman uses the ideas of the French psychoanalytic theorist Jacques Lacan to argue that characterising girls as 'pure' and 'ideal' is a way for boys to hold on to the 'lost object' of the mother. At the same time, this process of idealisation helps to sustain a rigid gender polarisation, in which qualities that are seen as feminine have to be expelled from the masculine self (Redman, 1999, pp. 10–11).

As mentioned earlier, there is a lack in the research literature of any detailed exploration of the part played by family relationships in the negotiation of young men's identities. This absence indirectly reinforces the association of young masculinity with the external world of school and the peer group, and of femininity with the domestic and personal spheres. However, a number of studies have touched in passing on boys' attitudes to family relationships. For example, Frosh *et al.* note that the young men in their study described their mothers as being more sensitive and emotionally closer to them than their fathers, who were seen as more jokey but at the same time emotionally more detached. The authors quote one young man as saying: 'I much prefer speaking to girls about my problems than I do boys, especially to older women ... like my mum, my mum's friends, even my nan' (Frosh *et al.*, 2002, p. 34). Despite this closeness to their mothers, boys tended to identify more with their fathers, while also expressing a desire for a closer relationship with them. This feeling of paternal absence is described by the authors as part of 'a broader sense of something missing emotionally in the lives of boys and young men – perhaps of men in general' (Frosh *et al.*, 2002, p. 259). Mac an Ghaill offers a striking quotation from one of his interviewees:

> I think in families the girls are closer to their mums and dads. But boys, who can they be close to? Like in our family and all my friends, the parents wouldn't be close to their kids. I don't know why. Like my dad spends all his time in the pub with his mates. Why doesn't he want to be with me? Why doesn't he say that he loves me? Fuck it, I don't know, it does my head in.
>
> (Mac an Ghaill, 1994, p. 100)

Frosh *et al.* conclude that 'there really does seem to be an embargo on close, dependent contact between young men and between them and their fathers, which feeds into an idealisation of girls and women that itself is stereotyped and alternates with overt misogyny' (Frosh *et al.*, 2002, pp. 263–4).

In her exploration of 'Shaun's story', Diane Reay describes the importance of one working-class boy's close relationship with his mother and argues that writing about young men has often overlooked such relationships, ignoring their important role in the formation of young masculine identities, particularly where (as in Shaun's case) the father is absent or abusive:

> Although schooling is salient in the construction of subjectivities, families are the first site in which masculinities are fashioned. It is impossible to write about Shaun's subjectivity without writing about his relationship with his family, in particular his mother. Unlike the other children that I interviewed, Shaun regularly referred to his mother and family life throughout the interviews without any prompting from me.
>
> (Reay, 2002, pp. 229–30)

Shaun's Year 6 teacher, Ms Keithly, pointed to the importance of his close relationship with his mother, and other female figures in his life, in enabling him to develop a more fluid and expressive masculinity:

> Someone like Shaun will come up to me, 'I just want to get away from the other boys for a little while, all of us are dragging each other down'. You know, he takes equal responsibility for it. Because of all the boys he's the one most in touch with his feminine side, believe it or not. I do think he's more in touch with his feminine side but then he lives with three women, his mum, who he idolises, his elder sister, who he idolises, and his baby sister, who he idolises, so his feminine side is very much to the fore. Also, he loves his girlfriends. I do think Shaun sees them as quite a calming effect but then he's very much in touch with that.
>
> (Quoted in Reay, 2002, p. 230)

My own research with young men working in childcare suggested a positive link between the influence of maternal figures in boys' lives and their ability to take on caring roles (Robb, 2001). This is in contrast to the tendency in debates about young masculinity to problematise the absence of fathers and to pathologise lone mothers (Dennis and Erdos, 1992).

These contradictory messages about young men's capacity for emotional expression and for intimate relationships suggest a need for further research into boys' lives beyond school and the peer group. As with our discussion of boys' homophobia, they are also a reminder of the need to situate the ways in which young men express their masculinity in specific contexts. Young men's 'emotionalities' (the ways in which they experience and express their feelings) may be as diverse and as context-specific as other aspects of their masculine identities, with differing ways of expressing emotions and engaging in relationships on display in the peer group and in the home, for example.

Key points

- Young men are often characterised as emotionally inexpressive, and research finds some evidence of emotional isolation, particularly in young male peer groups.

- There is some evidence that boys are able to express themselves emotionally given a more encouraging context.

- Young men often express an emotional closeness to their mothers and a sense of emotional distance from their fathers.

- There is evidence that boys express different 'emotionalities' in different social contexts, though more research is needed to explore this further.

5 Embodying young masculinities

Researchers working with young men have drawn attention to the ways in which young masculinity is embodied, or bound up with particular ways of talking about and presenting the body. One of the main findings from the study by Frosh *et al.* quoted above was that 'popular masculinity involves "hardness", sporting prowess, "coolness", casual treatment of schoolwork and being adept at cussing' (Frosh *et al.*, 2002, p. 10). Elsewhere, the writers expand on this finding, citing examples from boys' talk in which being good at football (and able to talk knowledgeably about it) is perceived as a key marker of boys' difference from girls:

RP: What boys are popular in your school in your class and how did they become popular?

Maurice: I dunno. David's quite popular cos he's like pretty hard, but he's quite good at sports as well. He's best in our year ... at football.

RP: Ah, is he, yeah?

Maurice: And he's fast an' that.

(Frosh *et al.*, 2002, p. 78)

Wayne Martino and Maria Pallotta-Chiarolli cite similar examples from their work with Australian boys:

> To be masculine you have to be strong and big and muscular ... you're sort of paranoid about your body image. To be popular in school you have to be big and strong and good looking, in a sense, so that all the girls think you're good and you'll be popular with them.
>
> (Michael, 13, in Martino and Pallotta-Chiarolli, 2003, p. 18)

In addition, many of the boys interviewed by Frosh *et al.* spoke at length about their own and other boys' appearance. Many boys mentioned wanting to look good in designer clothes and took styles of dress as a key marker of popularity. The researchers found that boys tended to associate popular masculinity with bodily display and style:

RP: Can you tell me what makes boys popular?

Joey: Clothes.

RP: Clothes? What sort of clothes then?

Joey: Designer clothes.

[...]

RP: Right. How do people become cool? What do they do to become cool?

Calvin: They like, get Adidas designer clothes and show-off.

> (Frosh *et al.*, 2002, p. 79)

In the second half of the twentieth century, a concern with personal appearance became increasingly acceptable as a feature of heterosexual masculinity, whereas in the past it was often coded as gay. The process has been incremental, being confined in the 1960s to particular subcultural groups, such as Mods (see Chapter 1). Since the 1970s, many elements of what was once explicitly gay style, such as earrings, have become recoded as acceptable for straight men. Over the same period young men have become an important target audience for the fashion industry. Writing in 1994, Mark Simpson declared:

> Nineties man, it almost goes without saying, exhibits no bashfulness about gazing at his own reflection – ask any girl who has been locked out of the bathroom by her preening brother. Nor is this self-regarding something that he keeps private. He is to be seen parading in front of mirrors in High Street clothes shops and examining his new haircut in the salon mirror with the kind of absorbed concentration that his fathers might have reserved for the

football results. In fitness studios and gymnasia, meanwhile, he pets, pampers and provokes his reflection in full-length wall-mirrors into a shape he finds more appealing.

(Simpson, 1994, p. 95)

Simpson comments on the implicitly homoerotic nature of many of the images that are used to sell fashion products to men:

Men's bodies are on display everywhere; but the grounds of men's anxiety is not just that they are being exposed and commodified but that their bodies are placed in such a way as to passively invite a gaze that is *undifferentiated*: it might be female *or* male, hetero *or* homo. ... Narcissism, the desire to be desired, once regarded as a feminine quality *par excellence*, seems, in popular culture at least, now more often associated with men than with women.

(Simpson, 1994, p. 4)

Young men are exposed to diverse and changing ways of presenting the young masculine body

The line between a 'masculine' interest in looking good and a concern with appearance that would arouse suspicions of effeminacy is a difficult one for boys to tread. As Frosh *et al.* say of their interviewees:

none said they or others boys found particular boys good looking. Indeed most boys who were asked this found the question strange and seemed uncomfortable.

(Frosh *et al.*, 2002, p. 14)

As with other aspects of young masculinity, there is a plurality of ways in which boys can present their bodies, but at the same time some forms of embodiment are more acceptable than others. Bodily practices are embedded within particular cultures, and different localities and contexts have differing ways of regulating the body – explicitly or implicitly determining legitimate physical activity. At the same time, regulating how young men present and use their bodies has always been a way in which dominant notions of masculinity have been enforced and policed. Once again, Connell's argument that masculinities are diverse, but that particular forms of masculinity are dominant or hegemonic in any given context (Connell, 1995) can help us to understand that ways of embodying young masculine identities can be plural and even contradictory. There might be tensions between the official bodily 'regimes', (the ways in which the body is viewed and regulated) for example of the school, and those of particular subcultural groups. The following example from personal experience may help to illustrate this.

> I grew up in a white, lower middle-class English home in the 1960s and 1970s. At the age of 11 I joined the Boys' Brigade company at my parents' Methodist church. Like the Boy Scouts, but more so, the 'BB' had a military-style uniform and its stated 'object' was to instil obedience, discipline 'and all that tends towards a true Christian manliness'. Activities included regular drill parades, physical education, sports and camping. However, in the summer that I joined – 1967 – other young men were developing a very different kind of embodied masculinity – one that revolved around creative expression, bodily decoration, and free love. In fact, I was aware of and attracted by all of this, listening to pirate radio under the pillow at night. The attraction grew so that, alongside my continued 'BB' membership, I also identified increasingly with hippy music, styles and ideas. Later, my identifications shifted through the long-haired progressive rock of the early 1970s to the sexually ambiguous 'glam' rock of Bolan and Bowie. Somehow I managed to negotiate the contradictions between these diverse 'cultures' of the body, wearing my long hair under my Boys' Brigade hat.

This personal example is included to demonstrate a number of points. First, it is an instance of the ways in which forms of masculinity are bound up with particular bodily practices (whether doing drill or wearing long hair). Second, the example provides an illustration of some of the ways in which young masculinity has been policed through particular ways of attempting to shape young male bodies. Frank Mort (2000) has described how youth organisations such as the Boys' Brigade and the Boy Scouts inculcated an early twentieth-century masculine culture based on rational command over mind and body, while Jeffrey Weeks (1980) has seen in the rise of these movements a means of policing youthful sexuality. The third point the example demonstrates is the dynamic and plural character of the bodily regimes associated with young masculinity. Increasingly, in a society in which boys are exposed to a range of models of masculinity in the media and elsewhere, there are competing versions of embodied young masculinity on offer. At the same time, as we have seen, older models based on self control and restraint are perhaps giving way to new consumer-driven models that permit a degree of bodily display and self regard. As Simpson and others have suggested, this new male narcissism may offer a further threat to the boundaries of heterosexual masculinity and fuel a need for even more vehement policing of themselves by men.

Activity 4   Embodying gender

Allow 30 minutes

Reflect on the ways in which your own body might have been 'regulated' in your youth. Think about the bodily regimes that were in play in your school, youth groups, peer group, locality, as well as in popular culture at the time. What kinds of body image were seen as desirable and undesirable? Then think about the forms of masculine or feminine identity that were being encouraged or discouraged through these processes.

Comment

Although your personal experience may have been very different from the example above, you were probably able to identify a variety of competing ways of embodying gender identity in your remembered experience, and perhaps a tension between official forms of physical regulation and the creative bodily expression of youth subcultures. (Subculture and style will be discussed in more detail in Chapter 8, 'Playing'.)

In what ways is the experience of embodiment different for young men and young women? Holland *et al.* suggest that young men appear to be more comfortable with their bodies than young women (Holland *et al.*, 1998, p. 8). They argue that current models of feminine identity tend to encourage a femininity that disempowers young women and leads to a silencing and disembodiment of female desire. Aapola *et al.* suggest that among young women control of the body is valued highly and that 'girls and young women constantly struggle to contain their bodies in acceptable ways' (Aapola *et al.*, 2005, p. 132). Despite the increasing emphasis on cultivating the body among young men, young male bodies are not subject to the same degree of objectification as those of young women: 'Young women are encouraged to relate to their bodies as objects that exist for the use and aesthetic pleasure of others, and to work on the improvement of their appearance' (Aapola *et al.*, 2005, p. 136). Girls have to perform a difficult balancing act between presenting their bodies in ways that please men and exhibiting responsibility in avoiding unwanted male interest. Like the boys in the study by Frosh *et al.*, girls keep 'a close eye on each other', but the emphasis for young women is on creating distinctions between good girls and 'slags', rather than between masculine and non-masculine boys.

Aapola *et al.* suggest that the growing preoccupation in Western culture with health, fitness and physical appearance has affected young women as much as young men. In fact, the pressures to 'get it right' are arguably greater for girls, in part because the cultural messages are often contradictory:

> Women are encouraged to overindulge themselves simultaneously as they are told to restrict themselves; to diet as well as to enjoy consumption; to stop smoking as well as to drink alcohol; to feel good about one's body as it is, as well as to try to modify it through exercise and so on. For a young woman whose body is changing rapidly, it is all the more confusing trying to create a balanced relationship with one's body.
>
> (Aapola *et al.*, 2005, p. 158)

The consequences of these pressures on young women's mental health will be explored more fully in Chapter 6. Aapola *et al.* are also keen to emphasise that, as well as being a source of anxiety for young women, the body 'can also be a very positive site of self-expression, identity creation and enjoyment', for example through participation in dance and sport (Aapola *et al.*, 2005, p. 157).

Key points

- Young masculinities are embodied in particular bodily practices and attitudes to the body.
- A certain kind of body image, combining physical 'hardness' and agility with the ability to look 'cool', seems to be a key component of contemporary young masculinity.
- Changes in the embodiment of young masculinity in recent years have been influenced by media and consumer pressures.
- Bodily 'regimes' reflect wider social attitudes and are plural and dynamic.
- The ways in which young women's gender identities are embodied reflect the continuing objectification of the female body.

Conclusion

We began this chapter by suggesting that young men have become a focus for public concern in recent years and that young masculinity has become problematised in media and policy debates. The chapter as a whole has been concerned with exploring how young men negotiate their gender identities against this background. Using a mainly social constructionist perspective on gender identities, we have drawn on recent research studies, which have included the voices and experiences of young men themselves, to explore contemporary young masculinities.

We have found that young masculinities (like young gender identities generally) are dynamic and diverse and need to be understood in relation to other aspects of boys' (and girls') identities, based on class, ethnicity and sexuality, as well as the contexts in which they are produced. At the same time, a hegemonic or dominant model of young masculinity has emerged, with a number of key features. Among these has been the continuing dominance of a fairly traditional image of what it means to be a young man, based on physical attributes such as 'hardness' and sporting ability. Hegemonic young masculinity also appears to be constructed as a defence against the feminine, demonstrated in the performance of routine homophobia. It is possible to see these features as at least partly a response to the unsettling of gender identities in contemporary society, and the loss of traditional routes to young manhood. One of the consequences seems to be a sense of emotional isolation for young men, although further research into young men's emotional lives and personal relationships is urgently needed.

More broadly, we have seen that gender identities and gender relations have changed in dramatic ways in recent years, and also that the impact of these changes has been complex and uneven. We have seen that the dominant story about girls benefiting from social change, while boys are disadvantaged, is open to a number of challenges. Transitions to adulthood remain deeply gendered, and gender inequalities persist on a number of levels.

What are the implications of these discussions for work with young men, and with young women too? One consequence might be a recognition of the complex and diverse ways in which young people negotiate the path to gendered adulthood, especially against a background of rapid change that can act to unsettle the traditional boundaries of masculinity and femininity. Young people need support as they attempt to establish their gender identities not only in relation to their immediate peer group, but also alongside broader identifications of class, ethnicity and culture. The plurality of young gender identities needs to be recognised and endorsed by those who work with young people, particularly in contexts in which official or dominant versions of masculinity or femininity may threaten diverse identities.

Certainly, there is a need to support those who find it difficult to identify with dominant models of gender identity, and who may become victims of homophobia or sexism. Lynn Segal (1990) has called for gender workshops for young people, to work on changing sexist attitudes, but the difficulties of such work should not be underestimated, especially given the defended nature of young gender identities – and particularly of young masculinities. However, examples from existing practice with both young men and young women demonstrate that it is possible to create spaces in which young people can explore their identities more thoughtfully, free from the pressures of the peer group (Spence, 1990, 2003). Several organisations working with young people have produced resources that acknowledge the tensions and difficulties that surround talking about gender, sexuality and relationships, while asserting the need to challenge homophobia and sexism (for example National Children's Bureau/Sex Education Forum, 2005). If, as we have emphasised throughout this chapter, context is crucial in the production of gender identities, then perhaps work of this kind can help to create environments in which the rigid gendering of young people's lives can be challenged and new models of young masculinity and young femininity encouraged.

References

Aapola, S., Gonick, M. and Harris, A. (2005) *Young Femininity: Girlhood, Power and Social Change*, Basingstoke, Palgrave.

Adkins, L. (2002) *Revisions: Gender and Sexuality in Late Modernity*, Buckingham, Open University Press.

Alexander, C. (2002) '"One of the boys": black masculinity and the peer group' in Taylor, S. (ed.) *Ethnographic Research: A Reader*, London, Sage/The Open University.

Archer, L. (2001) '"Muslim Brothers, Black Lads, Traditional Asians": British Muslim young men's constructions of race, religion and masculinity', *Feminism and Psychology*, vol. 11, no. 1, pp. 79–105.

Baron-Cohen, S. (2003) *The Essential Difference: Men, Women and the Extreme Male Brain*, London, Allen Lane Science.

BBC (2000) *Young men 'failed over suicide'*, www.bbc.co.uk/1/hi/health/716863.stm [accessed 29/03/06].

Benjamin, J. (1998) *The Bonds of Love: Psychoanalysis, Feminism and the Problem of Domination*, New York, Pantheon.

Biddulph, S. (1997) *Raising Boys*, London, Thorsons.

Bly, R. (1991) *Iron John: A Book About Men*, London, Element.

Bruner, J. (1990) *Acts of Meaning*, Cambridge, MA, Harvard University Press.

Buckingham, D. and Bragg, S. (2004) *Young People, Sex and the Media: The Facts of Life?*, Basingstoke, Palgrave Macmillan.

Butler, J. (1990) *Gender Trouble: Feminism and the Subversion of Identity*, London, Routledge.

Chodorow, N. (1978) *The Reproduction of Mothering: Psychoanalysis and the Sociology of Gender*, Berkeley and Los Angeles, University of California Press.

Connell, R. (1995) *Masculinities*, Sydney, Allen and Unwin.

Dennis, N. and Erdos, G. (1992) *Families without Fatherhood*, London, IEA Health and Welfare Unit.

Edley, N. (2001) 'Analysing masculinity: interpretative repertoires, ideological dilemmas and subject positions' in Wetherell, M., Taylor, S. and Yates, S.J. (eds) *Discourse as Data: A Guide for Analysis*, London, Sage/The Open University.

Edley, N. and Wetherell, M. (1995) *Men in Perspective: Practice, Power and Identity*, London, Prentice Hall: Harvester Wheatsheaf.

Foster, V., Kimmel, M. and Skelton, C. (2001) '"What about the boys?" An overview of the debates' in Martino, W. and Meyenn, B. (eds) *What About The Boys? Issues of Masculinity in Schools*, Buckingham, Open University Press.

Frosh, S., Phoenix, A. and Pattman, R. (2002) *Young Masculinities*, Cambridge, Polity Press.

Giddens, A. (1994) 'Detraditionalisation' in Beck, U., Giddens, A. and Lash, S. (eds) *Reflexive Modernization: Politics, Tradition and Aesthetics in the Modern Social Order*, Cambridge, Polity Press.

Hall, G.S. (1904) *Adolescence: Its Psychology and Its Relations to Physiology, Anthropology, Sociology, Sex, Crime, Religion, and Education*, New York, Appleton.

Hall, M. (2005) 'The lost boys; one in four lads say: "we are just yobs"', *Daily Star*, 26 January.

Holland, J., Ramazonoglu, C., Sharpe, S. and Thomson, R. (1998) *The Male in the Head: Young People, Heterosexuality and Power*, London, Tufnell Press.

Kehily, M.J. (2002) *Sexuality, Gender and Schooling: Shifting Agendas in Social Learning*, London, Routledge.

Mac an Ghaill, M. (1994) *The Making of Men: Masculinities, Sexualities and Schooling*, Buckingham, Open University Press.

Martino, W. and Pallotta-Chiarolli, M. (2003) *So What's A Boy? Addressing Issues of Masculinity and Schooling*, Maidenhead, Open University Press.

McLeod, J. (2002) 'Working out intimacy: young people and friendship in an age of reflexivity', *Discourse: Studies in the Cultural Politics of Education*, vol. 23, no. 2, pp. 211–26.

Mort, F. (2000) *Dangerous Sexualities: Medico-Moral Politics in England since 1830*, London, Routledge.

National Children's Bureau/Sex Education Forum (2005) *Sexual Orientation, Sexual Identities and Homophobia in Schools* (Forum Factsheet 33), London, NCB.

Nayak, A. and Kehily, M.J. (1996) 'Playing it straight: masculinities, homophobia and schooling', *Journal of Gender Studies*, vol. 5, no. 2.

Norberg-Hodge, H. (2000) *Ancient Futures: Learning from Ladakh*, London, Rider.

O'Donnell, M. and Sharpe, S. (2000) *Uncertain Masculinities: Youth, Ethnicity and Class in Contemporary Britain*, London, Routledge.

Potter, J. and Wetherell, M. (1987) *Discourse and Social Psychology: Beyond Attitudes and Behaviour*, London, Sage.

Reay, D. (2002) 'Shaun's story: troubling discourses of white working-class masculinities', *Gender and Education*, vol. 14, no. 3, pp. 221–34.

Redman, P. (1999) 'The discipline of love: negotiation and regulation in boys' performance of a romance-based heterosexual masculinity', paper presented to Second International Gender and Education Conference, University of Warwick, 29–31 March.

Redman, P. (2000) '"Tarred with the same brush": "homophobia" and the role of the unconscious in school-based cultures of masculinity', *Sexualities*, vol. 3, no. 4, pp. 483–99.

Redman, P. and Mac an Ghaill, M. (1997) 'Educating Peter: the making of a history man' in Steinberg, D.L., Epstein, D. and Johnson, J. (eds) *Border Patrols: Policing the Boundaries of Heterosexuality*, London, Cassell.

Robb, M. (2001) 'Men working in childcare' in Foley, P., Roche, J. and Tucker, S. (eds) *Children in Society: Contemporary Theory, Policy and Practice*, Basingstoke, Palgrave/The Open University.

Sedgwick, E.K. (1985) *Between Men: English Literature and Male Homosocial Desire*, New York, Columbia University Press.

Segal, L. (1990) *Slow Motion: Changing Masculinities, Changing Men*, London, Virago.

Sharpe, S. (2002) '"It's just really hard to come to terms with": young people's views on homosexuality', *Sex Education*, vol. 2, no. 3, pp. 263–77.

Simpson, M. (1994) *Male Impersonators: Men Performing Masculinity*, London, Cassell.

Spence, J. (1990) 'Youth work and gender' in Jeffs, T. and Smith, M. (eds) *Young People, Inequality and Youth Work*, London, Macmillan.

Spence, J. (2003) 'Feminism in work with girls and women' in Nolan, P.C. (ed.) *Twenty Years of Youth and Policy*, Leicester, National Youth Agency.

Thomson, R. (2004) *Tradition and Innovation: Case Histories in Changing Gender Identities*, unpublished PhD thesis, London, South Bank University.

Walkerdine, V., Lucey, H. and Melody, J. (2001) *Growing Up Girl: Psychosocial Explorations of Gender and Class*, Basingstoke, Palgrave.

Weeks, J. (1980) *Sex, Politics and Society: The Regulation of Sexuality Since 1800* (2nd edn), London, Longman.

Wetherell, M., Taylor, S. and Yates, S.J. (eds) (2001) *Discourse as Data: A Guide for Analysis*, London, Sage/The Open University.

Willis, P. (1977) *Learning to Labour: How Working Class Kids Get Working Class Jobs*, Farnborough, Saxon House.

Chapter 5

Belonging

Rachel Thomson

Introduction

> Identity is about belonging, about what you have in common with some people and what differentiates you from others. At its most basic it gives you a sense of personal location, the stable core to your individuality. But it is also about your social relationships, your complex involvement with others, and in the modern world these have become even more complex and confusing. Each of us lives with a variety of potentially contradictory identities, which battle within us for allegiance: as men or women, black or white, straight or gay, able-bodied or disabled, 'British' or 'European' ... The list is potentially infinite, and so therefore are our possible belongings. Which of them we focus on, bring to the fore, 'identify' with, depends on a host of factors. At the centre, however, are the values we share or wish to share with others.
>
> (Weeks, 1990, p. 88)

The aim of this chapter is to develop an understanding of what belonging may mean for young people, including dimensions of group membership, identity, identification and recognition as well as forms of 'dis-identification' and exclusion. The chapter employs a perspective that locates forms of identity and belonging in historical context, and through a comparative and empirical approach draws attention to the specificity of identity claims. The biographical necessity of belonging is illustrated through the voices of young people.

The core questions that this chapter will address include:

- Has the nature of belonging changed historically?
- How can we understand the different claims for recognition involved in conflicts over identity?
- What are the different forms that belonging may take for young people?
- Can a positive sense of belonging be fostered among young people?

1 Belonging: what's in a word?

What do we mean by belonging? Or perhaps we should ask, 'what don't we mean?' When preparing to write this chapter I did what many of you will do when faced with an unfamiliar term. I typed the word into a search engine. I looked at only the first ten of the 1,190,000 hits. The following gives you a flavour:

- the homepage of the BBC Wales soap opera *Belonging*, based in the Welsh valleys

- an exhibition of Scottish landscape photographs

- a link to one of the principles of an early years initiative, encompassing self esteem, a sense of community, self control, equal opportunities and anti-discriminatory practice

- the homepage of an extreme metal band called The Belonging

- an article outlining James Fowler's faith development theory, from experience of belonging (in childhood), through joining (early adolescence), searching (late adolescence) and owning (adulthood)

- the homepage of the actors' trade union Equity

- the publisher's website for a children's picture book in which a series of collages show the greening of an inner city environment over a year

- a link to an online language resource for year 8 pupils (12–13-year-olds) in which they are invited to discuss 'belonging to a club' in French, Italian and German

- a blog entry by a management consultant describing a virtual project that he and colleagues are engaged in, and the importance of participation, and the creation of their own logo and other visual insignia for a sense of belonging

- the homepage of a research cluster in the School of Geography at Leeds University, exploring citizenship and belonging.

Doing the same thing on a different day, in a different country, on a different search engine would bring up a different list. The possibilities are infinite. Defining and claiming the word 'belonging' is part of the contemporary zeitgeist. In this semi-random clutch of cultural references, we may be able to capture the dynamic interplay of factors and forces that make 'belonging' such an important, contentious and slippery concept. The list above includes:

- cultural representation as a reflection/affirmation of identity (the Welsh soap)

- symbols as a medium of identification between isolated individuals (the project logo)

- the centrality of the family to belonging, established in the earliest stages of childhood development (the early years initiative and the theory of faith development)

- the role of forms of collective organisation in establishing a sense of belonging (trade unionism, joining clubs)

- belonging as forging a connection between the land/landscape and individual identity (the picture book, the Scottish photographs, the TV soap)

- belonging as a new way of describing and thinking about inequality, discrimination, oppression and difference (the early years initiative, the School of Geography homepage)

- a connection between notions of belonging and religious faith (the theory of faith development, the extreme metal band).

Activity 1   Searching for belonging

Allow 40 minutes   Before reading any further spend ten minutes doing an internet search, using the words 'young people' and 'belonging'. Have a look at the first ten sites that come up. Make a note of what they are, and what you think they mean by belonging. What are the connections between them? We will come back to your list towards the end of the chapter.

1.1 Belonging and choice

One of the most powerful narratives of social change is the story of **secularisation**: put simply, this is the view that many modern societies are no longer dominated by religious institutions in the way they were in the past. In Chapter 3 we explored the argument that there has been a progressive decline in the influence of tradition and social institutions in the formation of values and identities, a process variously described as detraditionalisation (Heelas *et al.*, 1996), individualisation (Beck, 1992) and disembedding (Giddens, 1991). These theories are premised on the idea that in Western cultures, identities and forms of belonging are becoming fluid, uncertain and subject to choice. Where identity was once a given, it is increasingly chosen, resulting in the emergence of new ethical stories and communities (Plummer 1995; Tronto, 1993; Weeks, 1995). So, for example, we may positively choose to be vegetarian, to be an ethical consumer, to be part of a political or religious community.

Yet choice also brings anxiety. **Postmodernism** is defined as specific modes and styles of intellectual culture committed to forms of thinking and representation that emphasise fragmentation, discontinuities and the breakdown of universal narratives and grand theory. The sociologist

Zygmunt Bauman has argued that the ethical paradox of the postmodern condition is that it 'restores to agents the fullness of moral choice and responsibility while simultaneously depriving them of the comfort that modern self confidence once promised' (Bauman, 1992, p. xxii). The more we crave belonging, the less satisfaction belonging provides. So as Western societies become increasingly secular, there is also a rise in the number of people converting to orthodox religions and a proliferation of new forms of belief that may or may not be religious, but which do involve a search for meaning. The term 'belief without belonging' has been coined by British sociologist Grace Davie (1994) to capture the paradoxical process through which religious institutions lose their grip at the level of the social, while faith continues to be a feature of individuals' identities. For minority ethnic and religious groupings the same processes are in operation, yet 'choice' is complicated by ongoing practices of discrimination. As Tariq Modood, a leading commentator on South Asian communities in the UK, explains:

> Compared to their elders, the young are less likely to speak to family members in a South Asian language, or to regularly attend a place of worship, or to have an arranged marriage. Yet they do not cease to identify with their ethnic or racial or religious group, though they may redefine what that group is (say, from Pakistani to Muslim).
>
> For identity has moved on from a time when it was largely unconscious and taken-for-granted ... it is now more likely to be based on conscious and public projections, and the explicit creation and assertion of politicised ethnicities. Shaped through intellectual, cultural and political debates, such identities are fluid and susceptible to change with the political climate. However, to therefore think of them as weak is to overlook the pride with which they may be asserted, the intensity with which they may be debated and their capacity to generate community activism and political campaigns.
>
> (Modood, 2005, p. 69)

It is a highly dynamic political climate. Modood wrote this account in the light of the Bradford riots of 2001 and the impact of the terrorist attacks of September 11th. The politics of difference have since absorbed media reactions to the London bombings of July 2005 (with a focus on radicalised young Muslims apparently adrift from the culture of their parents) and then to the riots involving young people of North African descent that spread across France during the late summer of 2005. The reporting of these two events encouraged reflection on the different political traditions of multiculturalism in France and the UK. By the time you read this the agenda will no doubt have moved on again.

Young people are always central to narratives of social change. As we outlined in Chapter 3, the argument goes as follows: in Western societies several generations ago young people did not have to worry about who they were or where they belonged, as their 'normal biography' was already plotted out for them. Such a normal biography may have included periods of searching and questioning. Western psychologists such as Piaget and Erikson have tended to understand 'adolescence' as a period in which experimentation and a search for identity takes place. From this perspective adolescence is defined as a time limited period that is part of a normal biography. Adolescence then is understood as part of a journey towards adulthood in which identities and forms of belonging are fixed. The very different forms of identity work that may be involved for different groups of young people are dissolved in the idea of a universal and biologically underpinned developmental stage. Young people who do not fit this model are seen as deviant or difficult.

For late modern theorists the destination point for this developmental journey is fast disappearing. Rather than being a universal stage of development, they would argue that adolescence was/is part of a historically and culturally specific biography that is no longer dominant. This is not to say that young people are no longer searching, but rather that the security associated with belonging in the way outlined above is evaporating. From this perspective we are all teenagers, trying on identities, searching for an illusive security. It is a pessimistic view, aspects of which will resonate with some people and not with others. Yet does it provide an accurate picture of the past or the present? Is it really the case that people really knew who they were and where they belonged a generation ago, and that we are all so uncertain now? Or do tradition, innovation and free will combine in more interesting and unexpected ways?

Activity 2   Conversations about social change

Allow 90 minutes

Talk to someone you know from an older generation. Ask them what life was like when they were young. How did they develop their sense of belonging? What were the positive and negative influences? How did this developmental process influence their sense of belonging today?

Discussions of belonging may raise raw and intimate issues for both parties. It is the sort of terrain that is best approached indirectly and with sensitivity.

Comment

If your discussion is anything like the one that I had with my mother, you will find that although theories of social change may capture the broad sweep of social trends, they often fail to capture the complexity of actual lives. They may be true in general but not in the particular. As a child growing up during the war, my mother had little stability. She was moved frequently, evacuated, left with strangers, and was witness to a great deal of social and personal upheaval. Her main sense of belonging was to her family, who were very close, despite (or possibly because of) the amount of geographical mobility they experienced. My mother's family were nominally British yet she had been born and brought up abroad. She explains that she did not have a strong sense of nationality, nor even of locality. Nor was religion or churchgoing an important part of her life. Her family created their own myths that tied them together over time and place. Now in her sixties, my mother's sense of belonging is relatively unchanged. She identifies strongly with family and friends, but little with place. She is a typical late modern 'cosmopolitan', seeing herself as a citizen of the world, loving to travel and move house. Neither she nor her mobile ancestors fulfil the criteria of the stable, secure and predictable past assumed by theories of detraditionalisation.

Your conversation may have thrown up a very different picture or something similar. Either way, it is important to recognise that these kinds of theories tell a highly simplified story about social change, one that ignores the kind of diversity and detail that may in fact be crucial to making sense of identities and feelings of belonging.

Key points

- Like identity, forms of belonging are multiple and often contradictory.

- With detraditionalisation, belonging has the potential of being a matter of choice rather than fate.

- Paradoxically, the more we crave belonging, the less satisfying it may be.

- From the perspective of the traditional 'normal biography', the search for belonging was a defining characteristic of the 'phase' adolescence. However, in a postmodern age the search for belonging becomes a generalised condition.

- Theories can provide useful ways of seeing, but individual experiences rarely fit neatly into them.

2 Perspectives on belonging

The previous exercise may have left you with the feeling that 'belonging' is a very nebulous idea, that it means everything, anything and possibly nothing! You may be wondering what belonging means to and for young people. In this section we suggest how to break the idea of belonging into its component parts in order to help you find a way of thinking about it as an aspect of young people's identities. We do not want to present you with different theories of belonging; rather, we want to suggest that belonging can be understood from a number of complementary perspectives.

2.1 I, we, you and they: the personal pronoun model

The sociologist Norbert Elias developed an approach to social analysis that treats concepts as relational and multi-perspectival. In order to explain this he encourages us to think about the structure of language, referring to the distinction that exists in most languages between:

- the first person (I/we)
- the second person (you)
- and the third person (he/she/they).

Each of these positions in speech reflects a basic position in the web of relationship, positions from which the world is experienced and can be described. And although these positions and resulting perspectives are distinct, they do not negate each other. Rather they represent co-ordinates in a **figuration**:

> we can never think of people singly and alone; we must always think of them as people in figurations. ... everyone is interdependent – every person can refer to himself as 'I' and to other people as 'you', 'he' or 'she', 'we' or 'they'. ... One's sense of personal identity is closely connected with the 'we' and 'they' relationships of one's group, and with one's position within those units of which one speaks as 'we' and 'they'. Yet the pronouns do not always refer to the same people. The figurations to which they currently refer can change in the course of a lifetime, just as any person does himself. This is true not only of all people considered separately, but of all groups and even of all societies. Their members universally say 'we' of themselves and 'they' of other people; but they may say 'we' and 'they' of different people as time goes by.
>
> (Elias, 1970, pp. 127–8)

Let's illustrate this with an example of what belonging might mean to a contemporary young person living in a children's home.

The 'I' perspective leads us to consider the world through the individual young person's eyes, a perspective in which personal feelings of being wanted, needed and attached are to the fore. From this perspective, a sense of belonging is tied up with basic forms of security and attachment. At the core of theories of attachment is the idea that, in order to develop a secure sense of self (of I), we must first have a secure attachment to a dependable object (usually a parent). The lack of a secure attachment in early childhood is likely to translate into difficulties in subsequent relationships, in belonging to others and trusting that others belong to us.

If we think about belonging from the collective 'we' perspective, we get a rather different view. Here the young person's identifications and loyalties may come closer into view: relationships with family, religion, ethnicity and nationality, identification with other young people in the home or with a particular group of friends or gang.

If we then shift to the third person perspective (he/she/they), we look at the young person from the perspective of the social system of which they are a part. From this perspective we may think in terms of the administrative processes they are implicated in – for example, leaving care plans, a social work case load – or, in more collective terms, we may think of them as actors in wider social processes such as the making and remaking of inequality and social exclusion.

Elias says rather less about the second person perspective (you) than the position of the 'other'. But here we may think about the importance of audience for any statement of identity and belonging, and the relative power of those involved in the interaction. Our identifications are not simply essential aspects of ourselves, rather they are expressions of our social locations in relation to others. Thinking in this way can draw our attention to clashes between forms of belonging: for example, a young person asserting the identity of 'bad girl' in a school context that demands the identity of 'good pupil'. Here we are able to make sense of how young people may exclude themselves from and/or be excluded from forms of belonging. Examples of such exclusion might include young people's own rejections of help and support from professionals ('because they don't really care, only do it because they are paid to'), and rejection of learning identities at school (not wanting to be a swot), as well as the way in which young people may experience themselves as 'othered', for example labelled formally as 'at risk', 'vulnerable', 'special needs', and informally as 'slag', 'nutter', 'pikey', 'hard man'.

These perspectives on belonging are situated in particular places and times. Contemporary third person perspectives reflect current policy and popular narratives, and if we turned the clock back we would encounter very different concerns and categories. For example, the process through which young people in trouble with the law have been defined and redefined as criminals, juvenile delinquents and, most recently, young offenders, reflects the changing forms of expertise involved in defining this group of young people, as well as the way in which society, the state and professionals respond to their behaviour. Increasingly, the kind of terminology used to describe young people will differ according to locality, environment and policy jurisdiction, a tendency encouraged by the move toward increased devolution of social policy.

Formal categorisations of personhood (identities) may vary according to professional area. For example, the same young person may be defined as a:

- 'looked after child' and 'at risk' by social services
- 'user' in social, welfare and community settings
- 'student' and a person with 'special needs in education'
- 'patient' in health care
- 'client' in a training agency
- 'customer' in a commercial setting
- 'member' of a youth club.

These categories will be overlaid with informal categories of personhood, depending on context:

- 'daughter', 'sister', 'mother' within the family
- 'mate', 'girlfriend', 'rival', 'popular', 'a laugh' within the peer group
- 'skater', 'scally', 'slag', 'nutter' and so on within popular culture.

The kinds of identifications that we make depend on the kinds of identities it is possible to *inhabit*. In the following extract Stuart Hall describes how the forms of belonging available to him changed over time:

> When I was growing up in the 1940s and 1950s as a child in Kingston, I was surrounded by the signs, music and rhythms of this Africa of the diaspora, which only existed as a result of a long and discontinuous series of transformations. But, although almost everyone around me was some shade of brown or black (Africa 'speaks'!), I never once heard a single person refer to themselves or to others as, in some way, or as having been at some time in the past, 'African'. It was only in the 1970s that this Afro-Caribbean identity became historically available to the great majority of Jamaican people, at home and abroad. In this historic moment, Jamaicans discovered themselves to be 'black' – just as, in the same moment, they discovered themselves to be the sons and daughters of 'slavery'.
>
> This profound historical discovery, however, was not, and could not be, made directly, without 'mediation'. It could only be made *through* the impact on popular life of the post-colonial revolution, the civil rights struggles, the culture of Rastafarianism and the music of reggae – the metaphors, the figures or signifiers of a new construction of 'Jamaican-ness'. These signified a 'new' Africa of the New World, grounded in an 'old' Africa: a spiritual journey of discovery that led, in the Caribbean, to an indigenous cultural revolution; this is Africa, as we might say, necessarily 'deferred' – as a spiritual, cultural and political metaphor.
>
> (Hall, 1990, p. 231)

In order to have a rounded picture of young people's lives it is important that we are able to think in a **relational** and multi-perspectival way, understanding the range of forms of belonging that are at play and the ways in which they may cut across each other and combine within particular biographies at particular times and in particular places. In many institutions and bureaucracies (such as schools and health services) it is the third person perspective that dominates, with young people understood first and foremost as part of institutional processes. One of the aims of this chapter is to encourage an understanding of belonging that is historically and culturally aware, and biographically sensitive. In the following subsection we will work with an emotive example of how issues of belonging, identity, faith and institutional processes become entangled.

2.2 The headmaster and the headscarves

In 2004 the French government voted to ban all overt religious symbols including the Islamic hijab (headscarf) from state schools, a policy implemented from September 2004. A BBC documentary, *The Headmaster and the Headscarves*, explored how the policy was implemented in the Lycée Eugène Delacroix in Drancy, a suburb north east of Paris. The documentary featured a group of girls of North African origin, who felt strongly that they should have the choice to wear the scarf. One of these young women, Touria, explained, 'It's part of who I am. It's not just some bit of fabric on my head. It's everything' (quoted in Jones, 2005). The documentary also explored the feelings of some of the teachers including two who had been good friends but fell out over the implementation of the ban. One teacher vigorously defended the right of all French citizens to a secular education, expressing concern over restrictions on women's freedom and choices that she associated with Islam. Her former friend disagreed and supported the young women's right to self determination. Male teachers were also divided. The girls' campaign was encouraged by a young male teacher who felt that they were being discriminated against. Another teacher at the school refused to let girls in his class wear the headscarf, citing the example of a friend in Algeria who had 'been shot because she did not wear it'. The following extract is taken from the BBC website about the documentary.

> The headmaster, however, is under pressure from the majority of his teachers, who want a total ban on headcoverings. He has decided to hold a public meeting at the end of the school term so all interested parties can air their views.
>
> Among the speakers at the public meeting is Eric Finot, a history teacher at Delacroix with strong views on the subject.
>
> As he rises to speak, he says he wants to address the veiled girls in particular. 'We are only asking you to abide by the principle of secularism,' he says.
>
> To the anger of the girls, he then adds: 'We are thinking of those girls who we could maybe protect a little bit at school ... This law is

here to protect those girls who are compelled to do things they don't want to do – not to be forced into marriage, not to wear the veil.'

Separate issues

For the veiled girls, the public meeting confirmed their worst fears. The pro-law lobby was mixing everything Islamic in the same pot: Sharia law, forced marriage, veils.

They understood very well the feminist arguments condemning many aspects of their faith, but all of them insisted that they were under no pressure at home to wear the veil.

In fact, quite the opposite. Their parents would prefer them to de-veil rather than jeopardise their education.

Touria adds: 'People say that it's the women who wear the veil that are submissive ... but I think it is those women who are submissive, because it is what men want, women half naked.'

As the veiled girls agonised over whether or not they would de-veil, their headmaster became convinced that a compromise was possible.

When Lycée Eugène Delacroix opened for the new school year, it was one of the only schools in France to allow girls to wear a discreet bandanna.

But for veiled girls like Iptiseim, this was not the outcome she had hoped for.

'Now that I'm wearing a bandanna in school,' she says, 'when I come out I can't wait to put my veil back on. It was always important, but now even more so.'

(Jones, 2005)

Iptiseim (right) believes France wants to de-veil Muslim girls in order to veil its problems

---

Activity 3   Thinking through diversity: what do you think and feel?

Allow 30 minutes   What are your thoughts and feelings about this issue? Take a moment to summarise them. Now list arguments from both sides of the debate, as you have identified them.

Comment

These are a few comments taken from the BBC website:

> France has it absolutely correct. Religious clothing has no place in a modern society. I find the public display of religion somewhat disturbing, threatening even. Whatever the argument, schools are for learning and religious displays have no place there.
>
> (Laurie North, London)

I used to believe that keeping the veil out of school was the right thing to do, but I have changed my mind since I've been living in the UK. It doesn't bother me at all if people wear any religious symbols. It is a part of British society.

(Melodie, London)

I thought this documentary was very well-presented and informative. The young women who wanted to wear the veil were very articulate and showed courage. I was astounded when some teachers said how nice it was for schoolgirls to wear sexy clothes! I would argue that young women 'looking sexy' at school was far more inappropriate in a learning environment than a veil.

(Dr Lewis Turner, Lancaster)

I am seriously upset by this programme. The very idea of telling thinking women what they can or cannot wear fills me with anger.

(Mervyn Goode, Hove)

(Source: BBC News, 2005)

Now that you have written down your thoughts and feelings, think a bit about where they come from. Are they linked to your own feelings of belonging, the different kinds of 'we' that make up who you are? They may be linked to an idea of yourself as a citizen, a parent, a woman, a man, as progressive, as traditional, as black, as a feminist, as a person of faith. As Jeffrey Weeks points out in the quote at the beginning of the chapter, these forms of belonging are contradictory and battle for allegiance. What is perhaps more important than having the 'right' answer to this kind of complex question, is developing a better form of *understanding* in which all voices are heard.

Having watched the documentary I tried to think about this particular controversy through Elias's idea of a web of positions and perspectives that constitute this 'figuration'. Time and place are important. This documentary was made after the events of September 11th 2001, but before the riots that took place among young people of North African descent in cities around France in 2005. France has a complicated history regarding multiculturalism and secularism (Thomas, 2006). Although the question of whether Muslim girls have the right to wear headscarves in UK schools is also a controversial issue, the way the issue is configured is quite different. Both the UK and Ireland have a tradition of faith schools and religious worship in schools as part of the national curriculum. Post-colonial legacies, immigration, housing and equal opportunities policies also contribute to distinct national traditions. Yet at the same time events such as September 11th cut across cultures, and the formation of new kinds of religious and political identities are simultaneously global and local phenomena. In 2005 the European High Court ruled in favour of a British

Muslim young woman's right not to be excluded from school on the grounds of wearing traditional religious dress. In her statement on leaving court the young woman blamed the school's decision on hostility to Muslims after the September 11th terrorist attacks:

> As a young woman growing up in a post-9/11 Britain, I have witnessed a great deal of bigotry from the media, politicians and legal officials ... This bigotry resulted from my choice to wear a piece of cloth, not out of coercion, but out of my faith and belief in Islam. It is amazing that in the so-called free world I have to fight to wear this attire.

> (Halpin, 2005)

Activity 4   Thinking through diversity: imagining the other

Allow 30 minutes   In the table below I have tried to present the complexity of the situation captured in the *Headmaster and the Headscarves* documentary, focusing on two of the actors in the figuration: Touria and the headmaster. I have sketched out the range of forms of belonging that seem to be in play for Touria from the different perspectives of the first and third person. Now you try to fill in the table for the headmaster.

	Touria	Headmaster
I	Hero?	
We	The five girls campaigning to be allowed to wear the headscarf Member of Muslim community Residents of her estate French citizen? Woman? Minority who are discriminated against?	
You/they	Hostile teachers Worried parents Racist French society	
Context	Socially deprived Parisian suburb, ethnically segregated Post September 11th Defence of French secularism in context of New Europe	
Time	Second generation Algerian Final (examination) year of compulsory schooling	

Comment

Was it difficult to think about this situation through the eyes of the headmaster? I imagined that the headmaster saw himself in the position of a responsible manager and that he identified with being a teacher and a guardian of secularism. Less conscious **identifications** may have included being a white European, a citizen and a man. I speculated that, from his perspective (and that of many others positioned differently), 'they' may have appeared both as potential victims and as dangerous fanatics. And no doubt he felt pressure from the 'powers that be' in the media and the wider educational administration. Not an easy situation.

Now compare the two lists and see if anything strikes you. When I did this exercise I was struck by the number of excluded forms of belonging in Touria's part of the table. There were some forms of belonging followed by question marks. It was not clear to me that she felt a comfortable sense of belonging as a citizen or as woman (as opposed to a Muslim woman). I found it difficult to think of comparably excluded forms of belonging for the headmaster, but that may say more about me than about him. I was also struck by the extent of misunderstanding and lack of awareness that was part of the figuration. For example, the headmaster did not actually ask the young women what they thought, but made assumptions about them. For their part, the young women appeared to have little interest in or awareness of the arguments being put forward in defence of a secular curriculum. Obviously, the context is crucial for making sense of this figuration. If I had used an example that explored student demands for prayers in American schools, my feelings might have been different.

In the next subsection we will explore ways in which the politics of belonging may be understood.

2.3 From identities to identification and recognition claims

> What constitutes a social group is not internal to the attributes and self understanding of its members. Rather, what makes the group a group is the relation in which it stands to others.
>
> (Young, 1997, p. 389)

So far in this chapter we have considered the way in which the detraditionalisation of social structure impacts on identity, creating a paradoxical situation in which our desire for belonging increases as the efficacy of belonging declines. The detraditionalisation process can be understood as shifting us from approaching identity as a 'thing', an essential part of the self, towards thinking in terms of the process of **identification**. Identification need not be positive: people's refusal of identification (**dis-identification**) is equally significant (Skeggs, 1997).

The most important thing to ask about when considering the process of identification or dis-identification is the relational context in which it takes place.

Elias's approach of thinking about a situation or 'figuration' through the different co-ordinates that constitute it (the first, second and third person) can help us in this task. Which is the 'I' position, who or what is the 'you' that constitutes the audience? How might the situation be understood from a third person position? This kind of multi-perspectival and relational approach also fits with the type of narrative approach outlined in Chapter 3. What story is it possible to tell? Who is the speaker? Who is the audience? British sociologists Sarah Irwin and Wendy Bottero take a similar approach, treating identity and assertions of belonging as **recognition claims**.

> Gender, class, 'race', dis/ability, sexuality and age are themselves statements (claims) about difference: its nature and salience. They are inherently about power relations, inequality and the naturalisation/fixing of human made social relations. Values and assumptions about natural differences, about different competencies and appropriate behaviours, and about norms and transgressions, serve to normalise and naturalise hierarchy. The claiming perspective holds particular value since it helps throw into relief the historical and cultural nature of such arrangements.
>
> (Bottero and Irwin, 2003, p. 480)

From this perspective claims for recognition are made in particular situations and times, and are aimed at securing power and resources. A claiming perspective encourages us to look at the situation in which identities are asserted, and to ask why the claim is made and what is at stake. The answer to these questions is likely to be complicated. Think again about Touria and her friends and their claim for recognition as Muslim women students. What is at stake? What will be the implications of the identity claims that they make, for themselves and for others around them?

The circumstances in which claims for ethnic and religious recognition are being made are dynamic. In the UK, 2001 proved to be a significant year for the politics of belonging. There was a new Home Secretary (David Blunkett), there were riots in some Northern English cities and the events of September 11th unfolded. Anxieties associated with a multi-ethnic and multicultural society increasingly found official voice in policiesaround immigration. Several leading commentators from within the race relations industry explicitly criticised a tradition of multiculturalism for encouraging a segregation of communities. In 2004 Trevor Phillips, Chairman of the Commission for Racial Equality, argued that multiculturalism was out of date, made a fetish of difference and discouraged ethnic minorities from becoming 'truly British'

(BBC News, 2004). These views found a sympathetic audience at the time, and again in 2005 after the London bombings of 7 July. However, the British approach to multiculturalism was cast in a more positive light later in 2005 when comparisons were drawn between Britain and France in the wake of the riots in France mentioned earlier.

Each of these events operates as a collective 'critical moment' when understandings of diversity and belonging are reconfigured. Several commentators have sought to reflect on and reinvigorate the notion of multiculturalism for an increasingly complex society in which national identity is compatible with multiple ethnicities. One such example is the argument put forward by sociologist Tariq Modood in 'A defence of multiculturalism' (2005) in which he identifies three principles at the heart of a positive multiculturalism: 'equality', 'multi' and 'integration'.

Equality: of dignity and respect

Modood argues that the liberal defence of diversity is premised on a divide between the public and the private. This argument is also associated with the notion that differences we 'choose' (sexuality, religion) are properly the realm of the private, and differences we do not choose ('race', gender, disability) need to be protected via the laws of the public sphere. Yet as Modood points out, the distinction between ascribed and chosen difference is hard to sustain in practice. In his words, 'No one chooses whether to be born into a Muslim family. Similarly, no one chooses to be born into a society where to look like a Muslim or to be a Muslim evokes suspicion, hostility or failure to get the job you applied for' (Modood, 2005, p. 66). Modood also points out that one of the ways in which minority groups gain confidence and ultimately become 'integrated' into the polity is through having differences recognised in the public sphere. So, for example, the demands for lesbian and gay marriage and for the acceptance of religious insignia in public institutions can both be seen as demands for an equality of respect as well as an equality of rights. As Modood explains, 'Equal respect ... is an important part of the idea of equality ... It is the interpretation of equality as meaning that non-assimilation is OK; that minority identities ought to be included in the public sphere' (2005, p. 66).

Multi: recognition of plurality

The way in which individuals respond to discrimination and the absence of 'recognition' and 'respect' is diverse. Modood explains that 'Some will organise resistance, while others will stop looking like Muslims (the equivalent of 'passing' for white); some will build an ideology out of their subordination, others will not. Some Muslims may define their Islam more in terms of piety than politics' (2005, p. 66). This alerts us to the second element of Modood's idea of multiculturalism, the importance of recognising plurality within groups. He argues that within disadvantaged groups there are always intersecting identities 'combining elements based on origins, colour, culture, ethnicity, religion and so on' (p. 66). As Jeffrey Weeks observed in the introduction to this chapter, our forms of belonging are complicated and competing. Modood encourages an awareness of the stratification of minority ethnic groups – a sensitivity to social class, individual and family biography – 'the distinctive needs and vulnerabilities of different groups' (p. 67). A similar subtlety of thinking also needs to be brought towards understanding different kinds of racism – the racism expressed by a white working class teenager towards a black police officer may be very different from that expressed towards black neighbours. The hostility expressed towards asylum-seeking refugees by young people in Northern Irish urban communities is very different, though related, to the deeply embedded practices and prejudices of sectarianism. Rather than lumping together all such phenomena under the term 'racism', such practices need to be made sense of in context and in relation to the different forms of belonging and conflicting recognition claims that are involved.

Integration: without assimilation

The third element of the model of multiculturalism defended by Modood is the notion that diversity changes everyone, the majority as well as the minority. In his words:

> The traditional model of assimilation is one-way: here is a society, people come into it and they try to be like what already exists. The multiculturalist concept of integration is not one way but interactive. It is about fitting people together so that there is give and take, mutual change and the creation of something new. It also involves a redefinition of Britishness.
>
> (Modood, 2005, p. 67)

So, for example, the speech patterns, styles, habits and diets of young people in London, Leeds and Llandudno are increasingly constituted by a dynamic fusion of cultures that is much more than the sum of its parts.

We hope you can see connections between Modood's defence of multiculturalism and the multi-perspectival approach outlined in this section. You should also begin to get a sense of how these ideas may inform work with young people. From this perspective identities are not simply 'things' but are claims for recognition. It is an approach concerned as much with understanding as it is with taking a stand or judging young people. Yet it is also an optimistic position that associates recognition with participation and transformation. By acknowledging the presence of another's difference within the public sphere (which could be a school, a youth club, a health or welfare setting), the setting itself is changed, as are the actors involved.

Key points

- Young people's sense of belonging can be understood from different positions within a figuration, including the first person (I/we), the third person (he/she/they) and the second person (you).

- Context, timing and perspective are crucial to the meaning of belonging for young people.

- The identities of young people and those who work with them should not be understood as 'things' but as processes of identification and 'dis-identification', and as situated claims for recognition.

- Multiculturalism can be rethought through three key elements: equality of respect, plurality within different groups and integration without assimilation.

3 Forms of belonging

As we have seen, the forms of belonging that we may claim, enjoy and reject are infinite and may be more or less conscious. Rather than understanding what an identity or form of belonging is, it may be much more productive to ask why it is important in this particular situation, at this time. In order to ascertain the forms of belonging that have salience for a young person at any point in time, it is necessary to know more about their lives, their history and the context in which they live, that is, to take a biographical approach (see Chapter 3). In this section we will briefly explore two forms of belonging that have significance in young people's lives: belonging to place (including nationality, neighbourhood and combinations of these); and belonging to a sexual community. These examples are drawn from the *Inventing Adulthoods* study (London South Bank University, 2006) and provide a taste of the many forms of belonging that have salience for young people.

3.1 Imagining community: from nationality to neighbourhood

In the *Inventing Adulthoods* study, young people were asked about whether they had a sense of national identity. The study was located in five contrasting areas of the UK: a predominantly white public housing estate in the north of England; an ethnically diverse inner city area in the south of England; a predominantly white and middle class commuter belt area on the outskirts of a city in the south of England; an isolated rural area; and a Northern Irish city. The quotes in the next activity give a taste of the very different ways in which young people responded when asked either what it meant to be English or what it meant to be British.

Activity 5   Nationality as a form of belonging

Allow 30 minutes

Read the quotes and answer the following questions:

- What forms of positive identification do you see the young people making? What kinds of dis-identification can you detect?

- Can you distinguish between forms of belonging that are self defined and defined by others?

- What are your personal feelings about national identity? What positive identifications do you have? What dis-identifications do you make?

> I'm more or less British, really. English. It's just something I don't really think about that much. I suppose if I was a professional footballer, then I would think of it.
>
> (Gordon, 16, white, working class young man, living in public housing estate in north of England)

> Chips and meat pies. [laughs] Well, it depends really. If you go out abroad then the English tend to be either dead snooty or completely arrogant and just assholes, you know, so, nothing, you see some people when you're away and you think, oh he's British.
>
> (Owen, 17, white, working class young man, living in public housing estate in north of England)

> It's kind of like a bit confusing for me 'cause if I'm over here, I'll always be classed as a British oriental, or British Vietnamese person, and, like, I'll never be seen as fully British or fully Vietnamese 'cause I've always got something in me, even though I'm not, like, actually in my blood, but, like, actually, just because of where I live and stuff. And if I go to Vietnam, then I won't be classed as fully Vietnamese, and I wouldn't be classed as fully British, 'cause I'm Vietnamese so I'd be classed as a Vietnamese English person, or Vietnamese British person. So it's kind of always be a mix of something, 'cause, like, when I'm over here I think I'd rather be fully Vietnamese, like fully seen as Vietnamese person. 'Cause, like, with being kinda a bit British, they kind of expect me to act a certain way and, like, with Vietnamese, you act differently, and when I'm over in Vietnam, then I'd prefer to be fully Vietnamese as well, 'cause they'd treat me kind of as a person of theirs, instead of being, like, oh I'm like a half person, more or less, it makes me feel like a mixed race, being mixed race person, even though I'm not.
>
> (Su, 15, Asian, working class young woman, living in inner city area in south of England)

> I still, like, if someone used to say to me 'what are you', I say I'm half Asian and half West Indian, but I still feel that I'm more black, maybe 'cause I look more but I dunno just feel accepted by … I don't know what to call myself. If someone asked me I'd just say mixed race normally.
>
> (Jamal, 15, 'mixed race', working class young man living in inner city area in south of England)

In my identity I'm a British citizen, but I always let people know that I'm a Pakistani.

(Khattab, 17, south east Asian, working class young man living in inner city area in south of England)

I'd love to have a wider range of friends from different nationalities. I think that would be really interesting, but I'm not really given the chance because I don't mix with that many people from different countries, but that would be amazing. If I had lots of different friends.

(Judy, 16, white, middle class young woman living in affluent commuter belt)

I'm not very patriotic, I'm not 'look at me, I'm British, look at me, I'm great, we own the third world, we beat the Germans in the war', because you know I wasn't alive and I didn't contribute to the Second World War, or the British Empire, you know. I think we should keep our monarchy, just 'cause they're cool, aren't they?

(Elsa, 17, white, middle class young woman living in affluent commuter belt)

I'd say I'm an English person and I always have been and I'm quite happy to be that, I sort of come from this tiny little island that's normally raining.

(Shaun, 15, white, working class young man, living in isolated rural area)

My friends all think I'm really Irish you know, really loved and really proud and all.

(Deidre, 16, white, middle class, Catholic young woman living in Northern Irish city)

Cos the Northern Irish are British. I don't really care about non Irish. I definitely don't want to feel British.

(Dermot, 16, white, working class, Catholic young man living in Northern Irish city)

I feel more Welsh than I do British because my dad's Welsh but because, like, my mum's side is really strong Protestant, especially my granny and my granddad. I mean there's nothing wrong being proud of what you are, that's how you feel or whatever, I mean you don't have to have hatred, I just don't like hatred. Hatred is horrible and that's what made me go, hang on a minute, if that's what I'm supposed to be, if that's what I'm supposed to think, it's just not me.

(Carolyn, 17, white, working class, Protestant young woman living in Northern Ireland)

Comment

These quotes make it clear that national identity is complicated, emotional and does not mean the same thing to everyone. Your feelings about national identity are likely to have been contradictory and may have been

In Northern Ireland identity may be linked to religion and territory

quite strong. The responses of these young people will inevitably have been shaped in part by the context in which they were asked the question (who their audience was). However, their responses are also shaped by their social location – where they are speaking from (Rutherford, 1990). So locality, gender, ethnicity, religion and social class matter. They shape the forms of belonging available to young people. The subjective experience of belonging inevitably jars with the way in which researchers have 'objectively' located these young people within categories of age, gender, ethnicity, locality and social class – labels that the young people may neither recognise nor identify with.

In the first two examples we encounter the mixing up of Britishness and Englishness that was typical of many of the white English young people in the study. Here national identity is invisible and simply assumed until it is made visible or problematic in some way. This might be through sports such as football in which the nations that constitute the British Isles compete separately, or through travel and the idea of the English as seen through the eyes of others. Certainly, sport provides an arena where the complexities of national belonging are played out. Campaigns to kick racism out of football reflect the contradictory coincidence of the presence of minorities as world class athletes, their absence from particular sports and the expression of popular racism in sporting events.

Minority ethnic young people in the *Inventing Adulthoods* study tended not to claim the identity of English, preferring hyphenated identifications of British 'plus'. As the quotes from Su, Jamal and Khattab suggest, feeling British is complicated when you are not white. The process of identification is not one-way; we do not simply choose who we are. We also need to feel welcomed, recognised, to have a sense of belonging. For these young people cultural difference and a constant translation of ideas and values between forms of belonging is a part of everyday life. For others, such as Judy, cultural difference may be an ideal, a form of cosmopolitanism that can be aspired to or cultivated.

Many of the white English young people in the *Inventing Adulthoods* study had ambivalent feelings about nationality. On one hand they associated feelings of pride in the nation with an older generation, yet they also felt a connection with place, and could express hostility towards those classified as 'outsiders' even when this was not part of their everyday experience.

The *Inventing Adulthoods* study did not include young people in Scotland or Wales. National identity for young people in Northern Ireland is highly contested, and the forms of belonging expressed by these young people were shaped by a range of factors including religious affiliation, social class and family tradition. For example, middle class Deidre positively embraced Irish culture and identity, while working class Dermot emphasised his rejection of Britishness. Carolyn is torn between a positive identification with her national and religious identity and a dis-identification with much of the associated baggage.

For most young people a sense of belonging to place is tied to a more immediate locality. The locality in turn may influence what nationhood comes to mean. For example, in a study of two south London estates, sociologist Les Back (1996) suggests that white, black and Asian young people create a form of 'neighbourhood nationalism' in which racism may exist alongside a sense of shared belonging. Think back to the discussion of skinheads in Chapter 1. So, while working class, white young people may express prejudice in relation to unknown others (for example black and Asian youths from the neighbouring estate), they accept minority ethnic young people from within the community as exceptions to the rule. Watt and Stenson (1998) reinforce this point by pointing out the significance that young people attribute to 'knowing others' and 'being known' for the preservation of personal safety.

Sustaining a sense of belonging to this kind of locality is complicated, especially where there are few opportunities or resources available. In the *Inventing Adulthoods* study the researchers found differing orientations to place. In the rural and commuter belt sites young people complained of boredom and aspired to leave but generally hoped to return to their localities later in life. In less affluent communities young people tended to accept that you have to 'get out in order to get on', even though many subsequently stay. So, although young people who grow up in disadvantaged communities may not like them, they may not want to be anywhere else. Diane Reay and Helen Lucey describe this in terms of 'ambivalence and equivocation' about the places in which they live, expressing 'a shared sense of belonging ... undercut by a recognition of the stigma associated with living on large estates' (Reay and Lucey, 2000, p. 424). Robert MacDonald and Jane Marsh explain that young people in poor neighbourhoods often stress 'feelings of *inclusion* in localities that, by all objective definitions, were socially *excluded*' (2001, p. 385, original emphasis). These are themes that we will return to in Chapter 9, 'Moving' (see also Henderson, 2007; Henderson *et al.*, 2007).

Think for a moment about the neighbourhood(s) in which you grew up. What were your feelings about it/them? Did you want to get away? Did you feel a sense of belonging or loyalty to your neighbourhood? You may still be living there now. If so, what have been the consequences of staying local?

3.2 Belonging to a sexual community

Young people coming out as lesbian, gay, bisexual or transgender (LGBT) are often forced to look for friends and support outside their local community. They are more likely than their heterosexual counterparts to leave school and home early and often also escape their neighbourhood (McNamee *et al.*, 2003). Despite increasing visibility, such young people still experience high levels of bullying and intimidation at school, on the street and sometimes at home. This may be particularly acute for young people living in working class communities and/or belonging to ethnic and religious minorities. For this reason, such young people may look to the internet, specialist media and/or telephone lines as a way of making contact with others who share this particular experience. They may also leave school and home early in order to migrate to urban areas in which it is safer and easier to be 'out'. Those who make it to university may find it easier to come out in a more cosmopolitan environment. While young people may feel that being gay is an essential part of them, they still have to learn how to negotiate the many spaces and aspects of the gay scene. It may take time before they are able to find a form of belonging that is comfortable.

There were several lesbian, gay and bisexual young people in the *Inventing Adulthoods* study. Devon was unusual in that he had already come out as gay when the researchers made contact with him. Over the years during which he was involved in the study his identity as a young gay man evolved as he became increasingly confident and proficient in his belonging. When the researchers first met him in 1999 he had recently made contact with a lesbian and gay youth club and had moved into a shared gay household which was part of a leaving care scheme. Although he had 'come out' to his family, he did not dare be 'out' in his neighbourhood, where he had a long history of being bullied. As he gained in confidence he ventured into the commercial gay scene. Initially, he was careful to hide his sexual identity at work, having experienced discrimination in the workplace. Eventually, he found a job within the scene, working as a bartender in a gay nightclub.

The extracts in the next activity are from a series of biographical interviews carried out between 1999 and 2003.

Activity 6 Learning to belong

Allow 30 minutes Read the following extracts and as you do so make a note of how Devon's sense of belonging changes over time.

1999 (age 18)

At that point I still hadn't actually come to terms with it myself. I was just thinking maybe I am and erm ... So I saw this advert and I thought maybe I will give them a ring and I was talking to my social worker and she was talking about me and what I had in mind for myself for the future, instead of my family. So that was when I was always very, erm, thinking about my whole family rather than me. So she said: 'What are you gonna do for yourself?' And I said: 'Oh, I've seen this advert for a youth project, I thought maybe that just, you know, somewhere to go that's away from my family, just for me and be around people my own age'. And she's like: 'Oh that's nice. What's it called? Where is it?' And I said: 'Well, it's over west and it's only for gay people, so I'm gay.' And er, she started crying. Yeah. Just like, oh I'm so happy and blah, blah, blah.

[...]

I remember going shopping with my mum and that just seemed so normal actually. But when I first moved into a gay household, going shopping with them, it was ... I know it sounds so stupid, I got embarrassed by them, walking round and they were saying sort of the same things that my mum'd say, like. Talking about the special deals that was on, like loaves and bread and like that and ... Even like the points that you get on the cards and that. It was just so strange and because living in, like, a gay household, well, over a year, sort of, that's just normal.

2000 (age 19)

Even now I still think two men together is errrr, so I'm quite happy to have sex with men but the idea of you know setting up home with another man, bringing up kids with another man, having pets with another man, going shopping with another man! You know, as far as I am concerned that is what straight people do, that's not what we do. That's definitely not what I do.

[...]

I'm not out completely yet. I drop hints and say things like 'I'm single'. I go out to a place which is a gay place, if you're gay you'd know about it, if you weren't, it's just a bar. So dropping hints, not completely out still, and I'm not sure if I wanna be now.

[...]

He's exactly 15 days younger than me, but he'd been out on the scene for years before I even met him. So it was having his confidence out on the scene, me tagging along, which I only ever felt I did. I tagged along, being with him though, it helped me a lot. And sort of, after a while, I got confident that I didn't have to go out with him. You know, I could go out by myself, which I've never been a big fan of doing anyway. Or I could go out with other friends, meet friends in places, like. When I first started, if I made arrangements to meet with someone – like I'd been out somewhere else or with my parents and I'd arranged to meet them and they'd be waiting inside for me – it'd take me about ten minutes just to get inside to meet them, even though there was people in there. Horrible. But now, yeah, I'm confident enough to go out and spend the evening on my own.

[...]

We'd lived together for about 11 months, he and me, and loved it. It was such a laugh cause he was so camp, so, so camp. And he was one of those camp people that just don't give a damn about anything.

Interviewer: Was that the first time you'd encountered someone like that?

Yes, yes really, because I was sort of just, just starting to go out to the scene. So everybody else that I knew through the project, y'know, were all in the same situation as me. Basically, they were scared about being gay. And Shane came into my life and he was all, 'Oh I don't care about that, I'll do what I wanna do'. And that was pretty cool.

2001 (age 21)

[I helped Jamie with] things like getting to know the scene, getting to feel comfortable with other gay people and things like that. He was still learning about that and it wasn't something that he felt comfortable with. At that time I was still going out on the scene as much as possible and things. And I've sort of been, at his request, introducing him more to the scene and how to cruise people and things like that. It is nice. It's the same with sort of when there's new people. It's just having that little bit more knowledge. I love learning about new things anyway, so if it's something that I can actually use to sort of teach another person, I just love that – to sort of learn about the scene and learn about the city or how to pick up people.

2003 (age 23)

Yeah, before when I spoke to you last I was a user of the scene, and now I feel as though I'm part of it. When was it? Last Sunday I was going up to my parents' and just standing there at the bus stop listening to my walkman, lalalala, and this little guy – I don't know his name, could tell you what he drinks – came up to me and immediately recognised me from the pub. He came up to me and started talking to me, and I'm just standing there waiting for a bus. It was nice to talk to him.

[...]

I understand more of what it means by gay community. Whereas before it was just like a bunch of blokes going out and getting drunk. I was one of those blokes, but it didn't feel like a community, it just felt like a night out. This does definitely now feel – I feel like I am part of something outside my family.

Comment

These quotes suggest an uneven process of change. Initially, Devon's identification with other gay young people is very tentative and he struggles with powerful dis-identifications. He finds it hard to square his views of gay men with images of 'normal' heterosexual family life. Discovering 'camp' is an important part of the process of learning how to be confident and to operate on the gay scene. As Devon accumulates knowledge he is able to take up the position of a teacher to others struggling to negotiate the scene themselves. It is when he gets a job on the scene that Devon is able to make a shift from the position of 'consumer' and gain a real sense of belonging. Yet sexuality is only one part of Devon's biography and one form of belonging that exists in conjunction with identifications with family, social class, nationality and so on.

If we think back to Elias's personal pronoun model explored earlier in the chapter, we can see the ways in which Devon moves between different forms of belonging. Initially, he identifies primarily with his family and not with the identity of a gay man which he perceives as 'othered' and deviant (they). It takes him some time and considerable identity work in order to develop a sense of 'we' and belonging in the gay community. As time goes on it becomes possible for him to hold on to his sense of belonging to both family and community.

Key points

- Forms of belonging for young people can include the imagined communities of nationality, neighbourhood and a sexual community.

- Forms of belonging for young people are multiple, and may include both positive identifications and dis-identifications, inclusion and exclusion.

- Forms of belonging may be embodied and may develop slowly over time as young people gain in confidence and competence.

4 Fostering a sense of belonging in work with young people

We all belong to a range of communities. Sometimes we identify with these positively, others we are less comfortable with. Some forms of belonging are based on choice, for example being a fan of a particular kind of music or football team. Others we may feel we are born into but have the choice to stay with or leave, for example religion and family. Certain kinds of group membership may be experienced as being independent of our choices, for example being white, female, lesbian or gay. Still others are forced on us, perhaps by professionals (for example 'young offender', 'teenage mother') or perhaps by peers (for example 'slag', 'pikey'). It is possible to reclaim identities that are spoiled in this way, as has happened with terms such as 'queer', although the use of such language is circumscribed by prior meanings. It is this complexity that makes our experience of belonging intimate, sensitive and emotionally charged.

When working with young people it is important to understand that they will have a range of groups and **allegiances**, some of which are rooted in their own choices, others of which relate to family and community identity. Belonging is not an option for any of us – a sense of belonging is vital for our wellbeing. As we have seen, our forms of belonging are multiple, may be contradictory, and may move and change. Not all of our identities are positive or achieved. Here it is important to consider processes of identification and dis-identification and the recognition and claiming of identities. Exclusion from belonging may happen in a range of ways: it may be subtle and embedded (for example institutional racism) or it may be informal and explicit (for example bullying). Many of the institutions that young people are part of attribute identities, which may be more or less comfortable to inhabit. It is not simply in the power of professionals to 'give' young people a sense of belonging. In many cases such forms of identification are separate from (and sometimes in opposition to) the settings in which professionals encounter young people (recall the subcultures discussed in Chapter 1). In fact, the initial encounter between many professionals and young people may be characterised primarily by dis-identification! However, as we have seen in this chapter, belonging is fluid and complex, and we need to recognise that a sense of belonging can be nurtured by those working with young people. For this to happen a space needs to be made for reflection on these kinds of issues both within professional development and in work with young people.

Activity 7   Researching policy and practice examples

Allow 25 minutes

In Activity 1 you were asked to do an internet search using the terms 'young people' and 'belonging'. Look now at what you found. What are the main themes that link the various items identified in your search? In what ways do they present a picture of youth in the UK? You may want to look at some of the websites to find out more about different kinds of work taking place with young people.

Comment

When I did this exercise again I came up with the following list:

- another link to the article outlining James Fowler's faith development theory

- the response made by the National Youth Agency to the government's consultation *Strength in Diversity: Towards a Community Cohesion and Race Equality Strategy* that arose from the Cantle report into riots in Bradford in 2002

- a page on the Office of the Deputy Prime Minister's website outlining its action plan arising from the recommendations made by the Children and Young People's Unit's report *Learning to Listen* (2001), outlining four principles underlining children and young people's participation in decision making

- a county council's website link to information on voluntary youth organisations

- an academic article on how young people living in Kingston, Jamaica view their environment

- another reference to the BBC Wales soap opera *Belonging*

- a page on the organisation Homeless Link's website explaining the importance of finding young people accommodation in their local areas where they have 'support networks, a sense of identity and belonging and knowledge of local job markets'

- a fact sheet produced by the education and community service of a county council about involving young people in decision making and building citizenship.

This list gives a very definite 'flavour' of a moment in time. At the time of writing UK youth policy appears to be framing 'belonging' in the following ways:

- in terms of social inclusion (citizenship, participation in decision making, having a voice, having your identity respected)

- in terms of potential for social exclusion (not having access to informal sources of support, knowledge and so on, having your voice ignored, your identity, community or locality not respected or given any recognition)

- putting religion, ethnicity and locality at the centre of the stage

- viewing government (local and national), faith groups, the media and academia as 'brokers' in shaping what belonging might mean for young people.

Your list may look rather different. If so, it suggests that either the agenda in youth policy has changed, and/or the national context in which you are working is different. It may be worth reflecting a little on the extent to which both the experience and the representation of belonging are historically and culturally situated.

4.1 Positive suggestions

In concluding this chapter we can identify three lessons that can be drawn from our exploration of the meaning of belonging for young people, suggesting possible ways in which they may be applied in practice.

Promoting understanding and respect

Perhaps the most important lesson to derive from this chapter is that belonging is tied up with our most intimate feelings and that disregarding or disrespecting these is likely to produce defensiveness. For this reason it is important that those who work with young people gain an understanding of what belonging might mean to them, and hold back from making assumptions or acting on their own ideas of what this might be. This means attempting to make sense of the 'I/we' perspective, rather than imposing the 'he/she/they' perspective. It also means recognising the importance of the context in which claims for recognition are made and asking: 'Why this identity claim? Why now? What are the consequences for the young person and for those around them?'

Some forms of belonging are very visible, and in the field of youth policy and practice notions of belonging may be becoming a euphemism for black and minority ethnic issues. Yet belonging is a universal phenomenon: we are all implicated, workers, parents, policy makers too. Thinking about what belonging might mean for any group of young people involves working out what is important to them (what they value). What is threatening to them? What groups do they feel part of and what groups do they feel excluded by? Why are they investing in one thing rather than another? It also demands that workers reflect on their own values and forms of belonging to become aware of why young people react as they do and to identify the support they may need to develop a sense of belonging(s) (Turney, 2007).

We should also assume that young people feel torn by conflicting allegiances and that identities and forms of belonging are dynamic, in flux, changing. In this context taking up strong positions on contentious issues such as the wearing of religious or nationalist insignia may actually produce a hardening of identifications and dis-identifications. What may be more productive is working with young people to promote an understanding of how these processes of 'othering' work as well as looking for positive forms of identification that may cut across and complicate some of these boundaries. Group work and creative arts may provide an ideal medium.

Promoting inclusion: participation and voice

A practical way of nurturing a sense of belonging is through involving young people in the decision-making processes that shape the institutions and environments in which they spend their time. The principle of participation has become a mainstream commitment of central government, taken up enthusiastically by devolved administrations in Scotland and Wales, with children and young people actively involved in decision making through regular consultation. In England the Commissioner for Children is aiming to make a similar impact. There is a growing awareness that in order to reach the most excluded young people, participation needs to take place close to the ground and to be concerned with the everyday decisions that affect young people in school, at college and in neighbourhoods (see Montgomery, 2007).

Participation has also been proposed as an antidote to community disturbances such as those which took place in Bradford in 2002. It is also likely to be looked to as part of the response to the London bombings of July 7th 2005. Participation sits alongside a commitment to promote anti-oppressive training and education and the promotion of black and ethnic minority leadership at the heart of a raft of new strategies to promote 'community cohesion'. Participation alone can never be sufficient in situations where divisions are entrenched and resources scarce. As the experience of integrated school and cross-community initiatives in Northern Ireland shows, goodwill among young people is not enough to bridge divides that are institutional, economical and material (McGrellis, 2005). Promoting inclusion may also entail offering young people different kinds of belonging from those they are currently investing in; for example, a street gang may have less hold over a young man who has a strong sense of belonging to a peer education project. A young lesbian may manage to stay on at school to take GCSEs if she has access to a support group of gay school students.

Recognising exclusion: anti-oppressive practice

Finally, a commitment to inclusion needs to sit alongside a willingness to recognise the reality of exclusion, and the inequalities in power and resources that such exclusions are an expression of. This means challenging exclusionary practices such as homophobia and racism at an institutional

Challenging exclusionary practices

level. Zero tolerance policies on bullying are an important part of this. Exclusions are also material: for example buildings and activities that are inaccessible to disabled young people; timetables that exclude young people with caring responsibilities; rules and regulations that make young people choose between participation and belonging. Working to tackle exclusion may be particularly challenging where young people self exclude in order to protect themselves from rejection and/or failure.

Conclusion

In this chapter we have explored what belonging may mean for young people. We began by mapping different positions from which belonging might be understood, distinguishing between first, second and third person perspectives. We also traced the evolution of contemporary understandings of belonging, from treating identity as a *thing*, towards understanding identification as a *process* involving situated claims for recognition. These ideas were brought to life through examples of young people's lives, including Touria's struggles to be allowed to wear a hijab at school and Devon's account of becoming a confident young gay man. Forms of belonging may be multiple and contradictory, and in this chapter we have considered examples of how communities can be conceptualised, exploring forms of belonging involving religion, nationality, neighbourhood and sexuality.

References

Back, L. (1996) *New Ethnicities and Urban Culture: Racism and Multiculture in Young Lives*, London, UCL Press.

Bauman, Z. (1992) *Intimations of Postmodernity*, London, Routledge.

BBC News (2004) 'Debate call on "multicultural" UK', 5 April, http://news.bbc.co.uk/1/hi/uk_politics/3599925.stm [accessed 10/04/06].

BBC News (2005) 'Read your comments', 24 March, http://news.bbc.co.uk/1/hi/programmes/this_world/4366147.stm [accessed 01/05/05].

Beck, U. (1992) *Risk Society: Towards a New Modernity*, London, Sage.

Bottero, W. and Irwin, S. (2003) 'Locating differences: class, "race" and gender and the shaping of social inequalities', *Sociological Review*, vol. 51, no. 4, pp. 463–83.

Davie, G. (1994) *Religion in Britain since 1945: Believing without Belonging*, Oxford, Blackwell.

Elias, N. (1970) *What is Sociology?*, New York, Columbia University Press.

Giddens, A. (1991) *Modernity and Self Identity: Self and Society in the Late Modern Age*, Cambridge, Polity Press.

Hall, S. (1990) 'Cultural identity and diaspora' in Rutherford, J. (ed.) *Identity, Community, Culture, Difference*, London, Lawrence and Wishart.

Halpin, T. (2005) 'Muslim girl wins legal battle over school dress', *Times Online*, www.timesonline.co.uk/article/0,,2-1508573,00.html [accessed 08/0705].

Heelas, P., Lash, S. and Morris, P. (eds) (1996) *Detraditionalization*, Oxford, Blackwell.

Henderson, S. (2007) 'Neighbourhood' in Robb (ed.) (2007).

Henderson, S., Holland, J., McGrellis, S., Sharpe, S. and Thomson, R. (2007) *Inventing Adulthoods: A Biographical Approach to Youth Transitions*, London, Sage (Set Book).

Jones, E. (2005) 'Muslim girls unveil their fears', *BBC News*, http://news.bbc.co.uk/1/hi/programmes/this_world/4352171.stm [accessed 14/03/06].

London South Bank University (2006) *Inventing Adulthoods*, www.lsbu.ac.uk/inventingadulthoods [accessed 20/02/06].

MacDonald, R. and Marsh, J. (2001) 'Disconnected youth?', *Journal of Youth Studies*, vol. 4, no. 4, pp. 373–91.

McGrellis, S. (2005) 'Pure and bitter spaces: gender, identity and territory in Northern Irish youth transitions, *Gender and Education*, vol. 17, no. 5, pp. 515–29.

McNamee, S., Valentine, G., Skelton, T. and Butler, R. (2003) 'Negotiating difference: lesbian and gay transitions to adulthood' in Allan, G. and Jones, G. (eds) *Social Relations and the Lifecourse*, Basingstoke, Palgrave Macmillan.

Modood, T. (2005) 'A defence of multiculturalism', *Soundings. After Identity*, no. 29, March, pp. 62–71.

Montgomery, H.K. (2007) 'Participation' in Robb (ed.) (2007).

Plummer, K. (1995) *Telling Sexual Stories: Power, Change and Social Worlds*, London, Routledge.

Reay, D. and Lucey, H. (2000) '"I don't really like it here but I don't want to be anywhere else": children and inner city council estates', *Antipode,* vol. 32, no. 4, pp. 410–28.

Robb, M. (ed.) (2007) *Youth in Context: Frameworks, Settings and Encounters*, London, Sage/The Open University (Course Book).

Rutherford, J. (1990) 'A place called home' in Rutherford, J. (ed.) *Identity, Community, Culture, Difference*, London, Lawrence and Wishart.

Skeggs, B. (1997) *Formations of Class and Gender: Becoming Respectable*, London, Sage.

Thomas, E.R. (2006) 'Keeping identity at a distance: explaining France's new legal restrictions on the Islamic headscarf', *Ethnic and Racial Studies*, vol. 29, no. 2, pp. 237–59.

Tronto, J. (1993) *Moral Boundaries: A Political Argument for the Ethic of Care*, London, Routledge.

Turney, D. (2007) 'Critical practice' in Robb (ed.) (2007).

Watt, P. and Stenson, K. (1998) 'The street: "It's a bit dodgy round there": Safety, danger, ethnicity and young people's use of public space' in Skelton, T. and Valentine, G. (eds) *Cool Places: Geographies of Youth Cultures*, London, Routledge.

Weeks, J. (1990) 'The value of difference' in Rutherford, J. (ed.) (1990) *Identity, Community, Culture, Difference*, London, Lawrence and Wishart.

Weeks, J. (1995) *Invented Moralities: Sexual Values in an Age of Uncertainty*, Cambridge, Polity Press.

Young, I.M. (1997) 'Difference as a resource for democratic communication' in Bohman, J. and Rehg, W. (eds) *Deliberative Democracy*, Cambridge, MA, MIT Press.

Chapter 6

Wellbeing

Martin Robb

Introduction

The focus of this chapter is young people's health and wellbeing, a topic that has received much attention from commentators and policy makers in recent years.

Specifically, the chapter will set out to answer the following core questions:

- How has young people's health been constructed in public and policy discourse in recent years, and what are the implications for young people and those who work with them?

- What might an alternative, critical framework for understanding young people's wellbeing look like?

- How is young people's wellbeing shaped by diversity and inequality?

- What are the implications of a critical approach for promoting young people's wellbeing?

We begin with two newspaper stories that are fairly typical of recent media coverage.

Activity 1   Stories about young people's health

Allow 20 minutes   Below are two extracts from newspaper articles. Read through them and make notes about the kinds of issues they are concerned with and the general picture they present of the current state of young people's health.

> Depression, eating disorders, addiction, self-harm and the experience of frightening street violence ... these stories are all around me, as if they are now normal rites of passage for young adults. At times it seems there is hardly a single family unaffected. This child, so bright and optimistic so recently, is sunk in grey depression and won't go to school. That one, so athletic and cocky, has been violently mugged and now avoids walking anywhere, lurking inside his bedroom. Another cuts herself. Another suffers extreme bullying and has ballooned in size. Another was stabbed while walking the dog. The papers are full of stories of

the extreme edges of teenage trauma – the 12-year-old fathers and the child mothers; the suicide pacts made on the internet; the very young binge drinking; those who walk out and never come back.

(Ashley, 2005, p. 24)

Recent studies have painted a somewhat unsettling picture of life at 15: of the 788,000 15-year-olds in Britain, one in three have had sex, one in five regularly smoke cannabis, and most drink alcohol every week. Nearly 37% of 15-year-old girls consume soft drinks every day, and almost 3% are clinically obese. Last year, Childline counselled more than 14,000 15-year-olds on a variety of issues, including family relationships (14%), sexual abuse (12%) and pregnancy (10%). Between 2% and 8% of adolescents suffer from major depression.

[...]

A 25-year study of adolescent mental health by the Institute of Psychiatry at King's College London and the University of Manchester, published last summer, found that, compared to 1974 figures, today's 15-year-olds are more than twice as likely to display behavioural problems such as lying, stealing and disobedience, and are 70% more likely to experience emotional problems such as anxiety and depression.

(Barton, 2005, p. 2)

Comment

These two stories are concerned with a wide range of health related issues, including mental health, behavioural problems, victimisation, addiction and sexual health. The general picture they present is one of a decline in young people's physical and mental wellbeing, and their mood is generally pessimistic.

These extracts are fairly typical of recent media discussion of young people's wellbeing. Recent years have seen a succession of minor moral panics about the health related behaviour of teenagers. As in these extracts, the concerns have been wide-ranging rather than confined to a particular issue, giving a sense of an accumulation of overlapping problems afflicting young people today. However, we can identify a number of key images that recur in recent media coverage and public discussion of young people's health.

One key set of concerns relates to young people's physical health and is encapsulated in the popular media image of the young person as 'couch potato', eating too much (and too much of the wrong things) and not getting enough exercise. Here is a fairly typical selection of recent headlines from one UK newspaper, reflecting some of the contrary views on the issue.

Obese teenagers heading for heart attacks

(Guardian, 11.02.05)

MP outlines bill to ban junk food in schools

(Guardian, 18.05.04)

Children misclassified as obese

(Guardian, 6.09.05)

Childhood obesity fears 'exaggerated'

(Guardian, 16.02.05)

The image of the unfit and overweight teenager has become a staple of anxious media coverage and of popular cultural representation. The picture that comes to mind is of a young person slumped on the sofa in front of a TV screen or hunched over a PlayStation, snacking on unhealthy food, rarely going out into the fresh air or taking part in physical activity.

A second set of concerns focuses on the health implications of 'risky' behaviour by young people. As indicated in the two extracts above, attention has focused recently on activities as diverse as sex, drug taking and binge drinking. There is a detailed discussion of young people as 'risks' to themselves and others in the companion volume of this series (Robb, 2007).

A third and increasingly pervasive image is that of the anxious teenager. Concern about young people's emotional wellbeing has grown in recent years, with a number of research studies claiming that there has been an increase in mental health problems among young people. For example, one report claimed that the rate of emotional problems such as anxiety and depression among adolescents has increased by 70 per cent in the last 25 years (Collishaw *et al.*, 2004), while the Mental Health Foundation's *Bright Futures* study in the late 1990s claimed that 20 per cent of young people are experiencing psychological problems at any one time (Mental Health Foundation, 1999).

There is also a growing realisation that services set up to meet young people's mental health needs are patchy and inadequate. According to the *Bright Futures* report: 'There is huge variety in the quality and speed of mental health services, with some children having to wait a year to see a child psychiatrist' (Mental Health Foundation, 1999).

Taken together, these images – of the young person as physically unfit, risk taking and anxious – tell a story of an alarming decline in the state of young people's wellbeing. But how does this 'story' – reproduced in the media and increasingly in policy discussions – account for this apparent decline?

One explanation sees young people as under growing pressure to perform at school and to get a good job in an increasingly competitive jobs market. Other accounts speculate about failures on the part of parents. In the newspaper article cited in Activity 1, journalist Jackie Ashley wonders: 'Perhaps the move of more women into the labour market in recent decades, with fathers not compensating for the time lost with children, is ... a factor' (Ashley, 2005, p. 24). Another journalist, Madeleine Bunting, has suggested that 'an increasing minority of parents are unable or unwilling to provide the emotional nurturing which will ensure a resilient child'. She quotes Dinah Morley of the charity YoungMinds as claiming that 'there is a failure in attachment ... A growing number of us simply aren't bonding sufficiently with our babies' (Bunting, 2004, p. 17).

Thus concerns about the unhealthy young person have become a lightning rod for wider anxieties about key aspects of contemporary life, such as changes in parenting and family life, and an increasingly competitive and stressful society.

Activity 2   Researching media stories of young people's health

Over the next few weeks look out for media stories about young people's wellbeing. Do they reflect the kinds of concerns – about physical health, risk-taking behaviour and mental wellbeing – that we have noted here, or do they embody other anxieties? How do the stories account for changes in young people's experience?

Comment

Although you may identify some similarities to the articles quoted in Activity 1, it is likely that new concerns about young people's health will have emerged by the time you read this. Look out for similarities and differences in the responses of media commentators and in the explanations they offer.

Analysing popular images and stories about young people's health is important, not least because they can have an impact on young people's behaviour. For example, the intense public focus on obesity appears to be having an effect on young people's sense of the 'ideal' body weight. In March 2005 the *Guardian* newspaper reported research that suggested that girls as young as five were fretting (unnecessarily) about their weight.

Another reason why these public narratives are important is that they help to shape policy in relation to young people, leading for example to bans on 'junk' food in school or initiatives to reduce teenage alcohol consumption. The UK government's Green Paper of 2005 on youth reflected many of the concerns discussed above:

Young people today have more opportunities than previous generations. Most teenagers take advantage of this and make the transition to independent adulthood successfully ...

Yet in other areas there is little improvement or even poorer outcomes. This is the case, for example, with some aspects of teenagers' health such as drinking, sexual health and obesity. A minority of teenagers face serious or multiple problems and some become involved in anti-social behaviour and youth crime.

[...]

Some teenagers have health problems, including chronic clinical conditions such as asthma or diabetes. In the key areas of sexual health, obesity, alcohol, volatile substance abuse and mental health, the health of adolescents is either worsening or static. This is in contrast to marked improvements in the health of younger children and older people over the last thirty years. Some young people get into bad habits such as binge-drinking or drugs. Young people are in fact the heaviest drinkers, and are more likely than all other age groups to binge-drink. As well as harming their physical health, this can lead to violence and accidents.

[...]

Evidence suggests that at least 10% of young people have a diagnosable mental disorder. Mental problems can interfere with young people's ability to learn, develop and maintain relationships and to deal with the difficulties they face.

(DfES, 2005, pp. 12–13)

As in the media stories cited earlier, this extract reflects overlapping concerns about different kinds of health problems: physical, mental and emotional. There is also a blurring of concern for young people's health and a concern about the impact of their health problems on society in general.

How should we respond to these stories about the state of young people's health? What models of health and wellbeing do they assume, and what are their implications for policy and practice? Is it possible to offer an alternative way of thinking about young people's wellbeing, and what might be the implications of that model for work with young people? These are some of the questions that will be addressed in this chapter. Rather than offer a descriptive survey of the state of young people's health, or a detailed account of a range of health 'problems', the chapter will continue the critical analysis of current ways of constructing young people's wellbeing begun in this Introduction, and attempt to provide a critical framework for understanding and responding to young people's health needs.

Key points

- Recent media coverage has painted a picture of a decline in young people's wellbeing and of increasing concern about their physical and mental health.

- These images and stories influence young people's own perceptions and behaviour, and at the same time help to shape policy and practice.

1 Frameworks for understanding young people's wellbeing

In the Introduction we explored some of the images and discourses about young people's health currently in circulation. But what assumptions are being made in these stories about what it means for a young person to be healthy, whether physically or mentally? What kind of model of wellbeing is being used in these discourses, and are there alternative approaches?

1.1 Defining wellbeing

Wellbeing has become popular among policy makers as a generic term that embraces physical, mental and emotional health. Is this simply a matter of changing fashions in terminology or does it reflect particular assumptions about what it means to be healthy? Moreover, does the term have particular meanings when used in relation to young people? In this section we will analyse current ideas about what constitutes wellbeing for young people, and work towards producing a critical framework for understanding young people's health.

An early use of the term wellbeing as a synonym for health can be found in the definition adopted by the World Health Organization (WHO) in the years following the Second World War:

> Health is a state of complete physical, mental and social wellbeing and not merely the absence of disease or infirmity.
>
> (World Health Organization, 1948)

What work is the word wellbeing doing in this definition? First, it signals an attempt to bring together different aspects of health – principally the physical and the mental – and to demonstrate the connections between them. This is an implicit criticism of earlier, medical models of health which had viewed these areas as discrete and unconnected. Second, the use of the word wellbeing reinforces the sense of health as a positive concept – a state of 'wellness' – rather than the mere absence of illness. Once again, there is an implicit criticism of a negative, medical focus on health 'problems'. Third, the use of the word wellbeing represents an attempt to broaden the scope of what is meant by health, so that it includes not only physical and mental health but also what is here called 'social' wellbeing. Presumably, this means a sense of 'wellness' not only within the person but also in their social environment. This reflects an assumption that the causes of health, and of ill health, are not only located within the individual (as in the medical model) but also depend crucially on social factors, such as material resources and social relationships. There is an implicit recognition here of the part played by social disadvantages such as poverty in many people's experience of poor mental and physical health.

Writing in support of using the notion of wellbeing in public policy, Hetan Shah has argued that 'an incredible amount is spent on our "health" service, but most of it focuses on dealing with physical symptoms of sickness' and that 'we need to reconfigure the purpose of the system in order to promote wellbeing' (Shah, 2005, p. 39). Other writers have argued that the holistic concept of wellbeing is more in keeping with the way in which health is seen in the majority of societies and cultures in the world, than is the Westernised medical model (Frankel, 1986).

However, some commentators have been more cautious about adopting the positive model of health implied by the term wellbeing. Drawing attention to the emphasis on 'complete ... wellbeing' in the WHO definition, at least one writer has criticised this model for presenting an idealistic counsel of perfection that 'puts health beyond everyone's reach' (Lewis, 2001, p. 59). How many people can claim to have experienced a 'state of complete physical, mental and social wellbeing', and is such a state desirable? Arguably, promoting this ideal as a standard puts pressure on individuals to constantly strive for its vision of perfection, and to be forever dissatisfied with their current state of health. Thus a holistic model of wellbeing, while appearing to present a more social vision, may paradoxically promote an individualised approach in which good health is not only every person's right, but also their personal responsibility.

Certainly, it can be argued that much recent health related policy, with its promotion of healthy lifestyles and 'taking control' of your own health, seeks to shift responsibility for health on to individuals and away from society as a whole. Some critics have seen this as part of more general attempts to 'responsibilise' individual citizens in a number of areas (O'Malley, 1996), a notion we will return to later in the chapter.

How does this movement away from a medical model of health and towards a positive and holistic model of wellbeing relate to the experience of young people, and to the ways in which their health has been discussed and promoted? Significantly, the UK government has adopted the term wellbeing as a key concept in its strategy *Every Child Matters: Change for Children* (DfES, 2003), which it describes as 'a new approach to the wellbeing of children and young people from birth to age 19'. The five outcomes for children and young people which are at the heart of *Every Child Matters* are described as 'a positive vision of the outcomes we want to achieve'. The outcomes are:

- *being healthy*: enjoying good physical and mental health and living a healthy lifestyle

- *staying safe*: being protected from harm and neglect

- *enjoying and achieving*: getting the most out of life and developing the skills for adulthood

- *making a positive contribution*: being involved with the community and society and not engaging in anti-social or offending behaviour

- *economic wellbeing*: not being prevented by economic disadvantage from achieving their full potential in life.

(DfES, 2003, pp. 6–7)

This vision of wellbeing clearly goes beyond even the World Health Organization's definition and at the same time gives a particular meaning to 'social' wellbeing. As with the WHO definition, many people's first response to the government's five outcomes will probably be to see them as a progressive movement away from defining young people's health in negative terms, and as an advance on an individualised model which overlooked the impact on young people's health of other aspects of their lives, such as education and work. By contrast, this definition construes wellbeing as resulting from a combination of personal and social influences.

However, the model of the healthy young person that lies behind the five outcomes is also open to criticism. For example, some youth organisations have criticised the outcomes for being insufficiently youth focused and as having an inherent bias towards younger children, with their emphasis on protection and the absence of any reference to encouraging autonomy and participation. The National Youth Agency, for example, has argued that 'the Green Paper generally reflects children and young people as passive recipients of adult care, rather than as partners and active citizens with a full range of human rights and a need for encouragement and support to take increasing responsibility for their own lives' (National Youth Agency, 2003, p. 1).

Paradoxically, the vision presented in the five outcomes can also be criticised for over-emphasising young people's responsibility for their health. At least three of the outcomes focus on the individual's active contribution to their own wellbeing. The healthy young person presented in this vision is one who is 'achieving' in education and making a 'contribution' to their community, both positively through volunteering and negatively by staying out of trouble. Even the first and most directly health related outcome emphasises the individual's responsibility for 'living a healthy lifestyle'.

So this vision represents a move away from a traditional welfarist model of health in which responsibility rests with society to provide the conditions that promote young people's wellbeing. As Shah acknowledges, a shift to a focus on wellbeing often entails an emphasis on 'promoting self-efficacy' rather than viewing people as 'passive recipients of welfare' (Shah, 2005, pp. 35–6). There is very little role for the active state in this vision, but a major role for the active, achieving, enterprising individual. Although economic disadvantage is mentioned, economic wellbeing is less about the right to basic resources, as in traditional social democratic welfare policy, and more about supporting individuals to achieve economic wellbeing for themselves.

Nikolas Rose has charted the ways in which the 'private self' has increasingly become a focus of government intervention in late modern societies. Under **neo-liberalism**, a political philosophy associated with free markets and reduced government intervention, policy is directed towards the promotion of the enterprising individual:

> The theme of enterprise that is at the heart of neo-liberalism certainly has an economic reference ... But enterprise also provides a rationale for the structuring of the lives of individual citizens. Individuals are to become, as it were, entrepreneurs of themselves, shaping their own lives through the choices they make among the forms of life available to them ... The political subject is now less a social citizen with powers and obligations deriving from membership of a collective body, than an individual whose citizenship is to be manifested through the free exercise of personal choice among a variety of marketed options.
>
> (Rose, 1999, p. 230)

It can be argued that recent policies aimed at promoting young people's wellbeing have sought to encourage the notion of young people as 'entrepreneurs of themselves', largely responsible for their own health and happiness. Another criticism might be that government strategies such as the five outcomes seek to impose a particular model of wellbeing on all young people and to deny the viability of alternative ways of being young. Critics might argue that there is little room simply to 'be' in the Green Paper's vision of youth as a time of achieving and contributing, and that outcomes such as 'making a positive contribution' transform something that should be voluntary and spontaneous into a government directed duty.

Allow 20 minutes   What is your view of the UK government's five outcomes and their vision of young people's wellbeing? Can you think of any outcomes that might contribute to young people's wellbeing that are not included?

Comment

You might have noted that the five outcomes make only passing reference to the importance of basic material resources. They also have little to say about the impact on young people's wellbeing of personal and social relationships, despite the fact that most research into young people's mental health emphasises these as a 'protective' factor (see Section 3). The five outcomes also omit young people's rights, such as the right to participate in decisions affecting their health, and do not mention the impact of inequality and discrimination on wellbeing.

1.2 Towards a critical framework

Is it possible to construct an alternative framework for understanding young people's health, and if so, what resources might we need to draw on to do so? I suggest that the three theoretical perspectives introduced in Part 1 of the book can help us to develop a more critical and social understanding of what constitutes wellbeing for young people.

A *cultural perspective* can help us to see constructions of adolescent mental health as interwoven with histories of 'youth concern' (see Chapter 1). As we noted in the Introduction to this chapter, recent debates about young people's wellbeing can be seen as an extension of more general anxieties about the state of contemporary childhood (James and Prout, 1997). A Foucauldian analysis would view current notions of what constitutes health as part of changing institutional practices, serving particular social and political purposes (Foucault, 1967, 1973). For example, adopting this approach in relation to young people might prompt us to ask why recent policy has begun to focus so much on mental health and to construe young people's needs in these terms rather than others. What kinds of interventions does it make possible, and what wider purposes are served by this change of emphasis? Along these lines, the Iraqi-born child psychiatrist Sami Timimi has argued that 'the system of faith used in modernist child and adolescent psychiatry' has 'its cultural origins in Western history', and he adds, perhaps somewhat reductively:

> We must also accept that Western biomedical psychiatry represents the economic value system of capitalist, free market thinking

and be happy to go along with the pharmaceutical industry's drive to open new markets (children's mental health is a growth area).

(Timimi, 2005, p. 38)

A *comparative or cross-cultural perspective* can throw light on how concepts of health and wellbeing have developed in different societies and cultures. Research shows that many cultures do not distinguish between physical, emotional and spiritual health in the way that contemporary Western societies do. Even in the UK, ideas about young people's wellbeing have changed radically in the last century, as ideas about youth have changed. For example, in the Victorian period there was a strong association of children's wellbeing with notions of moral purity.

A *biographical* perspective situates wellbeing within the life story of the whole person, rather than seeing it as a separate issue, and at the same time invites us to view it from the young person's perspective. Chapter 3 posed the question of whether life was becoming more difficult for young people, and discussed Beck's argument that the downside of detraditionalisation is a loss of a traditional sense of security (Beck, 1992). This has obvious implications for attempting to understand an apparent increase in mental health problems among young people. The chapter drew on John Clarke's idea of the 'magical recovery', which saw youth subcultures as trying to resolve the contradictions of the older generation (Clarke, 1976). Arguably, this idea can also be related to phenomena such as the increasing incidence of eating disorders and self harm. There are some parallels here with a psychoanalytic explanation, which would see the unconscious anxieties of the wider society as projected on to young people, who then symbolically (and in some cases literally) 'embody' them. For example, eating disorders such as anorexia and bulimia might be seen as ways of 'acting out' societal anxieties about consumption.

Together, the three theoretical perspectives offer a challenge to generalised understandings of young people's wellbeing and simplistic explanations of the apparent increase in health problems experienced by young people today. The cultural, comparative and biographical perspectives all lend support to a view that locates young people's wellbeing in particular social contexts, while also challenging and interrogating what is meant by wellbeing. They contribute to a *critical* framework for understanding young people's health, one which starts from the following key assumptions:

- Definitions of wellbeing for young people can never be universal or absolute, but will depend on particular cultural and historical contexts.

- Concerns about young people's health need to be seen as interwoven with wider and changing discourses about youth.

- These concerns can be seen as, in part, projecting wider social concerns on to young people.

- Young people have real experiences of physical and mental ill health, but these experiences need to be seen as shaped by the particular contexts in which they occur.

1.3 Applying a critical approach

A critical approach to young people's health sounds fine in the abstract, but what might it mean in practice? How can such a framework help us to make sense of young people's actual experience of physical and mental distress?

To explore these questions, we will look at the apparent increase in the incidence of eating disorders, especially among young women. One of the advantages of this example is that it combines concerns about physical and mental health. This discussion will draw on a research study carried out by John Evans, Emma Rich and Rachel Holroyd with young women in the UK. In an article summarising their research the authors explore the link between the development of eating disorders such as anorexia nervosa and the 'practice and processes' of formal education. The article analyses the part played by what the authors term the 'performance codes' and 'perfection codes' deriving both from school culture and from wider social trends (Evans *et al.*, 2004, p. 127).

The study is an attempt to go beyond accounts of eating disorders that see them as having a purely psychological origin. Instead, the article places the development of anorexia within the varied contexts and settings of young people's lives. The authors focus on the ordinary experience of women and girls, not on the extraordinary 'disorder' which they claim is often the object of discussion. They see the key to understanding eating disorders in 'the varied, complex and socially conceptualised experience of individual girls and women' (p. 124).

Evans *et al.* examine the influence of what they describe as 'the enduring and powerful notions of body control through the marketing of a slender, or thin, ideal and its spread within and beyond the Western world' (p. 125). This is reflected in the following extract from one of their group interviews:

Lauren: You can't look through the pages of something like the *Daily Mail* without coming across 'The Little Black Dress Diet' or something like that.

Ellie: They say things like 'Lose weight, Feel Great, Keep it Off', it's always things like that.

Carrie: Yeah, and they always have comments from people who say, 'Oh, it changed my life, I feel like a better person.'

Ellie: And they have before and after pictures of people and they always make them look really horrible beforehand, like miserable and with bad clothes.

Carrie: They use pictures of naturally skinny people all of the time too, so it gives you the impression that if you do what they say that you will end up looking like that, and that's not the case.

(Evans *et al.*, 2004, pp. 133–4)

This extract demonstrates the power of media images and discourses in shaping young women's ideas of what their bodies should look like. However, the authors are also concerned to explore how this ideal 'finds its way into the socio-cultural fabric of schools' and how it intersects with the structures of contemporary schooling, particularly for middle class young women. In this context, being anorexic can be a way of achieving popularity and attention:

Hayley (15):   I always used to look at my friends and think that I wanted to be as good, or as pretty, or as clever as them. So I decided that not eating was a way that I could maybe achieve that.

(Evans *et al.*, 2004, p. 137)

Paradoxically, not eating can become a way of taking control over one's body and 'achieving self-determination within the culture of the school' (p. 136). As the authors put it, some of the girls were simply 'hungry to be noticed'.

Evans *et al.* examine the way that health promotion has been woven into the school curriculum and how it legitimises what they call the ideology of 'healthism', oriented to 'making young people more active, "fit" and thin, with young people responsible for their own health and "making healthy choices"' (p. 130). They claim that 'healthism' constructs the body as imperfect and unfinished, threatened and in need of being changed, and they make a connection between these 'perfection codes' and the 'performance codes' of the school, which create intense pressures on young women to succeed.

The argument set out in the article is distinctive in the way that it moves beyond conventional approaches to eating disorders which see them as rooted in the psychology of the individual 'sufferer', and considers the influence of wider contextual factors. The authors show that the ways in which this wider context operates is complex and multi-layered, interweaving the expectations of the immediate institutional context (in this case the school) with wider cultural images and discourses (reflected, for example, in advertisements). They see gendered power relations, and the

The 'performance codes' of school can create intense pressures for young women

ways that young women struggle for empowerment within them, as of vital importance in trying to understand how eating disorders develop.

Evans *et al.* also suggest that there are contradictions between different strands of government policy concerning the wellbeing of young people: for instance, between a wish that all young people should 'achieve' at school, and a desire to promote young people's physical and emotional health. The researchers see the intense pressures on young middle class women to succeed at school, combined with peer pressure to be popular, as at least contributing to the development of eating disorders. At the same time, they argue that the very health promotion agenda that aims to improve young people's wellbeing is in fact inculcating an ideology of 'healthism' which encourages a neurotic obsession with body image.

Evans *et al.* emphasise the part played by gender in the development of eating disorders, and they touch briefly on the way that gender intersects with class in framing young women's ideals and expectations. Other researchers adopting a critical approach to young people's wellbeing have placed a greater emphasis on class as a key factor in shaping young people's experience of physical and mental health. In their study of transitions to adulthood in poor neighbourhoods in the north east of England, Robert MacDonald and colleagues emphasise the importance of high rates of morbidity and mortality in structuring the lives of disadvantaged young people (MacDonald and Marsh, 2005; Shildrick *et al.*, 2005). They found that 'narratives of personal and family ill-health' were very frequent in their interviews with young people in poor areas, and that physical and psychological ill health, both of the young people and of their families and friends, were 'common but often incidental' elements in the interviews (Shildrick *et al.*, 2005, p. 5). Ill health often had a negative impact on young people's 'school to work' careers, as shown by the following quotation from Chrissie, aged 25:

> At the moment I'm suffering from depression, cos I've applied for loads of jobs and then you just don't get them, so you start feeling really, really low ... your chances are getting slimmer and slimmer because you hear about people closing factories down and all them people are looking for work

(Shildrick *et al.*, 2005, p. 6)

The researchers conclude that mortality and morbidity are 'significant elements of multiple social problems that affect young people in poor neighbourhoods – and their transitions to adulthood' (p. 15).

This research is another important reminder that young people's health is produced in and by diverse and unequal social contexts. A critical approach, by attending to the ways in which factors such as class and gender structure young people's experience of physical and mental wellbeing, undercuts the attempts to generalise either about the state of young people's health or about its causes that we saw exemplified in the media 'scare stories' quoted in the Introduction.

Key points

- A holistic model of young people's wellbeing, linking mental, physical and social dimensions, has begun to replace traditional medical models, which tended to promote an individualistic model of health.

- While this holistic model has positive aspects, it can be criticised for setting up an impossible ideal and placing responsibility for good health on the individual.

- The current UK government model of the healthy young person, while acknowledging a social dimension, replaces welfarist ideas with an individualistic vision of the active, achieving and enterprising individual.

- All definitions of wellbeing for young people need to be seen in their cultural and historical context and as embodying particular social and political priorities.

- A critical perspective sees young people's health as enmeshed in institutional and social structures and shaped in complex ways by relationships of power and difference.

2 Diverse and unequal experiences

This section will focus particularly on young people's mental and emotional wellbeing, as a way of exploring how social divisions create diverse and unequal health experiences for young people.

2.1 Young people's mental health: diversity and inequality

Earlier in the chapter we cited claims that young people today are experiencing an increase in mental health problems. What is certainly clear is that there has been an increasing *concern* in the media and elsewhere about young people's mental health, resulting in a range of reports and initiatives.

But how are we to view young people's experience of mental health difficulties? Should they be seen as a part of 'normal' adolescent development, or as a cause for concern? Is vulnerability to emotional distress a universal experience, or are certain groups of young people more at risk?

Allow 20 minutes

Read the following extract from the website of YoungMinds, a national charity that works to improve the mental health of children and young people. How is young people's mental health presented here?

> The period of late adolescence going into young adulthood is of crucial developmental importance. Major decisions affecting personal relationships, independent living, family and working life are made during this period. This transitional stage gives young people the opportunity to change direction and outlook. Socio-biological research suggests that there is a critical period extending into early adult life for the formation of self-image and social and reasoning skills.
>
> Peer relationships appear to be more important than those with parents and other adults. It can be difficult both for young people and their parents to adjust during this period of separating. Where these adjustments are not made, mental health problems can arise, such as eating problems and depression. More than 10% of young people in this age range will experience a mental health disorder and will need skilled help. Many others will go though difficult and upsetting times which they will survive with the support of family and friends. A small minority of young people will begin to experience the first symptoms of psychosis, and these may be on-going.
>
> (YoungMinds, 2006)

Comment

This extract presents a certain level of mental and emotional distress as part of the normal experience of growing up. Behind this assumption lies a developmental model (explored in earlier chapters) which views adolescence as a time of inevitable 'storm and stress' in the transition from childhood to adulthood and the formation of adult identities. However, the extract also suggests that a substantial minority of young people experience what it calls a mental health 'disorder' for which professional help is needed. Finally, the extract suggests that a much smaller minority will experience 'the first symptoms of psychosis' during adolescence.

Clearly, debates about what constitutes a mental health 'problem', 'difficulty', 'illness' or 'disorder' cannot easily be resolved, and a critical perspective on young people's wellbeing will emphasise that definitions change over time and vary between social groups. However, such a perspective would not deny the very real distress experienced by many young people, whatever its complex origins. At the same time, a critical approach does not view mental health difficulties as a universal experience. Instead, it aims to explore the ways in which social and contextual factors contribute to the experience of particular groups of young people.

Some commentators have seen the rising concern about young people's mental and emotional health as a mainly middle class issue. From this perspective, the moral panic about obesity and physical health problems is directed mainly at the 'unhealthy' habits and behaviour of working class young people. At the same time, concerns about mental health are seen to be focused on the stresses and strains of high-performing middle class teenagers under pressure to succeed in education and employment.

However, the research evidence would appear to contradict this easy stereotype, with a young person's chance of experiencing mental health problems significantly increased by the experience of social disadvantage. Class and social exclusion are, in fact, important factors in young people's vulnerability to mental health problems, and in their capacity to cope with them:

> Research has suggested that the chances of developing into a mentally healthy, emotionally stable, coping adult are seriously impaired by social adversity, poor parenting, low intelligence, poor achievement, impoverished social networks and threatening life events. Indeed these risk factors themselves expose children to more adverse life events.
>
> (Mental Health Foundation, 1999)

As our discussion of eating disorders in Section 1 demonstrated, young people's health and wellbeing are shaped in significant ways by social divisions such as class and gender. In the remainder of this section we look in detail at some of the factors that have an impact on young people's mental wellbeing and create diverse and unequal experiences. We will focus in particular on issues of gender and ethnicity.

2.2 Gender and young people's mental health

The discussion of eating disorders and schooling in Section 1 suggested that gendered relations of power, both in an institution such as a secondary school and in society at large, could contribute to the development of particular health problems for some groups of young people. The article by Evans *et al.* (2004) presented young people's wellbeing as strongly gendered, in that instance to the disadvantage of young women.

There is evidence that young women suffer disproportionately not only from anorexia and other eating disorders, but also from a range of mental health problems. As a review of the literature by the former

Health Development Agency (HDA, now part of NICE, the National Institute for Health and Clinical Excellence) concludes, 'gender plays a significant role in mental health issues' (HDA, 2001, p. 35). Based on research evidence, the HDA suggests that young women are twice as likely to suffer from a depressive illness as young men, despite the fact that most recent media coverage and policy concern has focused on the increase in depression among young men.

Deliberate self harm is four times more common in women than men, and much more common among younger than older adults. The HDA concludes that, in general, more young women than young men experience mental health 'disorders', although it acknowledges that the statistical differences are not enormous and may depend to some extent on how a 'disorder' is defined.

However, young men are disproportionately represented in the reporting of certain mental health problems. They are three times more likely to be dependent on alcohol or drugs than young women, and what is termed 'conduct disorder' (persistent bad behaviour) is twice as common among young men, with those who are in prison, homeless or unemployed being particularly vulnerable.

Much recent attention has focused on the apparent rise in suicide among young men. According to the HDA, the figures for suicide in the population as a whole have been going down in recent years. However, the period since the 1980s has seen a decline among women generally but a rise among men, with a significant increase in the 15–44 age group (HDA, 2001, p. 38). According to the Men's Health Forum, suicide is now the commonest cause of death in men aged under 35 in England, with suicide rates for men aged 15–24 more than doubling since 1971 (Men's Health Forum, 2002, p. 1).

Activity 5   Gender and the risk of suicide

Allow 20 minutes   Why do you think rates of suicide might now be higher among young men than young women? Make a list of any possible reasons that occur to you.

Comment

According to the HDA: 'Surprisingly little has been written about maleness in relation to the incidence of suicide among young men' (HDA, 2001, p. 39). However, some explanations have been advanced by researchers, and the range of arguments offered is surveyed below.

An explanation might be found in the dislocation felt by young men at a time of rapid social change (remember the discussion in Chapter 4 of the 'victim' discourse in relation to boys, and its use in debates about declining school performance):

> Changing patterns of employment, altered gender relations, new discourses of masculinity or femininity may undermine young men's sense of certainty and security, particularly when these are seen to damage opportunities for economic independence ... significant numbers of young men may need more support in finding their way on this rapidly changing terrain, and statistics on young men's suicide indicate that there is much work to be done to contain growing problems.
>
> (Bradford and Urquhart, 1998, cited in HDA, 2001, p. 39)

Other writers have suggested a link between higher rates of suicide and the nature of young masculinity itself. According to Debbi Stanistreet:

> in a culture that encourages men to obtain mastery over their environment, risk-taking behaviour may be construed as a popular operational definition of man's maleness. This type of behaviour may manifest itself in several different ways, including reckless driving, excessive drug use or, in a more overt form, commonly defined as suicide.
>
> (Stanistreet, 1996, cited in HDA, 2001, p. 40)

This argument sees young male suicide not primarily as a response to depression but as an extreme form of adolescent risk-taking behaviour.

Another possible explanation is that young men are less likely than young women to articulate their problems. According to the Men's Health Forum, research shows 'that men are not good at seeking help, and that male inexpressiveness leads to a reluctance in seeking medical or psychological help' (Men's Health Forum, 2002, p. 3). The image of the emotionally inexpressive young man was discussed in Chapter 4. Masculinity researchers such as Frosh *et al.* (2002) and Mac an Ghaill (1994) have identified a culture within young men's peer groups that discourages emotional openness and shuts down the possibilities for sharing personal problems.

Shildrick *et al.* (2005) found evidence of an unwillingness to seek counselling or psychiatric help among the socially excluded young men they interviewed in Teesside. They cite this quotation from Max, 28, who had lost friends in a car crash:

> Oh it was fuckin' bad. I'm glad that I'm working and that now, cos me head would be up me arse if I wasn't working like ... All the

shit I've had in me life, it's my mates that have got me through it. There's a lot of people who say, have you seen a counsellor? You know with the crash. I'm like, no I don't fuckin' need counselling, you know what I mean?

(Shildrick *et al.*, 2005, p. 14)

2.3 The mental health of young black men

According to the Health Development Agency, 'Young black men are over-represented in the mental health statistics' (Health Development Agency, 2001, p. 36), particularly in terms of diagnosis for schizophrenia, which is generally three times higher for the African-Caribbean population than for the UK white population (Nazroo, 1997). Young black men are over-represented in hospital admissions for mental health problems, contact with psychiatry via the police, courts and prison, and at the same time are under-represented in outpatient and self-referral services (Pilgrim and Rogers, 1999). They are more likely to be admitted to mental health facilities compulsorily, and once there, more likely to be placed in locked wards. African-Caribbeans generally are over-represented in statistics for psychiatric disorders and under-represented in neurotic disorders. Schizophrenia and 'cannabis psychosis' are often given as the diagnosis, but the validity of both of these has been questioned by researchers (Fernando *et al.*, 1998).

Activity 6	Young black men and mental health

Allow 15 minutes   How can we account for young black men's experience of the mental health system? Make a list of any possible explanations that occur to you.

Comment

Writers and researchers have offered a range of different reasons for young black men's apparently disproportionate experience of mental health difficulties, and for their particular experience of mental health services. The following provides a brief summary of some of the most common explanations.

Explanations that rely on racist stereotypes of black people in general, and young black men in particular, are now academically and politically discredited, but it can be argued that their influence lingers at the level of popular assumptions. In the fairly recent past it was not uncommon to read 'explanations' of poverty, unemployment or health problems among minority ethnic groups that pathologised black people, their family structures and cultures. This kind of stereotyping persists in more recent

Young black men are often treated unfairly by mental health services

debates about young people of Asian origin, which attribute their mental health and other problems to the supposed roles and relationships within Asian families. Avtar Brah has criticised this kind of 'ethnicism' which 'defines the experience of racialised groups primarily in "culturalist" terms', and views cultural needs as 'independent of other social experiences centred around class, gender, racism or sexuality', with the result 'that a group identified as culturally different is assumed to be internally homogeneous' (Brah, 1992, p. 129). Along similar lines, Waqar Ahmad criticises the 'racialization' of health research in which it is assumed 'that the population can be meaningfully divided into "ethnic" or "racial" groups, taking these as primary categories and using these categories for explanatory purposes', and which means that issues of class and income are overlooked and 'issues of institutional and individual racism as determinants of health status or healthcare become peripheral at best' (Ahmad, quoted in Kelleher, 1996, p. 72).

Critics of 'culturalist' explanations, such as Brah and Ahmad, tend to attribute young black men's experience of mental health problems to the impact of institutional racism. However, even if the impact of racism is admitted, there are at least two distinctive ways in which it can be said to have impacted on mental health.

One account offers what we might call a 'realist' model, seeing young black men's mental health difficulties as real rather than imaginary, and laying the blame squarely on their experience of institutional racism. For example, Tony Sewell (1997) argues that the UK school system provides young black men with a choice between two strong models, either to conform and be more British than white people or to play up to the stereotype of the rebel. He suggests that expectations by the wider society can create identity problems for young black men, and that these may lead to mental health problems. A more 'constructionist' argument is proposed by Fernando *et al.* (1998), who argue that young black men are misdiagnosed by the mental health system, which tends to operate on the basis of limited or inadequate knowledge of black communities and using stereotypical expectations of young black men's behaviour.

These two accounts are not necessarily contradictory. It is possible that young African-Caribbeans are *both* more vulnerable to mental health difficulties, due to their experience of racism at school and in the wider society, *and* treated in a discriminatory way by mainstream mental health services. As we saw in the case study of eating disorders in Section 1, a critical perspective on young people's wellbeing sees the development of health 'problems' as complex and multi-layered, with individual, institutional and broader social factors interacting with each other.

This section has used the example of mental health to explore some of the ways in which young people's wellbeing is shaped by social divisions, such as those of gender and ethnicity. Although class has not been discussed in this section, there is evidence from the work of MacDonald and Marsh (2005) and others that poverty and social exclusion also play a significant role in shaping young people's mental and emotional wellbeing. The ways in which diversity and inequality impact on wellbeing challenge generalised narratives that tell of a general 'decline' in young people's health. The complex interactions of social and cultural contexts with individual experience that we have seen demonstrated in these examples also undermine any attempts to produce straightforward or simplistic explanations.

Section 3 of the chapter moves on from analysing young people's experience to exploring ways in which their wellbeing can be developed and promoted, taking forward the critical framework that we have been using here.

Key points

- While mental and emotional difficulties can be viewed as a feature of 'normal' adolescent development, there is evidence that some groups of young people are more vulnerable than others and that the experience of mental health is influenced by factors such as gender, class and ethnicity.

- Young people's experience of mental health is strongly gendered, with young women at greater risk of eating disorders and self harm, and young men having higher rates of suicide.

- Young black men appear to experience a disproportionately high rate of mental health problems and to suffer from institutionalised racism at the hands of mental health services.

3 Promoting wellbeing

In the previous section we examined some of the factors that affect young people's chances of experiencing mental health problems. This section continues the focus on mental health but takes a more positive stance, exploring the factors that promote young people's mental health and that might enable them to cope with threats to their emotional wellbeing. However, it will be important to carry forward the conclusions reached in previous sections, about diversity and inequality in young people's experience, and about the 'situated' nature of wellbeing. For example, we should subject generalised statements about 'resilience' and 'protective factors' to the same kind of critical analysis that we have used to explore other aspects of current discourses about young people and their wellbeing.

3.1 The resilience model

In recent years the dominant approach to the promotion of young people's mental and emotional wellbeing has been to seek ways of developing resilience and of putting in place the protective factors that might reduce young people's vulnerability to mental health problems. Although the following statement from the Mental Health Foundation refers explicitly to children, the terms used are similar to those used in recommendations about the emotional wellbeing of young people:

> Children are less likely to develop mental health problems if they have good communication skills, a sense of humour, religious faith, the capacity to reflect, at least one good parent-child relationship, affection, a family environment without severe discord, appropriate and consistent discipline, family support for education, a wider support network within the community, good housing, a high standard of living, a range of positive sport and leisure activities and a high morale school offering a safe and disciplined environment alongside strong academic and non-academic opportunities.
>
> (Mental Health Foundation, 1999)

Simone Fullagar reports that policy responses to the high rates of suicide among young people in rural areas of Australia have focused on identifying risk factors such as previous suicide attempts, mental health problems and social isolation, and on promoting preventive factors such as social connectedness, problem-solving skills, and readily available mental health services (Fullagar, 2005, p. 32).

In some ways resilience has many similarities with the concept of social capital discussed in later chapters of this book. The statement by the

Mental Health Foundation portrays it as consisting of a 'package' of different components: personal qualities and skills, social relationships and support networks, and particular kinds of community and institutional environments. Clearly, the concepts of resilience and protective or preventive factors build directly on the holistic model of wellbeing that we analysed earlier, incorporating a similar combination of individual, material and social components. Like that model, the notion of resilience can be seen as a positive move away from conventional, medical models of health promotion that focused on the eradication of illness and on individual pathology.

However, it can be argued that some models of resilience are more 'social' than others. While some versions focus on the development of personal skills and strategies, such as emotional literacy or communication skills, others emphasise the importance of relationships and the development of a positive social environment. To some extent, the difference in emphasis depends on the political priorities of the moment. Governments operating within a 'welfarist' framework have tended to give priority to initiatives to eradicate child poverty and to improve access to education and employment, while those that are attempting to reduce state welfare spending encourage the development of skills that will enable the individual to thrive in a competitive world.

In keeping with the neo-liberal model of the 'healthy teenager' that we analysed in Section 1, recent initiatives to promote young people's mental health have tended to move away from an emphasis on social and material factors, and to focus more on personal skills and qualities. Two areas that have received increasing attention in recent years have been emotional literacy and spirituality.

There has been a growing interest, in both academic and policy circles, in emotional literacy and what some have termed 'emotional intelligence' (Goleman, 1995), and much of this attention has been focused on children and young people. There have been a number of programmes in UK schools aimed at helping children and young people to develop skills in dealing with and expressing emotions. Initiatives of this kind can be seen as reflecting the 'new emotionality' of contemporary culture analysed by many commentators. In their different ways writers such as Giddens (1991) and Rose (1999) have analysed late modern society's growing concern with the cultivation of the self, which is seen as something that needs to be worked on and developed, rather than simply as a 'given'. (Comparisons can be made with the notion of the body as unfinished noted by Evans *et al.*, 2004, and discussed in Section 1.) From this perspective, learning how to handle one's emotions is essential for success in learning and employment, and for achieving fulfilling personal relationships. As discussed in Chapter 4, educational programmes designed to assist boys often target the development of their social, emotional and communication skills (McLeod, 2002, p. 213).

One of the organisations working with the UK government to improve young people's emotional literacy is Antidote, which works with schools and other organisations 'to help shape learning environments that give young people the best possible opportunity to achieve and make a positive contribution' (Antidote, 2005).

It is noticeable (and no accident) that Antidote's aims echo the language of the government's declared aim of helping young people to 'achieve' and 'make a positive contribution' as stated in the five outcomes in *Every Child Matters*. Arguably, the government's encouragement of 'emotional literacy' programmes for children and young people is part of the new model of the healthy young person as a skilful, coping and enterprising individual that we analysed in Section 1.

Clearly, programmes that encourage young people to cope with their emotions more effectively are of value in promoting their emotional wellbeing. However, it can be argued that an exclusive emphasis on such programmes risks returning to a model that individualises mental health, locating the 'problem' and its solution in the individual young person's personal skills or lack of them, and drawing attention away from the social and contextual factors which require strategies and solutions at a societal level (as discussed in Section 1).

A second area that has become the focus for policy makers concerned to promote young people's emotional wellbeing is spirituality. The terrorist attacks in the USA on 11th September 2001 and in the UK on 7th July 2005 have been the catalyst for much public soul searching about the role of religion in late modern Western societies. However, even before these events, governments in the USA and UK were seeking to encourage the contribution of 'faith communities' to social policy, with both the Bush and Blair governments apparently keen to support 'faith-based' welfare initiatives. Recent education policy in the UK has sought to support the work of faith schools, and representatives of religious groups have been invited to contribute to policy forums. While involvement in formal religion has declined in most Western societies, recent years have also seen an upsurge of interest in issues of spirituality, with Eastern and 'new age' spiritual practices increasingly popular.

In this context the notion that faith and spirituality might be useful resources in developing individual and community wellbeing has become popular among policy makers. The Mental Health Foundation statement quoted at the start of this section included 'religious faith' as one of the positive factors that could safeguard young people against the experience of mental distress. A research report published in 2005 appeared to bear this out, with young people who had a religious faith apparently expressing a more hopeful and positive attitude to life than their more sceptical and secular peers (Francis and Robbins, 2005). In 2003 the UK government funded the National Institute for Mental Health in England (NIMHE) and the Mental Health Foundation to carry out a two-year research project to explore 'the importance of spirituality in a whole person approach to mental health' (NIMHE, 2003). Professor Antony Sheehan, Chief Executive of NIMHE and Group Head of Mental Health in the Department of Health, was quoted as saying: 'Spirituality is increasingly being identified by people with mental health needs as a vital part of their mental wellbeing and recovery from ill health; and is coming to greater prominence in our multi-cultural society' (NIMHE, 2003, p. 2). A YoungMinds study of the mental health of black and minority ethnic young people concluded that religious faith was a powerful resource for some groups:

> In the face of depressive and schizophrenic symptoms, prayer was perceived as particularly effective among African Caribbean Christian and Pakistani Muslim groups ... However, another study found that, relative to other kinds of help for depression, religious activity was not seen as particularly helpful, but that Muslims believed more strongly than other groups in the efficacy of religious coping methods for depression.
>
> (Street *et al.*, 2005, cited in Meier, 2005, p. 17)

As with the renewed emphasis on emotional literacy, it is undeniable that a positive and hopeful outlook on life, whether inspired by religious belief or anything else, is likely to protect young people against depression, and may help them to cope with the everyday anxieties of youth. On the other hand, it can also be argued that this emphasis on the value of a 'positive' faith, regardless of its content, has its dangers. It can be seen as denying the important part played by doubt, scepticism and intellectual exploration in the experience of adolescence. The emphasis on the value of faith is consistent with the emphasis on youth as a time of achieving, contributing and generally being positive and enterprising that was discussed earlier in the chapter.

Attempts to employ spirituality as a resource for promoting young people's mental health also run the risk of emptying belief of any content – viewing it simply as a neutral 'resource', like other forms of social capital – and glossing over awkward contradictions. Is acquiring or maintaining a strong religious faith necessarily a good thing for all young people, whatever the nature of that faith and its beliefs and practices? Does encouraging 'faith' as an element of social policy mean supporting religious groups that have illiberal attitudes to women and gay people? And if a strong sense of purpose is always a good thing, should we also encourage young people to join extreme political organisations?

It could be argued that, in some instances, a 'positive' faith might actually be detrimental to a young person's mental health, and that rigid adherence to a religious or political faith might be a symptom of mental distress rather than its solution. Writing about the lessons to be drawn from the London bombings of 2005, Richard Meier states:

> It was said of one of the suicide bombers, Hasib Hussain, that he 'went off the rails' as a young teenager but became a reformed character when he 'suddenly became devoutly religious' two years ago.
>
> (Meier, 2005, p. 17)

Reflecting on this quotation again leads us to question what exactly we mean by wellbeing in relation to young people. Was Hasib Hussain a more whole or healthy person before or after he became 'devoutly religious'?

This kind of critical questioning helps to undermine any universal notion of what constitutes wellbeing, and to be critical of attempts to impose a single set of healthy 'outcomes' on all young people, whatever their circumstances. It is also important to acknowledge that many young people experience youth as a time of difficulty and uncertainty, but that this may have no serious long-term consequences for them. If a young person has been brought up in an unquestioning religious faith or in a claustrophobic family environment, then their teenage years might be a time of necessary breaking away, with its own inevitable but perhaps short term distress. On the other hand, research into youth subcultures such as Paul Hodkinson's study of 'Goth' culture has demonstrated that affiliation to such groups can be a powerful source of identity and community for young people, even when the culture of the group may appear macabre and 'unwholesome' to adults (Hodkinson, 2002).

Religion versus youth subculture: which is healthier for young people?

3.2 Beyond resilience?

Initiatives to promote an individualistic model of resilience for young people can be seen as contributing to discourses of neo-liberalism that, to quote Fullagar, 'work to shape the understanding and management of emotional subjectivity' (Fullagar, 2005, p. 34). Drawing on the work of Nikolas Rose, Fullagar points to ways in which 'the language of increased self-esteem, greater locus of control and self-responsibility are linked to ideals of adult identity as active and resilient with a view of life as an "enterprise" of self-improvement' (Fullagar, 2005, p. 34).

However, it is one thing to offer a critical analysis of current models for promoting young people's wellbeing, and another to provide practical alternatives. While not denying the value of some strategies to promote personal resilience, a critical approach to wellbeing seeks to go beyond them. Discussing government responses to high rates of suicide among young rural Australians, Fullagar argues that an emphasis on identifying individual risk factors has tended to 'ignore the complex power–knowledge relations that govern the way particular young people do or do not seek help within rural or urban contexts' (p. 37). He argues that there is a need to acknowledge the influence of 'power relations that shape the way that young people are socially positioned and come to feel about themselves'. What might this mean in practice? In the next activity we explore this question by returning to the example of eating disorders discussed in Section 1.

Activity 7   A critical approach to preventing eating disorders

Allow 20 minutes   Look back at the analysis of eating disorders among young women in Subsection 1.3. Bearing in mind the authors' (Evans *et al.*, 2004) conclusions about the complex factors involved, jot down a few thoughts on strategies for preventing anorexia among young women in the secondary school context.

Comment

Any strategy to prevent eating disorders would certainly need to include supporting individuals and providing them with personal strategies for dealing with their anxieties about weight, body shape, image and so on, at least in the short term. However, if we accept the analysis offered by Evans and colleagues, a longer term and more effective strategy would also need to address the broader issues that the authors raise. This would mean taking a critical look at the official culture of the school, and the way that certain 'performance codes' and bodily 'perfection codes' were promoted both formally in the curriculum and informally through the messages conveyed in the day-to-day life of the school. It would perhaps mean working with young women to help them to challenge the expectations imposed on them both within the school environment and beyond, helping them to affirm positive identities that did not involve conforming to restrictive gendered images. However, this would need to be part of a wider struggle at a social and cultural level to change deeply embedded gendered power relations and expectations.

There is a clear role here for those working with young people, including those working in schools, as well as those responsible for the management and direction of schools and other institutions that impinge on young people's lives. But there are also elements in this suggested strategy that are beyond the power of the face-to-face worker: they are issues for politicians and policy makers, and for society as a whole. Thus a critical approach to promoting young people's wellbeing needs to acknowledge the limitations of interventions at the individual and local level, and simultaneously to challenge existing social structures and campaign for social and institutional change.

A similar model might be applied to work with young men at risk of suicide, focusing on providing support and strategies at an individual level, while also challenging dominant notions of young masculinity, and working at a policy level to change services so that they meet the needs of young men. In the case of young black men, a critical approach to promoting emotional wellbeing would involve working to eradicate racism at the institutional level, in schools and mental health services for example, and at the social level in the attitudes and expectations imposed on young black men. Thus a critical approach to promoting young people's health would certainly need to work at the policy level to address issues of social exclusion and inequalities of class, gender and ethnicity that, as we have seen, play an important part in shaping young people's mental health and wellbeing. In other words, the implications of taking a more critical, social perspective on promoting young people's wellbeing do not make for any easy, 'quick fix' solutions. Instead, they call for work by practitioners at the individual level, both supporting individuals and challenging attitudes and expectations, in combination with longer term initiatives at an institutional and wider social level.

Key points

- Initiatives to promote young people's mental health have focused on developing resilience and on a range of factors, from individual skills to social resources, reflecting holistic ideas of wellbeing.
- Some recent initiatives in this area have promoted a normative and individualised model of the 'healthy' young person and have tended to overlook wider social and structural issues.

- A critical, social approach to promoting young people's wellbeing needs to move beyond a 'resilience' model to address some of the structural issues that impact on young people's health and wellbeing.

Conclusion

This chapter began by analysing some of the ways in which young people's wellbeing has been represented in media and policy discussions. We then moved on to explore current constructions of young people's 'wellbeing' and presented an alternative critical, social framework for thinking about the health of young people. We analysed some of the ways in which class, gender and ethnicity help to shape young people's mental health. Finally, we discussed ways in which young people's wellbeing can be promoted by attempting to move beyond a focus on individual resilience to examine the wider social and structural processes that might improve the health and wellbeing of all young people.

References

Antidote (2005)
www.antidote.org.uk [accessed 09/08/06].

Ashley, J. (2005) 'It is adults who have made teenagers' lives a misery', *Guardian*, 3 February, p. 24.

Barton, L. (2005) 'S'alright ... Being 15', *Guardian G2*, 16 March, p. 2.

Beck, U. (1992) *Risk Society: Towards a New Modernity*, London, Sage.

Bradford, S. and Urquhart, C. (1998) 'The making and breaking of young men: suicide and the adolescent male', *Youth and Policy*, 61. Cited in Health Development Agency (2001)

Brah, A. (1992) 'Difference, diversity and differentiation' in Donald, J. and Rattansi, J. (eds) *'Race', Culture and Difference*, London, Sage/The Open University.

Bunting, M. (2004) 'Our teenage canaries', *Guardian*, 13 September, p. 17.

Clarke, J. (1976) 'The skinheads and the magical recovery of community' in Hall, S. and Jefferson, T. (eds) *Resistance through Rituals: Youth Subcultures in Postwar Britain*, London, Hutchinson.

Collishaw, S., Maughan, B., Goodman, R. and Pickles, A. (2004) 'Time trends in adolescent mental health', *Journal of Child Psychology and Psychiatry*, vol. 45, no. 8, pp. 1350–62.

DfES (Department for Education and Skills) (2003) *Every Child Matters: Change for Children. Summary*, London, HMSO, www.everychildmatters.gov.uk/aims [accessed 28/03/06].

DfES (Department for Education and Skills) (2005) *Youth Matters*, London, HMSO.

Evans, J., Rich, E. and Holroyd, R. (2004) 'Disordered eating and disordered schooling: what schools do to middle class girls', *British Journal of Sociology of Education*, vol. 25, no. 2, pp. 123–42.

Fernando, S., Ndegwa, D. and Wilson, M. (1998) *Forensic Psychiatry, Race and Culture*, London, Routledge.

Foucault, M. (1967) *Madness and Civilisation: A History of Insanity in the Age of Reason*, London, Tavistock/Routledge.

Foucault, M. (1973) *The Birth of the Clinic: An Archaeology of Medical Perception*, London, Tavistock.

Francis, L. and Robbins, M. (2005) *Urban Hope and Spiritual Health: The Adolescent Voice*, London, Ebury Press.

Frankel, S. (1986) *The Huli Response to Illness*, Cambridge, Cambridge University Press.

Frosh, S., Phoenix, A. and Pattman, R. (2002) *Young Masculinities*, Cambridge, Polity Press.

Fullagar, S. (2005) 'The paradox of promoting help-seeking: a critical analysis of risk, rurality and youth suicide', *International Journal of Critical Psychology*, vol. 14, pp. 31–51.

Giddens, A. (1991) *Modernity and Self Identity: Self and Society in the Late Modern Age*, Cambridge, Polity Press.

Goleman, D. (1995) *Emotional Intelligence*, New York, Bantam.

Health Development Agency (HDA) (2001) *Boys' and Young Men's Health: Literature and Practice Review: An Interim Report*, London, HDA.

Hodkinson, P. (2002) *Goth: Identity, Style and Subculture*, Oxford, Berg.

James, A. and Prout, A. (1997) *Constructing and Reconstructing Childhood: Contemporary Issues in the Sociological Study of Childhood*, London, Falmer Press.

Kelleher, D. (1996) 'A defence of the terms "ethnicity" and "culture"', in Kelleher, D. and Hillier, S. (eds) *Researching Cultural Differences in Health*, London, Routledge.

Lewis, G. (2001) 'Health: an elusive concept' in Macbeth, H. and Shetty, P.(eds) *Health and Ethnicity*, London, Taylor and Francis.

Mac an Ghaill, M. (1994) *The Making of Men: Masculinities, Sexualities and Schooling*, Buckingham, Open University Press.

MacDonald, R. and Marsh, J. (2005) *Disconnected Youth? Growing Up in Britain's Poor Neighbourhoods*, Basingstoke, Palgrave Macmillan.

McLeod, J. (2002) 'Working out intimacy: young people and friendship in an age of reflexivity', *Discourse: Studies in the Cultural Politics of Education*, vol. 23, no. 2, pp. 211–26.

Meier, R. (2005) 'Help when it's needed', *YoungMinds Magazine*, 78, Sept/Oct.

Men's Health Forum (2002) *Soldier It! Young Men and Suicide*, London, Men's Health Forum.

Mental Health Foundation (1999) *Bright Futures: Promoting Children and Young People's Mental Health. Updates*, vol. 1, no. 7, September, www.mentalhealth.org.uk/page.cfm?pagecode=PBUP0107 [accessed 28/03/06].

National Youth Agency (2003) '"Every Child Matters" – and every young person: the NYA's initial response to the green paper', *Spotlight*, Issue 16, September, Leicester, NYA.

Nazroo, J. (1997) *The Health of Britain's Ethnic Minorities*, London, Policy Studies Institute.

NIMHE (National Institute for Mental Health in England) (2003) *Inspiring Hope: Recognising the Importance of Spirituality in a Whole Person Approach to Mental Health*, Leeds, NIMHE.

O'Malley, P. (1996) 'Risk and responsibility' in Osborne, A., Barry, T. and Rose, N. (eds) *Foucault and Political Reason: Liberalism, Neoliberalism and Rationalities of Government*, London, UCL Press.

Pilgrim, D. and Rogers, A. (1999) *A Sociology of Mental Health and Illness* (2nd edn), Buckingham, Open University Press.

Robb, M. (ed.) (2007) *Youth in Context: Frameworks, Settings and Encounters*, London, Sage/The Open University (Course Book).

Rose, N. (1999) *Governing the Soul: The Shaping of the Private Self* (2nd edn), London, Free Association Books.

Sewell, T. (1997) *Black Masculinities and Schooling*, London, Trentham Books.

Shah, H. (2005), 'The politics of wellbeing', *Soundings*, Issue 30, Summer.

Shildrick, S., MacDonald, R. and Simpson, D. (2005) *Critical Moments, Poverty and Health: Biographical Experiences of Mortality and Morbidity in Marginalised Youth Transitions*, paper presented to British Sociological Association annual conference, April, University of York.

Stanistreet, D. (1996) 'Injury and poisoning mortality among young men – looking behind the statistics', *Working with Men*, (3), pp. 16–19.

Street, C., Stapelkamp, C., Taylor, E., Malek, M. and Kurtz, Z. (2005) *Minority Voices: Research into the Access and Acceptability of Services for the Mental Health of Young People from Black and Minority Ethnic Groups*, London, YoungMinds.

Timimi, S. (2005) 'The new practitioner: the emergence of the post-modern clinician' in Malone, C., Forbat, L., Robb, M. and Seden, J. (eds) *Relating Experience: Stories from Health and Social Care*, Abingdon, Routledge/The Open University.

World Health Organization (1948) *Constitution of the World Health Organization*, www.searo.who.int/LinkFiles/About_SEARO_const.pdf [accessed 24/10/06].

YoungMinds (2006) 'Young people's mental health', www.youngminds.org.uk/index.php [accessed 28/03/6].

Part 3
Practices

Chapter 7

Working

Rachel Thomson

Introduction

My son is five years old and has recently begun formal schooling. He doesn't like it very much. When I ask him why, his answer is always the same: 'It's too much work! I like playing!' For him, work is experienced in terms of a formalisation of activity, and the element of compulsion that distinguishes entry into the national curriculum from early years education. It is a shift that he resists. As a rather spoilt, only child, he has few domestic responsibilities. As such his understanding of 'work' is forming through the experience of schooling, rather than via domestic chores and responsibilities. This simple example is intended to alert you to the way in which work is often constructed in opposition to other categories such as play and rest. These kinds of definition are always culturally and historically situated, with meanings varying between and within communities. They also hint at the ways in which work is gendered, the different value that is placed on work that is public (outside the home) and private (within the family), and a blurring of boundaries between education and employment.

In this chapter we will explore 'working' as a practice. The focus will be primarily on the school to work transition and on paid employment. We will not explore voluntary work, domestic work, educational work or informal economic activity, although these are a vital part of young people's experience. We will focus on what work means to young people, seeking to gain insights through the three perspectives set out in Part 1 of the book: the cultural, comparative and biographical perspectives.

Core questions addressed in this chapter will include:

- What part does 'working' play in contemporary young people's transitions to adulthood?
- In what ways do young people's experiences of work reflect, compound and challenge existing inequalities?
- How do young people experience work?

1 The subjective meaning of work

Allow 1 hour   Think back to an early job or experience of paid work. Try to remember what the work was like and how you got the job. What most marks your memories of it? What did you get from it, in either a positive or a negative sense? Make a note of all these points. Now ask someone else about their first job – how they got it and what they learned from it – and make a note of this too. How do the two accounts compare? What is similar and what is different?

Comment

My first 'proper' job was in 1980 as a Saturday girl at a hairdresser's, although I had had a few summer jobs before that, including leading donkeys on the beach. I got the job through my hairdresser, who knew my mother. It was supposed to be just a Saturday job, but it was also a Wednesday afternoon/night job (training evening), and soon filled up my holidays and any time I decided to skip school. The job taught me to make conversation with total strangers, which was a big thing for the shy little girl I was then. It also taught me to smoke during those precious five-minute breaks between clients, a habit that took some 20 years to break. I loved working at the hairdresser's. In a boring small town working in a trendy hair salon drew me into what seemed a very glamorous and adult world. I had wages for the first time in my life, which meant that I could circumvent any control my mother had over what I wore. It also meant that I could change my hair colour every week, free of charge, which gave me a degree of distinction among my contemporaries. It was exactly what I needed to survive being a teenager in a small seaside town. But

Hairdressing – a way of surviving being a teenager in a small seaside town

it also drew me away from school, which seemed very boring in comparison. My critical moment came when I had to choose whether to take on a formal apprenticeship or carry on my education and stay a Saturday girl.

I also did this exercise with a friend. His first job had been as a paperboy in the mid-1970s and he remembers the thrill of being the only person up and about in the house in the morning, and the pleasure of being on the empty streets. He then got a job in a fruit and vegetable market which was in a different neighbourhood. That meant that he would stay over at a school friend's house the night before and they would drink and play cards and have a laugh with a different group of friends. The job itself entailed fast mental arithmetic, which he enjoyed (including learning how to take a cut for himself to supplement the low wages). When he left school he worked for a time on a building site alongside much older men. He was the 'young one', a 'mascot' really. He remembers learning a lot about work. Some of the men had a strong work ethic and he would work hard and fast alongside them. Others would encourage him to slow down, explaining that he should not kill himself for this kind of money. He told me that his body changed doing the work and he learned how to drink. He also discovered that he did not want a long term job that involved physical labour, even though he was earning what seemed a great deal of money to a teenager.

Both of us experienced work as opening up new social worlds, enabling us to develop new skills (and vices) and to feel more grown-up. We both used work as a way of experimenting with our future identities, trying on and exploring the nature of different pathways and immediate versus deferred gratification. For both of us, these early jobs can be reflected on as learning experiences, but also as play and experimentation. The kinds of work that we were involved in were very gendered as were some of the skills we developed.

The memories that you documented will probably be both similar and different. The way in which you experienced (and remember) your first job will be dictated in part by whether you were entering what you thought to be a 'job for life' or an interlude between spells of initial and further education. As the youth labour market has changed, so too have the meanings attached to work for young people. Ideally, this activity has given you a sense of the way in which work, especially paid work, provides young people with skills, opportunities and risks. It should also have shown you how important context is in determining the extent of the risks and the nature or limits of the opportunities.

The subjective experience of work is the focus of an Australian study of the experiences of young hairdressers. The author of the study, Jo Lindsay (2004), suggests that this group of workers negotiate a continuum between the 'serious' and the 'spectacular' in both their work and social lives. In her words:

> The 'serious' involves an emphasis on security and conventional, socially acceptable behaviour and a commitment to traditional aspirations such as job security and marriage. By contrast, the 'spectacular' involves an emphasis on fun, freedom, unconventional behaviour and consumer culture. The 'serious' includes social restriction and responsibility, and correlates with the economic or relations of production. By contrast, the 'spectacular' includes freedom and rebellion and correlates with the cultural or relations of consumption. ... the serious and spectacular are not either/or categories [but] enable us to explore the diverse range of possibilities in hairdressers' work and social lives [and] the ways in which their practices are constrained by wider social forces.
>
> (Lindsay, 2004, pp. 261–2)

Think about how your experiences of your first job fit with the serious/spectacular categorisation. The following table categorises some of the young Australian hairdressers' comments.

Hairdressing as serious	Hairdressing as spectacular
'It's a trade. Once you've done your time, you've done your apprenticeship, you've got it. You can come back to it whenever you want.' (Liz)	'I socialise with a lot of hairdressers as well and because it's such a scene as well, the hairdressing, like all the big names, they hang around sort of together.' (Andre)
'I've got a son I've got to provide for. I have to. Even though it's not a very well paid job, it's still a job.' (Nicole)	'It's a fun out-going social scene. In the salon everyone can just have so much fun.' (Maria)

(Source: based on Lindsay, 2004, p. 267)

Key points

- The meaning of 'work' varies according to time and place and tends to be defined in relation to other activities such as 'play' and in opposition to the private domain of home and family.

- The subjective experience of work is important: for example, hairdressing has both 'serious' and 'spectacular' aspects of work for young people.

- Work may open up new social worlds for young people and provide them with a range of new experiences, relationships and skills.

2 Putting work into context

Contemporary Western understandings of work are underwritten by a range of social divisions such as gender, social class and ethnicity. For example, girls tend to do much more domestic labour than boys (Fenton *et al.*, 2002). Working class young people may contribute the wages from their employment to the family budget while middle class young people may spend theirs on leisure (Hutton and Seavers, 2002). In some communities young people may be expected to work long hours in family businesses from an early age (Song, 1999). Yet despite this diversity, there is nevertheless a popular understanding of where work fits into the contemporary life course: children play, then 'work' at school, and then, as they get older, may take on some part time employment. Adult status is associated with the kind of financial independence made possible by full time paid employment. But this is a Eurocentric view, and one that does not apply to large parts of the world historically or contemporarily.

2.1 Historical narratives: from 'one-step' to 'yo-yo' transitions

In Britain, the period between the end of World War II and the mid 1970s witnessed an employment market which was relatively stable. Young people seeking entry into employment managed to do so with relative ease. There was a demand for labour which exceeded the supply. This stability allowed young people to be able to predict, to some extent, what sort of employment they were likely to attain. At one level it meant that the majority of young men could predict that they would become employed on a full-time basis. At another level, young people were even socialised into expecting particular types of work, as done, for example, by their family and friends ... thus young working class boys expected to get jobs typically done by members of the working class. Since the 1970s, however, the labour market has changed significantly. The extent to which young people can predict their future employment status has declined as the demand for full-time employment has, in many instances, been overtaken by the supply of those looking for it. Many young people today are thus in a more uncertain position ... This uncertainty relates to how these young people will fare in the labour market. For young men, this uncertainty is of not becoming an established member of the full-time employed labour force. For young women this uncertainty relates to changes in forms of labour market participation, but also to a decline, or at least the deferring of leaving the labour market to raise a family.

(Pollock, 1997, pp. 615–6)

The nature of the youth labour market has changed dramatically over the course of a generation. Economic restructuring has meant that new part time service sector jobs have tended to be filled by adult women, with education and training seen as the solution to youth unemployment. These changes have affected different groups of young people in different ways. The clearest shifts have taken place in relation to the experiences of working class young men, who a generation ago would have left school and entered full time manual work in what was a relatively buoyant labour market. In Phil Mizen's words:

> For those who could not secure a job or who were unprepared to take up a place in an expanded further education, a training scheme rapidly became the only viable option. In entering a government programme, the young unemployed were subjected to a methodical attempt to recompose the very nature of their labour. Through these programmes, wages were depressed, insecurity was institutionalised and skills training emptied of much of its previous technical or craft content.
>
> (Mizen, 2004, p. 75)

The labour market position of young women is complicated by a trend away from early marriage and parenthood, which makes it appear that young women's labour market opportunities are greater than in an earlier generation (Bynner, 2001). Gill Jones (2005) has characterised these changes as making young people's transitions to adulthood:

- more *extended*, with economic independence deferred
- more *complex*, in that there is no longer a conventional timetable, dependence and independence may combine, and critical moments make a difference
- more '*risky*', involving backtracking, risk taking and parent/child conflict
- more *individualised*, in that young people have more choice but are not equal in their ability to capitalise on it
- more *polarised*, with inequalities more sharply defined in relation to more elite 'slow track' transitions and more risky 'fast track' ones.

As a discipline, youth studies has tended to tell a relatively simple story of social change in which young people's transitions to adulthood were previously collective, one-step, linear and predictable, and now are individual, extended, non-linear and uncertain. Andy Furlong and Fred Cartmel capture this through an extended metaphor of travel, a shift from the 'train journey' transitions of the past to the 'car journey' transitions of the present:

> With the impression of having control over the timing and routing
> of their journeys and with the experience of passing other
> motorists, what many of the drivers fail to realize is that the type
> of car which they have been allocated at the start of the journey
> is the most significant predictor of the ultimate outcome.
>
> (Furlong and Cartmel, 1997, p. 7)

It is a story that fits in with theories of individualisation and
detraditionalisation, which depend on constructing the contemporary
period as fragile and full of risk in contrast to a past that was robust,
predictable and certain. Increasingly, sociologists and historians are
questioning this picture, arguing that if we go back to original source
material we find that uncertainty and risk were a feature of the past too.

One example of this can be found in a paper by Sarah Vickerstaff in which
she draws on oral history interviews with individuals who had been teenage
apprentices in the 1960s. She suggests that what in the youth studies
literature is often portrayed as a 'golden age of smooth, unproblematic, one-
step transitions from school into the labour market' (Vickerstaff, 2003,
p. 269) differs from the experiences of young apprentices who accounted
for around 35 per cent of male school leavers in the period 1945–75. The
accounts that she draws on show that these young people's transitions to
adulthood were far from easy, involved considerable hardship and often a
form of extended dependency. As Vickerstaff comments:

> The range of choices was different: employment opportunities in
> the labour market, especially for young men, were more plentiful
> and more secure, leading to greater homogenization of possible
> pathways ... It does not necessarily follow, however, that young
> people experienced this greater certainty of employment as
> giving them choice or freeing them from individual risks and
> dilemmas.
>
> (Vickerstaff, 2003, p. 272)

Even though the labour market was generally buoyant, young people still
feared unemployment, and apprenticeships were often taken up as a result
of chance and family pressure rather than by choice. Nor did these young
people's transitions to adulthood fit the one-step model that is often
contrasted with more contemporary 'yo-yo' structure of contemporary
transitions where young people move back and forth between education
and work, and between dependence and independence (Du Bois-Reymond
and Lopez Blasco, 2003). Apprenticeships in the 1960s were typically five
years, having been reduced from the seven years of the 1940s and 1950s
when they were usually followed by national service. As one interviewee
put it, 'you were always "the boy" going through the apprenticeship'

Traditional apprenticeships were a feature of youth employment up to the end of the 1970s

(Vickerstaff, 2003, p. 275), and all notions of economic independence, marriage and family were deferred to the future. Apprenticeships could be harsh and gruelling experiences, with apprentices having to negotiate the vicissitudes of junior status. Vickerstaff shows us that past experiences are a means of gaining insight, and should not simply be employed as a means of creating contrasts with the present. She cautions us against accepting the simplistic pictures of the past that are created by theories that emphasise social change. As we have already found in our discussions of 'belonging' in the past and present, theories of late modernity may be good at painting broad social trends but they often fail to account for the specificity of experience.

2.2 From youth unemployment to vocationalism

The story of the changing youth labour market has been highly gendered and differentiated by social class and ethnicity. In a review of the period Mizen explains:

> In 1979, a young male leaving school with no qualifications was between four and five times more likely to be unemployed than a graduate; for unqualified women it was double. Twenty years later the gap had widened even further. Unemployment also fell heavily on young blacks. Study after study revealed the scale of the problem facing black school leavers, with general rates of

unemployment among both young people of African-Caribbean and Asian descent running between two and three times the level of their white peers.

(Mizen, 2004, p. 53)

Mizen argues that a political move away from seeking to provide 'jobs for all', towards a form of 'vocationalism' that looked to the market to provide solutions for workless youth, did little to solve youth unemployment but provided the state 'with the political means to disengage itself from any continuing responsibility for the employment fortunes of the young' (Mizen, 2004, p. 74). There are now few expectations that young people can leave school at 16 and find work. Instead they are directed towards training schemes and further education. Many move between schemes and courses. Despite the introduction of modern apprenticeships, there is no institutionalised 'training culture', which in countries such as Germany prepares those young people not going on to higher education for adult employment. As John Bynner observes, the flexibility of the UK system:

> favours those who want to keep their options open and have the resources to recover when the choices they make work out badly. It also leaves open the possibility of second chances for those who drop out early. But others, whose situation prevents them ever taking this step, face the risk of being steadily squeezed out of the system – losing sight, when young, of the ever-present conveyor belt that is taking the majority along.

(Bynner, 2001, p. 8)

In a comparative review of youth transitions in OECD (Organisation for Economic Co-operation and Development) countries, David Raffe *et al.* (1998) characterise the UK youth labour market in terms of *flexibility*, including:

- flexible outcomes (there being no formal graduation from vocational pathways)
- flexible inputs (qualifications can be accrued incrementally in different institutions)
- flexible pathways (movement between academic and vocational routes)
- flexible choices and markets (emphasis on student choice).

In recent years there has been a rise in members of most ethnic groups gaining entry to university (Modood and Acland, 1998; Reay *et al.*, 2001; Reay, 2005). A relatively high proportion of black and minority ethnic young people are now in higher education, the highest participation rates being among black British young women (66 per cent) and the lowest among white males (34 per cent) (Connor *et al.*, 2004). However, it continues to be the case that more than 50 per cent of young people in the UK do not enter higher education but instead seek to enter paid employment. Of those young people who do not stay on in education after the age of 16, approximately 10 per cent fall into the NEET category (not in education, employment or training). The rest find some kind of employment, often temporary or short term.

In the next section we will focus on the changing nature of the youth labour market and the significance in this context of the local labour market.

Key points

- School to work transitions have changed for young people since the 1970s. Where previously the demand for labour outstripped supply, now supply outstrips demand, and as a result of economic and political restructuring, further and higher education have expanded to absorb those who once went directly into the labour market.

- Youth transitions have become extended, complex, uncertain and polarised (with both fast and slow tracks). These changes are complicated by changes in gender and family relations and translate into an overall improvement in employment opportunities for young women, and the effective disappearance of employment traditionally taken up by working class young men.

- Patterns of youth unemployment are differentiated by social class, gender and ethnicity.

- Youth transitions of the past were less homogenous than often portrayed in contemporary accounts of social change.

3 Labour markets and local structures of opportunity

Much current policy attention is focused on the ability of individuals to shape their destinies: to make the right choice of subjects; to make the most of work experience opportunities; to get good career guidance; and to make the most of opportunities in higher education. Policies such as the Connexions service (in England) have been designed in order to maximise the opportunities available to the most marginalised young people. Yet young people tend to make choices in conditions that are not of their choosing. The environment in which young people grow up is crucial in framing what is possible for them and what 'success' means for them.

In order to explore this more we will consider two studies of young people that have taken place in different labour markets.

3.1 The metropolitan experience

Stephen Ball and colleagues studied a group of young Londoners as they moved through their final year of mandatory schooling and into their first year of post-16 experience. The study looked at their choices, the market behaviour of local education and training providers, and those who help and advise young people on these choices. The authors draw attention to the specificity of London, and the different old and new economies that operate within it. In particular, they focus on the opportunities that London offers young people for new kinds of work. They describe these as follows:

> The new urban, post-industrial labour markets engender both opportunity and risk, while excluding some 'others' altogether ... They have their own internal hierarchies and structures. Modelling, DJ-ing and hair styling each offer some potential for a 'glossy future' or they may equally well produce low-wage, serial, sub-employment. Luck, tenacity and talent are important but 'success' also depends on who you are and who you know ... London and other global cities are characterized by a plethora of service/style outlets; from fast food bars, cafes and restaurants, cyber-cafes, haircutters, fashion retailers, clothes manufacturers to specialist music/night time venues. These are staffed by young people and target young people. They offer new kinds of employment but entail new kinds of risk and new kinds of discrimination.
>
> (Ball *et al.*, 2000, pp. 282–3)

Ball and colleagues explore the ways in which young people are positioned differently in relation to the city's highly complex labour market by contrasting the cases of three young white Londoners: Michael (a hairdresser), Wayne (a DJ) and Rachel (a model). Michael, a working class Londoner, left school early as a result of bullying, and went into hairdressing as part of a longer journey towards training as a fashion designer. His life is entirely urban and concerned with the 'look' of things. Rachel is a middle class academic high flier, whose initial ambitions to go to the 'best university' were revised to include a route to an elite lifestyle through modelling. Wayne struggled at school, yet experiences a sense of competence and fulfilment when DJ-ing in what Ball *et al.* call 'a liminal world somewhere between work and unemployment, adolescence and adulthood, independence and living at home'

(2000, p. 292). For Wayne this is a local and family affair (his father is also a DJ). So, although each of these young Londoners is engaging in the new urban economies, they do so from very different positions:

> Despite living in the same locality, each of the three young people works within different and stratified horizons and time spans, Wayne: local, Michael: urban, Rachel: global. Their accounts of their 'choices' and decisions in the London education and labour markets, exposes the different 'opportunity structures' which frame these 'choices' and their different 'futures' and identities towards which they are struggling. The relationship between opportunity and education is different in each case and related to different 'learner identities'. In effect, 'these people inhabit co-existing social spheres, coeval and overlapping in space, but with fundamentally different time horizons and time-spans' (Albrow, 1997, p. 47). The material, social class differences between them are reflected in, and compounded by, time-space inequalities. Michael's and Rachel's social relations are increasingly disembedded from local contexts of action.
>
> (Ball *et al.*, 2000, p. 298)

3.2 The post-industrial experience

Let us now compare this with another local economy, that of the north east of England. Les Johnston and colleagues, and Robert MacDonald and Jane Marsh, investigated the experiences of young people in two deprived parts of Teesside (Johnston *et al.*, 2000; MacDonald and Marsh, 2001). Once a thriving centre of heavy industry, it is now a locality where there are high rates of long term unemployment, lone parent households, poor health, crime and very low levels of educational attainment. Johnston *et al.* describe the area they studied as follows:

> Built in the 1920s [this] neighbourhood of Teesside was for fifty years an unremarkable but successful example of local authority housing and a 'respectable' working class community. Since the 1970s the dramatic economic restructuring of local manufacturing industry has stripped away the economic security which underpinned social cohesion. Joblessness in [the area] is estimated at around 40 per cent and its wards are in the top 10 per cent most deprived in the country. Employment opportunities for school-leavers and young adults are particularly limited. [The area] has become notorious for high rates of crime and drug-related offending. Teesside in general and [this area] in particular provide extreme examples of rapid economic decline and long-term structural unemployment and, as such, this locality provided the

opportunity to study a place where the problems of social exclusion for young people are thrown into sharpest relief.

(Johnston *et al.*, 2000, quoted in Joseph Rowntree Foundation, 2000)

Only nine of the sample of 88 young people followed by Robert MacDonald and Jane Marsh (2001) had never been unemployed. Yet unemployment was not a permanent position for many; rather young people's careers were characterised by moving in and out of jobs, college courses and training schemes: 'many were started but fewer were completed' (p. 386). They define the whole sample as 'economically marginal', experiencing the brunt of the post-industrial 'flexible' labour market:

> Their school to work careers were characterized by the cyclical movement around various permutations of government schemes and college courses, low-paid, low-skill and often temporary jobs (e.g. in food processing and textile factories, fast-food outlets, garages, shops, hairdressing salons, offices, construction sites and bars), recurrent unemployment (with or without benefits) and, for a minority, occasional voluntary work or irregular 'fiddly work' ... The frequency of changes ... differed across the sample but the nature of their school to work careers was much the same (i.e. leaving school with poor educational qualifications and then circulating around the various 'options' available at the bottom of the local labour market). All were included in these insecure, unstable and marginal careers.
>
> (MacDonald and Marsh, 2001, p. 386)

MacDonald and Marsh illustrate their findings through 'cameos', or potted biographies, of three young people – Martin, Jason and Sarah – in order to argue that they are all disadvantaged, yet:

> there is not one single, uniform way of growing up in [this area]; a context of social exclusion does not generate just one sort of youth transition ... The transitions to adulthood that these three were making are quite different. Sarah is a single mother who has re-engaged with education after teenage years marked by turbulent relationships with family, friends and partners and a very unsettled housing career. Jason is serving his 10th term 'inside': an outcome of extended and dangerous criminal and drug-using careers. Martin is now married, in steady employment and working hard for the local youth organization he founded.
>
> (MacDonald and Marsh, 2001, p. 382)

We will reproduce the cameo of Jason in order to communicate how illegal careers (in this case petty crime, drug dealing and taking) can offer the structure, reward and progression that were once provided by the skilled manual work that characterised the economy of Teesside. For young people like Jason crime is normal, it is work.

> Jason was 21 years old when we talked to him in a Young Offenders Institute. He was born in East Kelby and had lived there all his life. His school experiences were limited and negative. At the age of 11, Jason started 'getting into trouble': he and his older friends stole from cars and were involved in other 'petty crimes'. By the age of 13, he was truanting 'most of the time'. He was then 'in and out' of secure units and Young Offender Institutes throughout his teens and left school with no GCSE passes. In the mid 1990s, he returned from one spell 'away' to find that his friends had progressed from 'recreational' drug use (i.e. cannabis, amphetamine, ecstasy, LSD) to dependent, intravenous heroin use. He first smoked heroin at the age of 16 then quickly progressed to injecting. Fuelled by the need to fund his heroin dependency, Jason's criminal activities intensified, and became more serious and more chaotic. By the age of 19, he was using crack cocaine alongside heroin. He had served 10 sentences between the age of 14 and 21 years (most recently, 21 months for burglary).

Given this criminal and drug-using career, it is not surprising that Jason's success at school and in the labour market had been limited. He had held a job as a packer in a factory but left after 3 days. He could not cope because of the health consequences of his heroin use (e.g. he had once been hospitalized after an overdose and at the age of 19 weighed just 8 stone). He had also had a labouring job that lasted some months and paid 'good money', but he was made redundant from this. The following extract is from an interview with Jason and his friend Stu, who was also serving time for similar offences. They describe their plans on release.

JM: Where do you see yourself in the future, do you see yourselves going straight at all?

Jason: Nah ... God, 'where do I see myself?' I see myself wisening up, using different ways of getting money where I can get more money. I couldn't see myself changing or settling down or anything like that ... and I have to take the shit that goes along with that. Going away every now and again. I've been doing it for too long to stop now.

JM: What about you Stu?

Stu: Exactly the same as him. Staying the same. I'd like a motorbike as well.

JM: When you say 'wisening up' do you mean getting into other crimes to make money?

Stu: Yeah, there's so many [dealers] out there now. You'd have to give it [the drug dealing] a year and use your 'ead, get drug free, not smack but coke, and make your money!

Jason: We'd be selling drugs that we used to take and spending the money.

[...]

There were 11 other people in the sample who recounted very similar biographies; ones that involved the interdependency of drug using and criminal careers, and virtually 'empty' school to work careers. Significant life events, often in the spheres of home and family, acted as catalysts that initiated a chain of experiences (typically, disengagement from school and engagement with street-based peer groups) that ended up in persistent, heavy drug use, repeated and increasingly serious criminality, and imprisonment.

(MacDonald and Marsh, 2001, pp. 379–80)

Activity 2   Your local labour market

Allow 30 minutes   Think for a moment about the local labour market in the area in which you live and/or work. What kind of full time employment opportunities are there for young people? How has this changed over the course of a generation?

Comment

The nature of your answer will depend on the characteristics of the area in which you live. In rural areas the industrialisation of farming has eliminated a great deal of the seasonal manual work that once existed. The changing fortunes of the British seaside has seen towns once dependent on fishing switch to tourism and ultimately to servicing the welfare sector. Some areas of former heavy industry have become employment wastelands, others have become sites of new service industries. In some areas the labour market is ethnically segmented, such as the Tower Hamlets area of London, where it is estimated that up to 70 per cent of young Bangladeshis are unemployed. Yet whatever the changes, the new forms of employment available to young people tend to be highly flexible, temporary and low paid.

In a study of young men in Scotland who had experienced a period of extended unemployment early in their careers, Furlong and Cartmel paint a picture of 'vulnerable young men in fragile labour markets' (Joseph Rowntree Foundation, 2004). For these young men, finding work was not the problem, but holding on to a job was, as employment was usually terminated as a result of changes in the demand for labour and not their employers' dissatisfaction with their performance. These young men tended to be unskilled, working in temporary positions or for agencies. This kind of extreme flexibility eroded any sense of security, as one young man, Tony, explains of agency work:

> You had to look at the board at the end of the week to see if you had a shift for the next week. It was unbelievable. You didnae know by the Friday if you were working ... Every week yer heart it wis in yer mooth, wondering if you were gonna have a job for the next week.
>
> (Furlong and Cartmel, 1997, quoted in Joseph Rowntree Foundation, 2004)

The authors of this study suggest that the problem here is not labour supply. The young men were all keen to find work, even though the kind of work did not help them accumulate skills. Rather the problem is primarily with labour demand and the trend towards the casualisation of employment.

Key points

- Local economies provide the 'structures of opportunity' within which young people's transitions take place.

- In some parts of the UK and the Irish Republic there is little demand for young people's labour.

- In any single place there are multiple forms of transition, with different young people forging very different futures.

- For some young people, crime and drug taking can offer an alternative 'work' career.

- Flexibility in the UK labour market and education/training systems may reward those with the most resources

4 Resources in the school to work transition

In this section we present two longitudinal case studies of young people taken from the *Inventing Adulthoods* study (London South Bank University, 2006). The interviews took place in the early years of the twenty-first century. Both young women, Maeve and Jade, are academically able, with high aspirations for education and work. Typical of their generation, they both see education as their route to a successful future, yet they are positioned very differently in terms of family and socio-economic resources. Maeve is the youngest daughter of an intact middle class family living in Ireland. Jade is the only child of a single mother living close to the centre of a major English city. As you will see, family support and relationships are an important factor in shaping how the two girls balance the demands of work and education.

| Activity 3 | Comparing two school to work transitions |

Allow 1 hour   Read through the two case studies and as you do so make notes on the different jobs that Maeve and Jade take, and the different resources that they are able to draw on. After the two accounts there are some further questions to help you compare the two cases.

Maeve

First interview, aged 16

Maeve is not working so is supported by her parents. She gets £6.50 a week from her parents and a monthly clothing allowance of £100. She receives social support from a wide range of friends in lots of different areas of her life, including school, drama group and choir. These groups travel about the country and so she has greatly expanded her experience. Her sister has moved to study in England. As the only child in the house now she is the centre of her parents' attention, which is sometimes a good thing, sometimes not. Her ambition is to go to medical school and become a doctor.

Second interview, aged 17

Maeve has now got a part time job in a shop. This gives her great independence as she no longer gets financial support from parents. Her relationship with her boyfriend is becoming much closer. She is glad that she has been able to maintain this relationship without any negative impact on her friendships. Her parents are giving her more freedom and she talks to her mother about relationships and friendships. She is still part of a lot of social and cultural groups, which all make her feel very 'connected'.

Third interview, aged 18

Maeve has got a place at medical school. She gave up her job at the end of the summer so that she could concentrate on her A levels. Her parents now give her £80 a month to spend as she wishes. She has passed her driving test and has access to the family car. This is important now that the family have moved to the countryside, further away from friends. She sees this move as a future asset, a good place to come home for a rest and holidays when she goes to university and to bring her children to when she is at that stage in her life. She does not see a lot of her sister now – only at holiday times. Her large group of friends continue to provide an extensive social outlet. Following the death of one of them, friendship patterns changed, with some people needing a lot more support than others (the school provided counselling). Maeve turned to her mother and her own inner resources.

Fourth interview, aged 19

For the summer holidays Maeve has a part time job in a hotel close to home. It is poorly paid and Maeve considers it hard work and not really worth it; she has an interview for a clerical job at a local firm. She is saving for a holiday to Amsterdam with friends later in summer. She hasn't had a part time job at university, but hopes to get one next year. She doesn't get a grant or loan, so depends wholly on her parents. They pay her accommodation costs and give her £200 a month to live on. She can manage on this, but is prepared to run up big debts (for extras such as holidays) in anticipation of securing a well-paid job when she graduates. Her music has been a resource for her: she joined the university orchestra, made new friends and also made some money playing in a small group at weddings and other gatherings.

Fifth interview, aged 21

During the past two years Maeve has continued to rely heavily on her parents for financial support. They currently give her an allowance of €750 per month from which she pays fees and rent, buys books, clothes and so on. As her second year in medical school was very demanding, she was not able to work – she worked in a shop for two months but gave up as it was interfering with her course. She took a part time job in a local hotel in summer 2003, and then went to Dublin for the latter part of that summer and worked in a pub and club for six weeks. She managed to break even and returned to university for her third year. Due to the demands of the course she only took a pub job for the last few months of the third year, when pressure eased. She worked in a pub earning €7.50 an hour. With the financial assistance from her parents she has so far managed to avoid taking out a bank loan. An insurance policy cashed in last year paid for her accommodation. She plans to pay back her parents when she starts earning. With the guarantee of a well-paid job at the end of her six years' training she plans to take out bank loans in her last two years so she can afford to live more comfortably and pay for good clothes, which she needs for ward rounds. During the summer of 2004 she travelled around Europe, working in a shop in Ibiza for six weeks, a job 'passed on from one Irish person to another'. She hopes to get two weeks' work now in the local hotel before she returns to university. At the beginning of summer she invigilated exams at her old school, work she got through her parents.

Jade

First interview, aged 15

Jade is the only child of a single mother and has just finished year 10 at school where she is doing well academically. Her career ambitions are to 'do well', go to university and possibly become a fashion designer. She has never worked. Financial resources seem to be limited: she gets money from her mother, but does not have an expensive social life. She is close to her aunt, who has no children and will take Jade on holiday next year. Her godmother is also a significant figure, and will pay for her driving lessons when she is 17. Personal resources (purpose, determination and so on) seem to be very significant. She has a sense of being in a warm and close network of women who are mutually supportive, and this is echoed in her group of girlfriends.

Second interview, aged 16

Jade is now in year 11, studying for 10 GCSEs. Her ambition is to be a scientist. Her mother and her aunt appear to be getting tired of supporting her financially, probably because she is going out much more now, clubbing and so on, and obviously needs more money. They want her to get a job as soon as possible, but she is thinking that she should be more sensible and try not to go out so much because she has a lot of work to do and needs to revise for GCSE exams. If she had a job she would not be able to do so much. She really only needs money from her mother for school. She had a work experience placement at a clothes shop and the employer paid her for her work.

Third interview, aged 17

Jade has passed her GCSEs with flying colours. Her ambitions have shifted but she still wants to go to university. She is studying science A levels in the sixth form. She is in receipt of an educational maintenance allowance (EMA) of £30 per week. The only job she has had was for the Christmas period and up to the end of January, when she worked at B&Q on the shopfloor and as a cashier. She was paid something over £3 an hour, working from 6–10 pm in theory, on a four-day week, but said she was often there until 11 pm for no extra money. She earned quite a lot over Christmas by doing overtime (several hundred pounds), but this made her very tired and it affected her schoolwork. She reported that teachers were sympathetic over Christmas, but are generally not so if this carries on into normal term time. Now she has only £40 left, and her mother and aunt will not give her any money, so she is hoping to get a job at the local supermarket next week, which she says pays more than B&Q.

Fourth interview, aged 18

Jade is now in her third year in the sixth form having not done as well in her exams as she had hoped. She recently left home to live with her aunt due to friction with her mother. Jade is not working at present: she gave up working at B&Q earlier in the year and is living on £30 per week EMA while preparing to resit her A levels. She is about to work in a clothes shop for three weeks during the sales. Her main resources are her boyfriend and her family – but her mother as a resource is less close than she was because Jade left home to live with her aunt. She has paid her own way for some time now, so that represents some independence. She cooks for herself sometimes, or else her aunt cooks for them both. She says she is eating more healthily since she left home.

Fifth interview, aged 20

Jade is now at university in her home city, studying for a degree in environmental studies. She is living in student halls and also sometimes with her aunt. She relies on her full grant of £1600 per term and has access to a £1000 hardship grant from the university, but she has a lot of debt. She doesn't know where the money goes: she pays £700 per term in rent and is now £1100 overdrawn. She explains that some people have taken out two student loans, but she doesn't want to as she will be even more in debt. Her mother has given her £200, which she wants to pay back, although her mother says she can have it. Jade is looking for a job close to the university, but at present does some work at B&Q in her neighbourhood for £5.30 an hour (it's just gone up). She says she doesn't spend much on clothes or clubbing, but she and her friends seem to spend a lot on food. She feels that being an adult is about money, spending money. She does not like the responsibility that she now has for paying for everything.

Now compare and contrast Maeve's and Jade's experiences, bearing these questions in mind, and write your conclusions in the table.

- How do their work patterns change over time?
- What issues affect their choices of work?
- How are tensions between paid work and educational work managed?
- What is the role of their families?

	Maeve	Jade
Work pattern		
Choices		
Tensions between work and education		
Family		

Comment

Maeve's approach to work is very strategic. She has a clear goal – medical school and a professional career – and part time and temporary work is managed in order to fit in around this. The case study suggests no sense of doubt about this ultimate goal and it is clear that Maeve's parents play a crucial role in supporting her emotionally and financially towards this end. Maeve also seems to be proficient at trading in her skills and resources. So, for example, she uses her training in music to make some money, picks up a job through contacts while travelling and cultivates contacts that fit in with other aspects of her plan such as taking a low paid job because it is in the area where her parents live. You may have been surprised at how much part time and temporary work Maeve does, given that she is from a comfortable middle class family. Her case study suggests the level of expense involved in the very extended form of semi-independence demanded by a professional training such as medical school. It also demonstrates a kind of 'professionalisation' of biography in which all activity is purposeful and part of building up a good CV.

Jade recognises the same tensions between work and education, which Maeve is so proficient at juggling. Part time and temporary work is an integral part of student life, but the key is to ensure that it does not erode academic performance. Jade has fewer material resources to draw on than Maeve even though she has access to benefits such as EMAs aimed at less well-off students. Her family are loving and supportive but are not able to support her indefinitely and they let her know that this is the case. Research by Gill Jones (Jones, 2005) has found that parents of working class young people, most of whom have not gone to university themselves, often struggle to know how to support their children through the kind of extended transitions that are demanded by the expansion of higher education.

The housing situations of the two young women differ significantly. Maeve leaves home to go to university, yet 'home' continues to be her parents' house where she returns in holidays (even though they have moved). Jade studies locally and, wishing to establish some independence from her mother, moves in with her aunt. She also then lives in student halls some of the time. Jade's options for part time work also seem to be more limited; both young women take jobs that are very low paid. Where Maeve is able to access several labour markets (near her parents' old and new homes, in her university town and surrounding area and on holiday), Jade is more fixed in a single neighbourhood, although she is beginning to look for work near the university. Paid work is clearly important to both young women, and an integral part of being a student, reflecting the relatively high levels of part time work among UK students compared with their peers in the rest of Europe (Bynner, 2001).

4.1 Staying local

One of the main reasons young people give to explain their decision to study locally and live at home is that it is a debt avoidance strategy (Patiniotis and Holdsworth, 2005). Yet the trend for middle class young people to study at a distance from their parental home and for working class young people to live and work locally can be seen as one way in which differences in resources are amplified during the period after leaving home. Jackie Patiniotis and Clare Holdsworth have tried to explain this paradox by looking at how working class young people's decisions to 'study local' can be seen as a way of maintaining a sense of security and minimising risk when venturing into the unfamiliar territory of higher education. Yet it is a choice that ultimately exacerbates existing inequality. Their analysis draws on Pierre Bourdieu's typology of different forms of capital: material (what you have); social (who you know), cultural (demeanour, etiquette, knowledge). The value of this capital is judged within different social fields and it is mutable (can be converted from one form to another) (Bourdieu, 1986). These theoretical tools have been used widely in educational and cultural studies to explore the production and reproduction of inequality within education, where the absence of cultural capital is explored as a central feature limiting ambition and achievement (Reay *et al.*, 2001; Skeggs, 1997).

> Students with little or no family knowledge of university life, who do not possess the 'right' kind of legitimated cultural capital, are more likely to experience HE as alien and a risky venture.
>
> [...]
>
> The push towards widening participation is directly encouraging students without the 'right' cultural capital to go to university. While this message may not resonate in communities and families where higher education has traditionally held little value, ... neither is it failing completely. Although commentators have argued that the real success of expansion has been to facilitate less-bright students from middle-class backgrounds, universities are increasing their intake of students from varied cultural and social backgrounds. At a time when traditional working-class routes to independence and adulthood are disappearing, continuing in education has replaced apprenticeships and employment as the most viable means to higher earning potential.
>
> (Patiniotis and Holdsworth, 2005, pp. 84–5)

They go on to argue that those without the 'right' cultural capital will need to adopt strategies that make the experience more comfortable. The decision to continue to live at home may reflect the need to maintain the security of family life while stepping into the unknown territory of higher education.

Think back to the two case studies. Can you see examples of cultural capital in operation? It may be that higher education is more of a risk and an expense for Jade in relative terms and that her decision to study locally is a risk avoidance strategy. If so, how does her decision to leave home and live with her aunt fit in? Maeve also faces certain risks and has to find ways of managing them. You may also want to question whether everything can be reduced to 'cultural capital' and whether it is impossible for working class students to get on through education. Are they always fated to simply reproduce their social class location? If we look at this question through a historical lens, then the structure and dynamism of the wider society becomes important. There certainly have been periods when social mobility from the working class to the middle class took place (think of the 'baby boomer' generation and all the working class grammar school educated children who are now in positions of power). However, research suggests that despite the progressive rhetoric of New Labour, the UK is in fact going through a period in which social mobility is declining (Blanden *et al.*, 2005). It may be that the main form of social mobility that is taking place in this period is downward, making sense of the ways in which middle class parents seek to ensure an educational advantage for their children.

Key points

- The rapid expansion of higher education is one of the most dramatic changes to affect young people's lives over the course of a generation.

- An increasing number of working class and minority ethnic young people are now entering universities, and this is associated with extended dependency on their parents.

- There are high levels of part time work among students, and young people struggle to balance part time work and education.

- Patterns of work have changed over time and families differ in whether they provide support at strategic moments in order to protect educational performance.

- The expansion of further and higher education means that there are now many young people who are the first in their families to go on to post-16 education.

- Decisions by these students to attend local universities may be linked to minimising the risks of being in an unfamiliar environment.

5 Work: youth policy and practice

There is a long history of government policy aimed at the 'socialization of young people with poor educational prospects into adult occupational roles' (Bynner, 2001, p. 17). It is a tradition that the New Labour government that came to power in 1997 has continued. In 2004 John Bynner and colleagues conducted a review of government policy relating to young people, drawing on published evaluations of relevant interventions. In the area of education and employment policy they identified the following interventions:

> *Active labour market policies* directed at young people, such as the New Deal and Modern Apprenticeships, have been effective in reducing unemployment and increasing employability, though their success has been helped by economic conditions that ensure the continuing availability of jobs.

Education-based policies are designed to enable young people to remain in education. New Start and Connexions offer counselling services involving personal advisers. Connexions offers an information, advice and guidance service for all young people, while targeting support for disadvantaged young people, especially those at risk of entering the NEET group. Educational initiatives such as Connexions and the Educational Maintenance Allowance (EMA) show positive returns such as increasing participation in education among young people at most risk of dropping out or leaving school without qualifications.

Area-based policies represent a move away from universal services, replacing them with strategies directed at raising standards in traditionally poor performing localities. Some key components of the policies reviewed are clearly benefiting many of the young people for whom they were primarily intended. The success of such programmes as Excellence in Cities in helping to raise standards is reflected in the take-up outside the programme of components such as Learning Mentor and the extension of the programme from secondary to primary schools.

[...]

Reducing social exclusion among young parents. Participation in education and training more than doubled between 1997 and 2002, but has since fallen back. Sure Start Plus (SSP) in particular appears to be relatively successful in working with pregnant young women, helping them out of social isolation and enabling them to access appropriate benefits. Early evidence also suggests Re-integration Officers are a valuable means of encouraging young mothers to return to education. Support with the cost of childcare, through Care to Learn, is clearly crucial to young parents who want to return to education, training or employment.

(Bynner *et al.*, 2004, p. 4)

If I had been writing this chapter ten years ago I would have focused this section almost entirely on youth unemployment. Although the youth unemployment rate continues to be high, it is increasingly the case that education is seen as a solution to it, and in turn work is now seen as a solution to social exclusion and welfare dependency. The 'welfare to work' agenda has caused particular controversy in some areas: paid work being prioritised over the unpaid yet socially important work of childcare in the case of young parents (Bunting, 2004a); the proposed withdrawal of invalidity benefit; the moves to tie a wide range of benefits to 'purposeful activity' through the use of 'opportunity cards' (DfES, 2005). Work, it appears, is becoming the social policy solution to all forms of social exclusion (Bunting, 2004b).

connexions

13-19? Living in England? If you want information and advice designed just for you, or just someone to talk to, then Connexions has it all – and if you're 16 why not sign up for an exclusive Connexions Card?

Connexions Direct	Connexions Card	Practitioners
Confidential advice, support and information for 13-19 year olds – search our website, contact us by phone, text, e-mail, or webchat or get in touch with a Personal Adviser in your area.	Rewards and discounts for 16-19 year olds who stay in learning plus loads of useful information including how to build an effective CV	Information for Connexions practitioners plus contact details for local Connexions Partnerships and access to Connexions publications
Go to the site > >	Go to the site > >	Go to the site > >

Increasing participation in education and training

Activity 5 From biography to practice

Allow 1 hour

The following case study is taken from the *Inventing Adulthoods* study (London South Bank University, 2006) and recounts the school to work transition of Sandra. As you read the case study you will see that Sandra has been touched by several of the policy interventions described above. However, you will also see that there are other factors that shape the course that Sandra's life takes. As you read this case study, bear the following questions in mind:

- Is Sandra's a story of success?

- What interventions and incentives (personal, policy and so on) appeared to be decisive in the direction she took?

- What is the role of 'serious' feelings of security, comfort and belonging in the decision-making process?

- What is the role of the 'spectacular' in her decision making, the desire for fun, danger, excitement?

- How does work contribute on the one hand to feelings of maturity and competence and on the other to feelings of freedom and immaturity?

Sandra

First interview, aged 14

When we first interview Sandra she is in year 9 at school and living at home with her mother, stepfather and two older sisters in a disadvantaged public housing estate. Her father lives locally but provides no material or emotional support. Because of arguments between Sandra and her mother, the latter is not currently the key emotional resource she has been in the past. Her stepfather is a key material resource (money and clothes). Her sisters enable her to imagine different work and educational futures: one left school early and is 'on good money', the other has the kind of adult life Sandra would like in terms of career, personal style and appearance, consumption, home and children. This is the year when Sandra decides her GCSE options, but having done well educationally in the past, she is beginning to 'mess around', failing to hand work in. Sandra is a very attractive young woman, and popular. When we first met her in year 8 she had a relationship with a boy she described as 'the cock of the school'. Now in year 9 she has a boyfriend in her class, who is 'nice', reliable and does not put any sexual pressure on her. She has also recently started a part time job collecting glasses in a local night club until 3–4 am on a Saturday night. She describes the job as fun and experiences no problems with it. She is home by 5 am. At this point her ambition is to go to sports college and train as a PE teacher. In the future she anticipates having a husband and children but first she wants to be a children's holiday rep working abroad.

Second interview, aged 15

Sandra is still living at home and studying at school for her GCSEs. She is with the same boyfriend and the relationship is not yet sexual. She has settled down again as result of action taken by her mother, who offered her money for achievement. Sandra is taking maths a year early. She had good results in her mock exams. Mentoring was introduced in school and she now has a mentor. She has work experience coming up but doesn't know what she might be able to do and will leave it to the school to place her. The night club she was working in closed and her mother got her a summer job cleaning five nights a week (£52 per week). The job was too much when she returned to school and she is currently looking for a new part time job. Her career plans have changed. She now wants to take a year out travelling before going to college. Although she still wants to be a PE teacher, she also wants to have some fun, and time to think about what she really wants to do.

Third interview, aged 16

Sandra is still living at home. Since the last interview she has experienced a 'critical moment' where a drinking binge resulted in her being hospitalised. This coincided with her splitting up with her long term boyfriend, being broken hearted and losing her virginity. Since this episode her parents have exerted greater control over her behaviour. She has done reasonably well in her exams and has looked around for a sports college. Her mother secured her a weekend cleaning job at the old people's home where she works. It's for five hours a day on Saturday and Sunday for which she earns £250 per month. Immediately after the drinking incident they worked together and became close again. Now her mother works different hours so that she can be at home more when Sandra is there. Her mother has also encouraged her to do her training before going travelling, which has now been postponed until after college and teacher training. There is a great deal of reciprocal support within the household: her stepfather gives her a lot of money including 'putting to' for a computer for her. Sandra plans to get her sisters to 'put to' with her to pay for their parents to go away for her mother's fiftieth birthday. She still wants to be a PE teacher but travelling is an even greater desire now.

Fourth interview, aged 18

Sandra is still living at home but will soon be the only child left as her sister is about to move in with her boyfriend. Although she did well in her GCSEs (5 A–C grades), she has decided that she wants to earn immediately and therefore not go on to further and higher education. She secured a job in the hairdressing salon in which her sister already works. Leaving school and starting work as a hairdresser on a modern apprenticeship in a 'posher' area has confirmed Sandra in her desire to stay and 'be local'. She loves her job and has risen to the challenge of being 'posher' as required by the locality she works in and of conversing with a generational mix of clients. Her confidence has increased. At this point Sandra is enjoying herself and having an active social life. She now has an older, 'bad boy' boyfriend whom she phones every day but only sees at weekends (after going out clubbing with her girlfriends). Her mother and stepfather continue to provide Sandra with most material things even though she works. She spends most of her wages on clothes (she loves designer labels), cigarettes and going out. She borrows money from her stepfather but always pays him back at the end of the week. She is not required to do domestic chores but sometimes vacuums the house on her day off (Monday, having spent all Sunday in bed). She plans to carry on as she is until at least her late twenties and then to settle down in the locality. Sandra talks of going to Australia where she has family.

Fifth interview, aged 20

Sandra is still living in the parental home and her sister has moved back after difficulties with her boyfriend. She has now finished her hairdressing training and is working as a junior stylist in the same salon, which her sister now owns. Sandra still loves her job and has no desire to progress to trendier, more glamorous salons. Her week is still very regulated: she works long days and now supplements her income by doing the hair of family and friends most evenings. She pays £10 a week towards her keep but still does no domestic tasks. Her stepfather has clearly been a source of stability in the family. She still borrows from and repays him rather than building up credit card debt. She recently split up with her 'bad boy' boyfriend, who had told her to go and have other relationships. She acted on this advice and his pride was hurt. The desire to travel has returned, but Sandra cannot envisage living away from her mother. She talks again about going to Australia when she's a stylist.

Comment

The question of whether Sandra's story is successful goes to the heart of contradictions that exist within contemporary youth policy. On the one hand, Sandra does not become a pregnant teenager, nor does she fall into drug taking or criminal behaviour, so in terms of agendas concerning social exclusion she is a 'success'. It may be that her jobs (however inappropriate they may seem for one of her age) were both fun and distracting. On the other hand, Sandra does not pursue the path to higher education that she initially anticipated, and from this perspective she might be seen as 'failing'. From a policy position that emphasises the value of community cohesion, Sandra can be seen as a good 'social capitalist': she wants to 'stay local', relies on family networks and engages in reciprocal support with other family members. From the perspective of social mobility, she has failed to 'get out in order to get on'. At a personal level, hairdressing has provided her with money (which helps her feel adult), a skill and a social life. She sees hairdressing as a transferable skill that is 'mobile' and could enable her to work in Australia. Thus hairdressing satisfies her desire for both the serious and the spectacular at this point in her life. Higher education may be something that she reconsiders in the future. It is difficult to judge the significance of the impact of policy interventions such as having learning mentors in schools. It may be that without a mentor Sandra's career trajectory might have been different. The narrative that she provided researchers with appeared to emphasise the importance of her mother's intervention at a critical moment and the resources that the family were able to harness.

Activity 6   Practice proposal

Allow 10 minutes

Outline a single practice or policy intervention that might have supported Sandra. You will need to describe what the intervention is and who might undertake it. For example, it could be something that is shaped by national policy and policy makers, or a much more local intervention led, for example, by voluntary youth workers.

Comment

I thought of two things: the first was a good work experience placement that might have given Sandra an idea of what she might do in the future, but would also have provided her with personal contacts that she could have drawn on. The second was some kind of initiative involving Sandra's mother, who seems to be the most important person in this story in terms of providing advice and resources. Could there have been a way in which mother and daughter could have collaborated on a work placement? Once Sandra left school it was unlikely that she would have had any sustained contact with professionals concerned with her welfare unless she had become unemployed and fallen into the category of NEET. But this does not mean that she would not have had needs, or that policy and practice interventions could not have helped her. Did you come up with a strategy that was not linked to school?

Key points

*   Contemporary government youth policy includes labour market policies, education policies, area based policies and policies aimed at reducing social exclusion.

- When translated into practice there appear to be contradictions in contemporary youth policy that construct the same young person's life as a success and a failure, depending on the policy area.

- By taking a biographical approach over time it is possible to think creatively about opportunities for positive intervention.

Conclusion

In this chapter we have taken a broad approach to exploring young people's school to work transitions. Education is understood as a form of work, and paid work as an essential part of what most young people experience as students. The chapter has emphasised how social class, gender, ethnicity and locality are crucial factors in shaping the overall pattern of employment related transitions.

We have explored young people's experiences of work using the three perspectives laid out in Part 1: cultural, comparative and biographical. From a cultural perspective we have explored how school to work transitions have altered significantly since the 1970s when there was a shortage of labour and working class young people were mostly able to find jobs on leaving school at 16. For the majority, education now is extended and with it dependence on family resources. Depending on their acccss to resources, part time work can be a critical means of survival and/or way of finding new opportunities.

The comparative perspective employed in this chapter enabled us to understand the specificity of youth transitions in the UK and the Irish Republic. These young people face a more flexible labour market and educational system than in the rest of Europe, an advantage for some but a disadvantage for others. We also saw how a cross-cultural perspective can work when looking at labour markets *within* one country. Comparisons between London and Teesside demonstrated the importance of the environment in which young people live to the kind of 'opportunity structures' around them.

The chapter also employed a biographical perspective through which we explored how young people's engagement with work changes over time, and how it forms part of a wider biography. We saw how the demands of education and paid work may compete with each other, as well as competing with the demands of family, and the need for fun and romance. Importantly, we focused on the subjective experience of work including feelings of maturity, competence and pleasure. We also saw how leisure, drug taking and ultimately a criminal career may take the place of a legal 'school to work biography' through the case study of Jason. In the final section we attempted to apply these insights to practice.

References

Albrow, M. (1997) 'Travelling beyond local cultures: socioscapes in a global city' in Eade, J. (ed.) *Living in the Global City: Globalization as a Local Process*, London, Routledge.

Ball, S., Maguire, M. and McRae, S. (2000) 'Space, work and the "New Urban Economies"', *Journal of Youth Studies*, vol. 3, no. 3, pp. 279–300.

Blanden, J., Gregg, P. and Machin, S. (2005) *Intergenerational Mobility in Europe and North America*, report supported by the Sutton Trust, London, London School of Economics.

Bourdieu, P. (1986) 'The forms of capital' in Richardson, J.E. (ed.) *Handbook of Theory of Research for the Sociology of Education*, New York, Greenwood Press.

Bunting, M. (2004a) 'Something has to give', *Guardian*, 6 December.

Bunting, M. (2004b) *Willing Slaves: How the Overwork Culture is Ruling Our Lives*, London, HarperCollins.

Bynner, J. (2001) 'British youth transitions in comparative perspective', *Journal of Youth Studies*, vol. 4, no. 1, pp. 5–24.

Bynner, J., Londra, M. and Jones, G. (2004) *The Impact of Government Policy on Social Exclusion among Young People: A Review of the Literature for the Social Exclusion Unit in the Breaking the Cycle Series*, London, Social Exclusion Unit, Office of the Deputy Prime Minister.

Connor, H., Tyers, C., Modood, T. and Hillage, J. (2004) *Why the Difference? A Closer Look at Higher Education, Minority Ethnic Students and Graduates*, Research Report 552, London, Department for Education and Skills.

DfES (Department for Education and Skills) (2005) *Youth Matters*, Green Paper, London, HMSO.

Du Bois-Reymond, M. and Lopez Blasco, A. (2003) 'Yo-yo transitions and misleading trajectories: towards integrated transition policies for young adults in Europe' in Lopez Blasco, A., McNeish, W. and Walther, A. (eds) *Young People and Contradictions of Inclusion: Towards Integrated Transition Policies in Europe*, Bristol, The Policy Press.

Fenton, S., Bradley, H., West, J., Guy, W. and Devadason, R. (2002) *Winners and Losers in Labour Markets: Young Adults' Employment Trajectories*, Swindon, Economic and Social Research Council.

Furlong, A. and Cartmel, F. (1997) *Young People and Social Change: Individualization and Risk in Late Modernity*, Buckingham, Open University Press.

Hutton, S. and Seavers, J. (2002) *How Young People Use, Understand and Manage Money*, Research Briefing 10, Swindon, ESRC Youth, Citizenship and Social Change Research Programme.

Johnston, L., MacDonald, R., Mason, P., Ridley, L. and Webster, C. (2000) *Snakes and Ladders: Young People, Transitions and Social Exclusion*, Bristol, The Policy Press/ Joseph Rowntree Foundation.

Jones, G. (2005) *Young Adults and the Extension of Economic Dependence*, policy discussion paper, May, London, National Family and Parenting Institute.

Jones, G., O'Sullivan, A. and Rouse, J. (2006 forthcoming) 'The changing role of parents in partnership formation', *Journal of Youth Studies*, vol. 9, no. 4.

Joseph Rowntree Foundation (2000) 'The impact of social exclusion on young people moving into adulthood', *Findings*, October, www.jrf.org.uk/knowledge/findings/socialpolicy/030.asp [accessed 13/04/06].

Joseph Rowntree Foundation (2004) 'Vulnerable young men in fragile labour markets', *Findings*, March, www.jrg.org.uk/knowledge/findings/socialpolicy/344.asp [accessed 13/04/06].

Lindsay, J. (2004) 'Gender and class in the lives of young hairdressers: from serious to spectacular', *Journal of Youth Studies*, vol. 7, no. 3, pp. 259–78.

London South Bank University (2006) *Inventing Adulthoods*, www.sbu.ac.uk/inventingadulthoods [accessed 20/02/06].

MacDonald, R. and Marsh, J. (2001) 'Disconnected youth?', *Journal of Youth Studies*, vol. 4, no. 4, pp. 373–91.

Mizen, P. (2004) *The Changing State of Youth*, Basingstoke, Palgrave.

Modood, T. and Acland, T. (1998) 'Conclusion' in Modood, T. and Acland, T. (eds) *Race and Higher Education*, London, Policy Studies Institute.

Patiniotis, J. and Holdsworth, C. (2005) '"Seize that chance!" Leaving home and transitions to higher education', *Journal of Youth Studies*, vol. 8, no. 1, pp. 81–95.

Pollock, G. (1997) 'Uncertain futures: young people in and out of employment since 1940', *Work, Employment and Society*, vol. 11, no. 4, pp. 615–38.

Raffe, D., Biggart, A., Fairgreave, J. and Howieson, C. (1998) *OECD Thematic Review: The Transition from Initial Education to Working Life*, Edinburgh, Centre for Educational Sociology, University of Edinburgh.

Reay, D. (2005) 'Beyond consciousness?: The psychic landscape of social class', *Sociology*, vol. 39, no. 5, pp. 911–28.

Reay, D., Davis, J., David, M. and Ball, S. (2001) 'Choices of degree or degrees of choice? Class, "race" and the higher education choice process', *Sociology*, vol. 35, no. 4, pp. 855–74.

Skeggs, B. (1997) *Formations of Class and Gender: Becoming Respectable*, London, Sage.

Song, M. (1999) *Helping Out: Children's Labour in Ethnic Businesses*, Philadelphia, Temple University Press.

Vickerstaff, S. (2003) 'Apprenticeship in the "golden age": were youth transitions really smooth and unproblematic back then?', *Work, Employment and Society*, vol. 17, no. 2, pp. 269–87.

Chapter 8

Playing

Mary Jane Kehily

Introduction

In this chapter you will be introduced to the notion of *playing* as a social practice in which young people engage. We will explore the concept of play in young people's lives. This will entail looking at issues of leisure, pleasure and consumption as key sites of social practice that constitute play. Many studies of children and young people use the term 'play' to refer to children's activities, while young people are viewed as engaging in leisure activities and youth subcultures rather than play. This chapter will consider some of the ways in which this split has emerged and discuss some of the implications. It will address the following core questions:

- What is play and how does it feature in young people's lives?
- How are the play activities of young people viewed and understood by adults and professionals who work with them?
- In what ways can young people at play be regarded in a positive or negative light?

Children's play is commonly viewed as benign – imaginative, exploratory and a 'safe' way of dealing with difficult emotions. Play is often regarded as one of the most distinctive features of childhood. Indeed, for many people children's capacity to play, their enthusiasm for playing and the importance attached to being allowed to play define childhood.

The Romantic movement in eighteenth-century Europe fostered the idea of play as essential for children, most famously in Jean-Jacques Rousseau's words, 'Is it nothing to jump, play and run all day? He will never be so busy in his life' (Rousseau, 1979 [1762], p. 107). Building on the Romantic idea that play encourages self expression, educationalists in the West suggested that play was a natural way for children to learn. Child developmentalists in particular attach significance to play as a central way in which children learn the complex skills required to reach adult maturity. From the twentieth century onwards, the consensus among professionals working with children views play as significant and necessary – *the work of childhood*. Play and work may appear to be separate; however, in the lives of children and young people they can become fused and blurred. While Chapter 7 pointed to some of the playful aspects of work, a recurrent theme of this chapter is the *work* involved in play. In this respect the chapters are in dialogue with one another in their exploration of the relationship between work and play. Jean Piaget (1896–1980) (first mentioned in Chapter 5, Subsection 1.1) viewed play as an opportunity for children to practise and consolidate newly emerging skills, in contexts where shortcomings need not have serious consequences, such as when a young child practises building a tower of bricks. One of Piaget's main contributions to understanding children's play has been his attempt to link types of play to the wider process of intellectual development, which he defines in terms of age and cognitive ability (Piaget, 1951).

From a psychoanalytic perspective, play has been characterised as significant for children's emotional development and psychological wellbeing. Building on his psychoanalytic work with adult patients, Sigmund Freud explored the possibility that the inner world of a child's psyche could be revealed through play. Freud believed that children enact difficult and troubling situations during play in order to control them. Freud (1995 [1920]) described his observations of his 18-month-old grandson whose play repeated the same action of throwing an object out of view, accompanied by a long-drawn-out sound which Freud interpreted as an attempt to say the German word *fort*, meaning 'gone'. Later, Freud observed his grandson repeating the game with a cotton reel on a piece of string. The child threw the reel out of his cot until he had lost sight of it, said 'gone' and then pulled the cotton reel back into view. Freud suggested that the game represented the boy's attempt to come to terms with loss and particularly with the absence of his mother. Other psychoanalysts, such as Melanie Klein and Anna Freud, also placed significance on play and incorporated play activities and games into their therapeutic work with children, a practice that continues to be part of the professional's repertoire in many Western settings.

In contrast to the creative and constructive ways in which children's play is cast, young people's play and leisure activities are commonly seen as potentially threatening and disturbing. The notion that young people *need* to play and that this may serve useful functions is rarely indulged. Rather, young people 'at play' can become a source of evidence to indicate that they are unfit for adulthood, a symbol of what is wrong with the neighbourhood, the country or the world. The focus on subcultures in Chapter 1 demonstrates how the idea of youth can be associated with 'moral panics', threat and danger. This chapter considers the role of play and leisure in young people's lives. It explores different examples of young people at play and asks how these activities should be viewed and interpreted. It is possible to suggest that young people's play can be seen as imaginative expressions of late childhood/early adulthood which have many points of continuity with children's play. However, it is also the case that some aspects of young people's leisure activities, such as drug taking and joyriding, can be potentially damaging for young people and those around them.

1 The growth of leisure time for young people

This section will take a brief historical overview of the growth of leisure time and leisure activities for young people. The construction of the 'teenager' is commonly regarded as a Western, post Second World War phenomenon. The 'birth' of the teenager remains part of the mythology of the postwar years, existing as a well-worn cultural narrative of modern times. For the first time, so the story goes, young people found themselves with free time and a disposable income. In the past, young people moved from school to work and from the family home to the marital home, with little time or money for carefree pleasure. The transition from childhood to adulthood was a seemingly straightforward affair, marked by entry into the job market and growing economic independence. But the optimism and relative affluence of the postwar years provided space for something else to emerge: a space in which the conformity of the postwar period gave way to the conflict and change associated with the 1960s. Increased employment opportunities and greater financial independence provided young people with some of the raw materials for 'playing', and the mass production of everyday items such as food, clothes, music, books and magazines added to these. Consider this description of the period from Jonathon Green, UK based writer and activist in the 1960s:

> 'Adolescence' ... meant simply becoming an adult. It was a passage, not a status. 'Teenage' conferred that status; one lingered, indeed, moving on was a regret, and no reward. A word so emblematic of the modern world ... The years between thirteen and twenty had never existed in so totemic and autonomous a way. Now, in the post-war decades, teenage life began its gradual move to centre-stage ...

> ... Once upon a time in the traditional, pre-1950s society, being mature was what mattered; being young was no more than an unfortunate period through which one had to proceed, best left behind as soon as possible ... Those who lived longest had to be the wisest since they had worked out the various ways of best surviving in a world which was, in its essentials, pretty immutable ...

All of which collapsed in the face of a new phenomenon: the consumer society. The old, set in their ways, well aware that life, however much one garlanded it with distractions, was still essentially tedious, were the last people the merchants wished to consider. The young, on the other hand, still firmly of the belief that life was to be lived, that life was fun, that 'new' (like themselves) was what really mattered, were very much to their taste. Suddenly it was the young who 'always know best, and one of their tasks is to repress, educate and control anyone older than themselves'. As for the idea that those who had learned the tricks of survival were the wisest: far from it – it was the young, as yet free from such pragmatic cynicisms, who were the wise. These 'absolute beginners' as MacInnes [1961] christened them, had the real knowledge. 'In consumer culture,' notes Bradbury [1962], 'there are no fathers any more'. The authority/father figure is dead.

(Green, 1999, pp. x, 1–2)

Green describes a period marked by the growth of consumerism and leisure industries to attract and cater for a new market – the teenager. Music, fashions, dance venues and coffee bars proliferated as ways to express being young, living life and having fun. Green presents the preoccupations and pursuits associated with being a teenager as an interesting inversion of the past. The young become the new inheritors of a commodity-orientated world; as consumers with a fresh outlook, they dismiss tradition, embrace new values and embody the emergent spirit of the age. However, Green's commentary extends beyond an iconoclastic celebration of being young and having fun. He suggests that young people in the 1960s invested in disrupting the past in order to create a better future. In his portrayal, young people can be seen to have adopted a politicised and somewhat utopian vision of the future that was dramatically different from the present: a future free from the atomic bomb, men in suits and the restraints of an outmoded era; a future that was premised on ideas of revolutionary change and the building of an 'alternative' society. In Western societies, this period saw the emergence of youth as a cultural phenomenon. Certain preoccupations and pursuits came to be associated with young people as *expressive cultures*. These usually included a combination of protest and rebellion, style and attitude, sex and romance, and having fun. The following activity invites you to look back at your own youth and think about it in these terms.

| Activity 1 | Youth cultures and leisure |

Allow 15 minutes

Look back on your own youth and identify any leisure activities and/or youth cultures you participated in. Did they have a distinctive name or label? What were their particular characteristics: for example, dress, hairstyle, music or behaviour? How old were you at the time of your involvement? If you weren't yourself a member of such a culture, what do you remember of those who were? What do you see as the equivalent cultures that attract young people today?

Comment

The youth cultures available to you as a young person would have depended to a large extent on the period you grew up in and on other factors such as where you grew up, your socio-economic background, your relationship to media forms and the ideas with which you identified at the time. The two youth cultures that were prominent during my teenage years in a small town in Warwickshire were 'mods' and 'rockers', probably a pale, provincial and much diminished version of the subcultures Stanley Cohen (1972) describes in *Folk Devils and Moral Panics* (discussed in Chapter 1). Neither of these appealed; I saw them as a choice between obsessively neat but ugly clothes or an excess of leather and grease. I was more influenced by the legacy of the hippy culture than by youth cultures that offered the possibility of membership in Leamington Spa. By the mid-1970s the idea of being a hippy was on the wane but the hippy ethos was much in evidence. My friends and I were against wars, governments and 'selling out', and for all things 'mind expanding'. We wore long hair, long dresses, lots of velvet and patchouli oil – and having a purple bedroom wall was compulsory. Intimacy was very much in vogue and I recall many tender moments huddled up with friends listening to The Velvet Underground. While I am tempted to make fun of this time in my youth and see it as a resource for humour, I also recognise that identification with a youth culture can be a formative period in an individual's life and highly generative of identities, ideas and perspectives that shape their life.

But what about youth cultures today? If I were young now would I be part of a cultural group and, if so, which one? Well, the appeal of new-age hippies is an obvious one for me – yards of floaty clothing, tie-dying and lots of piercings – I'd be in heaven. But on a less shallow note, the stylised 'what we stand for' of new ageism is also appealing. Environmental protest movements, animal rights activism and the global anti-capitalist demonstrations of recent years owe a great deal to the hippy era and can be seen as a reworking of earlier themes and issues. What can we learn from such reminiscences? One thing I realise from my own reflections is that young people at play are forging values and identifications that may have a life-long impact on them as individuals. In my account there is a tension between leisure as mass consumption and leisure as active, politicised endeavour involving shared peer group values and choices. The playful activities of youth may also be part of a wider generational process involving collectives with deep connections to each other. Being a student, for example, can be transformative at a personal level while also involving individuals in a generational movement as part of a student body. Finally, it is also important to appreciate that the styles and values of young people can become personal resources to be reworked and reconfigured over time.

Key points

- In contrast to children's play, young people's play and leisure activities are frequently seen as potentially threatening.

- The construction of the 'teenager' is commonly viewed as a Western postwar narrative, carrying traces of myth as well as moments of lived experience amid widespread social change.

- Economic change, increased affluence, the growth of consumerism and leisure industries play a part in shaping contemporary notions of youth.

2 Young people at play

This section will focus on different forms of leisure and pleasure in young people's lives. Activity 1 in Section 1 indicates that youth as a category is far from being homogeneous despite shared age; social positioning and matters of class, ethnicity and gender may serve to fragment and differentiate young people's experiences. Young people's leisure activities illustrate some of the different ways in which they construct a sense of identity and create distinctions between themselves and others. In the following extract, writer and broadcaster Ray Gosling describes his experiences as a young person growing up in Nottingham in the 1960s:

> I was a Ted, not in the hard core. I was only a follower, part of a wave, but I was a believer. I was also in a group of working-class grammar-school boys christened the 'grubbies' or 'arty-farties'. We were interested in things of the mind. It was a rather élite set. None of them had Teddy-boy interests and they pooh-poohed me a bit – though we were all moved by James Dean. One of these grubbies, his parents may have been a little deaf, lived in a flat which was unusual with a front room looking on to a main road. The room had a high ceiling. There was a record player

with speakers, and his collection was classical. We used to sit there on the floor, sometimes in darkness, three or four of us grammar grubs and we'd play as loud as we could doom-laden Stravinsky and Vaughan Williams and read Thom Gunn and loving all the big boom. And a feeling that something was going to happen, the same feeling – that we were capable of changing the whole way the world was. Of changing our own life. A new world. If we'd been ten years later I think we would have been listening to the Pink Floyd with heavy drugs and something would have happened. Maybe. Maybe ... And we would just sit there, holding ourselves, posing to ourselves, some of us smoking, and let this huge sound sink into us. Doing nothing else ... but you had the sense that something was ... going to happen.

(Gosling, 1980, pp. 45–6)

Gosling's description of how he spent his leisure time at this point in his life provides us with another layer of understanding to add to the extract from Green in the previous section and my comments about being a teenager in Leamington Spa. Interestingly, Gosling indicates that it was possible to be a member of different youth cultures at the same time. He had allegiances with the Teddy boys and 'grubbies'. These two groups in themselves were not entirely congruent – Teds were associated with the working class, popular culture and living in the moment, while the grubbies appeared to be forging a more elitist sensibility based around classical music and the anticipation of personal and political change. Dual membership for the young Ray, however, made sense for him as a working class grammar school boy. He also suggests, very touchingly, that the important points of connection were *conviction* and *feeling*: you had to be a 'believer' and this produced a shared sense of emotional togetherness between you and your peers. Implicit in Gosling's narrative is the idea that what is possible in the present and the future is contingent on time and place. He suggests that ten years later the scenario may have been different for him and his friends. It would also have been different for boys in other locations outside the UK and, indeed, for other boys in different socio-economic contexts within the UK. As we saw in Chapter 5, in discussions of belonging, identity is shaped by a combination of historical, local and interpersonal dynamics that change over time.

I was struck by the parallel between Gosling's description of listening to music with the grubbies and my own memory of listening to music with friends. In many ways we are describing a similar experience but recounting it in different ways. I am a little embarrassed about owning the feelings of the time and recall them with a mock humour, sending myself up as a hippy clone with pretensions. Gosling, on the other hand, is a little more emotionally honest, more open about capturing his feelings at the time and less embarrassed about describing them and taking responsibility for them. This passing comparison of the two experiences tells us something about the nature of memory. Memories are always reconstituted in the present and are as much a comment on the present as on the past, commonly revealing something about the relationship between the two in the biography of the individual.

Finally, it may be productive to ask what the grubbies were doing when they got together to listen to Stravinsky. Can it be seen as late adolescent play and, if so, with what purpose? An obvious point is that the boys were forming a subgroup within the culture of the grammar school. They gave themselves a name and an identity as boys who were different from the rest. They adopted a certain sensibility based around leisure interests and attitude. Above all, they shared a sense of impending change – the expectation of something about to happen. This could be interpreted in broad terms as a rehearsal for adulthood; grubbies may have been trying out identities available to them as high-achieving young men awaiting their place in the adult world. They could also have been enjoying the sensory pleasure of being together: listening to loud music, reading poetry, feeling excited. In Subsection 2.1 we will consider further examples of boys at play and ask a similar question: what purpose do these activities serve?

2.1 Playing boy

The gendered nature of young people's leisure is evident in a wide range of play and leisure-time activities enjoyed by adults and young people. Rule-governed games such as football, baseball and basketball, while played by girls and women, are commonly seen as boys' games. The popular and highly lucrative world of organised football most notably remains a predominantly male domain, spawning hundreds and thousands of mini football games in which boys around the world aspire to be heroes of 'the beautiful game'. In this subsection we will consider some of the ways in which gender may be constructed through play.

Studies of boys and young men in Western societies point to the significance of hegemonic masculinities (Connell, 1995) as a consensual form of social power through which males achieve and maintain dominance in social relations. (The concept of hegemonic masculinities was first explored in Chapter 4.) An examination of game playing, 'play fighting' and sporting prowess indicates that these forms of 'play' remain a salient feature of intra-male peer groups. Many of these interactions involve boys using language and physicality competitively, where the 'game' becomes an arena for competing masculinities. Ellen Jordan's (1995) study of seven-year-old boys in Australian schools suggests that a 'warrior' discourse informs the fantasy play of most boys. In games drawing on, for example, the adventures of King Arthur, Superman and Ninja Turtles, boys position themselves as heroes of their own text and position others as cowards and 'baddies'. Jordon suggests that boys not capable of positioning themselves within these narratives risk being excluded from peer play. In studies that focus on older boys, the fantasy element may be less evident but the notion of the omnipotent masculine hero remains. The play of adolescent boys commonly involves play fighting and competitive duelling that can be verbal and physical. While appearing playful, studies suggest that young men may be engaged in a considerable amount of **identity work**: social interactions which promote and produce a sense of self. Researchers working with adolescent boys have identified the following forms of play:

- 'back slap and chase' – hitting a boy hard on the back and running before the slap is returned (Back, 1990)

- 'sounding' – the verbal trading of ritualistic insults among African-American boys in the USA; the insults are usually directed against a boy's mother (Labov, 1972)

- 'blowing competitions' – a UK equivalent of the above (Kehily and Nayak, 1997)

- 'dozens' – the ritual exchange of insults among male fraternities in the USA, usually involving sexist jokes (Lyman, 1987)

- 'punch 'n' run' – an intra-male contest to see who can deliver the most blows, usually to the upper arm (Kehily and Nayak, 1997).

Les Back's (1990) study of young people in a youth club setting in the UK comments on these forms of play in the following terms:

> Duelling play is a process whereby young people test out the boundaries of interpersonal relationships ... These exchanges have greater significance than just play for play's sake. They not only mark the boundaries of tolerance within friendships but they also mark those who are included in the peer group – those who are 'alright' – and those who are excluded – 'wallies'.
>
> (Back, 1990, p. 10)

Activity 2   'Box-out' and 'taxing'

Allow 30 minutes   The following extract by Roger Hewitt takes up many of the themes discussed above. It is based on research with 14-year-old boys in a secondary school in south London, and describes a play activity known as 'boxing-out'. As you read the extract make a note of the ways in which boxing-out can be used by boys to construct a particular masculine identity.

Boxing-out

... the practice of boxing (striking) any item out of another player's hand. The boxer could then claim possession either of the object boxed or of an equivalent value in cash. Such a 'box-out' could happen at any time during the school day and anywhere within the school. A boy could be writing in class when suddenly his pen might be boxed out of his hand. The boxer could then call 'box-out', thus making a formal claim to the nature of the event – it was not an accident; it was not merely to be annoying; it was an act within the game ...

The ability to play the game was said to involve a watchfulness, quickness and opportunism that not all could boast ... The taxing part of the game came about whenever a debt incurred through a box-out was not met by a stipulated time ... What this schoolboy culture had created was, therefore, a mechanism in which the simplest basis of social coherence was derived from the collective exploration of individual gain. The game also had an associated imagery that drew upon connotations of the adult world of the street hustler. The basis of the box-out itself was the exploitation of the momentary weakness or inattention of others. Furthermore the severity of the taxing system was based on the principle that the debtor had no choice ... The game thus acted out in shadow form the street level perception of success at the expense of others, the merciless ethic of pawnbroker economics, of victim against victim.

(Hewitt, 1997, pp. 32–3)

Comment

Hewitt notes that the game is played by about half of the boys in the school year group. Among these boys the playing of the game offers scope for group activity and co-operation that is premised on an unbridled form of competitive individualism. Boys who are successful at the game demonstrate a vigilance and opportunism that is entirely motivated by self interest. But why? What is the point of a game that involves constant hassle and the risk of financial penalties? Hewitt goes on to suggest that the game has parallels with trickster figures in different societies. The male figure of the rogue, living on his wits and doing 'what a man's gotta do' informs the rule making and rule breaking of 'box-out' and 'taxing'.

2.2 Playing girl

In contrast to the physicality of young men at play, girls' leisure activities are commonly seen in terms of *sociality* rather than physical activity. Young women's leisure activities are more likely to be cast in terms of fashion and dance rather than the intense rough and tumble of young men's play. Within Western societies, a wide range of feminist researchers over many decades remind us that girls are interested in spending time with each other, talking to each other and supporting one another. In an early study of young women's participation in youth clubs, Angela McRobbie (1978) suggests that the working class girls who attended the youth club formed a clique that was zealously guarded and difficult to access. McRobbie describes them as huddled together in the margins of the youth club, talking and reading magazines, while boys played table-top games in the central space. McRobbie's analysis of emergent femininity in this setting points to the importance of the female friendship group as a site of support and solidarity in young women's lives, acting as a buffer zone in the face of the demands placed on them by a sexist and patriarchal culture. McRobbie argues that, through a shared enjoyment of popular culture and the practice of female friendship, young women prepare for their future roles in the domestic sphere as wives and mothers. From this perspective, young women's leisure activities perform an important preparatory function in enabling working class girls to cope with the exigencies of patriarchal power and subordination.

In her later work, McRobbie (1994) suggests that the relationship between gender practices and social structures have undergone dramatic change since the 1970s. In keeping with other feminist scholars, McRobbie (1994, p. 157) indicates that 'there is now a greater degree of fluidity about what femininity means and how exactly it is anchored in social reality'. McRobbie uses the example of rave culture to illustrate some of the differences in what she terms 'changing modes of femininity'. The following activity invites you to think about these changes in the light of girls' leisure time activities.

Activity 3	Girls and rave culture

Allow 45 minutes

The following extract from McRobbie (1994) focuses on the presence of girls in the rave scene that flourished in the UK and mainland Europe from the mid-1980s to the early 1990s. As a point of contrast to the economic boom of that period and the corporate boast of Thatcherism, rave, in its initial stages, eschewed commercial culture and capitalist ethics. Rave parties were organised by young people themselves and commonly held in disused buildings in out-of-town locations. New technology was used to inform ravers of the 'secret' location and also as a strategy for deflecting police involvement and dispersal. Read the extract and think about it in relation to the description above of McRobbie's earlier work. Then answer the following questions:

- How has the experience of being a girl changed in the period from the 1970s to the mid-1990s?

- How are *changing modes of femininity* reflected in the leisure activities of young women?

- How far can girls' participation in rave culture be seen as an expression of late childhood or early adulthood?

Strip down and sweat
out: girl at rave

Rave dance legitimates pure physical abandon in the company of others without requiring the narrative of sex or romance. The culture is one of childhood, of a pre-sexual, pre-oedipal stage. Dancing provides the rationale for rave ... in rave everything happens within the space of the party.

There is always something arbitrary and almost absurd about the objects or favoured ritualistic practices of subcultural choice ... the sight of rave girls in hot pants and bra tops dancing with a 'dummy' in their mouths, and a whistle round their necks, is as unexpected as it is unprecedented in the visual repertoire of stylish femininity (the rave equivalent perhaps to the laddered fishnet tights and suspenders of punk). This is a drug culture which masquerades its innocence in the language of childhood. Ice lollies help the 'revellers' to chill out or cool down. All three of these objects, the lolly, the dummy and the whistle, also mediate between the drug E and its absorption by the physical body. The symbols and imagery are self-consciously childlike and direct. Primary colours, psychedelic doodles, images taken from familiar advertisements, phrases and tunes lifted from children's TV programmes like *The Magic*

Roundabout, *Sesame Street* and others, all of these along with electronically produced music with a dance-defying beats-per-minute ratio are crafted together creating a rapturous response on the part of the 'revellers'.

... What kind of image of femininity, for example, is being pursued as female ravers strip down and sweat out? Dance is where girls were always found in subcultures. It was their only entitlement. Now in rave it becomes the motivating force for the entire subculture. This gives girls a new-found confidence and a prominence. Bra tops, leggings and trainers provide a basic (aerobic) wardrobe. In rave (and in the club culture with which it often overlaps) girls are highly sexual in their dress and appearance ... The tension in rave for girls comes, it seems, from remaining in control, and at the same time losing themselves in dance and music. Abandon in dance must now, post-AIDS, be balanced by caution and the exercise of control in sex. One solution might lie in cultivating a hypersexual appearance which is, however, symbolically sealed or 'closed off' through the dummy, the whistle, or the ice lolly.

(McRobbie, 1994, pp. 168–9)

Comment

There are striking differences between girls' participation in rave culture and McRobbie's description of young women in the youth club of the 1970s. The girls in the earlier study existed on the fringes of male-dominated space and did not attempt to play a part in the activities on offer at the youth club. They did their own thing on the margins. By contrast, girls at raves have moved from the margins to the centre. Their participation in the party is that of a full-on reveller, like their male counterparts. Separate roles are not designated to boys and girls; rather, there appears to be a common entitlement to the pursuit of pleasure and excitement. McRobbie suggests that this gives young women status and an increased sense of confidence. Within the context of the rave, young women can engage in free and uninhibited expressions of pleasure. McRobbie suggests that the point of tension for girls exists around sexuality. Young women may dress in sexually provocative ways while simultaneously regulating their sexual behaviour.

McRobbie draws a direct comparison between the rave party and childhood. Both states share a love of carefree abandonment, and some of the paraphernalia of childhood, such as dummies, primary colours, lollies and songs from children's television programmes, can be found among the accessories of ravers. But how can we interpret this? Rave can be seen as a counterpoint to high capitalism and the globalisation of youth cultures. Taking over the defunct relics of industrialisation and using them to stage illicit all-night parties can be regarded symbolically as youthful play and youthful protest. McRobbie's analysis speculates that young women may be symbolically sealing themselves off from sexual activity with the self-conscious adornment of childhood effects acting as a protective membrane around the body. However, many other interpretations are possible. These depend on whether young people are positioned as young *adults* or older *children*. Youth researchers have been keen to give young people adult status and see their actions in adult terms. It is also possible to see rave as an extension of childhood and a postponement of adulthood. In the context of the wider culture in which youth transitions to adulthood are becoming extended, non-sequential and uncertain, rave may be a way of immersing oneself in the perpetual present of an in-between state.

Since the demise of rave in the 1990s there has been a resurgence of interest in 'going out' in the traditional sense of a 'night on the town'. Town and city centres across the UK have spawned a range of theme bars, pubs and clubs aimed at young people. Binge drinking and the ensuing social problems associated with excess alcohol consumption have become a feature of nightlife in these locations. Widespread public criticism has censored pubs and clubs for promotional offers encouraging young people to drink cocktails and spirits in greater volumes. Alcohol manufacturers have also been accused of targeting the young with 'alcopops' – sweet-tasting drinks heavily laced with vodka or other spirits and also heavily advertised. The extent to which young people are drinking has given rise to concern among health professionals, while police and local authorities express concern about rising levels of violence and public order offences. We will return to the subject of young people and drinking patterns later in the chapter.

Key points

- The play activities of young people can become important resources for individuals.

- The leisure activities pursued by young people can be seen as gendered, enabling young people to shape or fuse different versions of masculinity and femininity.

- Young people's play develops in dialogue with the wider culture and can be seen as a comment on societal events and practices.

3 Organised sport and structured play

So far we have focused on examples of young people at play that mark out the teenage years and early adulthood as different from other stages in the life course. Some of these examples, such as being a grubbie, can be seen as a celebration of being young and wanting to do things differently. Other examples, such as being a hippy and participating in rave culture, can be interpreted as a form of protest and a comment on adult society. In this section we will focus on football and organised sport as points of continuity with the past and the future. Rather than inspiring rebellion, organised sport commonly exists as a leisure activity for young people that promotes conformity. For many young people, organised sport remains a way of learning about the adult world of rules, teamwork and fair play. Sport also exists as an aspirational form of *work* among young people who dream of an imagined future as a professional footballer or cricketer – the *Roy of the Rovers* hero scoring the winning goal, or the next David Beckham. Like the game playing that has serious intent as a form of identity work, in organised sport the boundaries between work and leisure can also become blurred.

Organised sport can be a way of managing risk and excitement. The rise in popularity of extreme sports such as mountaineering and white-water rafting legitimises a range of legal dangers for young people that can produce a natural 'high'. At the same time, young people's participation in organised sport can regulate and discipline young bodies in ways that meet with adult approval and even praise. Organised sport commonly features as part of the repertoire among professionals who work with young people.

From the sad-looking table tennis set at the local youth club to adventure holidays in foreign parts, organised sport has 'good for you' appeal as a way of communicating with young people that can have a transformative effect on their lives.

3.1 Figurational sociology and sport

In Chapter 5 you were introduced to the work of Norbert Elias and particularly his understanding of social relationships as *relational* and *multi-perspectival*. The notion of figurations was developed by Elias (1978a, 1978b) to explore the relationship between 'individual' and 'society', emphasising forms of interdependency and pluralities of connection and experience. Elias is best known for his theorisation of the 'civilising process' in Western Europe. This thesis suggests that the period from the Middle Ages to the twentieth century saw an improvement in manners and standards of behaviour that became normalised across society as a whole. Individuals were encouraged to exercise control and restraint for their own sake rather than relying on feudal relationships to impose control. Elias associates this change with the development of 'conscience' as a moral arbiter of behaviour, prompting individuals to take responsibility for their own actions. In a parallel development, Elias suggests that violence became more taboo and less socially acceptable than in the past. It is this aspect of his thesis that directly comments on sport.

Elias claims that, over time, pastimes became sports as part of an ongoing political development in which conflict and feudal disputes were replaced by parliamentary systems. Feudal societies were marked by forms of *segmental bonding*, characterised by high levels of violence and strong boundaries to locate insiders and outsiders. Parliamentary systems, by contrast, are shaped by forms of *functional bonding*, exhibiting high levels of control over violence that grows organically out of the interdependencies implicit in complex divisions of labour. In Western societies the transition from segmental to functional bonding is marked by the organisation of less violent and more civilised forms of enjoyment. The 'sportisation' of pastimes involved more organised forms of game playing, the establishment of rules and the presence of a referee to ensure fair play. Elias and other sociologists suggest that eruptions of violence in contemporary sport can be understood as a link to the emotional content of the game in the past. A significant feature of pastimes in the modern era is that they are shared leisure pursuits that can be enjoyed by *everyone*. The popularity and passion attached to football in the UK led to it being known as 'the people's game' – a democratic sport with a huge working class following, providing work, leisure and points of connection for communities. Many local clubs ran youth teams for boys in the area and offered 'apprenticeships' to promising young footballers. In recent years the close relationship between the football club and the local community has been tested and severed in many ways. The following subsection looks at some of the changes and considers the impact on young people.

3.2 The beautiful game

Like other sports, football has undergone dramatic change in the twentieth century. Graham Scambler (2005) cites the role of television as central to the hyper-commodification of contemporary football. The increased commercialisation of the game has called for new levels of professionalism among players and managers and new ways of operating as a club. The business ethic much in evidence in the modern game has weakened the once strong regional ties that existed between football club and fans. While it is generally recognised that the local club is more likely to be global in composition (especially among the Premiership sides), affective affiliations live on in the passion and commitment of supporters – as documented by Nick Hornby in his novel *Fever Pitch* (1992).

For young people, football is likely to carry many different associations: player or 'wannabe' player, fan, marker of regional/national identity, and consumer. Football can provide a link with the past through parents and grandparents, but it can also be a powerful way of shaping an identity in the present. Many football fans draw distinctions between supporters of the same team. Anoop Nayak's (2003) study of white masculinities in the north east of England identified three subgroups of young people in the locality: the Real Geordies, the B-boys and the Charvers. Each group positioned themselves differently in relation to the local football team. The Real Geordies saw themselves as the natural inheritors of the Newcastle brand. As season ticket holders and the sons and daughters of season ticket holders, they regarded themselves as the *true* fans by right. They had (and claimed) pedigree as supporters and as authentic, working class Geordies, members of the labour aristocracy despite widespread de-industrialisation and the absence of skilled labour. The B-boys, by contrast, preferred to play basketball and, although retaining a regional identity to some extent, refused to embrace the nostalgia and authenticity invoked by the Real Geordies. B-boys focused outwards rather than inwards; they looked to the USA to provide them with new ideas, new sporting activities and a different sense of aesthetic to escape the parochialism of a northern city in post-industrial decline. The Charvers can best be described as an underclass. Their relationship to the locality was one of struggle. Charver kids commonly dropped out of school before the age of 16, became involved in criminal activity and lived life on the margins of social exclusion. Unable to afford tickets to football games and unlikely to participate in organised sport, Charvers had a volatile and troubled relationship with the Real Geordies and the B-boys and more generally with authority. While

Charvers may be the obvious recipients of youth based initiatives involving sport, erratic school attendance and the pursuit of 'alternative' careers made them a difficult group to access and work with in a professional capacity. We will return to issues of professional practice later in the chapter.

3.3 Structured play

While organised sport can help young people to learn the rules of adult society, the importance of play as an adult activity in itself is relatively unacknowledged. Celebrations such as New Year's Eve, St Patrick's Day and carnival can be seen as opportunities for adult play. Such festivals provide moments in which normal societal rules are suspended in the pursuit of pleasure. Brazilian carnival in particular serves as an example of a society at play. Carnival exists as an inversion of normal life where the idea of 'normal' is turned on its head and replaced by utopian anarchy in which anything is possible, if only temporarily. Brazilian culture stresses the importance of carnival (*carnaval*) as 'playtime', a time when the fun of childhood innocence and the sex play of adolescence and adulthood can be indulged. Richard G. Parker's (1991) study of sexuality in Brazilian society illustrates these connections:

> Through the notion of play ... the experience of *carnaval* is linked, simultaneously, to the innocent and carefree play of children and to the sexual play of adults ...

> ... Linking the pleasurable experiences of infancy to the erotic pleasures of adulthood, oral symbolism abounds. For young and old alike, the oversized *chupeta* (pacifier) is among the most common *brinquedos* (toys) used during the *carnaval*, and since its original recording in 1937, *Mamãe Eu Quero* ('Mommy I Want'), with all of its possible meanings, has continued as perhaps the most popular of all *carnaval* songs:

> [...]
> Mommy I want,
> Mommy I want,
> Mommy I want to suckle.
> Give me the pacifier,
> Give me the pacifier,
> Give me the pacifier,
> So that the baby won't cry.

> Recreating a world outside of time, a world where wishes and desires can always be satisfied, this emphasis on sucking and suckling breaks down the lines that separate children from adults and the divisions that separate one individual body from another.

(Parker, 1991, p. 143)

Brazilian *carnaval*: an inversion of normal life

Parker's observations suggest that play can be claimed as an important aspect of adults' happiness and wellbeing. The need to indulge in play, to regress to the world of childhood and adolescence and to make emotional demands forms part of the *feel-good* factor of Brazilian carnival. It is also worth thinking about Parker's comments on pacifiers in relation to McRobbie's (1994) discussion of dummies and rave culture in Section 2. McRobbie's claims that young women are seeking refuge in childhood as a protection against sex appears to overlook the sexualised nature of sucking and the sexual symbolism inherent in suckling. More recently, professionals working with young people have taken on the idea of structured play as an aspect of youth work. Alternative therapies such as Indian head massage, reflexology and 'pampering' sessions engage professionals and young people in the joint quest of *feeling good*, relaxing and *letting go*.

Key points

- Organised sport for young people promotes conformity and provides an aspirational form of work for some, particularly young men.

- Organised sport can be seen as a feature of the 'civilising process' in Western Europe.

- Football carries many associations for young people and can be used as a marker of difference and distinction between subgroups in particular localities.

- Structured play points to the significance of play for young people and adults and can be creatively adapted for use in youth work settings.

4 Sex play

Earlier sections of this chapter have considered some of the ways in which masculinity and femininity may be constructed through play. In the case of femininity, McRobbie's example of girls' participation in rave culture focused on sexuality as a point of tension for young women who embraced the rave scene. In this section we will consider sexuality in more detail: we will look at some of the ways in which sexuality is invoked by young people at play.

4.1 Expressing sexuality through fashion

For many young people sexuality occupies a significant place in their lives and can be seen as a resource for play, a site of humour, playfulness and fun. Crossing the boundary between the domains constructed as 'private' and 'public', Anthony Giddens (1993, p. 181) describes sexuality as 'a terrain of fundamental political struggle and also a medium of emancipation'. Brian McNair (2002) expands on this observation by adding that, despite the intimate nature of sexuality, these struggles have taken place in public and are increasingly part of the public domain. McNair's analysis suggests that the post Second World War period in the West has been characterised by the transformation of desire into commodities, witnessed in the increased sexualisation of culture across a range of local and global media. Central to McNair's argument is the role of the media and particularly new media technologies. He suggests that new media technologies have aided the growth of a more commercialised, less regulated and more pluralistic sexual culture, promoting, in his terms, 'a democratisation of desire' (McNair, 2002, p. 11). For McNair, the 'democratisation of desire' describes the present period in which there is popular and widespread access to diverse forms of sexual expression – the availability of pornography through the internet, for example. Simultaneously, there are more ways of being a sexual subject within Western cultures. As an illustration of his argument, McNair documents and discusses the ways in which pornography and homosexuality no longer have subterranean or subordinate status; they now exist as part of mainstream media culture.

If we think about these themes in relation to young people's lives, it is possible to suggest that young people are the new sexual citizens of a democratised and richly diverse sexual culture. But are they? How do young people feel about sexuality and what role does it play in their lives? The following activity invites you to reflect on these ideas.

Activity 4   'With a rebel yell'

Allow 30 minutes

The following extract is taken from an article in the *Guardian* newspaper. It describes some of the changes that have taken place in young women's fashion in Japan over the last three decades. Read the extract and answer the following questions:

- How does sexuality feature in Japanese young women's fashion from the 1980s to the present period?
- How do young women use sexuality and fashion as forms of self expression and what can this tell us about how they feel?

[I]n-your-face sexuality has surely been a hallmark of female expression for decades. Japanese journalist Yo Yohata has railed against this subculture in Sekai magazine. Neo-masochism defines the young, he says, and picks on the 'number one fashion among Japanese youth', Gothi-Loli, which, as the name suggests, is a combination of the Gothic and the Lolita look, as symbolising 'something we call the tendency towards the dark'.

Youth fashion has, certainly, expressed the challenge to convention and tradition as effectively as anything, going through several incarnations. In the 1980s the dominant style was Kawaii, meaning cute and essentially childlike, adorable, innocent and vulnerable. There seemed to be little subversive about it in its early saccharine form. But according to journalist Sharon Kinsella, 'It evolved to a more humorous, kitsch and androgynous style', and in due course became 'the more knowing Chou-Kawaii' (super-cute).

Kogal followed in the early 1990s, defined by knee-length socks, bleached hair, distinct makeup and short school uniform skirts. This had the required effect of appalling older Japanese with its 'impertinent panache, independence, sexuality and self-confidence'.

From the Kogal fashion came subversive graffiti photos taken by and featuring very young women, using basic little cameras. In them, the young women caricature sexy poses and classic beauty, or they subvert femininity altogether by pulling grotesque faces and attempting to look repulsive.

Associate professor Laura Miller, a specialist in Japanese Studies at Loyola University, Chicago, explains the motivation behind this rebellion: 'Japanese girls are constantly bombarded with messages from a beauty industry and the media that exhort them to be feminine and sexy. They are simultaneously admonished at home and at school to be chaste and submissive through confining gender norms.' Through fashion, comics, graffiti and language, they can show their disdain for such contradictory messages, she says.

(Neustatter, 2005, p. 8)

Comment

The extract describes some of the ways in which young women in Japan have used fashion and adornment to express themselves sexually. From the 1980s' 'cute' style to super-cute, Kogal and Gothi-Loli, young women are commenting on sexuality and femininity through what they wear and how they look. In adopting particular styles of dress, young women can play with and subvert normative sex-gender roles and expectations. The

Using fashion and adornment to express sexuality

Kogal style specifically challenged notions of femininity with an assemblage of mischievous and overtly sexual styles. In keeping with other memorable youth styles, it had the added value of outraging the establishment. In the light of McNair's argument on sexuality and new technologies, it is interesting to note that young women themselves were active in promoting the playfully pornographic images of themselves through their use of photography. Interpretations of the Kogal style are couched in terms of youthful rebellion; the young women's style can be understood as a protest against the competing and contradictory demands placed on them by the beauty industry, parents and teachers.

4.2 Playing it straight

Elizabeth Wilson (1985) points out that the combination of oppositional dress and sexuality has long been a feature of rebellion and protest in the West, observing that this tendency can be traced to the beginning of the nineteenth century when dress codes were clearly demarcated, denoting both gender and social class, and were also more strictly adhered to by all members of society. Wilson cites the 1970s as a critical period in the development of gay identities, linked to political activism of the Gay Liberation Front (GLF):

> The GLF ideology was that forms of cross dressing broke down stereotyped gender roles; to wear a skirt and high heels was to give up 'male privilege' ...
>
> Because society had already made their sexuality into a problem, it was perhaps easier for young homosexuals to act out this attack on gender than it would have been for others. The problem with full scale drag still remained: although it caricatured traditional drag, it still often caricatured women as well, and could be offensively sexist.
>
> (Wilson, 1985, pp. 201–2)

Wilson's comments alert us to the ways in which gender and sexuality can be located on the body. Wilson asserts that fashion matters; what you wear can be political, even transgressive. Drag occupies and has become symbolic of the transgressive terrain between male and female. The double-take between looking and being can produce moments of challenge and confusion. More recently, Judith Butler (1990, 1993) has drawn on the example of cross-dressing to illustrate the ways in which gender itself is a 'performance' reliant on the repeated stylisation of the body to give it the appearance of substance. In our discussion in Chapter 4, 'Gender', of research I carried out with Anoop Nayak (Nayak and Kehily, 1996), we explored Butler's notion of bodily performance in relation to the homophobic game playing of young men in school. Nayak's and my ethnographic observations of young men in secondary school in the UK document the many ways in which they engage in homophobic displays. We found that homophobic practices were regarded by teachers and students as 'natural', routine activities in the informal peer group cultures of young men. Many of these enactments were physically performed in extrovert displays that were much repeated during the course of the school day. These included the routine verbal abuse of some students, the continual reference to a gay male stereotype as a source of humour and derision, the incessant bodily practices of making crucifixes and moving away from other males, and endless efforts to 'look big' and appear masculine.

While homosexuality is usually seen by straight culture as a performance encompassing various degrees of camp and effeminacy, we suggested that the young men revealed something of the ways in which heterosexuality can also be seen as performative. We argued that the homophobic displays of young men in school can be viewed as an act of self production, an exhibition of the 'natural' that is ultimately flawed. For many of the young men who engage in these oppressive actions, heterosexual masculinities are consolidated through display. The performance provides a fantasy of masculinity that can be sustained only through repetition, yet always resonates with the echo of uncertainty. We felt that the young men in our research were engaged in an endless struggle with the self, a struggle which affected their lives as well as those around them. The constant need to perform also invokes the hollowness of the masculine ideal, where bodies can only approximate the illusion of substance in fraught exhibitions. From this perspective, the homophobic game playing of young men in school can be interpreted literally as a way of 'playing it straight'.

Key points

- Sexuality occupies a significant place in young people's lives as a resource for play, humour and fun.

- Young people use fashion and adornment to express themselves sexually.

- The bodily expression of sexuality among some young men can give rise to homophobic performances.

5 Consumption

Tim O'Sullivan *et al.* offer the following definition of consumption:

> The act or fact of using up the products or yield of any industry in the support of any process.
>
> Production and consumption are terms borrowed from political economy, and they are now widely used (often uncritically) to describe the parties to and the transactions of communication. Thus meanings, media output, texts and so on are said to be produced and consumed. Media professionals are seen as industrial producers while audiences or readers are seen as the consumers of meaning.
>
> ... Meanings and communication, however, are not consumed as finished products. The consumption of messages, therefore, is simultaneously an act of production of meanings.
>
> (O'Sullivan *et al.*, 1994, p. 244)

In this definition notions of production and consumption have been applied to the world of culture, cultural products and communication. O'Sullivan and his colleagues suggest that we are all consumers of meanings and messages that saturate our everyday cultural worlds. Furthermore, as consumers of messages we also *create* and produce meanings by interpreting them in ways that make sense to us as individuals. In this section we will work with this contemporary understanding of consumption as part of a cultural process involving activity and agency.

The consumption of cultural products is an active process through which individuals make sense of the world around them and define themselves and their place within it.

A very early study of practices of consumption (Veblen, 1970 [1899]) explored the world of the nouveau riche in late nineteenth-century America. Thorstein Veblen's analysis suggests that this group bought products to impress others and were more concerned with issues of taste, display and status than with function or use value. Ideas of taste have been further explored in more recent work by Pierre Bourdieu (1984) who suggests that identities are produced through practices of 'distinction'. Bourdieu argues that culture is concerned with the processes of identification and differentiation that allow individuals to distinguish themselves. Through the practices of consumption, individuals and groups exercise cultural capital, express taste and articulate a sense of identity. Bourdieu uses the concept of 'habitus' to capture a sense of the cultural environment that is structured in terms of taste and distinction, learned in childhood and applied in later life. Viewed from this perspective, the practices of consumption involve young people in participation with a 'habitus' wherein they organise themselves and others into a classificatory system marked by moments of identity and difference. Young people's particular consumption of clothes, music, alcohol and drugs becomes an expression of values and taste that distinguishes them from other young people. However, this emphasis on style is also affected by socio-economic forces. The ability to consume is crucially linked to access to resources – being a postmodern subject within a post-industrial economy remains a difficult if not contradictory position for many young people. The following activity looks at what happens to young people's patterns of consumption in the late modern era when traditional working class jobs are in decline.

Activity 5   'Friday night, Saturday night'

Allow 45 minutes

The following extract is taken from a study of young people's leisure activities in the north east of England. This area of the UK has traditionally been associated with coalmining, steel manufacture and shipbuilding. In the industrial past, working class young people in the region had identities waiting for them as workers in these industries. The research specifically focuses on the 'night out', the significance of going out for young people and the changes in patterns of behaviour since de-industrialisation.

- From your reading of the text, identify why going out is important to young people in the north east.

- How has the meaning of going out changed in post-industrial times?

[W]e argue that the meaning of going out has altered significantly in relation to wider economic and cultural transformations.

... The two [predominant] meanings our overall sample gave to explain what going out means to them were an emotional or subjective characteristic (with 73% saying this), and socialising with friends (62%). Getting drunk or high was [a] distant third (35%), followed by going out to dance or listen to music (25%) and just meeting people (20%). Surprisingly, only 18% gave meeting potential sexual partners as one of the three main reasons why they went out. The same percentage said it was a relief from work or education, while 10% stated they simply wanted to get out of the house.

The idea that the social context and meaning of going out has changed significantly perhaps helps to explain these findings, some of which might contradict common-sense views on this subject. For example, our argument that going out has become less of a rite of passage from youthfulness to adulthood and more a permanent fraternisation ritual, supports the idea that the meaning of nights out for people has shifted away from some of its traditional functions to become more of a permanent way of life in terms of socialising within one's own post-adolescent community. While young people may continue to use nights out to signal their movement into adulthood (i.e. the celebration of one's 18th birthday), evidence of the changing nature of their social condition is reflected by the ritualisation and extension of this activity to include 21st, 25th and even 30th and 40th birthdays!

[...]

In conducting this research we were struck by the importance of friendships and group solidarity on nights out. Many local respondents were willing to undergo debt and conflict with family members and partners in order to go out regularly with their gang on a Friday night. People's recollection of their best night out often revolved around the atmosphere created through going out in the company of a large group of friends. The significance of nights out as a socialising circle was also underlined by the fact that group members were more likely to have met one another in pubs/clubs as they were to have been workmates. Close-knit groups also organised around musical tastes, dance and clothing styles or through student circles. The primary 'raison d'être' of these 'mini-communities' was companionship and fraternisation achieved through an engagement in ritualised activity over extended periods of time.

The importance of explaining the meaning of going out in terms of emotional and subjective categories is also related [to] a changing social context. While going out has always contained an air of excitement, it has been argued that economic uncertainty, rapid social change and the experience of modernity has resulted in the emergence of new 'risk cultures' amongst young people (Beck, 1992). Some of these cultures might be described as the quest for excitement in an unexciting world and the role of the city as a site for this experience may be important here. Many of our respondents used terms like 'getting a buzz', 'experiencing the crack', 'letting your hair down', 'being in with a crowd' to explain the experience of going out. Responses like 'getting out of the house' and 'relief from work and education' also fit into this notion of relieving boredom and monotony.

The role of drink is also connected with the idea of socialising rituals, as well as risk cultures. Drink, as the anthropologist Mary Douglas (1987) reminds us, literally creates community. However, its social significance lies not so much now as a rite of passage into the adult community, but rather as an extended ritual signifying one's membership into an intermediate zone of 'post-adolescence'. Drinking, and increasingly drug use, in this sense becomes less of a transition rite and more a ritual signalling this separate phase of life. As such young adults can continue to engage elements of the rite such as over-indulgence, combine it with symbolic aspects of a kind of risk culture ('live for today' attitude), and ritualise both as a permanent feature of a Friday night 'booze up' or 'getting high'.

(Hollands, 1995, pp. 34, 36)

A night on the town

Comment

Robert Hollands' study highlights the impact of social change on former industrial areas such as the north east of England. In industrial times going out signalled the move into adulthood as a wage earner with money to spend. Sharing a drink with workmates existed as a rite of passage that celebrated a worker identity. The emphasis, in Hollands' terms, was on production; industrial labour enabled an adult identity to be consolidated. In contrast to industrial times, de-industrialisation has produced a significant shift in the social meaning of going out. Hollands suggests that young people now regard themselves as consumers rather than producers. Their identity is shaped by the social practices of consumption rather than the work they do or the money they earn. Hollands' study reverberates with the themes of late modernity. Young people no longer move from youth to adulthood by virtue of their position in the labour market. Rather, they experience a protracted period of extended youth that has become more of a 'permanent way of life'. The fraternity of the workplace seems to have been replaced by the ritualistic bonding of going out drinking with your mates. The importance attached to going out is indicated by many respondents' willingness to incur debt and conflict with family members in order to enjoy the excitement of a Friday night on the town.

Key points

- Consumption involves young people in the exercise of agency and practices of distinction.
- Social change has an impact on young people's practices of consumption.
- Young people's patterns of consumption sometimes incur risk, and this can be a cause for concern.

6 When pleasures become 'problems'

The final section of this chapter will focus on the overlap between young people's leisure activities and perceived social problems. This can be a fine line, as we saw with the Kogal fashion among Japanese young women: offending adult sensibilities can be an aim for many young people or simply a consequence of the pursuit of a particular aesthetic. Chapter 1 discussed the ways in which, historically, youth has been constructed as a problem category. The cyclical nature of 'moral panics' has the effect of promoting and maintaining the idea of youth as troubled and troublesome. However, it is also worth noting that oppositional styles, such as multiple piercing and tattooing, can quickly and easily be assimilated into mainstream culture.

From the perspective of professionals and concerned adults, young people's leisure activities can all too easily tumble into risk taking, 'problem' behaviour and criminality, as indicated by the brief discussion of binge drinking in Subsection 2.2. To explore these themes in more detail we will focus on two examples: so-called 'happy slapping' and joyriding.

6.1 Happy slapping

The following news report from the BBC looks at happy slapping and asks the important question – does it exist or is it a media creation?

> **Does 'happy slapping' exist?**
>
> *Reports suggest a new craze in which young people slap strangers and film the assault on mobile phones is on the increase. But does this trend actually exist or is it the product of media hype?*
>
> A new breed of violence is sweeping the nation, if media reports are to be believed.
>
> 'Happy slapping' is thought to have originated as a craze in south London six months ago, before becoming a nationwide phenomenon, police and anti-bullying organisations have claimed.
>
> Videos of the slaps are reportedly sent to other mobile phones and posted on the internet.
>
> Earlier this week, Surrey Police made an arrest after an 11-year-old child was slapped at a Leatherhead school.
>
> Reports of such violence are becoming increasingly common.
>
> A school in Tonbridge, Kent, warned that a boy's hearing had been damaged by an attack.
>
> Other reported incidents have included a youth punching a woman in the face after approaching her at a bus stop.

Amid mounting concern about the phenomenon, St Martin-in-the-Fields School in Lambeth, south London, has banned pupils from carrying mobile phones to school altogether.

'Pain and humiliation'

Nicola Kerr, who works for children's charity Kidscape, said the trend was difficult for schools to control because pupils were bringing video phones into school.

'Some schools have tried getting the children to hand their phones into their form teachers at the beginning of each day,' she said.

The assaults have prompted an ITV documentary on the subject.

Academic Dr Graham Barnfield, a media lecturer at the University of East London, has blamed television programmes such as Jackass and Dirty Sanchez – which are aired on MTV – for the craze.

[...]

Mr Fawcett [from Victim Support] said the use of mobile phones to film an attack added a new dimension because it meant there was 'no other reason for the assault, such as money or drugs, other than the gratification of inflicting pain'.

(Akwagyiram, 2005)

It appears clear from this account that happy slapping does indeed exist and cannot be attributed to the media. It seems likely that it exists as an elaboration of bullying and mugging behaviour with the added twist that

Happy slapping, communicated by mobile phone

new technologies offer for dissemination and display. The media, of course, still play a role in the reporting and interpretation of events. In keeping with the notion of 'moral panic' discussed in Chapter 1, the presence of young people becomes an object of concern at a general level.

6.2 Joyriding

The following extract from Bea Campbell's *Goliath: Britain's Dangerous Places* (1993) also considers some of the ways in which young people at play can be problematic. Her book focuses on the 1991 riots in UK cities and particularly the activities of young men in these localities. The extract below captures something of the experience of joyriding for young people. In her analysis of the allure of the car chase, Campbell presents joyriding as a masculine appropriation of space. Campbell regards this activity as an assertion of masculinity among young men who have been dispossessed – they have lost their traditional place in the labour market and are no longer the breadwinner and authority figure in the domestic sphere.

> The driver was dressed, the car was ready, the time was right. It was ticking towards eleven o'clock and the fortified police carrier with a dozen officers aboard was pulling out of the Blackbird Leys 'arena' when the hooded driver, known as the Don, revved a stolen two-litre Maestro and skated past the police and a watching crowd at 60 mph. This was the most audacious incident during the Oxford riots, when the Don drove into a square recently cleared by riot police.
>
> This master of joyriding did indeed bring great joy to his audience, who savoured the chagrin of the officers doomed to do nothing but watch man tango with machine. Rude and red, the Maestro was the perfect dancing partner for the mystery man. This was not a star among cars, it had been selected from the common chorus, but it was strong, it could swing. It was utterly recognisable as a mainstream motor – and that made the performance witty as well as piquant. The Don made the car *more* than a Maestro when he tossed it into an immaculate handbrake-turn, hit the horn and swept into the wings, to safety. It was not the car's status, it was the Don's performance that mattered.
>
> [...]
>
> 'That Maestro! In front of all the TV and the riot police! That was to show that we ain't skinning teeth, we're not fucking around, we're doing what we want!' explained the Don.
>
> (Campbell, 1993, pp. 254–5)

Like happy slapping, Campbell's depiction of joyriding is infused with elements of display and performance. Happy slapping and joyriding both rely on an audience to give the event significance as a spectacular and aberrant drama. For happy slappers, the audience is created by the mobile phone and the internet, while joyriding draws its audience from the immediate locale of the neighbourhood in the hope of making regional, if not national, television news. Happy slapping and joyriding exist as daring examples of young people at play, transgressing the norms of acceptable behaviour through the dramaturgical staging of anti-heroic events. The Don's choreographed performance behind the wheel of the Maestro becomes a celebrated moment of defiance within his community, a moment when a working class lad outwits the police, making law and order look and *feel* impotent.

Key points

- Young people's leisure activities can tumble into risk-taking behaviour and criminality.

- New technologies provide a further site for the dissemination and display of 'problem' behaviour.

- Transgressing the norms of acceptable behaviour can involve young people in the dramaturgical staging of anti-heroic events.

Conclusion

This chapter has focused on the idea of *playing* as a social practice for young people. It has explored the concept of play in young people's lives by focusing on leisure, pleasure and consumption as key sites that constitute play. Many discussions in the chapter indicate that play for young people involves *work*. Young people at play are engaged in identity work that is shaping their lives in the present and for the future. Many aspects of this identity work will touch on and be in dialogue with matters of gender, ethnicity, sexuality and socio-economic status. Additionally, play may be used by professionals as a way of working with young people.

Traditionally, organised sport has been a way of communicating with young people, encouraging participation and inciting reflexivity. In recent years, professionals working with young people have increased their repertoire to include alternative therapies, drama and the arts. Potentially, this could provide a legal form of excitement and a more positively life-enhancing stage for the drama of youth than the joyriding arena courted by the Don on the Blackbird Leys estate. The discussion of football indicates that, within families, organised sport can provide a point of continuity with the past or a moment of rupture and change.

Finally, it is worth pointing out that the division between work and play is becoming increasingly blurred for many young people. The drinking cohorts in Hollands' study appear to have substituted consumption for production, in a manoeuvre whereby going out becomes the new *work*. For other young people, such as the ravers and footballers, the world of leisure and organised sport fuses work and play as a site for learning the skills needed to work in that environment in the future. These themes were explored in Chapter 7, 'Working'.

References

Akwagyiram, A. (2005) 'Does "happy slapping" exist?', BBC News, http://news.bbc.co.uk/go/pr/fr/-/1/hi/uk/4539913.stm [accessed 28/03/06].

Back, L. (1990) 'Racist name calling and developing anti racist initiatives in youth work', *Research Paper in Ethnic Relations*, no. 14, Coventry, University of Warwick.

Beck, U. (1992) *Risk Society: Towards a New Modernity*, London, Sage.

Bourdieu, P. (1984) *Distinction: A Social Critique of the Judgement of Taste*, London, Routledge & Kegan Paul.

Bradbury, M. (1962) 'All dressed up and nowhere to go', publisher unknown.

Butler, J. (1990) *Gender Trouble: Feminism and the Subversion of Identity*, New York, Routledge.

Butler, J. (1993) *Bodies that Matter: On the Discursive Limits of 'Sex'*, London, Routledge.

Campbell, B. (1993) *Goliath: Britain's Dangerous Places*, London, Methuen.

Cohen, S. (1972) *Folk Devils and Moral Panics*, London, Paladin.

Connell, R.W. (1995) *Masculinities*, Sydney, Allen & Unwin.

Douglas, M. (1987) *Constructive Drinking*, Cambridge, Cambridge University Press.

Elias, N. (1978a) *What is Sociology?*, London, Hutchinson.

Elias, N. (1978b) *The Civilising Process, Volume 1: The History of Manners*, Oxford, Basil Blackwell.

Freud, S. (1995 [1920]) 'Beyond the pleasure principle' in Strachey, J. (ed.) *The Standard Edition of the Complete Psychological Works of Sigmund Freud*, vol. XVII, London, The Hogarth Press.

Giddens, A. (1993) *The Transformation of Intimacy*, Cambridge, Polity Press.

Gosling, R. (1980) *Personal Copy: A Memoir of the Sixties*, London, Faber & Faber.

Green, J. (1999) *All Dressed Up: The Sixties and the Counterculture*, London, Pimlico.

Hewitt, R. (1997) 'Box-out and taxing' in Johnson, S. and Meinhof, U.H. (eds) *Language and Masculinity*, Oxford, Blackwell.

Hollands, R. (1995) *Friday Night, Saturday Night: Youth Cultural Identification in the Post-industrial City*, Newcastle upon Tyne, University of Newcastle upon Tyne.

Hornby, N. (1992) *Fever Pitch*, London, Gollancz.

Jordon, E. (1995) 'Fighting boys and fantasy play: the construction of masculinity in the early years of school', *Gender and Education*, vol. 7, no. 1, pp. 69–86.

Kehily, M.J. and Nayak, A. (1997) 'Lads and laughter: humour and the production of heterosexual hierarchies', *Gender and Education*, vol. 9, no. 1, pp. 69–87.

Labov, W. (1972) *Language in the Inner City: Studies in the Black English Vernacular*, Philadelphia, PA, University of Pennsylvania Press.

Lyman, P. (1987) 'The fraternal bond as a joking relationship: a case study of the role of sexist jokes in male bonding' in Kimmell, M. (ed.) *Changing Men*, London, Sage.

MacInnes, C. (1961) *Absolute Beginners*, London, MacGibbon & Kee.

McNair, B. (2002) *Striptease Culture: Sex, Media and the Democratisation of Desire*, London, Routledge.

McRobbie, A. (1978) 'Working class girls and the culture of femininity' in Centre for Contemporary Cultural Studies, *Women Take Issue*, London, Hutchinson.

McRobbie, A. (1994) *Postmodernism and Popular Culture*, London, Routledge.

Nayak, A. (2003) *Race, Place and Globalisation: Youth Cultures in a Changing World*, Oxford, Berg.

Nayak, A. and Kehily, M.J. (1996) 'Playing it straight: masculinities, homophobia and schooling', *Journal of Gender Studies*, vol. 5, no. 2, pp. 211–30.

Neustatter, A. (2005) 'With a rebel yell', *Guardian* ('Arts/Features'), 30 May, p. 8.

O'Sullivan, T., Hartley, J., Saunders, D., Montgomery, M. and Fiske, J. (1994) *Key Concepts in Communications and Cultural Studies*, London, Routledge.

Parker, R.G. (1991) *Bodies, Pleasures and Passions: Sexual Culture in Contemporary Brazil*, Boston, MA, Beacon Press.

Piaget, J. (1951) *Play, Dreams and Imitation in Childhood* (trans. C. Gattegno and F.M. Hodgson), London, William Heinemann.

Rousseau, J.J. (1979 [1762]) *Emile or On Education* (trans. A. Bloom), New York, Basic Books.

Scambler, G. (2005) *Sport and Society: History, Power and Culture*, Maidenhead, Open University Press/McGraw-Hill.

Veblen, T. (1970 [1899]) *The Theory of the Leisure Class: An Economic Study of Institutions*, London, Allen & Unwin.

Wilson, E. (1985) *Adorned in Dreams: Fashion and Modernity*, Berkeley and Los Angeles, CA, University of California Press.

Chapter 9

Moving

Heather Montgomery

Introduction

The first three chapters of this book looked at three different ways of understanding young people's lives. Chapter 1 looked at them from a cultural perspective, examining how the category of young people was created and understood. Youth has been characterised by the growing movement towards independence, and as a transition between the social, economic and political dependence of childhood and the autonomy of adulthood. Chapter 2 looked at rites of passage in young people's lives, especially the complex and contested transitions from childhood to adulthood, and the movement from one status to another. Chapter 3 examined the importance of biography in discussing young people's lives, how biographers create narratives around the lives and the critical moments in them. As that chapter made clear, many of these critical moments are in fact a series of processes and stages, so that leaving home, although a defining event in many young people's lives, does not happen overnight but through a series of negotiated stages and movements over time. Yet it is still an important way of marking a boundary between childhood and adulthood, and as such, can be seen as a key moment in young people's biographies. This chapter will return to some of these ideas, taking as its core the role of movement in young people's lives and, in particular, the critical moment of leaving home.

Ideas about movement are central to understanding young people's lives. On the one hand, there are practical problems, for example, 'how do I get home after a late night party when I am too young to drive, but too old to be picked up by my parents?', or indeed for a disabled young person, 'how do I negotiate space in a society which is often unhelpful or ignorant of my needs?' On the other, in the realm of fantasy, the idea of exotic foreign travel and 'seeing the world', which even if never realised, shapes the dreams of many. Writing about the study *Inventing Adulthoods* (London South Bank University, 2006), Rachel Thomson and Rebecca Taylor (2005) looked at different types of movement including driving, travelling and moving away – all of which were central to young people's understandings of themselves, the communities they lived in and their future aspirations.

> From the outset of the study it was clear that mobility (ranging from discussions of travel, transport and migration) was central to the material and symbolic practices through which young people have very different orientations towards mobility – differences that can be ascribed both to the material and cultural characteristics of the environments within which they live and to particularities of family culture and individual social location.
>
> (Thomson and Taylor, 2005, p. 328)

This chapter will explore the final two areas identified in that study, those of moving away and travelling, with particular emphasis on leaving home, whether that be through a forced change in the country of residence (as a refugee, for example), or as a care leaver, or from a more privileged position as a young person making an active choice to travel during a gap year. All three cases are linked theoretically by the idea that, despite very obvious differences, they show that moving is not simply about changing surroundings or individual challenges but is concerned with transitions, the management of these transitions and their social and political implications. Understanding movement means understanding social change. As more young people undergo a period of extended economic dependency on their parents, due in part to the demand for them to participate in further education or training, then young people such as refugees or care leavers become increasingly anomalous and marginalised. In contrast to their peers, they are forced to make accelerated transitions to adulthood, they have no safety net in the form of family, and extended dependency is simply not an option for them. The core questions in this chapter therefore are:

- What effects do moving, and especially leaving home, have on young people?

- Why are young refugees and care leavers particularly vulnerable in these circumstances?

- Why is turning 18 such a significant event?

- What comparisons can be made between young people who choose to take gap years after school and their peers in more vulnerable situations?

Activity 1   Movement

Allow 10 minutes

Think back to your youth. What did moving and/or travel mean to you? Write brief notes on the different types of movement in your life during that period.

Comment

This is clearly a personal activity and it will be hard to generalise from your own experience. However, when I did this, I came up with three distinct issues that summed up moving for me. The first one was the difficulty of getting back home after an evening out, especially late at night. Living somewhere with few transport links meant getting the relatively early last train back to my parents' house, or the unreliable, and frequently rather frightening, night bus. Having my parents come out to meet me would have been unthinkably embarrassing, so one of my abiding memories of my teenage years is running at full pelt across the concourse at Victoria station in London, trying desperately to catch the last train, having left wherever I was a little too late.

Moving to me also meant travelling, partly going on family holidays, but more important than this, the imaginary travelling I did in my head. I dreamed constantly of going away, of travelling to places I had never been to, and also of a future life, living in London or New York. This type of movement, even if it was imaginary, was a source of inspiration to me and defined the sort of person I wanted to be and the kind of life I wished to live. If anyone asked me what I wanted to do after school or university, I would always answer that I wanted to travel.

Finally, moving to me meant being independent for the first time. It meant leaving home, going away to university and establishing myself in a household away from my parents and being my own person. Regardless of the fact that I still went back to my parents in the vacations and still referred to their house as home, I felt I had made a significant transition.

You will have come up with very different forms of movement, of course. My life history reflects a particular white, middle class trajectory which did not include other pertinent issues of movement, some of which will be discussed in this chapter.

There are many different types of movement, each of them linked to much wider issues of class, gender or ethnicity, as well as to wider social, political and economic factors. Movement, in the way someone like me experienced it as a young person, was generally a positive issue, engaged in through choice and reflecting the privileged background I came from. Moving for me was a way of enriching my life and increasing my own social capital. It was also very much a matter of personal choice and personal fulfilment. Generally speaking, I travelled and moved on my own terms, when and where I wanted (late night trains notwithstanding). For many young people, however, movement represents the exact opposite. It is something they are forced into, often unwillingly, and even if they make a positive decision to move, they find it very problematic. Far from being a way of increasing social capital, it becomes a source of marginalisation and social exclusion.

The importance of home has been well documented in sociological studies (Henderson *et al.*, 2007) and it is not surprising that leaving home is a significant step for many young people. The idea of leaving home is inevitably tied up with ideas of movement, of leaving an environment which, while it may not necessarily have lived up to the ideal of a 'haven in a heartless world', is nevertheless familiar. Moving away from that familiarity means re-evaluating and reconstructing ideas about both home and the self. As the authors claim:

> The cycle of exchange and movement influences young people's construct of what home is, and how it might be shaped according to links with other places and other times. Memories, history and emotion (personal, familial and community) all come to play a significant role in the meaning of a home – aspirationally elsewhere (as in a desired return to the homeland), or as a passport to a variety of other locations (through diasporic family connections).
>
> (Henderson *et al.*, 2007, p. 128)

Throughout this book ideas about youth, and indeed adulthood, have been shown to be related to issues of class, race and socio-economic factors, as well as ideas about sexuality and gender. In exploring leaving home and moving, it is also important to keep all these factors in mind, and the three cases under discussion in this chapter show the very real differences between those who have the opportunities and financial and social capital to move out of choice and those who have moving forced on them. As Sheila Henderson *et al.* (2007) have argued, traditional sociological studies of the links between class, social mobility and geographical movement tended to draw sharp distinctions between working class localism (young people tending to stay near their families and socialising within their communities (for example Young and Willmott, 1957) and middle class cosmopolitanism (characterised as being more geographically mobile and socialising with new friends and work colleagues while maintaining links with family). However, this simplistic distinction between working class immobility and middle class mobility is now being questioned (see Thomson and Taylor, 2005; Henderson *et al.*, 2007; Szerszynski and Urry, 2002). Increasing expectations, the globalisation of information and television all mean that it is possible to be cosmopolitan without actual physical movement. Travel and mobility are not necessarily confined to the rich elite; they are as much about states of mind and access to information.

1 Young people and migration

The focus in this chapter is on the social and physical movement involved in leaving home. Many young people move houses or change areas as they grow up. Some also change country and move with or without their parents to another part of the world. The Office for National Statistics does not keep count of migrants by age, but in 2002, 513,000 people migrated into the UK and 359,000 left the country (Office for National Statistics, 2004). These figures suggest that there has been a net inflow of migrants into the UK. Typically, migrants tend to be young and are changing countries for better jobs or lifestyles. The removal of barriers to the movement of labour when the UK joined the EU has meant that any person, wherever they are in the European Union, has the right to live and work in the UK, and vice versa, and although numbers are hard to ascertain, many young people move into and out of the UK to work, live or study. Again, there are few figures to indicate how long people from other EU countries stay in the UK or how long UK nationals live and work abroad, but what is obvious is that young people have a much greater freedom of movement than their parents, and their choices about where to live or work are bounded much less by geography than they were a generation ago. Outside the EU young people are encouraged by some governments to travel on extended holidays and are allowed to apply for special working holiday visas, only available to young people (usually under the age of 26) on the understanding that they will leave at the end of their visa scheme. The UK has reciprocal working visa relationships with many countries, for example Australia and New Zealand, allowing young people to come and live or work in the UK for up to two years. Despite certain criticisms of these schemes, based on the fear that overseas travellers may take jobs that could be done by local people, governments are generally very supportive of such programmes, and in countries such as Australia, an 'OE' (overseas experience) is widely recognised as an important part of a young person's education and a rite of passage that many go through. The Australian government defended its programme of allowing young people in temporarily as follows, arguing that it benefited not only individuals but Australia as a whole:

> Young people from overseas benefit from a working holiday by experiencing the Australian lifestyle and interacting with Australian people in a way that is likely to leave them with a much better understanding and appreciation of Australia than would occur if they travelled here on visitor visas. This contributes to their personal development and can lead to longer term benefits for the Australian community.
>
> Through contact with working holiday makers, Australians, particularly those living in regional areas, are able to gain a better appreciation of other nationalities, languages and cultures. The relationships established and positive impressions gained during a working holiday can help to generate increased tourism interest in Australia and future business and commercial links with other countries. In some cases, it stimulates interest in future migration to Australia.
>
> (Commonwealth of Australia, 1997, p. 48)

Activity 2   Young people and migration

Allow 15 minutes   Write a list of the advantages of migration for (a) individual young people, and (b) the communities and countries to which they travel.

Then do the same for the disadvantages. What are the drawbacks of migration for individuals and the communities in which they come to live?

Comment

As suggested in the quote above, and as will become clearer in the final section of this chapter, on gap years, migration can bring enormous benefits to young people. They can travel, learn about different countries and cultures, learn new languages and different skills. It can also be a rite of passage for them in their transition to adulthood, and an important time of their life in terms of growing up and beginning to be independent. For the communities they come to live in, migration can also be beneficial. Many businesses in the UK, such as those in the catering industry and in agriculture, rely heavily on immigrant labour. As increasing numbers of British young people choose not to do this sort of work, gaps in the labour market have to be filled by other sources and often young migrant workers are happy to take on these sorts of jobs. More generally, young workers pay taxes and contribute to the economy, and socially they bring another dimension to multicultural Britain.

The disadvantages of immigration are generally given more coverage, although, as will be discussed below, it is a certain type of immigrant that is seen as problematic. For some individuals, especially those who for financial or social reasons cannot return home, migration can be a lonely experience. If there are language and cultural barriers, this is likely to be intensified. Some migrants have unrealistic expectations of the opportunities that are on offer to them in the UK, and are disappointed in the reception they receive or the jobs available to them. When migrants are brought in illegally, they may undertake hazardous or illegal jobs that expose them to danger. Furthermore, aware of their status as illegal workers and possibly afraid of the people who had brought them to the UK, they do not go to the police or to any other authorities who could help them. In 2004, 23 Chinese cockle pickers (mostly under the age of 30) drowned in Morecambe Bay. Unaware of the tides and unable to communicate with local people who could have warned them, they were trapped in the bay and drowned.

While such people contribute to the UK's economy by undertaking work that young Britons will not do, they may not become integrated in the UK either economically or socially. Those immigrants whose sole purpose is to find work may not pay taxes, and any money they earn may be sent back to their home country and not spent in the UK. Socially, they may not integrate and they contribute little to the long term future of the country, although, as mentioned above, often they are doing jobs that British workers will not do and therefore they contribute to the economy in this way. It is also important not to overemphasise their lack of integration: they still spend money in the UK and their work contributes to the overall economy. Business needs a ready supply of cheap labour: in California, for example, it is estimated that the state would go bankrupt if it were not for the contribution of illegal workers.

More problematic are the perceptions and assumptions made about some immigrants by the host populations. Often as a result of reports in the media, some migrants, especially those seeking asylum, are vilified and blamed for crime (Valentine and McDonald, 2004). Whether the problem is as severe as some newspapers claim, migration is often viewed as a problem because of this. Furthermore, the majority of young asylum seekers are single young men. When they are placed in detention centres, or when they live in local authority sponsored accommodation, they are more likely to be perceived as a threat than women or families. A study carried out in 2004 by Stonewall (a group which campaigns for equality for all and focuses particularly on prejudice against gays, lesbians and other minorities) reported that 13.6 million people in the UK claimed to be prejudiced against asylum seekers, with many complaining that they were associated with organised crime and 'disrespectful attitudes towards women' (Valentine and McDonald, 2004, p. 12).

It would be misleading to see migration only in terms of the problems it presents. As the Australian government report emphasised, encouraging people to live and work abroad when young can have enormous benefits for the countries concerned as well as for the individuals. Yet this positive attitude is in short supply when it comes to young migrants who are poor or non-English speaking, or who claim asylum. In 2002, the then Home Secretary David Blunkett said of young refugees from Kosovo and Afghanistan:

> If these people are dynamic and well-qualified, and I don't dispute that they are, they should get back home and recreate their countries that we freed from tyranny, whether it be Kosovo or now Afghanistan ...
>
> I have no sympathy whatsoever with young people in their 20s who do not get back home and rebuild their country and their families.
>
> (Quoted in Tempest, 2002)

As with so many statistics about migration, it is difficult to establish numbers of refugees effectively. It is generally estimated that 95 per cent of the world's refugees and displaced persons live in Africa or Asia, and that many more millions are internally displaced (Hart, 2002). The United Nations High Commissioner for Refugees (UNHCR) offers support to 7.7 million refugee children, and in addition the United Nations Relief and Works Agency (UNRWA) looks after 1.5 million Palestinian refugee children. It is also estimated that around 25 million people are internally displaced, and of these between 40 and 50 per cent are likely to be under the age of 18. Although there are special protection measures for young people under the age of 18, there is nothing in place for those between the ages of 18 and 25, even though these young people may be particularly vulnerable to certain types of risk. The UNHCR offers no policy on young people after the age of 18, and many of the national and international treaties designed to protect and provide for children offer no help or support to young people once they have reached this age.

It is difficult to discuss issues concerning young refugees in the UK because of the ways statistics are collected and support is given. There are clear policies and guidelines on how to provide help for the under 18s, but little on support for young refugees who may technically be adults but are still vulnerable. A child under the age of 18 is entitled to a number of additional rights, which recognise his or her particular vulnerability as a child. They are expected to be placed in suitable accommodation (not in a hostel or a bed and breakfast with older youth) and to have access to specialist social workers as well as to education. A young person over the age of 18 has none of these rights. What makes it worse for many young people is that even if they come to the UK when they are under 18, once they reach that age their status abruptly changes and they lose all the privileges that being a child confers on them; they may then be deported or uprooted from their foster home and sent to another part of the country. A particularly acute instance of the effects of this abrupt change in status is given by Dennis:

> Artur arrived as an unaccompanied minor and was placed by social services with an accommodation provider in the Midlands. Although Artur began to settle in, social services did not discuss the future with him and did not visit him after he'd been housed. The rent payments to his landlord by social services ended on Artur's 18th birthday. As a result Artur was evicted on the same day.

(Dennis, 2002, p. 16)

Furthermore, many refugees and asylum seekers either come from countries where their births are not registered, and therefore do not know their exact age, or travel on faked passports or documents, which can lead to them being denied rights on entry to the UK because they are perceived as adults and not entitled to special protection measures. Not surprisingly, many agencies report that the biggest fear of many such young people is the uncertainty of not knowing what will happen to them once they turn 18, whether they will be allowed to stay in the country and where they will be allowed to live.

Key points

- Migration is not necessarily a problem in young people's lives; it can also be a positive force for change and for good.

- Hostile perceptions of migrants make it hard for young people to settle into new communities, especially if they do not speak English and are perceived as different.

2 Unaccompanied minors

Unaccompanied children have been arriving in the UK without their parents for many decades. During the Spanish Civil War (1936–9) 4000 children were given refuge in the UK, and before the Second World War, 10,000 Jewish children were allowed into the UK in the famous Kindertransport programme. A few hundred Hungarian young people came to the UK after the 1956 uprising, and in the 1970s there were unaccompanied children among the Vietnamese boat people, who were settled in the UK as 'quota refugees', their numbers agreed on as part of international resettlement agreements. More recently, war in the former Yugoslavia led to thousands of refugees leaving the country and many separated children being resettled in the UK (Ayotte and Williamson, 2001). In the 1990s young people from over 70 countries came to the UK as unaccompanied minors, although the most significant numerically have been from Kosovo, Afghanistan, Somalia, China, Albania, Turkey, Sierra Leone, Sri Lanka, Romania, Eritrea, Ethiopia, Iraq, Nigeria, Angola and the Democratic Republic of Congo (Ayotte and Williamson, 2001, p. 16). Getting an accurate picture of the numbers of unaccompanied minors is difficult. The Home Office does not keep overall statistics on the number of unaccompanied minors in the UK, only on those who apply for asylum. Between 1992 and 1997 only young people who applied for asylum at their port of entry were included in official statistics. Since 1997 the Home Office has also included in-country applications in its figures. Furthermore, it also defines unaccompanied minors as those with no family members to care for them, so that if a young person is living with a sibling (even if the sibling is also young), they are not classified as a separated child or unaccompanied minor. The figures that do exist, however, suggest a steady rise in the number of young people applying for asylum. In 1992, 190 children applied for asylum, in 1995 there were 603 applications, and from 1999 (after the rules had changed to allow in-country applications to be counted as well) there were 3349 applications for asylum by separated children (45 per cent of these were from Kosovan young people). Other estimates suggest that only 11 per cent of these young people were girls and that 66 per cent were 16 or 17 years old.

The reasons why young people come to the UK as unaccompanied minors are various, but the list of countries that they come from suggests that war and violence are major push factors. In several of these countries young people, especially boys, are in danger of forced recruitment into military or paramilitary groups and flee to escape this. Some have seen their parents killed or imprisoned and fear for their safety in their home country, others fear sexual assault or forced prostitution. The government, through the Home Office and the Immigration and Naturalisation Service, has produced clear guidelines on the treatment of unaccompanied minors in line with both international treaties such as the United Nations Convention on the Rights of the Child (UNCRC) and national legislation such as the Children Act 1989.

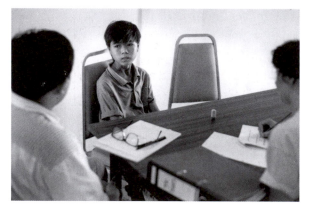

Young refugees are often unaccompanied

Activity 3   Unaccompanied minors

Allow 20 minutes   Read the following case study, which is based on first hand testimony from Jacques, a 17-year-old African boy. Afterwards make notes in answer to the questions below. Give your personal reactions to this case and think about why you have arrived at such viewpoints rather than looking for the 'right' answer or guessing the outcomes of the case.

Based on the information here, how strong is Jacques' case that he is a refugee fleeing because he fears persecution? What decisions do professionals have to make in this case? Why do you think there is a discrepancy between the various agencies? To what extent does it matter whether or not Jacques is under 18?

Ordeal of an unaccompanied minor

Jacques is from an African country. Before coming to the UK, he had been detained after the authorities came looking for his mother, whose religious activities they disapproved of. As a result of what happened to him during this time in prison and subsequently, Jacques had mental health problems before arriving in the UK, for which he took prescribed medication.

He arrived in the UK when he was 16 years old and, after sleeping rough in Croydon over the weekend, he claimed asylum on the first working day after his arrival. His age was disputed from the time of his screening interview and he was referred to the Refugee Council's Children's Panel. Although he was supported by social services, the Home Office did not accept that he was a child.

When his application for asylum was refused, Jacques attended an appeal hearing at the IAA [Immigration Appellate Authority]. Despite the fact that Jacques was being supported by social services, the adjudicator came to the conclusion that Jacques was over 18 because of his physical appearance, and his appeal was dismissed. The negative outcome of his asylum application had a detrimental impact on Jacques' mental health, which deteriorated rapidly and was exacerbated by the fact that his medication had run out. On one occasion, he was unable to report as he was too ill. Despite providing evidence of his illness, Jacques was detained about one month later and after two nights in a police cell, then two at Tinsley House [a removal centre near Gatwick airport], he was transferred to Harmondsworth [another removal centre] where he remained for nearly nine months.

During his time in Harmondsworth, Jacques' mental health deteriorated further still, but rather than being released or hospitalised he was segregated for his own safety and that of other inmates. After around six months in detention, Jacques was revisited by an advisor from the Refugee Council Children's Panel. As a result of this visit, he was moved to the hospital section within Harmondsworth where he remained for a further two and a half months. Eventually his solicitor made an application for bail and Jacques was released and taken back into the care of social services. He is receiving medication for his mental health problems but remains very vulnerable.

(Crawley and Lester, 2005, p. 20)

Comment

There is a great deal that we are not told about Jacques' case, so the question of how strong his claim is, is a very subjective one. However, it is rarely the case that even adjudication panels have the full facts, and many decisions about young asylum seekers are based on assumptions and on how far the panel accepts the young person's version of events. Professionals have to base decisions in these cases on a number of factors, founded on little or contradictory information. The definition of a refugee is a person who,

> owing to a well-founded fear of being persecuted for reasons of race, religion, nationality, membership of a particular social group or political opinion, is outside the country of his nationality and is unable or, owing to such fear, is unwilling to avail himself of the protection of that country.

(United Nations, 1951, Article 1)

However, this is hard to verify externally.

In this case professionals have to decide on two issues: first, whether or not a person is a refugee, that is, whether they have a well founded fear of persecution, and second, whether they are in fact under 18. In both cases there is unlikely to be much in the way of supporting evidence. Many children in African countries have no birth certificates and it is highly likely that Jacques would have entered the country on false papers. As many panels base their assessment on the veracity and honesty of the person claiming refugee status, Jacques is likely to be at a disadvantage. The fact that different professionals will take different positions on his case, and on whether or not he is under 18, underlines the difficulties that such cases present. Neither social services nor the Home Office can prove Jacques' real age and therefore such factors as his physical appearance are considered as a way of deciding how old he is.

It matters very much, therefore, whether or not Jacques is over or under 18. In moral terms perhaps it should not, and it is obvious that he is an extremely vulnerable young person. However, the counter argument to this is that even though he has mental health problems, he is not a UK citizen and therefore there is no duty of care towards him from the UK and the state has no obligation to look after him. This changes, however, if he is deemed to be under 18. If he could still be classified legally as a child, then under the terms of the UNCRC, the UK would have a responsibility to protect him. Indeed, the government's Green Paper *Every Child Matters* (DfES, 2003) (written in the wake of the inquiry into the death of Victoria Climbié, who was a migrant to the UK) acknowledged unaccompanied minors and asylum seekers to be among the most vulnerable young people in the UK. If Jacques was under the age of 18 he would be given special protection and additional rights, he would be suitably housed and; probably given leave to remain at least until he was 18 (although it is possible he would then be deported). Most importantly, he would not be kept at a detention centre, an experience Jacques describes as follows:

> At first I could manage it. But I couldn't sleep and I deteriorated. In detention you never see immigration. You are in limbo ... you never know if they are coming to get you. Every time they gave me removal directions, I would wait for them to come and get me, but they didn't. I didn't know why I was there.
>
> I spent eight months and 24 days [in detention] ... it was the hardest time of my life. It's hell. Prison is better than detention ... In prison, you have rights, not veiled rights. In detention, you have no rights.

(Quoted in Crawley and Lester, 2005, pp. 1, 19)

Although Jacques' story is just one small case study, research into young people and immigration has suggested that the numbers of young people held in detention in disputes over their ages has risen, that a significant proportion of these young people are separated from their families, and that this has a wide range of implications for their mental health, their educational prospects and for more general child protection issues.

There is now a substantial body of research emanating from groups such as the Refugee Council, Save the Children and Barnardo's about the problems faced by young asylum seekers in the UK. Unaccompanied young people may be at particular risk, but all young asylum seekers face obstacles in settling into a new life in the UK, either with or without their families. Research has suggested several areas of concern in which, despite legislation, local authorities are routinely failing to protect and support young people. One of the major difficulties facing young asylum seekers is the lack of provision of education. The 1996 Education Act stipulates that local councils must provide a school place for all children of compulsory school age (5–16 years). For young asylum seekers who are 16 or 17 when they arrive, therefore, there is no compulsory obligation for the council to send them to school, and even though schooling, with its routines and disciplines, may be one of the best ways to enable young refugees to assimilate and become involved in their local area, many of them cannot gain access to it. Providing young people with education would also help alleviate some of the fears of the host communities. As one youth worker put it:

> They are a population of young men who are denied a legitimate income and denied meaningful daytime activity, they are outside of parental and family guidance, it is a problem waiting to happen ... They look menacing in the centre of town in groups but they are not, they are desperately bored.
>
> (Quoted in Stanley, 2001, p. 83)

The Refugee Council conducted a survey of 150 young asylum seekers and found that almost 50 per cent were receiving no education at all in the UK. Even those who were receiving some support were not always given as much access to schooling as they might have liked, settling for one or two days a week instead of going full time. The report highlights one such case:

> Peter was 14 when he arrived as an unaccompanied child from Sierra Leone. He was already fluent in English. After waiting seven months for a place in school, Peter had to take the only place he was offered, which was in a project for children whose behaviour had led to them being educated outside of the usual classroom setting. Peter receives one and a half days' education in key skills and has no prospect of getting qualifications.
>
> (Dennis, 2002, p. 7)

Even when they are formally entitled to go, some young refugees cannot afford bus fares or the price of the uniform and are thus effectively excluded from school.

In areas such as housing, support for young refugees is limited. Councils are required under the Children Act 1989 to provide certain levels of support and help to young asylum seekers, but in practice this help is patchy and does not always fulfil the criteria set out in the Act. Research by the Refugee Council suggests that while, on the whole, foster care arrangements are successful, young people living in unsupported housing have greater problems. They may have to live with adults they do not know, from different cultural or religious backgrounds. Such accommodation may be difficult for them in practical terms in that it may not have cooking facilities and much bed and breakfast and other emergency accommodation offers limited privacy. Few young people in this sort of accommodation are given any help in settling into the community, or with learning how to shop, cook or budget. Councils are also allowed to contract out the care and support of young asylum seekers, which can mean that young people are housed at considerable distances away from areas where they may have friends or access to social workers.

Young asylum seekers have also voiced concerns about racial harassment and stigmatisation by the majority society and also by asylum seekers of other nationalities. Furthermore, the Refugee Council is concerned not only with the levels of financial support available to them, but the fact that this support comes in the form of vouchers rather than cash. These are seen as stigmatising, not all shops will take them and young asylum seekers report feeling self-conscious and unhappy using them. There is also no provision in some councils' budgets for travel or leisure allowances, meaning that some asylum seekers have no money at all for these activities, thus increasing their sense of social exclusion.

Key points

- Unaccompanied minors are particularly vulnerable and often fall through the gaps between policy and practice.
- It is not always possible to know the age of young refugees and if it is decided that they are over 18, they are not entitled to special protection despite their vulnerability.
- Unaccompanied minors face particular problems with education, health and discrimination.

3 Leaving care

Leaving care can be a worrying transition

So far, this chapter has concentrated on young people's involuntary movement across national borders. Young refugees who are forced to move face a series of dramatic and sometimes very traumatic changes over which they have little control. These changes can make them vulnerable and often they do not receive the services they are entitled to by law. It is important to emphasise, however, that some young refugees make the transition extremely successfully and refugees should also be celebrated for the diversity and skills that they bring to the UK. Many are highly motivated, determined to succeed and bring important long term benefits to the UK. To claim that they are vulnerable and sometimes let down by the services provided for them is not to undermine their resilience, but to point out the very great obstacles they must overcome. The same is true for another group of vulnerable young people in the UK: those leaving care. Like young refugees, they too may be resilient and successful (for a discussion of the concept of resilience see Chapter 6, 'Wellbeing'), and go on to manage the transitions they face very successfully. Nevertheless, they too face problems with support and services after the age of 18 and may also be forced to leave their homes abruptly. Although their geographical movement may be more limited, leaving home is also a dramatic change that brings with it many problems similar to those faced by young refugees. Like refugees, these young people have little control over the moves they are forced to make, and movement for them can be stressful and fraught with anxiety.

At any one time thousands of children in the UK will be in care of social services. This form of care can range from being adopted, to being placed on the 'at risk' register while living at home but being supervised by social services, or being taken away from parents and living in residential care or a foster family for a period of days, months or years. Anyone under the age of 18 whose parents do not have the financial, social or emotional facilities to look after them adequately is entitled to the help and support of the local authority's social services department. In cases where children are removed entirely from their parents' care (or do not have parents who can care for them), social services must find new homes for them. In the past many such children were put in institutional care, run either by local councils or by charities such as Barnardo's (see Evans (2007) for a fuller discussion of institutional care for young people). There has been a great deal of research indicating how damaging this sort of care is for children and today the most commonly accepted viewpoint is that institutional care should be the last option for children. Instead, social workers aim to place young people in conditions that closely mirror family life, and in the UK two thirds of children in local authority care are in foster homes rather than institutional care (Brindle, 2001). Nevertheless, thousands of children each year are placed in local authority homes, and each year approximately 8000 young people leave the care of local authorities (Biehal and Wade, 1999). In 2000 the Office of the Deputy Prime Minister claimed that 'young people who have been in local authority care are likely to be more profoundly and widely disadvantaged than young people without a care background' (Office of the Deputy Prime Minister, 2000).

Although many young people who leave care successfully make the transition to independence, they face many problems. Research has shown that they have a lower level of educational attainment than those without a care background. Their education is likely to have been disrupted by being taken into care as well as by the events which led them to be taken into care. Frequent changes of schooling once in care, stigmatising by peers, low aspirations on the part of care givers, worries over family and a lack of motivation and confidence have all been shown to be factors leading to low educational outcomes for young people leaving care (Allen, 2003). They are also more likely to be unemployed and many have difficulty finding a job and holding on to it once they have it. Former care leavers are also disproportionately represented in the prison population. Lack of support and encouragement to stay in work is especially difficult and can lead to further problems such as relationship breakdown or substance abuse. Lack of qualifications often means that young people leaving care take badly paid, menial jobs which do not provide them with enough money to live on (Allen, 2003). Care leavers are more likely to be homeless: one study in London found that up to one third of rough sleepers had been in care, often for much of their childhood. They are also more likely to live on or near the poverty line than their peers (Allen, 2003).

As with the case of young asylum seekers, there is legislation in place to protect the rights of these vulnerable young people, and yet, as with asylum seekers, there are also gaps in the practice, meaning that many young people do not get the support they need. An arbitrary cut-off age of 18 also causes problems for these young people, who are expected to grow up overnight and move from being in care to independence very quickly. Increasingly, local authorities are realising that making young people leave care at 18 when they are not fully equipped with life skills is inappropriate and leads to serious results for both the young people and society. Such accelerated transitions, undertaken without the help of families or social workers, have severe consequences. Therefore many local authorities have now implemented 'pathways' out of care whereby young people continue to receive help until their mid-twenties from a named social worker.

For young people leaving care, the gaps in provision remain large. Although they should ideally receive continuity of care and have a named social worker, often this is not possible as staff leave or change jobs. Social services departments are also very stretched and may have a number of vulnerable young people to care for, and often those in care, like young asylum seekers, are not given top priority. There are groups to help young people make this transition which have been effective in bringing the concerns of young people leaving care into the public and policy arena. What is apparent, though, is the gap between policy and practice; what is in place in the legislation for these young people and what actually happens. Increasingly, young people coming out of care are beginning to challenge the services and provision offered to them. One such group is called RAGE, which stands for Rights, Advisory, Group Experts (but whose acronym reflects the members' opinion of their treatment by social workers). They are a small group of young people who were raised in care who set out to discover the extent to which those who had left care were satisfied with their experiences. They found that the majority were in debt, over 44 per cent were not satisfied with where they were living, 46 per cent felt their education had been harmed by being in care and 39 per cent said that the quality of care they received was 'very poor', while only 7 per cent rated it as good (Dyer and Parker, 2005).

Activity 4   Leaving care and homelessness

Allow 1 hour   The physical movement away from care is often very hard for young people. There is a very high correlation between young people leaving care and becoming homeless or living in short term, substandard accommodation. Read through the following account and make notes on what you think are the links between homelessness and leaving care. Also think about the difference between voluntary and involuntary movement and how useful such a distinction is in discussing the movement between leaving care and homelessness.

Problems of living independently

If we focus solely on care leavers' entry into the housing market, their difficulties in this arena are evident in the high degree of mobility in their early housing careers and in high rates of homelessness.

Although some mobility is normal for this age group and may be positive, some care leavers make repeated moves for negative reasons. Within two years of leaving care, over half of the young people in our study had made two or more moves and a sixth had made five or more moves. Some moves were made when better accommodation became available, or when young people moved from intermediate households into independent tenancies. Some benefited from the support available in hostels or supported lodgings, while many of those in independent households managed reasonably well, especially if they received professional support. However, a number found it hard to budget, to cope with their new-found autonomy and isolation, and the lack of structure and day-to-day support at such an early age. Problems such as these led some young people to make repeated moves because they felt unable to manage tenancies of their own, found it hard to cope even in supported accommodation, or because they were fleeing violence and harassment. Instability in one area of young people's lives sometimes undermined positive developments in other areas, as moving often brought with it the disruption of further education, training or work, leading to a downward spiral.

For some the early transition to the housing market rapidly led to homelessness. Fifteen per cent of our survey sample had experienced homelessness within nine months of leaving care and over a fifth of those in our interview sample were homeless at some point within two years of leaving care, some of them on more than one occasion (Biehal et al., 1995) ...

Young people with a care background appear to be at higher risk of sleeping rough (Anderson et al., 1993; Strathdee and Johnson, 1994; Markey, 1998). Among those in our interview sample who became homeless, two-thirds slept rough or stayed in hostels for the homeless, while another study of homeless care leavers found the vast majority had slept rough and had used emergency hostels (Kirby, 1994). These findings suggest that young people with a care background are likely to have fewer support networks available to them in times of crisis.

For those who leave care at 16 or over, there is some indication of a relationship between an early entry to the housing market and patterns of homelessness. Our survey found a significant association between leaving care early, at only 16 or 17, and subsequent homelessness. This may be related to the manner in which younger care leavers left their final placements. All but one of those in our interview sample who left care as the result of a placement breakdown or other crisis did so before the age of 18. The crisis-driven manner in which they left precipitated them rapidly into independent living, often in emergency accommodation in bed and breakfast hotels, bedsits or board and lodgings, and most of these arrangements were short lived. Leaving care at only 16 or 17, particularly if this happens in an unplanned way, clearly increases the risk of homelessness for care leavers.

We also found a significant association between a high mobility while looked after and subsequent homelessness. For those who made numerous moves between residential and foster placements, preparation for leaving care may have been inadequate if they were not settled long enough to receive it. Young people who are looked after may also experience instability through persistently going missing from care placements. Recent research has shown that going missing from residential care is a serious problem for local authorities and that among those young people who do go missing, a large minority do so repeatedly (Wade et al., 1998) ... Persistently going missing from care is associated with involvement in crime and substance misuse and with truancy and exclusion from school (Wade *et al.*, 1998), all of which may make it particularly difficult for this group of young people subsequently to find employment and adapt to independent living at an early age. If young people are often missing from their care placements, then attempts to equip them with the kinds of practical and social skills they will need and to make effective plans for their futures may be impossible to achieve.

A consideration of the routes into homelessness for the young people in our interview sample who experienced it suggests that many were ill-prepared or unready for independent living. Some did not have the skills to sustain a tenancy or found it hard to cope with the loss of structure in their lives, which either led to their eviction or to their leaving their accommodation on impulse. Others had stayed temporarily with their families, but relationships had rapidly broken down. Other studies have also found that some care leavers became homeless after an initial return to the family home and that for those who return home, aftercare support is less consistent than for those moving to other accommodation (Kirby, 1994; Social Services Inspectorate, 1997).

It should therefore be clear that accelerated transitions – particularly where they occur in an unplanned, crisis-driven manner – bring with them a risk of homelessness at an early age. Those care leavers who became homeless are likely to have had unsettled care careers involving multiple placement moves or a history of going missing and, as a result, are ill-prepared for independence. In addition, homelessness among those with a care background must be understood in a wider policy context. Policy changes in the fields of housing and social security have reduced the availability of affordable housing for single people and increased the risk of poverty for unemployed young people, both of which have serious consequences for those without access to family support (McCluskey, 1994).

(Biehal and Wade, 1999, pp. 84–7)

Comment

Research on young people leaving care and homelessness shows a very high correlation between having been looked after by the local authority and an increased likelihood of becoming homeless later. Although legislation is in place to help these young people, clearly there are gaps in the provision of care for them and it is apparent that they need help and support long after they have left care or reached the age of 18. Although local authorities now have a statutory duty to support those aged between 18 and 21, many formerly looked after children will need support long after this because of the disruption in their lives.

The issue of homelessness also shows up the difficulties of making distinctions between forced and unforced movement in young people's lives. While it may be argued that young people do generally move a lot between the ages of 18 and 25, and may choose to do so, if they do not have the educational, social or financial resources to make choices, then their changes of residence can be seen as enforced and problematic.

Both young refugees and young people leaving care can be seen in terms of social exclusion and as lacking in social capital (this term was introduced in Chapter 6). They have neither the material resources nor the social resources of their peers. Consequently, they cannot rely on parents or family members to house them if they become homeless, they cannot rely on handouts from their families and they lack the education and skills that might enable them to overcome their backgrounds. Some academics have referred to asylum seekers as the 'imported underclass' (Chile, 2002), suggesting that their poverty is not simply material but also structural, and not just about lack of money but about existing in a culture of poverty which is unable to connect to the mainstream. Young people leaving care can be seen as similarly excluded and disadvantaged, and while much of the same legislation applies to both young people leaving care and the young homeless, it is often inadequate in practice. Independence for both groups is a traumatic process of accelerated transition whereby they are pushed into leaving home without necessarily being equipped with the right skills, whether they be social, financial or emotional, to cope with their new environment. Unlike the young people discussed in the next section, they do not have the safety net of home to fall back on if things go wrong. As one young care leaver has written:

> After growing up moving from family to family, school to school and social worker to social worker the most exciting thing for me was the thought of getting my own tenancy – having my own place for the first time. And if it wasn't for the support from nice people around me and many second chances I would not have managed with the money and the forms and the cooking type of stuff. It's taken me nearly 4 years of living alone to get things right but I still notice that my mate's family still give him loads of emotional and financial support even though he is 22 like me.
>
> (Quoted by A National Voice, 2005)

Key points

- Young people leaving care face many of the same problems as young refugees.

- They are more likely than their peers to be homeless, to be in prison and to have worse educational attainment.

- In order to overcome many of these problems, most local authorities have pathways out of care which continue until a young person is in their mid-twenties. These are designed to ensure support for vulnerable young people and recognise the particular problems they face.

4   Gap years

Gap year experiences

The previous sections of this chapter have considered involuntary movement in young people's lives, looking at how in two different circumstances – leaving care and becoming a refugee – physical movement brings with it an accelerated transition to adulthood. While some young people leaving care and some young refugees arriving in a new country negotiate the transition smoothly, they face greater obstacles than other young people, and as the previous sections have suggested, policy which is in place to protect them is sometimes inadequate. The critical moment in their biography is fraught with danger and the possibility of social exclusion, and economic, political and social marginalisation.

The final section of this chapter looks at a very different form of critical moment, one which is also linked to social mobility but in much more positive ways. It is linked to the other sections, however, because a study of gap years shows how a young person's social, political and economic resources have an important impact on their experiences of movement and leaving home. Leaving home is not necessarily negative, but it is transformational. If you think back to the first activity of the chapter, you were asked to think about the role of movement in your own life and your understanding of it as a young person. The example given and discussed was of a privileged middle class, white person for whom movement, travel and leaving home were positive steps which enhanced social mobility and cultural capital. Travel and movement were voluntary activities undertaken through choice and were seen as beneficial and a way of increasing knowledge and education. This section will discuss this in more detail, in particular the role of the gap year in many young people's lives and how it is now seen as an important step in the transition between childhood and adulthood and leaving home for the first time.

Foreign travel is now a common part of many young people's experiences. What was once the preserve of the very wealthy has become an achievable aspiration for many. The idea of travel and having a holiday is important to many young people, and indeed in 2000 the Joseph Rowntree Foundation used the lack of a holiday at least once a year as a marker of social deprivation and exclusion (Gordon *et al.*, 2000). A gap year, however, tends to be more than a holiday. It is an extended period of travel or work, usually undertaken by those between the ages of 16 and 25, which can be defined as 'any period of time between 3 and 24 months which an individual takes "out" from formal education, training or the workplace, and where the time out sits in the context of a longer career trajectory' (Jones, 2003, p. 25). For many young people in the UK, this year is a period without exams or assessment, taken as a gap between the structure and discipline of school and before university. In many ways it fits into the classic rites of passage model in which a young person leaves the familiar world behind, removes themselves from the community and then returns with a different, more adult, status. As importantly, it is also for many people the first extended period away from home in which they have to be self sufficient and self reliant, and as such it provides an easier transition into university life, where they will have to live more independently. It can thus be seen as a critical moment in young people's biographies, when they learn independence and make the symbolic break between being a dependent child at home and a competent adult in the outside world.

The idea of a gap year is a relatively recent phenomenon with a large rise in numbers of students taking them since the late 1980s and early 1990s. Some estimates suggest that at least 50,000 young people each year take a gap year but this figure could be as high as 200,000 (Jones, 2003). Gap years can take many forms and not all of them involve travel to exotic places, although this is what the media stereotype often portrays. The introduction of university top-up fees in 2005 means that for some young people a gap year is a way of saving up in order to go to university and they use their time to live at home, taking relatively menial jobs in order to save money. Others use it as a chance to 'temp' or volunteer in the sort of industry in which they wish to pursue a career. However, for most people the idea of a gap year does involve leaving home and travelling, particularly overseas. Again, this can take many forms, from an extended holiday to a structured work placement overseas or voluntary work in a developing country.

Activity 6	The gap year traveller

Allow 10 minutes

William Sutcliffe published the novel *Are You Experienced?* in 1999 which dealt with backpackers on their gap years. Below is a quote from the book in which Dave (who is backpacking around India) gets talking to a journalist at a train station. The journalist sums up the experiences of gap year students in a cynical, but not unrecognisable, way. Read the quote and write your reaction to it. To what extent do you agree with the journalist? Do you think he is being unfair?

> University of Life. Year one: Advanced Adventure Playgrounds. Part One Exam: go to the Third World and survive. No revision, interest, intellect or sensitivity required ... it's not hippies on a spiritual mission who come here any more, just morons on a poverty-tourism adventure holiday ... going to India isn't an act of rebellion these days, it's actually a form of conformity for ambitious middle-class kids who want to be able to put something on their CV that shows a bit of initiative ... Your kind of travel is all about low horizons dressed up as open-mindedness. You have no interest in India, and no sensitivity for the problems this country is trying to face up to. You also treat Indians with a mixture of contempt and suspicion which is reminiscent of the Victorian colonials. Your presence here, in my opinion, is offensive.
>
> (Sutcliffe, 1999, pp. 138, 140)

Comment

The view presented here is obviously extreme and yet it is one that many people will identify with. The perception of a gap year student, especially one travelling abroad, is generally one of self indulgence and middle class privilege. How far you agree with this will probably depend on your personal experience, whether you or your friends or family took a gap year, what you did and how you feel it benefited you (or not). Certainly some groups of young people are over-represented among those who take a gap year, and generally the idea of gap year students is quite negative.

The stereotype of a gap year student is of a white, middle class, privately educated young person being funded by their parents to enjoy a year away from responsibilities. The gap year can be seen as a direct descendant of the eighteenth-century 'grand tour', an essential part of the education of every young gentleman. Typically, visiting Paris, Rome, Venice and Florence, British young men would spend the years between leaving school and coming into their inheritance travelling around Europe, ostensibly seeing the sights of these cities, improving their languages and their knowledge of high culture and art. The Victorian travel writer Thomas Nugent describes the grand tour as 'a custom so visibly tending to enrich the mind with knowledge, to rectify the judgment, to remove the prejudices of education, to compose the outward manners, and in a word form the complete gentleman' (quoted in Buzard, 1993, p. 98). It was also an opportunity for young men to 'sow their wild oats' away from England, to womanise, gamble, drink and generally misbehave in places where they could bring no shame to their families back home. It also represented the commodification of culture by the wealthy as something to be defined, visited and collected, so that certain cities and certain monuments were defined as the epitome of good taste that everyone of the right social background should enjoy and recognise as important. A gap year, although by no means still the preserve of the wealthy, does share some similar features. There are certain areas of the world which are very much on the tour (South East Asia, India and Australia), while almost no one travels round the UK during their gap year. The type of gap year during which a young person travels to exotic parts of the world, to broaden their mind and learn about a new culture, is often extremely useful and life changing for the individual concerned. It can also be seen, however, as another form of middle class advantage, an option for those with the money which excludes those who do not have enough.

Research on gap years is limited and remains somewhat speculative. Nevertheless, it has shown that gap year participants are likely to have the following characteristics:

- predominantly white with few ethnic minority participants
- women outnumber men
- from relatively affluent middle class backgrounds
- over-representation of private and grammar school backgrounds
- under-representation of disabilities.

(Jones, 2003, pp. 49–50)

There is a suggestion, however, that the kinds of people taking a gap year are changing and, in particular, the number of young people from non-selective state schools is increasing. Nevertheless, certain groups remain under-represented. Not surprisingly, those from the poorest socio-economic backgrounds are the least likely to take a gap year. Fear of debt, lack of knowledge of the choices available to them, and lack of confidence in career opportunities after college are all likely to deter these young people from taking time out. They are also the group whose participation in

university is the lowest, suggesting that they are likely to go straight from
school to employment out of financial insecurity. Black and ethnic minority
young people are also less likely than their white counterparts to take a gap
year, and in the case of black young people, are also less likely to go on to
university than their white or Asian peers.

There is as yet limited research on the benefits and drawbacks of taking a
gap year and its importance as a rite of passage or critical moment in young
people's transitions to adulthood. Some academic studies of travel or youth
culture mention gap years, but specific information on them and young
people's experiences of them have only recently started to be published.
Anecdotal evidence suggests, however, that having a gap year has
important benefits for some young people. Many claim it as a critical
moment in their lives and see it as the start of independence. Many parents
(while worrying about the dangers and the expense) also view gap years
positively, both in terms of their children's personal development, and also
because, as suggested above, they see it as a way of broadening their
education and increasing their cultural capital.

There are now a multitude of companies which offer to organise gap years
for young people, either in community placements in the UK or abroad,
sometimes combining work and holiday so that, for example, a young
person may travel to Thailand for six months to work on a conservation
project for two months and travel the rest of the time. Other organisations,
such as Raleigh International, are set up specifically to place young people
in projects in the non-industrialised world, and young people are expected
to raise money through sponsorship and/or working in order to fund
themselves during this time. All of these companies emphasise the positive
aspects of a gap year and promise personal development. Andrew Jones
(2003) lists some of the benefits they claim to offer:

- improved educational performance
- formation and development of educational and career choices
- reduced likelihood of future 'drop out' from education, training or
  employment
- improved 'employability' and career opportunities
- non-academic skills and qualifications
- social capital
- life skills
- developing social values.

Such claims are difficult to verify and, of course, even if a young person has
a miserable time on an ill thought out and unstructured project with little
support, it can still be claimed that they have learned valuable life skills
from it. In 2003 the Department for Education and Skills commissioned a

report into gap years in which the author, Andrew Jones, interviewed 200 students about their experiences of a gap year and looked at the social and economic characteristics of young people who took gap years. He examined the claims listed above and found some evidence to support each of them. The lack of longitudinal research, however, means that it is difficult to draw any conclusions about future employability or reduced likelihood of drop out. It is also possible that those young people who were the most organised and used their gap year to improve their CV are also those motivated students who would do well regardless of whether they had a gap year. There needs to be more research on whether gap years benefit a small minority or the advantages are spread across the social classes.

Jones's findings emphasised the benefits of certain types of gap years, especially in terms of career prospects later on. He found that employers valued structured gap years where young people did voluntary or paid work and learned valuable work skills. It is harder to make generalisations about the benefits for young people themselves. For those going on to study languages at university, time spent in the country of choice learning the language brought useful skills which were likely to enhance their university career. For those on voluntary projects overseas or at home, there was the personal satisfaction of being more involved in the community and gaining useful skills, and there was some evidence that young people who had undertaken voluntary work remained more committed to the idea of community participation at later stages in their lives. Even for those who simply travelled there were positive benefits which came from appreciating different experiences and different lifestyles. Tom Griffith, one of the founders of the website www.gapyear.com, writes:

> There's this dinosaur opinion that you've got to do some good volunteering, yet there's a lot of people who actually just want to go off and see the world. I did some of that during my year off and I matured; I grew up. Some people say that's a wasted year: it's not; it's a growing year.

(Quoted in Curtis, 2004)

The opportunity to spend a year 'growing' needs to be seen in context, however. It is doubtful that it is an option for the less privileged or those who cannot afford a year without working.

Despite the benefits, the evidence on the impact of gap years is not uniformly positive. Many of the companies that organise them charge steeply for the service. It can also be argued that if the purpose of a gap year is for young people to gain skills, knowledge and independence, then simply paying money for what amounts to a package tour with some voluntary work attached does not fulfil its purpose. More problematic is the question of the relationship between the young person and the community they are working or travelling in, especially if this community is poor.

Some of the academic literature on tourism suggests that backpacker and gap year tourism is invasive and harmful:

> One criticism of backpackers is that, in ensuring that their funds will last for the duration of their travels, they become excessively concerned with bargain hunting ... They may regard haggling as a game, to the extent that they exploit artisans and traders so desperate for a sale that they accept unreasonably low prices for their products (Bradt, 1995). According to Riley 'Status among travelers is closely tied to living cheaply and obtaining the best "bargains" which serve as indicators that one is an experienced traveler' (Riley, 1988, p. 320).
>
> (Schevyens, 2002, p. 147)

Not only do gap year travellers value cheapness, they also value 'authenticity' and the excitement of travelling to places not usually frequented by others. Some authors have argued that this is, in fact, more invasive than mass package tourism. In resorts, tourists are catered for and the local people generally know what to expect of them. In so-called unspoilt places, backpackers may put a strain on local communities unused to foreigners. Other criticisms of backpackers concern their behaviour and flouting of local norms and customs. If gap year travelling can be understood as a rite of passage, then the time abroad is a liminal state (recall the discussion of the term 'liminal' in Chapter 2) in which young people have a freedom to act outside the social constraints and norms of their home society. This, however, may bring them into conflict with local customs and there are complaints from many communities about the inappropriate and provocative dress of Western young people, their use of drugs and alcohol, their casual sexual encounters and their ignorance of local religious or cultural norms, all of which can give offence to the local people. Although independence and cultural awareness rank high on most gap year participants' expectations of travel, it is ironic that it is these backpackers who often unwittingly cause the most insult to local people.

Key points

- Gap years are a period of time which a usually young person takes 'out' from formal education, training or the workplace. Many involve overseas travel, although they can also be spent in the UK, earning money for future study.

- Gap years are a rite of passage for many young people.

- Although the background of those who take gap years is changing, white, middle class girls tend to predominate.

Conclusion

Leaving home and travelling are often critical moments in many young people's lives. Movement defines many aspects of their lives, both at the present moment and in the future, as a lived reality and as an aspiration. In some instances it relates very closely to traditional rites of passage, as discussed in Chapter 2. In the case of gap years young people move away, spend time in a liminal place and then return home, transformed and ready to take on a new status and a different role in life. In other instances movement is less of a formal rite of passage and more about crisis and moments of critical and accelerated transitions when young people are forced to make decisions and move against their will or without fully knowing the consequences. Nevertheless, such movements are key moments in their biographies and help to define their lives, their identities and their sense of belonging (or not) within their communities.

Physical movement from one place to another, especially between countries, is an important feature of many young people's lives today. Whether undertaken from a position of privilege, as a chance to see the world and gain new experiences, or as a last resort when a community can no longer provide any sort of home, moving is an important transitional phase of young people's lives. In a globalised world the idea of travelling many thousands of miles to completely different countries and cultures is an option for young people today in a way it simply was not in the past. Some young people have to navigate and negotiate very different physical transitions and while care leavers may not move far, the steps they have to take and the obstacles they have to face are more difficult than those confronting others. For them, too, the physical movement away from the confines of a residential home may be liberating but also problematic and it is not surprising that the same legislation applies to both them and young asylum seekers or that both groups are recognised as the most vulnerable in society. Movement need not always bring disruption and problems, and in the case of gap year students, may result in the opposite, but it does usually bring transformation. How these changes are handled and how best to support young people through these stages, and how policy and practice can fully overlap, are, however, still under scrutiny.

References

A National Voice (2005) *There's No Place like Home*, Manchester, A National Voice, www.anationalvoice.org/professionals/pdf/NPLH_Summary.pdf [accessed 28/02/06].

Allen, M. (2003) *Into the Mainstream: Care Leavers Entering Work, Education and Training*, York, Joseph Rowntree Foundation.

Anderson, I., Kemp, P.A. and Quilgars, D. (1993) *Single Homeless People*, London, HMSO.

Ayotte, W. and Williamson, L. (2001) *Separated Children in the UK: An Overview of the Current Situation*, London, Refugee Council and Save the Children.

Biehal, N., Clayden, J., Stein, M. and Wade, J. (1995) *Moving On: Young People and Leaving Care Schemes*, London, HMSO.

Biehal, N. and Wade, J. (1999) '"I thought it would be easier": the early housing careers of young people leaving care' in Rudd, J. (ed.) *Young People, Housing and Social Policy*, London, Routledge.

Bradt, H. (1995) 'Better to travel cheaply?', *Independent on Sunday*, 12 February, pp. 49–50.

Brindle, D. (2001) 'Stability the key to good results', Guardian Society, *Guardian*, 2 May, p. 6.

Buzard, J. (1993) *The Beaten Track: European Tourism, Literature, and the Ways to Culture, 1800–1918*, Oxford, Clarendon Press.

Chile, L.M. (2002) 'The imported underclass: poverty and social exclusion of black African refugees in Aotearoa New Zealand', *Asia Pacific Viewpoint*, vol. 43, no. 3, pp. 355–66.

Commonwealth of Australia (1997) *Working Holiday Makers: More Than Tourists*, Canberra, Australian Government Publishing Service.

Crawley, H. and Lester, T. (2005) *No Place for a Child. Children in UK Immigration Detention: Impacts, Alternatives and Safeguards*, London, Save the Children.

Curtis, P. (2004) 'Use your gap year wisely, students told', *Guardian*, 27 July, p. 8.

Dennis, J. (2002) *A Case for Change: How Refugee Children in England are Missing Out*, London, The Children's Society/Save the Children/Refugee Council.

DfES (Department for Education and Skills) (2003) *Every Child Matters*, Green Paper, London, HMSO.

Dyer, A. and Parker, V. (2005) 'The state and care leavers. The views of care givers', paper presented at the conference *Children, Families and States*, London, Institute of Education, 12 May.

Evans, H. (2007) 'Institutions' in Robb, M. (ed.) *Youth in Context: Frameworks, Settings and Encounters*, London, Sage/The Open University (Course Book).

Gordon, D., Levitas, R., Pantazis, D., Payne, S., Townsend, P., Adelman, L., Ashworth, K., Middleton, S., Bradshaw, J. and Williams, J. (2000) *Poverty and Social Exclusion in Britain*, York, Joseph Rowntree Foundation.

Hart, J. (2002) *FMO Research Guide: Children and Adolescents in Conflict Situations*, October, www.forcedmigration.org/guides/fmo008/title.htm [accessed 10/04/06].

Henderson, S., Holland, J., McGrellis, S., Sharpe, S. and Thomson, R. (2007) *Inventing Adulthoods: A Biographical Approach to Youth Transitions*, London, Sage (Set Book).

Jones, A. (2003) *Review of Gap Year Provision*, Research Report No. 555, London, DfES.

Kirby, P. (1994) *A Word from the Street*, London, Centrepoint Soho/Community Care.

London South Bank University (2006) *Inventing Adulthoods*, www.sbu.ac.uk/inventing adulthoods [accessed 20/02/06].

Markey, K. (1998) 'Somewhere to call home', *Big Issue in the North*, No. 201, March, pp. 16–22.

McCluskey, J. (1994) *Acting in Isolation: An Evaluation of the Effectiveness of the Children Act for Young Homeless People*, London, CHAR.

Office for National Statistics (2004) 'International migration estimates 2002', 29 April, www.statistics.gov.uk/pdfdir/ime0404.pdf [accessed 10/04/06].

Office of the Deputy Prime Minister (2000) *Leaving Care: A Time for Change: Government Response*, www.odpm.gov.uk/staging/index.asp?id=1150118 [accessed 04/04/06].

Riley, P.J. (1988) 'Road culture of international long-term budget travelers', *Annals of Tourism Research*, vol. 15, no. 2, pp. 313–28.

Schevyens, R. (2002) 'Backpacker tourism and third world development', *Annals of Tourism Research*, vol. 29, no. 1, pp. 144–64.

Social Services Inspectorate (1997) *When Leaving Home is also Leaving Care: An Inspection of Services for Young People Leaving Care*, Wetherby, Department of Health.

Stanley, K. (2001) *Cold Comfort: Young Separated Refugees in England*, London, Save the Children.

Strathdee, R. and Johnson, M. (1994) *Out of Care and on the Streets: Young People, Care Leavers and Homelessness*, London, Centrepoint.

Sutcliffe, W. (1999) *Are You Experienced?*, London, Penguin.

Szerszynski, B. and Urry, J. (2002) 'Cultures of cosmopolitanism', *Sociological Review*, vol. 50, no. 4, pp. 461–81.

Tempest, M. (2002) 'Blunkett: refugees should rebuild their own countries', *Guardian*, 18 September, http://politics.guardian.co.uk/homeaffairs/story/0,11026,794462,00.html [accessed 05/05/06].

Thomson, R. and Taylor, R. (2005) 'Between cosmopolitanism and the locals. Mobility as a resource in the transition to adulthood', *Young: Nordic Journal of Youth Research*, vol. 13, no. 4, pp. 327–42.

United Nations (1951) *Convention Relating to the Status of Refugees*, Geneva, www.ohchr.org/english/law/refugees.htm [accessed 10/04/06].

Valentine, G. and McDonald, I. (2004) *Understanding Prejudice: Attitudes Towards Minorities*, London, Stonewall.

Wade, J., Biehal, N. with Clayden, J. and Stein, M. (1998) *Going Missing: Young People Absent from Care*, New York, Wiley.

Young, M. and Willmott, P. (1957) *Family and Kinship in East London*, London, Routledge and Kegan Paul.

Chapter 10

Relating

Martin Robb

Introduction

This final chapter explores the part played by personal relationships in young people's lives, at a time of rapid social change. Young people's relationships have already been discussed in earlier chapters in this part of the book. Chapter 7, 'Working', dealt with young people's relationships in the workplace, while Chapter 8, 'Playing', explored relationships within peer groups and youth subcultures and Chapter 9, 'Moving', explored the impact of mobility on family and other relationships. The everyday practices discussed in these chapters clearly had a relational component: the practices of playing, working and moving were influenced by, and also helped to shape, key relationships in the lives of young people.

In this chapter, we bring young people's relationships into the foreground. In doing so, and in making this the final chapter of the book, we are suggesting that relationships are a vital component of young people's lives. Like those of adults, young people's lives are caught up in, and profoundly influenced by, a network of key relationships. In some ways, these are similar to those of adults and of younger children, but in many ways they can be seen as distinctive, both in scope and in meaning.

Activity 1	The scope of young people's relationships

Allow 30 minutes

Think about a young person you know or about your own experience when you were a teenager. Make a note of what you think are (or were) the most important relationships in their (or your) life.

Comment

When I did this activity, I thought about my 13-year-old son. Perhaps self-centredly, I thought first of his relationships with his parents – his mother and myself – and with his younger sister. I imagine that these are the most important relationships in his life at the moment – in terms both of 'quantity' (time spent) and 'quality' or intensity. He lives with us, interacts with us every morning and evening and almost continuously at the weekends and during holidays. He depends on us for both material and emotional support. He also has quite close relationships with members of his wider family, particularly his grandparents. The other significant set of relationships in my son's life at the moment are those with his friends, most of whom he has met through school. Again, he spends a large proportion of his time with them. Among his quite wide circle of acquaintances at school, there are perhaps five or six close friends that he mentions regularly. Beyond these two sets of close relationships with family and friends – and much less close – would be relationships with other adults, such as teachers.

Answers to this activity will obviously vary enormously, depending on the personal circumstances of the young person involved. For example, young people's experience of family life is extremely diverse. While a majority may live with two biological parents, others live with a lone parent, or have a close relationship with a non-resident parent or step-parent. For some young people, such as those in care or custody or lacking support at home, relationships with key workers, teachers or youth workers may be more significant. Other differences can arise from the age of the young person. At 13, my son still spends most of his time at home or school, but as he grows older friendships will probably become more important and may even replace family relationships as his main source of emotional support. Moreover, as a fairly young teenager, my son hasn't yet begun to form romantic attachments (at least, not to my knowledge), but this can't be far off.

Doing this activity helps to convey a sense of the importance of personal relationships for young people. Despite the variations in experience that we have noted, it is probably fair to conclude that, for most young people, relationships with family members, with friends and, at some stage, with romantic or sexual partners, will be the most significant sets of relationships in their teenage years, and these will form the main focus of this chapter. Unfortunately, space does not allow an in-depth consideration of young people's relationships with key adults outside their families. However, you can find detailed discussion of such relationships in Robb (2007).

This chapter will explore the ways in which young people 'do' personal relationships and what those relationships mean to them, in the context of change and diversity. The remainder of this Introduction will briefly discuss theoretical approaches to young people and relationships, while the sections that follow will explore, in turn, the three key areas of family, friends and romance. In our discussion we shall be looking for answers to the following core questions:

- What meanings do relationships with family, friends and partners have for young people?

- What impact is social change having on the nature and significance of young people's personal relationships?

- How are young people's personal relationships influenced by differences of class, gender and culture, as well as by wider social contexts and discourses?

Part 1 of the book introduced you to a range of theoretical perspectives on youth. The first three chapters also developed between them a critique of developmentalist approaches based on psychological theories that assume a universal and unchanging model of young people's experience. Relationships play a central role in developmentalist thinking, and we will elaborate and critique some key assumptions of this approach in later sections of the chapter.

By contrast with the static model offered by developmentalism, the cultural, comparative and biographical perspectives advanced in Part 1 suggested that young people's lives are shaped by the changing social and cultural contexts in which they find themselves. A cultural perspective enables us to see that ways of thinking about young people's relationships have changed over time, and to situate those relationships within particular cultures which embody specific ways of 'doing' relationships. A comparative perspective reminds us that young people relate to adults and to each other in different ways across different societies and cultures, and that the meanings of those relationships are specific to the cultural contexts in which they are played out. A biographical perspective emphasises the importance of seeing the ways in which young people 'relate', and think about relationships, as part of the process of negotiating a personal biographical narrative. The detailed implications of viewing young people's relationships within this broad theoretical framework will be worked out in detail in the sections that follow.

Late modern theorists such as Giddens (1991, 1992), Beck (1992), whose work you were introduced to in earlier chapters, and Beck-Gernsheim (1998) have made the transformation of personal relationships a major focus of their analysis of social change in Western societies. A key element in late modern thinking is the apparent decline in importance of relationships based on social obligations, whether of class or community, and the increasing emphasis on relationships that are freely chosen and oriented to the fulfilment of personal needs: what Beck-Gernsheim (1998) calls 'elective affinities' and Giddens (1992) terms the 'pure relationship'.

One of the questions explored by this chapter will be the extent to which this thesis of change can be applied young people's relationships, and later sections will discuss its relevance to different kinds of relationships.

Key points

- Personal relationships are an important feature of young people's lives, with family relationships, friendships and romantic relationships assuming the greatest importance for most young people.

- While a developmentalist approach assumes a universal and unchanging model of young people's relationships, cultural, comparative and biographical perspectives suggest that young people's personal relationships are dynamic and diverse, shaped by social contexts and located within individual biographies.

- Late modern theorists maintain that relationships based on traditional ties and formal obligation are in decline and that personal relationships marked by a search for mutual self fulfilment are increasingly important.

1 Families

The developmentalist tradition has seen relationships between young people and their parents as one of the key arenas for adolescent development. As discussed in earlier chapters, this perspective views adolescence as a period of inevitable 'storm and stress' in which young people seek to break free from dependence on their parents and achieve independent status as autonomous adults. Despite this, as Sinikka Aapola, Marnina Gonick and Anita Harris comment, 'the realm of family life as the context for young people's growing up process has been a neglected area of youth research' (Aapola *et al.*, 2005, p. 84). In fact, as Val Gillies has pointed out, the location of research on young people and on families in separate academic disciplines – youth studies and family studies – has reflected 'the assumption that youth is a period marked by increasing autonomy and independence from family ties' (Gillies, 2000, p. 219).

The dominant theme in the research that has been undertaken in this area is one of dramatic change, reflecting an emphasis in writing about the family more generally. As Gillies notes: 'Contemporary theorising about family life revolves around the theme of social change, with discussion centring on the impact of broader structural and societal changes on personal relationships' (Gillies, 2003, p. 2). Echoing a persistent theme in this book, Gillies cautions against seeing family relationships entirely through the lens of social change and suggests, for example, that the same statistical data that have been used to emphasise increased diversity in family structure 'can also be used to demonstrate an enduring continuity of traditional ties, with the majority of families still composed of a heterosexual couple'. Gillies claims that 'diversity and plurality have always been a feature of family relationships' and cites theorists who see change 'in terms of a slow, uneven but cumulative influence on the way individuals live their lives' rather than radical transformation (Gillies, 2003, p. 3).

Generalised stories about dramatic changes in family life have often been accompanied by assumptions that the impact on young people of these changes has been largely negative. However, there is evidence from research to contradict this. Val Gillies, Jane Ribbens McCarthy and Janet Holland interviewed young people aged 16–18 and their parents from a variety of households and found that the vast majority 'described their family relationships in positive terms, emphasising the supportive and emotionally meaningful nature of their lives together' (Gillies *et al.*, 2001, p. 7). Although it is important not to generalise from one set of research findings, these conclusions stand as a useful corrective to negative discourses about young people and family life.

This section will explore change and diversity in young people's experience of family life, in an attempt to produce a more complex and many-layered picture than that suggested by popular and policy discourses. We will do this by examining in detail two key areas of change that have been the focus of much recent attention. The first area is changing relationships of dependence between young people and their parents, and the second is the impact of family change on young people, with a particular focus on the impact of parental divorce.

Inevitably, in one short section, there is not space to consider other important aspects of young people's experience of family life. For example, we can only refer in passing to the fact that many young people form families of their own when they become parents at a young age. Another way in which family life changes dramatically for some young people is through the loss of a close relative, an area that has been the focus of important recent research (Ribbens McCarthy, 2006). However, perhaps some of the general conclusions in this section about change and diversity can be related to other aspects of family life and relationships such as these.

1.1 Dependence and autonomy

According to Gillies, the developmentalist tradition has tended to see adolescence as a process of 'achieving individual autonomy and independence from parents'. On this view, 'successful' adolescent development 'depends on a "natural" loosing of parental ties' (Gillies, 2000, p. 213). The same perspective has portrayed youth as a time of inevitable rebellion against adult authorities, including parents: 'If a young person does not demonstrate a sufficient level of independence in relation to his/her parents, s/he is labelled as having a problematic transition to adulthood' (Aapola *et al.*, 2005, p. 92). As we shall see, this view can be seen as culturally and historically specific, rather than reflecting universal experience among young people.

There is also a widespread assumption in the literature on young people and family life that young people are now dependent on their parents for longer, and find it more difficult to achieve independence from them, than in previous generations. According to government statistics, in 2004, 58 per cent of young men aged 20 to 24 and 39 per cent of young women of the same age in England lived at home with their parents (Office for National Statistics, 2006). In the UK, it is argued that '**extended dependency**' has been brought about by changes in the nature of work, changes in the extension of further and higher education, and social policies that have altered the structure of financial benefits available to young people (Furlong and Cartmel, 1997).

There is both continuity and change in young people's experience of family relationships

However, drawing on findings from recent research, Gill Jones has argued for a more complex and uneven picture. She suggests that young people 'have never been a homogeneous grouping, though sometimes presented so' and argues that 'the broad trend towards the extension of dependent youth is not across the board. While for many the pathways to adulthood are getting longer, for others adulthood comes early, in effect still following traditional working class patterns. The result is a polarisation of experience in youth' (Jones, 2004, p. 16).

Jones suggests that extended dependency is a mainly middle class phenomenon, one affecting those families that can afford to fund an extended period of financial support. For others, the pattern of early transition to adulthood, traditionally associated with working class families, has continued.

Val Walkerdine, Helen Lucey and June Melody argue that leaving home is harder for the working class girls they interviewed than for middle class girls:

> If the girls had fantasies of independence, then the middle-class
> girls could actually make this happen through a carefully
> constructed and assiduously maintained set of social and class
> norms: they could go to university or go travelling and actually
> take their time moving out of the parental home. ... The physical
> separation of moving out of the parental home was much harder for
> the working-class girls. It was more dramatic in the sense that there
> was no gradual transition.
>
> (Walkerdine *et al.*, 2001, p. 197)

Young people's experience of negotiating independence from parental support also varies according to cultural assumptions and practices. On the basis of research in England, Spain and Norway, Clare Holdsworth (2004) has argued that, although family support is a key factor in young people's lives in all three countries, the ways in which that support is negotiated varies. For example, she found that 'greater emphasis is placed on young people learning about responsibility in Britain and Norway, while Spanish families identify more closely with maintaining young people's material well-being' (Holdsworth, 2004, p. 909). According to Holdsworth, 'British and Norwegian parents often cite the importance of "learning about responsibility" as the main determinant of how much parents should help children' and equate too much support with 'spoiling' children (p. 919).

Aapola *et al.* argue that concepts of dependence and autonomy vary enormously between cultural groups: 'Rebellion against or separation from one's parents are not necessary precursors in young people's development into adulthood, even if the individualist ideology places strong emphasis on a young person's growing independence over decisions affecting his/her life, as well as his/her gradual separation from the family' (Aapola *et al.*, 2005, p. 92). They add that 'in many cultures the parent–child relations are seen differently' and quote one young woman, the daughter of Vietnamese American parents, as saying: 'To be an American, you may be able to do whatever you want. But to be a Vietnamese, you must think of your family first' (Zhou and Bankston, quoted in Aapola *et al.*, 2005, p. 93). For some cultural groups in the UK too, as in some southern European countries, the transition to adulthood may be marked not by the achievement of complete independence from parents, but rather by a shift in continuing relationships of interdependence between generations, marked, for example, by continued residence in the parental home after marriage. Gillies suggests that an emphasis on adolescence as a time of achieving autonomy and 'breaking away' from parents is culturally biased, reflecting 'an individualistic ideology central to Western social and economic organization'. She notes that 'in many other cultures, the transition to adulthood is seen in terms of developing greater responsibility to other family members, rather than as a quest for individual autonomy' (Gillies, 2000, p. 214).

Young people also negotiate the balance between independence and autonomy differently according to gender. In the contemporary context, Aapola *et al.* argue that 'for girls and young women there are increasing tensions between their simultaneous but contradictory positions within the family as "dutiful daughters" and "autonomous young adults"' (Aapola *et al.*, 2005, p. 86). They claim that in conventional psychological theories of adolescent development 'girls have been seen as more dependent on other people, particularly their families, than boys' and add that 'developmental theories have ... emphasized the autonomous individual at the expense of relationships, neglecting the centrality of the family in young women's lives' (p. 92).

For young disabled people, too, achieving 'independence' can mean something very different from what it means for able-bodied people. According to Jenny Morris: 'Many young disabled people have no experience of an independent social life and few opportunities to make friends: they spend most of their time with family or paid carers and have no independent access to transport, telecommunications, or personal assistance over which they have choice and control' (Morris, 2002). This means that they are much more dependent on family support than their able-bodied peers, and the notion of 'independence' is a distant ideal, particularly for those who are severely disabled: 'Young disabled people rarely get the opportunity to move into a home of their own. Instead they are more likely to be "slotted into" available service provision' (Morris, 2002).

Even within the mainstream of young people's experience, it can be argued that young people themselves do not see achieving increasing independence as the most important feature of their relationships with their parents. Gillies *et al.* found in their research that: 'young people interpreted increasing independence as individual freedom as well as an obligation to accept personal responsibility' and 'both teenagers' and parents' understandings of independence were shaped by a strong sense of connection to each other, through mutual obligation and commitment' (Gillies *et al.*, 2001, p. 18).

These research findings make for a complex picture, in which young people and their parents negotiate a delicate balance between support and independence, against the background of changing social and economic pressures, and in which differences of class, gender and culture play a vital part.

1.2 Divorce and family change

Although it is important not to overlook continuities with the past, it remains true that young people are growing up in families that are in many ways visibly different from those experienced by previous generations.

Among the most significant changes in family life in recent decades have been the steady increase in the divorce rate, the growth in the number of lone-parent families, and the proliferation of stepfamilies. According to government statistics, between 1974 and 2004 the proportion of children living in lone-parent families in Great Britain tripled to 24 per cent, while in 2001, 10 per cent of all families with dependent children in the UK were stepfamilies (Office for National Statistics, 2006).

We have already noted the influence of discourses about the negative impact of contemporary family life on young people. The increase in divorce, in particular, has been blamed for a wide variety of social ills, including increases in mental health problems and antisocial behaviour among young people. These assumptions have been challenged by some writers and researchers. Bren Neale (2002) criticises the tendency to see divorce as something that is inevitably bad for children, rather than focusing on the quality of relationships between parents and children in all families:

> Parental conflict is no longer the prime culprit; it is divorce itself, seen as the 'break up' of the family and the potential for loss of contact between the child and the non-residential parent, that is deemed to cause harm. The nature of the potential damage wrought by divorce is never very clearly spelt out. But it is said to be wide ranging, incorporating images of the 'passive and innocent victim' (educationally, economically and emotionally disadvantaged) through to the 'potential threat' (descent into delinquency, substance abuse or teenage pregnancy). Children with divorced parents have thus come to be seen as vulnerable 'children in need', whose interests must be safeguarded for them by the law.
>
> (Neale, 2002, p. 458)

Activity 2   Critiquing discourses of young people and divorce

Allow 30 minutes   Read through the following extract from the same article by Bren Neale. What are her key criticisms of 'blanket formulations' about young people and divorce? Make a note of your thoughts.

> Blanket formulations such as those outlined in the preceding paragraph are not flexible enough to accommodate the diversity of children's circumstances. Nor do they allow for children's own constructions of their welfare to be taken seriously. In effect they assume a commonality of children's experiences, while glossing over the complexities and pluralities of real lives. If the law presumes to know in advance what arrangements are best for children, then the need to consult with them becomes somewhat superfluous. As a result, the child of legal discourse has become a somewhat generalized, theoretical child rather than a real,

embodied, biologically unique and socially differentiated child. Family law thus operates according to a welfare paradigm that allows for a limited notion of children's agency, one that recognizes children's competence to speak but only in carefully prescribed circumstances and according to adult agendas.

(Neale, 2002, p. 458)

Comment

Neale's first criticism is that the prevailing discourse is abstract and theoretical and does not reflect the diversity and individuality of young people's actual experience. A second criticism is that by constructing children as victims, their agency is denied or limited and as a consequence their opportunity to be consulted is confined within adult agendas.

Elsewhere, Bren Neale and Carol Smart (2001) draw on their own research into young people's experience of divorce to argue that there is little evidence to support the negative claims of this dominant discourse. Moreover, even if young people's wellbeing *is* affected by such experiences, they question whether it is divorce itself that is to blame. Although the children and young people in their study attached great importance to family relationships, it was the *quality* of relationships in families, and not necessarily the precise personalities involved, that seemed to matter most. Neale and Smart found that young people 'placed value on relations of care in their families, based on affection, emotional support, moral guidance and protection' (Neale and Smart, 2001, p. 11). At the same time, they found that young people manifested a strong ethic of respect and reciprocity in family relationships and regarded the quality of relationships as more important for their happiness than the details of family arrangements (pp. 11–12).

Jennifer Flowerdew and Bren Neale (2003) have also argued that the experience of parental divorce needs to be seen in the context of, and as shaped by, other transitions occurring in young people's lives, such as those relating to friendships, education and housing. They discuss the ways in which young people can 'get used to' the presence of new partners in their families. Conversely, they suggest that children who have become used to living with a lone parent experience a sense of loss when that parent finds a new partner: 'There is clear evidence in our study that with several years of post-divorce family life behind them, children's sense of what constitutes the "complete" family has often shifted radically. What was an "extraordinary" period of transition in their lives had become wholly "ordinary"' (Flowerdew and Neale, 2003, p. 151).

Activity 3   Not a big problem?

Allow 30 minutes   In support of the view that divorce should be seen as an 'everyday problem', Flowerdew and Neale include the following extract from their interview with Jake, aged 14. Read through what Jake said. What is his view of divorce? Why do you think divorce has not been a 'big problem' for him, and why does he think it might be for others?

> I have to say I didn't have feelings about the divorce then and I don't now ... As far as I can see, the divorce hasn't been a big problem to me. Providing parents act properly, divorce shouldn't be a problem ... I mean I don't want to criticize what you're doing, but there's a lot of fuss nowadays about talking about things. And I think that in some ways, for younger people, talking about things can just make them worse. Because I think a lot of people really can just sort of deal with things providing they're not going over and over them ... I think if you're like suicidally depressed, or compulsively cutting yourself, then it [talking about problems] is a good thing, obviously. But I think in a lot of instances it's just best to let go. The going over of what are really everyday problems, problems that affect millions of people, is not something appropriate for everyone. Is it a third or two-thirds of marriages that end in divorce?
>
> So you can't say it's something shocking. I suppose I think it's strange to be singling people out to talk about this. It's interesting in a way because you wouldn't say all this in an ordinary conversation. It's not awkward for me but I do feel it's unnecessary – unnecessary for me. But if it helps someone else, that's fine.
>
> (Quoted in Flowerdew and Neale, 2003, p. 158)

Comment

Jake sees divorce as normal and as a fairly common experience. It seems not to have been problematic for him because (by implication) his parents acted well. He believes that talking about the problem (as in this interview) might make things worse and implies that this might construct experiences as a problem. However, he can see that talking might help if the experience of divorce is accompanied by feelings of depression.

What counts as 'normal' family life is not fixed and can change for young people, depending on the quality of their experience. Parental divorce and repartnering need not be wholly negative events in the life of a young person and can come to be seen as quite 'ordinary'. Young people like Jake are not passive victims of events but are capable of actively constructing a range of meanings out of their experiences of family change.

Similar conclusions emerge from a study of stepfamilies by Jane Ribbens McCarthy, Rosalind Edwards and Val Gillies (2003). Although most of the authors' interviews were with parents, their discussions focused on responsibility for children, and they included some interviews with young people in reconstituted families. One of their main conclusions is that 'diversity of family forms may not necessarily mean diversity of family lifestyles: people in stepfamilies may be drawing on images and meanings of "ordinary" family in how they create and understand their lives together' (Ribbens McCarthy et al., 2003, p. 1). Like Neale, they argue that the existing literature tends to focus on differences from 'normal' family life, rather than on similarities with it. Their interviews with young people in stepfamilies show them characterising their families as 'normal'. For example, 11-year-old Katie said:

> I think it's just like a normal family really, because we all do respect each other, respect each other's privacy and everything, and we will listen to each other, help each other out, look after each other and everything. So I don't think there's any real difference, it's just I have an extra brother, an extra sister, an extra mum and an extra dad really.
>
> (Quoted in Ribbens McCarthy et al., 2003, p. 65)

Criticising late modern theory's emphasis on individualism and personal fulfilment as the driving forces behind contemporary relationships, the authors claim that the stepfamilies they interviewed 'still adhered to notions of family as being about ties that bind ... Our interviewees' "family practices" were framed by a set of long-standing ideas about the nature of family life, rather than around negotiating fluidity and diversity' (Ribbens McCarthy et al., 2003, p. 130). They suggest that 'moral imperatives' around parenting and caring for children featured very strongly, and criticise Beck-Gernsheim's (1998) vision of the modern family as being based on 'elective affinities' for its class bias, arguing that working class understandings of family life have been marginalised in much recent writing. As with Neale's work on young people and divorce, this research suggests that the impact of family change depends on the quality of relationships rather than on external arrangements, and is also influenced by the ways in which both young people and their parents construct the meanings of their experiences.

Of course, it is important to remember that the divorce or separation of parents can be a traumatic experience for some young people. However, the research discussed in this section is a reminder that what matters is not so much the experience itself as the way in which it is managed, and in particular the quality of relationships between adults, and between adults and children. Moreover, young people should not be seen as the passive victims of family change, but as active agents, able to make their own meanings out of the experience and to devise strategies for dealing with it.

Key points

- Although family relationships have often been seen as a key arena for adolescent development, to date there has been little research on young people's experience of family life.

- The ways in which young people negotiate the transition from dependence to autonomy varies along lines of gender, class and culture.

- Although it is important not to overstate the extent of change, it is broadly true that young people experience greater variety and fluidity in family forms now than in the past.

- Popular and policy discourses assume that the impact on young people of divorce and family change is mainly negative, but there is evidence that it depends on contextual factors and that young people value the quality of family relationships above external structures.

2 Friends

In the last section we mentioned the relative lack of research into young people's family relationships. The same cannot be said of young people's friendships, which have been the focus of a number of important studies, reflecting both developmentalist assumptions about the importance of friendships in adolescence and the disciplinary divide that we noted earlier. Although much of the writing on young people's friendships has focused on peer groups and gangs, recent years have seen an increase in the attention devoted to close personal friendships, especially those of young women, reflecting the influence of feminism on social research.

Developmentalist thinking tends to see adolescent friendships as an important framework for the development of individual identity. From this perspective, young people select friends on the basis of similarity, in order to 'mirror' and thus confirm certain aspects of their own identity. As we shall see, this view is open to challenge on a number of grounds. However, the connection between friendship and identity is an important one. In this section, we take gender as our main lens for exploring the ways in which young men and young women use friendships as a framework for negotiating their identities. Using gender as a focus will also be a way of examining one aspect of diversity in the ways in which young people practise friendship.

2.1 Friendship, gender and identity

There is evidence that young men and young women think about and 'do' friendship differently. Chapter 4, 'Gender', discussed Julie McLeod's longitudinal study of friendships among young Australian men and women. You will recall from that discussion that McLeod explores the increasing pressure on both boys and girls to be emotionally competent, and to value qualities of intimacy and relationship which in the past have been associated with girls and women. She argues that: 'Friendship and interpersonal relations are practices for the playing out and policing of gender identities ... For young women, the demand for intimacy is mediated by a historical alignment of femininity with the affective, and this is linked to a perceived dilemma of choice between autonomy and connection' (McLeod, 2002, pp. 222–3).

Although women and girls have traditionally been associated with the affective side of experience, and assumed to have a greater interest in close personal relationships, McLeod argues that this is changing, due to the impact of feminism and the rise of the men's movement. As Chapter 4 suggested, recent years have seen growing discussion of men's capacity for emotional expression, and McLeod argues that, increasingly, boys and men are seeking to reclaim qualities of:

> being in touch with their feelings, of being expressive and able to forge close bonds with one another ... In other words, the desire now is for men and boys to be able to conduct their personal and social relations with the kind of emotional openness said to characterise women's personal and social interactions.
>
> (McLeod, 2002, p. 213)

Although the evidence from McLeod's study of secondary school students appears to be that boys and girls still think and talk about friendships in quite traditionally gendered ways, she claims that 'alongside these traditional gender patterns there are also signs of change emerging in how young men and women negotiate friends and relationships', which in turn 'signal rearticulations of femininity and masculinity' (McLeod, 2002, p. 216).

Valerie Hey's research into girls' friendships in British secondary schools in the late 1980s also argued against an idealised and essentialist picture of young women's relationships. Although girls' capacity for intense friendships is often taken as a demonstration of a 'natural' feminine capacity for caring, Hey claims that this overlooks the 'violence and passion' in girls' friendships (Hey, 2002, p. 68). Her research included an analysis of notes exchanged between girls in class, which she argues constituted 'visible evidence of the extensive emotional labour invested by girls in their friendships' (p. 76).

Here is an example of one of the note exchanges collected by Hey:

> Bernice if you must know I don't like you. And I know what you are going to do tomorrow tell your sis.
>
> No, I am not going to tell my sis of you. Marcia's started again (not really) Bernice.
>
> Oh yeh I bet you are. If you feel like being moody go ahead.
>
> I like you, you are being childish.
>
> (Hey, 2002, p. 67)

In exchanges like these, girls characterise each other as 'nice' or 'bossy' and Hey sees in them evidence of what she calls the 'ideological imperative to be good' (Hey, 2002, p. 78). She argues that in these 'clandestine cultural productions' girls were 'learning not only to constitute their feminine subjectivities in conditions of surveillance as specifically classed forms of niceness, they were also defining themselves against the noisier and messier forms of boys' overt behaviours' (p. 78).

Hey also argues that this process of negotiating feminine identities is carried out in the context of gender inequality: 'Negotiating feminine friendship and its associated powers is a delicate business, being always already constituted through the socially coercive presence of the male gaze, which endlessly seeks to position girls within its regulation'. She gives the example of a note in which girls discuss a friend's appearance and argues that 'a key sanction to disqualify a girl from friendship is to relegate her from claims to femininity by implying that she looks insufficiently attractive' (Hey, 2002, p. 85).

However, Hey also claims that there is an ethic to girls' friendships:

> The central premises of girls' friendship are: reliability, reciprocity, commitment, confidentiality, trust and sharing. The repertoire of emotions that are provoked if these rules are broken are as powerfully felt and as dramatic as those that have characteristically been claimed as the sole prerogative of sexualized relations ... Girls' 'divorces' are messy.
>
> (Hey, 2002, p. 86)

Hey is arguing that girls' friendships are a key context in which young feminine identities are worked out. However, it is important to note that this process incorporates and works through externally imposed ideas of what it means to be a 'good' girl, working within but also ultimately reproducing unequal gender relations.

Similar conclusions arise from an exploration by Mary Jane Kehily, Mairtin Mac an Ghaill, Debbie Epstein and Peter Redman (2002) of the

Are friendships more important for girls than for boys?

'relationship cultures' of older junior school girls. Though not specifically about teenagers, their findings can be seen as relevant to understanding the friendships of older girls. The researchers conclude that girls' friendships are 'both a material relation of power and a technique for the regulation of normative gendered sexualities' (Kehily *et al.*, 2002, p. 169). As in Hey's research, friendships between girls enabled certain femininities to emerge and be sustained. Focusing particularly on the 'diary group' who (in a strategy that has some parallels with exchanges of notes among Hey's group of young women) kept records of their interactions, the authors argue that this group acted as a 'performative space' for the enactment of different versions of femininities: 'Through talk in this self regulated arena, diary group members try out different identities that may be perceived as empowering and constraining' (Kehily *et al.*, 2002, p. 176).

To suggest that girls' friendships are a framework for working out gendered identities is not necessarily to reinforce a developmentalist view of young friendships as primarily about confirming adolescent identities. Whereas developmentalism sees identity as something that emerges mainly from within the individual, and is mirrored in the 'other', the research cited here suggests, rather, that girls use their friendships to actively work out and negotiate their identities as young women. However, this process of negotiation is always performed within, and shaped by, the norms of particular local contexts, such as the secondary school, and is constrained by wider gendered relationships of power and inequality.

Do friendships have different meanings and purposes for young men? The study by Peter Redman, Debbie Epstein, Mary Jane Kehily and Mairtin Mac an Ghaill (2002) of 'boys bonding' was also carried out among older junior school children, but it has some useful things to say about boys' friendships at a time of change in gender relations. The authors use as a case study the friendship of two white boys, Ben and Karl, in a mostly Asian school. Arguing that boys' friendships are relatively under-researched compared with those of girls, and that there is a frequent assumption 'that boys are primarily group oriented in contrast to the claimed individual orientation of girls', they claim that Ben's and Karl's 'passionate friendship' challenges this view: 'If this friendship lacked the full-blown qualities of the specifically romantic sensibility implied by this term ... it was nevertheless intimate, devoted, faithful and the subject of strong feelings' (Redman et al., 2002, p. 180). The authors suggest that the friendship between the boys can be understood as 'a dialogic space in which the boys sought recognition from each other for particular versions of masculinity ... as a medium through which they jointly negotiated the overlapping currents of schooling processes, the microcultural relations of the school, aspects of their biographies and home backgrounds, and wider social relations' (Redman et al., 2002, p. 181).

While this particular relationship may not be typical of boys' friendships, and may be even rarer among older boys, this study at least suggests that boys can experience intimacy through their friendships, and that their friendships can be invested with the same amount of intensity as those between girls. However, McLeod argues that it is important not to overlook new possibilities for friendship that are emerging for older boys, under the influence of changes in social conditions and gender relations. McLeod cites the experience of Mark – a young Australian man whom she characterises as working class, white, rural and fairly conservative. McLeod emphasises the importance of 'mates' for Mark, in the changing social context of growing youth unemployment and insecurity in the jobs market: 'In such an economic context, "mates" and interpersonal relationships become increasingly important and in a sense occupy the space once filled by the sociality and purposefulness of paid work. Mark's work experiences are also depicted in terms of his positive and affirming interactions with workmates' (McLeod, 2002, p. 220).

On the one hand 'Mark appears to embody a relatively traditional, even an emphasised and intransigent form of white, provincial, working class masculinity' in which being with his mates 'is linked with a repertoire of masculine activities and values that appear relatively unchanged by a "transformation of intimacy" and feminism'. On the other hand, McLeod claims that 'his marginal connection to the labour market and the pleasure he derives from his relations with friends and workmates point to a retraditionalised masculinity that is anchored not in paid work, but in relationships' (McLeod, 2002, p. 220). This argument has some resonance with the claim made in Chapter 8 that, in areas of high unemployment in the UK, 'going out' with a group of friends has assumed the importance in young people's social lives that was once the province of paid work.

As with young women's friendships, it is important not to see young men's relationships with their 'mates' in a static and essentialist way, but to be aware of the ways in which ways of thinking about and performing friendship are also shaped by changes in the social context and gender relations, while at the same time acknowledging the persistence of socially structured gender differences and inequalities.

2.2 Stability, difference and change

Are young people's friendships simply a framework for negotiating young identities, or do they also have other meanings and purposes? Do young people always seek 'likeness' in their friends, or might young people also see value in maintaining relationships that encompass difference and change? Rachel Brooks (2002) carried out research into young people's friendships at a time of 'repositioning', as they make choices about and move on to higher education. Her research focuses on how young people manage their friendships at a time when differences in academic achievement and aspiration can create tensions in long-standing relationships. As Brooks says, conventional thinking about the purpose of young people's friendships, with its emphasis on the search for likeness and confirming identity, would tend to suggest that 'as the young people became aware of such differences in social location, the equality of their friendships would come under increasing pressure and, in such circumstances, would be likely to change' (Brooks, 2002, p. 459).

However, Brooks's research appears to demonstrate the remarkable stability of many friendships during this period of transition: 'instead of forging new friendships more congruent with their emerging social locations, the students used a variety of strategies to manage their existing friendships' (Brooks, 2002, p. 459). Although wary of making general claims on the basis of one group of young people, Brooks argues that these findings might prompt a rethink of the nature of young people's friendships.

Brooks is challenging the general assumption that young people's friendships change as they grow older, in line with other changes in their lives. Instead, she argues that, for many young people, friendships through adolescence are remarkably stable, and that young people adopt a range of strategies aimed at maintaining friendships during periods of transition, though this may sometimes prove difficult. Brooks's research challenges the view, based on developmentalist thinking, that young people's friendships are substantially different in nature from those of adults. On this view, major transitions which opened up differences between friends would lead to the leaving behind of old friendships and the forging of new ones to match new situations and identities.

However, what if, Brooks asks, young people's friendships are actually much like those of adults, and are seen by young people as valuable and worth sustaining in and for themselves? What if – as in Ribbens McCarthy and colleagues' (2003) view of stepfamily relationships – they are as much about a sense of *obligation* as about seeking personal fulfilment? As with Neale's (2002) work on family relationships, Brooks resists equating particular life events with particular meanings for young people and instead suggests that the significance of an event will depend on young people's response to it and the strategies they use to manage critical moments in their relationships. For example, Brooks describes the strategies used by the participants in her study to maintain existing friendships through challenging times:

> The strategies adopted by the young people had the overall aim of maintaining their friendships during a period in which the equality of the friendship tie was being threatened by emerging differences and a growing awareness of different social locations, both now and in the future. Strategies were used to mask, or at least to deflect attention away from, the various types of emerging difference – such as probable HE [higher education] destination, level of academic attainment, view of university life, and the implied status differences associated with these specific areas.
>
> (Brooks, 2002, p. 456)

The aim of these strategies on the part of young people was to maintain friendships, even as differences between friends became more obvious. Brooks claims that these findings contradict both developmentalist claims about friendship as identity confirmation, and late modern theories about contemporary relationships being solely about emotional fulfilment: 'Far from using their friends as "mirrors" to establish their own identity, or building fully open, honest and emotional "pure relationships", the young people managed their friendships in highly pragmatic ways, aware of the tensions, difficulties and points of difference inherent in their social bonds' (Brooks, 2002, pp. 463–4).

Brooks acknowledges that her conclusions are tentative, as they are based on one study with a particular group of young people. Nevertheless, her research is a challenge to the tendency to treat young people's relationships as completely different from those of adults. Although (as we have seen) young people's friendships can play an important part in the negotiation of identities, they may also have other purposes, as well as being seen by young people as an important end in themselves. Brooks's work is valuable in encouraging us to see young people as moral agents, able to enter into moral commitments and obligations to others, and as active agents, able to devise strategies for maintaining valuable friendships even as their circumstances change.

Activity 4	Reflecting on stability and change in friendships

Allow 30 minutes

Think back to your own friendships when you were young. Make a list of your close friends when you were in your early teens. Then think about your friendships in your late teens and early twenties. Were you still friends with the same people, or did you have new friends? Try to think of any reasons why some friendships persisted and others did not.

Comment

When I did this activity, I thought, first, about the friends that I had in my early years at secondary school. I realised that I was still friendly with most of them when I was about 17 or 18, despite our changing interests and experiences (some leaving school to start work, others preparing for higher education). Starting work at 18 and then university when I was 19 brought me into contact with new friends who shared my changing interests. At this stage, maintaining friendships with the first group became more difficult, but we still made efforts to keep in touch, thus providing some support for Brooks's thesis, even if my greater investment in my 'new' friendships reflected a search for 'likeness' and confirmation of my emerging adult identity.

Key points

- Young people's friendships have been seen as an important framework for developing and confirming identities.

- Gender identities are negotiated in the framework of boys' and girls' friendships, but always in the context of wider gender relations.

- There are important differences, as well as similarities, in the nature and significance of friendships for young men and young women, but the ways in which those differences are played out are changing.

- Like those of adults, young people's friendships are often characterised by stability and obligation and by strategies for actively maintaining relationships of difference.

3 Romance

The final aspect of young people's relationships that we will be exploring in this chapter is love and romance. Here we are concerned less with young people's sexual experience, and more with the ways in which they imagine and practise intimate relationships. What do love and romance mean to young people, and what influences their experiences and expectations of intimacy?

Once again, the developmentalist perspective places importance on 'young love' as part of the process by which young people detach themselves from dependence on their parents and progress towards forming family groupings of their own. On this view, one of the developmental tasks of adolescence is finding a sexual partner. By contrast, sociological perspectives have charted the impact of social change on young people's experience of intimacy. The past 200 years have seen a shift in Western, industrialised societies away from the model found in 'traditional' societies, in which the transition to adult status is associated with the identification of a lifelong sexual partner, often sanctioned by parents and the wider community. Fuelled by a discourse of romantic love, this model has been replaced in Western societies by an understanding of youth as a time of searching for 'true love' before 'settling down' with a stable partner. More recently, the kinds of changes that we noted in Section 1, including the extension of the time that young people live at home and remain in full time education, have accentuated this tendency. Perhaps it is because intimate relationships offer one of the few areas in which young people, remaining for longer in the pre-adult worlds of home and education, can begin to express and experience something of an adult identity, that they are invested with such intense emotional energy.

Alongside these wider social changes, there have been other changes specifically affecting romantic and sexual relationships. For example, over the past few decades people have tended increasingly to marry later in life. According to government statistics, the average age for first marriages in England and Wales in 2004 was 31 for men and 29 for women, compared with 25 and 23 for men and women respectively 40 years earlier (Office for National Statistics, 2006). In addition, fewer people now see marriage as their ultimate goal. As we noted in Section 1, more marriages than ever end in divorce, and serial monogamy – a succession of exclusive but not lifelong partnerships – is now common.

For young people then, romantic relationships may now be less about finding a partner for life, or experimenting with temporary relationships before 'settling down', and more about beginning a pattern that will continue into early adulthood: a series of relationships of differing seriousness and length, none of them necessarily oriented towards long term partnership, family or children. At the same time, the liberalisation of legislation and social attitudes have contributed to changes in young people's expectations and experiences of intimate relationships. The lowering of the age of sexual consent, and the easier availability of contraception and legal abortion, have also contributed to these changes.

Of course, as with the other developments discussed in this chapter, we need to be cautious about assuming universal change across the board. As in the case of family relationships, it can be argued that the picture of dramatic change needs to be balanced with a sense of important continuities of experience, particularly for certain groups of young people. As with assumptions about extended dependency, there is some evidence that delaying marriage and 'settling down' is more applicable to middle class than to working class experience. Later in this section we will discuss ways in which patterns and expectations of love and partnership are at least partly shaped by educational and employment trajectories and by the extent of social and geographical mobility (Willmot, 2003, 2007). In addition, young people from particular cultural or faith backgrounds may find themselves caught between contemporary secular notions of romantic exploration and inherited beliefs about monogamy and sexual abstinence outside marriage. In the discussion that follows, it will be important to bear in mind the ways in which culture shapes both expectations and experiences of 'love' and 'romance'.

In this discussion, we will again be using the lens of gender through which to explore similarities and differences between young men's and young women's experiences of romance, and the meanings with which they invest it. Conventional wisdom and popular discourse constructs young women as being intensely invested in love and romance, and young men by contrast as seeking relationships to satisfy sexual desire. Until recently, there has been little research into the meanings of intimacy for young people, and especially for young men, but this is beginning to change. As a result, a more complex picture is beginning to emerge.

3.1 'One day you wake up and think: Wow!': young men and romance

If research on young people's intimate relationships has been lacking until recently, there has been a particular absence of research into what such relationships mean for young men. However, Peter Redman (1999, 2001) carried out research on young men and romance in a sixth-form college and analysed the young men's narratives of 'love' as a product of the school culture and of a maturing late-teen identity. Drawing on the work of the French psychoanalytic theorist Jacques Lacan, he interprets young men's romantic yearnings in terms of a desire to find a 'pure' object to replace the lost mother. At the same time, Redman situates the production of narratives of romance in social and class contexts – in his case, in a group of middle class male sixth-formers.

The young men interviewed by Redman tended to see falling in love as something that just happened:

> Nick: [falling in love] is a natural process, yeah, it clicks. It's not something you can achieve. It's something that falls into place. One day you wake up and think, 'Wow!' You know, you can work at it but it can't be the same as real, natural love. It just comes naturally ... It just happens ... it comes from inside you definitely. It's just a magnetism.
>
> (Redman, 1999, p. 1)

Redman expresses some surprise that all the boys interviewed for the study expressed an investment in 'what appeared to be romantically organised relationships' (Redman, 1999, p. 2), admitting that he had expected boys to reflect a more instrumental or sexually predatory attitude to girls. Although this element was certainly present in their responses, he concludes that 'being in love was ... an important and acceptable way of being a young man in this college, at this particular time' (p. 2).

However, Redman does not follow his interviewees in seeing 'being in love' as a natural process. Instead, he sees it as closely related to what he calls the 'disciplinary regime' and individualist ethos of the college (Redman, 2001, pp. 187–8). Redman sees the movement towards serious romantic relationships in these young men's lives as linked to their move from compulsory education to the more adult environment of the college and as reflecting an aspiration towards adult attributes of commitment, mutuality and emotional intimacy (p. 188).

Redman's research is useful in demonstrating the significance that young men, as much as young women, attribute to love and romance. It also suggests that the ways in which young people (young men in this instance) think about intimate relationships is not natural and spontaneous, but is linked to the contexts in which they find themselves and the discourses (in this case of individualism and adulthood) embodied in those environments.

However, Redman's conclusions are also open to challenge. By implication, Redman is denying the importance of romance in the experience of younger teenagers, suggesting that at an earlier age boys are more interested in casual relationships and sexual exploration. Although Redman acknowledges the context-bound nature of these middle class young men's romantic feelings, his identification of romance with the aspirations of later youth perhaps overlooks the ways in which ideas of love and romance can be important for younger men, and women, in different social groups and different social settings.

The lack of research evidence in this area makes it difficult to substantiate this critique with anything more than anecdotal and observational experience. Based on my own experience of growing up on a lower middle class housing estate, and on observation of my own children and their friends, I would suggest that ideas of 'romance' might be important at a younger age for boys from different social backgrounds. Speaking personally, I clearly remember my first painful and exquisite experience of 'being in love' at the age of 14 (which involved writing bad poetry and endlessly playing romantic records in my bedroom) and would suggest that this experience was not atypical. Observation of my children and their friends also suggests that the age at which boys and girls become interested in romantic attachments may be lower than it was a generation ago, perhaps due to increased exposure among younger children to the discourse of love and romance in the mass media.

The lack of evidence of romantic attachments among young people, and especially young men, may be due not to the absence of such feelings but to the lack of safe spaces in which to articulate them. As Stephen Frosh, Ann Phoenix and Rob Pattman suggest, teenage boys are adept at policing their own and each other's masculine identities, and although in some instances heterosexual activity can act as a badge of masculinity, 'too much' interest in girls can attract accusations of femininity (Frosh *et al.*, 2002, pp. 115–20). Research by David Buckingham and Sara Bragg (2004) into young people's response to sexual representations in the media appears to demonstrate the importance of romance for those as young as 12. Writing about Valentine's Day in the diaries that they kept for the researchers, one girl, Courtney, aged 12, 'even confessed to buying her boyfriend a box of chocolates, as it was their "two month anniversary"' (Buckingham and Bragg, 2004, p. 51), while others felt depressed at being left out. The authors add: 'Needless to say perhaps, such emotions were not expressed by any of the boys, even if they may have felt them' (p. 51). But perhaps they might have been, if the diaries had been private and not meant for the researchers' eyes?

Writing about research on sexuality carried out with young people in southern and eastern Africa, Rob Pattman (2005) concludes that 'boys were much more misogynistic and likely to talk about girls in derogatory or impersonal ways when being interviewed rather than when writing diaries – and when being interviewed in groups rather than when being interviewed individually' (Pattman, 2005, p. 507). He adds: 'In group interviews (both mixed and single sex), for example, some boys boasted about sleeping with and dumping girls, yet in the individual interviews they kept quiet about this' (p. 507). Significantly, and unlike the boys in Buckingham and Bragg's study, Pattman notes that the boys *were* more open about romantic feelings towards girls in the diaries that they kept for researchers:

In the diaries they kept, where they were asked to record everyday details about significant events, emotions and relationships, many of the boys – particularly in South Africa – wrote highly romanticized accounts of their girlfriends or potential girlfriends, as well as heartrending pieces about being dumped by them. These were conspicuous by their absence in the interviews.

(Pattman, 2005, pp. 507–8)

While it is important to remember the ways in which cultural differences might have shaped the different uses made of diaries, this counter-example at least suggests that younger teenage boys invest in romantic attachments as much as older boys.

Activity 5   Remembering first love

Allow 15 minutes

Think back to your own first experience of being in love. How old were you? What did it mean to you, and how do you think it was related to other things that were happening in your life at the time?

Comment

I remember my experience of 'first love', occurring when I was 14, as all-consuming. It happened at about the same time that I was becoming interested in rock music, youth culture and 'alternative' ideas, and perhaps embodied a similar youthful idealism and energy, and an attempt to construct a 'youthful' identity to replace my childhood self.

Romance can offer young people a chance to try out adult identities

3.2 'I knew then I wanted to spend the rest of my life with him': young women and romance

The ways in which young women think about love and romance are also shaped by social contexts and discourses, rather than simply arising naturally or spontaneously, as might be suggested by a psychological perspective. Helen Willmot's study of the 'discourses of intimacy' articulated by young women highlights the importance of seeing young people's thinking about and practice of 'love' as embedded in diverse social discourses, which themselves reflect particular social locations and personal trajectories (Willmot, 2003, 2007). Willmot found that two opposing discourses of love and intimacy ran through her respondents' narratives on the timing, development and purpose of intimate relationships. The first was what she terms a 'romantic discourse' which had three main elements:

> Firstly, 'love at first sight' (Leach, 1981: 115; see also Giddens, 1992: 40). Secondly, the notion of exclusivity in terms of potential partners, that is, 'the one', or 'Mr Right' (Giddens, 1992: 46). And thirdly, 'foreverness', or at least 'a long-term life trajectory, orientated to an anticipated yet malleable future ... a course of future development' (Giddens, 1992: 45), which is commonly associated with marriage.
>
> (Willmot, 2003)

As examples of this discourse, Willmot quotes Janet, aged 27, a young white, married woman studying a secretarial and business course: 'I knew immediately ... I knew then I wanted to spend the rest of my life with him' (Willmot, 2007).

The second discourse identified by Willmot is one of 'contingency': 'The basic principle of this discourse is that far from being a force external to oneself, love and intimacy are contingent on and influenced by everyday, mundane, domestic life, and bigger life choices, as are other relationships such as friendships' (Willmot, 2003). This second discourse is reflected in an unforgettable statement by Anais, 29, a young woman of mixed parentage, studying in higher education and currently in a relationship: 'my pizza wasn't ready and I was looking for someone to talk to ... I was just wandering around [the take away] and I happened to pick on him' (quoted in Willmot, 2007).

According to Willmot, the reasons why particular young women invest in particular discourses of intimacy are not random but rooted in their material experience. Investing in a discourse of contingency was often related to the experience of geographical mobility: 'For example, the fast turnover of living arrangements that was, broadly speaking, part of the experience of going away to university, tended to be the situation which led respondents to "end up" living with a partner' (Willmot, 2003).

By contrast, the geographical stability associated with leaving full time education at the age of 16 or 18 and finding employment locally tended to encourage investment in a romantic discourse: 'Relationships tended not to be embarked upon with a finite time scale in mind when moving away was not imminent or planned. This left the way clear for the purpose of intimate relationships to remain more consistently, and romantically, at finding "foreverness"' (Willmot, 2003).

An additional factor for some young women was the framework of religious beliefs or cultural practices associated with belonging to a particular social group:

> The young Christian women in this study believed strongly in marriage as well as the 'foreverness' central to a romance discourse. Ethnicity is salient here too ... For example, the one Asian woman in this study was a Muslim and explained that part of her faith is that she had an arranged marriage. Such arranged marriages are not based upon love, romantic, contingent or otherwise. They are, however, based on one aspect of a romance discourse: foreverness.
>
> (Willmot, 2003)

The upshot of Willmot's study is that, like Redman, she is critical of the notion of complete 'free' choice in the practice of love and romance, believing that it is constrained by the kinds of influences outlined above.

Activity 6   Discourses of love

Allow 30 minutes

Think of a romantic relationship of your own, perhaps one that occurred when you were in your teens or twenties. How did you and your partner meet, and do you view this as reflecting a discourse of romance or a discourse of contingency – or perhaps a mixture of the two? Can you see ways in which your investment in this discourse was related to your wider experience at the time – for example, your involvement in work or education, or your geographical mobility?

Comment

I thought about the way I met my wife, when we were in our early twenties and found ourselves part of the same small group of postgraduate students at university. We started off as friends, only later progressing to 'going out', and then becoming long-term partners. Although as a teenager I had often invested heavily in a 'discourse of intimacy', I tend to think of the way I met my wife within the framework of a 'discourse of contingency' when I reflect on the combination of circumstances that led to our coming together. However, I am aware that, with hindsight, I often draw on elements of a discourse of intimacy when I describe this key event in my life to myself and to others.

Like Willmot, Louisa Allen (2003) is concerned to show the ways in which young people's attitudes to romantic and sexual relationships are shaped by social discourses and are strongly gendered. Her research compared the ways in which 17–19-year-olds in New Zealand thought about sex and relationships, and as a result she suggests that 'the notion that young women want only love from relationships and young men prefer sex is outdated' (Allen, 2003, p. 231).

Allen argues that young people draw on dominant discourses of (hetero) sexuality in their talk about themselves as sexual, but also that some young people 'took up subject positions that involved more resistant conceptions of the sexual self' (Allen, 2003, p. 215). Furthermore, the potential to do this 'was partly contingent upon young people's location in contexts that offered access to, or opened space for, other ways of constituting themselves as sexual' (p. 215). These contexts might be a particular school, or a focus group which provided a safe space for exploring alternatives.

Caitlin, aged 18, conformed to a conventional image of young women's attitude to intimate relationships when she said: 'to me it's really the emotional side which is important and that's why I like to cuddle and that rather than have sex ... like sometimes I just can't be bothered and just want to get it over and done with' (quoted in Allen, 2003, p. 219). However, others constituted their sexual selves differently. One example was Rosalind, aged 17, who attended a school known for its alternative pedagogies: 'I mean you have got your stereotypical, women want commitment and love and guys just want a fling, but I think that girls are pretty much like that as well [laugh]' (quoted in Allen, 2003, p. 221).

Allen argues that the persistence of a 'sexual double standard' meant that 'talk about female desire and pleasure occurred mainly in environments where young women felt they would not be negatively stigmatized' such as exclusively female groups or 'safe' mixed gender groups (Allen, 2003, p. 223). Pattman's analysis of the diaries written by young women in southern Africa suggests that they offered a similar safe space in which to articulate a more active sexual identity: 'Whereas for the boys the diaries seemed to provide a safe space to be "romantic", and to show how much they were affected by girls who dumped them, for the girls they seemed to provide an opportunity for articulating sexual desire' (Pattman, 2005, p. 509).

3.3 Young gay relationships

Our discussion in this section has not distinguished between heterosexual and same-sex relationships, though much of the available research is focused on the former. However, a large part of what has been said could be applied equally to young gay and lesbian relationships. Notions of love and romance for gay and lesbian young people are similarly shaped by prevailing discourses and contexts, and by the ways in which ideas about intimacy and sexuality continue to be deeply gendered. In the previous section we also noted the intensity of some same-sex friendships, such as that between Ben and Karl, and the similarities with romantic relationships. It is important to hold on to a sense of the fluidity of relationships and their meanings for young people, and not to draw rigid lines between friendships and romance, and between heterosexual and same-sex relationships.

At the same time, we need to remember the impact that the persistence of discriminatory attitudes and practices can have on the capacity of young people to develop and sustain openly gay relationships. Chapter 4 discussed Mac an Ghaill's (1994) interviews with young gay men in the sixth form of an English secondary school. The interviewees reported that homosexual desire was effectively silenced and effaced by the institution, rendering it invisible. The homophobia of the institution was a key influence on the young men's capacity to express same-sex desire and to form relationships. The same process of silencing is partly responsible for the relative absence, to date, of research data on young gay relationships.

However, Mac an Ghaill is keen not to paint young gay men simply as victims but to represent them as young people who devised 'creative strategies' for resisting homophobia and affirming their sexual identities (Mac an Ghaill, 1994, p. 167). Alongside the continuing difficulties for young people in openly developing and sustaining gay relationships, particularly in the school context, there are also signs that attitudes are changing and that new opportunities may be opening up. Aapola *et al.* claim that a 'changing climate' of social attitudes means that 'lesbian and bisexual young women in Western societies are finding it easier and easier to come out and form positive sexual relationships' (Aapola *et al.*, 2005, p. 157). They point to the positive role played by new technologies, such as the internet, in providing alternative, safe spaces for young lesbian women to form relationships, citing this example of an Australian 15-year-old, Liz, from research by Hillier:

> I actually met my first girlfriend via the net. I'd accidentally clicked 'reply all' on a long chain letter and, days after, received an e-mail from this girl. After general chit blah blah blah we discovered we were at the same school, met up, built up a friendship and things developed from there. I guess without the net I never would have met her.
>
> (From Hillier, quoted in Aapola *et al.*, 2005, p. 157)

In this section we have discussed the importance and significance of intimate relationships for young people. We have seen that romantic attachments can provide a realm of autonomy for young people at a time when they are suspended in a pre-adult status in so many areas of their lives. We have also seen that the ways in which young men and young women think about and practise intimacy are decisively shaped by the contexts in which they live their lives and by social discourses.

Key points

- Young people's expectations and experiences of intimacy have been affected by widespread social, legal and attitudinal changes.

- Love and intimacy can provide important experiences of autonomy for young people at a time of extended dependency.

- The ways in which young people think about love and romance are shaped by social contexts and discourses.

- Although experience and attitudes continue to be gendered, there is evidence that some young men and young women are able to resist stereotypical attitudes towards intimacy and sexuality, given a supportive context.

- The experiences of gay and lesbian young people are framed by the persistence of homophobia, but there is some evidence of new freedom and opportunities to develop relationships.

Conclusion

This chapter has shown the centrality of relationships with family, friends and partners to young people's lives. In all of these areas, young people's relationships are changing in dramatic but often quite complex ways. Change is uneven and its impact is interwoven with factors such as age, gender, class and ethnicity. There is a need to challenge simplistic assumptions about linear social change and to pay equal attention to continuities and constraints. The meanings given by young people to their changing experience of relationships often undermine the generalised assumptions of dominant theoretical and policy discourses. An informed understanding of young people's relationships needs to pay attention to these meanings, and also to the diverse ways in which young people perform family relationships, friendships and intimate relationships. Although our discussion has provided some confirmation of late modern ideas about changes in personal relationships, we have also discussed evidence that challenges straightforward generalisations, particularly when these are applied to the experience of young people.

References

Aapola, S., Gonick, M. and Harris, A. (2005) *Young Femininity: Girlhood, Power and Social Change*, Basingstoke, Palgrave.

Allen, L. (2003) 'Girls want sex, boys want love: resisting dominant discourses of (hetero) sexuality', *Sexualities*, vol. 6, no. 2, pp. 215–36.

Beck, U. (1992) *Risk Society: Towards a New Modernity*, London, Sage.

Beck-Gernsheim, E. (1998) 'On the way to a post-familiar family: from a community of need to elective affinities', *Theory, Culture and Society*, vol. 15, no. 3–4, pp. 53–70.

Brooks, R. (2002) 'Transitional friends? Young people's strategies to manage and maintain their friendships during a period of repositioning', *Journal of Youth Studies*, vol. 5, no. 4, pp. 440–67.

Buckingham, D. and Bragg, S. (2004) *Young People, Sex and the Media: The Facts of Life?*, Basingstoke, Palgrave Macmillan.

Flowerdew, J. and Neale, B. (2003) 'Trying to stay apace: children with multiple challenges in their post-divorce family lives', *Childhood*, vol. 10, no. 2, pp. 147–61.

Frosh, S., Phoenix, A. and Pattman, R. (2002) *Young Masculinities*, Cambridge, Polity Press.

Furlong, A. and Cartmel, F. (1997) *Young People and Social Change: Individualization and Risk in Late Modernity*, Buckingham, Open University Press.

Giddens, A. (1991) *Modernity and Self-Identity: Self and Society in the Late Modern Age*, Cambridge, Polity Press.

Giddens, A. (1992) *The Transformation of Intimacy: Sexuality, Love and Eroticism in Modern Societies*, Cambridge, Polity Press.

Gillies, V. (2000) 'Young people and family life: analysing and comparing disciplinary discourses', *Journal of Youth Studies*, vol. 3, no. 2, pp. 211–28.

Gillies, V. (2003) 'Family and intimate relationships: a review of the sociological research', Families & Social Capital ESRC Research Group Working Paper No. 2, London, South Bank University.

Gillies, V., Ribbens McCarthy, J. and Holland, J. (2001) *Pulling Together, Pulling Apart: The Family Lives of Young People*, London, Family Policy Studies Centre/Joseph Rowntree Foundation.

Hey, V. (2002) '"Not as nice as she was supposed to be": schoolgirls' friendships' in Taylor, S. (ed.) *Ethnographic Research: A Reader*, London, Sage/The Open University.

Holdsworth, C. (2004) 'Family support during the transition out of the parental home in Britain, Spain and Norway', *Sociology*, vol. 38, no. 5, pp. 909–26.

Jones, G. (2004) *The Parenting of Youth: Social Protection and Economic Dependence*, ESRC (End of Award Report R000238379), www.esrcsocietytoday.ac.uk [accessed 29/06/06].

Kehily, M.J., Mac an Ghaill, M., Epstein, D. and Redman, P. (2002) 'Private girls and public worlds: producing femininities in the primary school', *Discourse: Studies in the Cultural Politics of Education*, vol. 23, no. 2, pp. 167–77.

Leach, W. (1981) *True Love and Perfect Union: The Feminist Reform of Sex and Society*, London, Routledge & Kegan Paul.

Mac an Ghaill, M. (1994) *The Making of Men: Masculinities, Sexualities and Schooling*, Buckingham, Open University Press.

McLeod, J. (2002) 'Working out intimacy: young people and friendship in an age of reflexivity', *Discourse: Studies in the Cultural Politics of Education*, vol. 23, no. 2, pp. 211–26.

Morris, J. (2002) *Young Disabled People Moving into Adulthood*, Foundations: Ref 512, Joseph Rowntree Foundation, www.jrf.org.uk/knowledge/findings/foundations/512.asp [accessed 15/05/06].

Neale, B. (2002) 'Dialogues with children: children, divorce and citizenship', *Childhood*, vol. 9, no. 4, pp. 455–75.

Neale, B. and Smart, C. (2001) *Good to Talk? Conversations with Children After Divorce*, London, Young Voice.

Office for National Statistics (2006), www.statistics.gov.uk [accessed 10/05/06].

Pattman, R. (2005) '"Boys and girls should not be too close": sexuality, the identities of African boys and girls and HIV/AIDS education', *Sexualities*, vol. 8, no. 4, pp. 497–516.

Redman, P. (1999) 'The discipline of love: negotiation and regulation in boys' performance of a romance-based heterosexual masculinity', paper presented to Second International Gender and Education Conference, University of Warwick, 29–31 March.

Redman, P. (2001) 'The discipline of love: negotiation and regulation in boys' performance of a romance-based heterosexual masculinity', *Men and Masculinities*, vol. 4, no. 2, pp. 186–200.

Redman, P., Epstein, D., Kehily, M.J. and Mac an Ghaill, M. (2002) 'Boys bonding: same-sex friendship, the unconscious and heterosexual discourse', *Discourse: Studies in the Cultural Politics of Education*, vol. 23, no. 2, pp. 179–91.

Ribbens McCarthy, J. (2006) *Young People's Experiences of Loss and Bereavement: Towards an Interdisciplinary Approach*, Maidenhead, Open University Press.

Ribbens McCarthy, J., Edwards, R. and Gillies, V. (2003) *Making Families: Moral Tales of Parenting and Step-Parenting*, Durham, sociologypress.

Robb, M. (ed.) (2007) *Youth in Context: Frameworks, Settings and Encounters*, London, Sage/The Open University (Course Book).

Walkerdine, V., Lucey, H. and Melody, J. (2001) *Growing Up Girl: Psychosocial Explorations of Gender and Class*, Basingstoke, Palgrave.

Willmot, H. (2003) 'Young women and intimacy: milieux, experiences and discursive constructions of love and intimacy', unpublished paper.

Willmot, H. (2007 forthcoming) 'Young women, routes through education and employment, and discursive constructions of love and intimacy', *Current Sociology*, vol. 55.

Acknowledgements

Text

Pages 26, 29 and 34: Hall, S. and Jefferson, T. (1975) *Resistance through Rituals,* Taylor & Francis Group; pages 51–2: Hall, T. (2003) *Better Times Than This: Youth Homelessness in Britain*, Pluto Press; pages 59–61: Bourgois, P. (1998) 'Families and children in pain in the US inner city' in Sargent, C. and Scheper-Hughes, N. (eds) *Small Wars: The Cultural Politics of Childhood*, The University of California Press; page 64: Mandela, N. (1994) *Long Walk to Freedom*, Little, Brown; page 68: reprinted by permission of Ms. Magazine, © 1999; pages 81–2: Thomson, R., Holland, J., McGrellis, S., Bell, R., Henderson, S. and Sharpe, S. (2004) 'Inventing adulthoods: a biographical approach to youth transitions', *The Sociological Review*, Blackwell Publishing Ltd; pages 98–9: Thomson, R., Holland, J., McGrellis, S., Bell, R., Henderson, S. and Sharpe, S. (2002) 'Critical moments: choice, chance and opportunity in young people's narratives of transition', *Sociology*, vol. 36, no. 2, pp. 335–54, Sage Publications; page 157: taken from http://news.bbc.co.uk/1/hi/programmes/this_world/4352171.stm; page 293: Crawley, H. and Lester, T. (2005) *No Place for a Child*, Save the Children; pages 300–1: Biehal, N. and Wade, J. (1999) '"I thought it would be easier": the early housing careers of young people leaving care' in Rugg, J. (ed.) (1999) *Young People, Housing and Social Policy*, Taylor & Francis Ltd.

Illustrations

Page 19: © Mary Evans Picture Library; page 19: image from an unknown source; page 28: Photofusion Picture Library/Alamy; page 36: image from an unknown source; page 48: © Mary Evans Picture Library; page 57: © Photofusion; page 63: UWC-Robben Island Museum Mayibuye Archives; page 75: taken from http://www.bbc.co.uk/humber/videonation/archive/003_ben_borthwick.shtml; page 85: © Per-Anders Pettersson/Getty Images; page 88: © George Marks/Getty Images; page 88: © Steven Lam/Getty Images; page 88: courtesy of Deb Bywater and Anne Howells; page 91: Boston Women's Health Book Collective (1973) *Our Bodies, Ourselves*, Simon & Schuster Ltd; page 99: © Image Source/Alamy; page 112: © John Powell Photography/Alamy; page 118: © Comstock Production Department/Alamy; page 131: © Image Source/Alamy; page 137: © Rex Features; page 137: © Fox Photos/Getty Images; page 157: taken from www.news.bbc.co.uk/1hi/programmes/this_world/4352171.stm; page 177: reproduced with kind permission of Stonewall;

Index